Photo of Adam is courtesy of the Hollywood Historical Society & Michael Hopkins of Gerlinde Photograph

Missing Person

DONATIONS FOR

REWARD

NOW TOTAL MORE THAN

$100,000.00

FOR INFORMATION
LEADING TO THE SAFE RETURN
OF

Adam Walsh

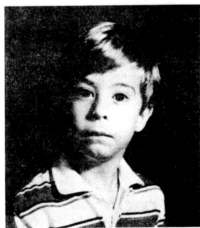

DESCRIPTION: Age: 6 years old
Height: 3' 6''
Weight: 45 lbs.
Eyes: Hazel
Build: Slight
Hair: Straight Sandy Blond

Other: Missing one top
tooth with second
tooth coming in

CLOTHING WORN WHEN LAST SEEN:
Pants: Green shorts
Shirt: Short sleeve pullover,
predominantly red & white striped
Shoe: Rubber Sandals
(Yellow Bottoms and Blue Straps)
Hat: Beige Colored
Boat Captain's Hat

PLEASE help us find Adam Walsh. Last seen and missing from Hollywood Mall Sears
Toy Department, Monday, July 27, 1981, around 12 noon.

We are willing to negotiate ransom on ANY terms. Strict confidentiality. DO NOT FEAR
REVENGE! We will not prosecute. We only want our son. If desired, contact any radio
or T.V. station, newspaper or any other media as a neutral party for negotiations or information. We want Adam home. If you think you see him, ask him his name.

If you have any information, PLEASE call or write either:

Hollywood Police Department
3250 Hollywood Boulevard
Hollywood, Florida 33021
Detective Bureau: (305) 921-3911

Parents:
John and Reve Walsh
2801 McKinley Street
Hollywood, Florida 33020
Phone: (305) 922-4454

File poster from the Hollywood Police Department, Florida

FRUSTRATED WITNESS!

The Real Untold Story of the Adam Walsh Case

WILLIS MORGAN

ll bookbaby

BookBaby is a self-publishing, print on demand, and book distribution services platform.

Self-published by author through BookBaby.com
E-mail: JusticeForAdam@AOL.com
Facebook: Frustrated Witness
Websites: JusticeForAdam.com & FrustratedWitness.com
Website design by Isa Swait at IsaDreaming.com
Photos that required restoration were done by Phojoe.com
Reader's Favorite review on back cover by Jessyca Garcia

Book cover design was created by me because I wanted to use my own photo of the location where I believe Adam was murdered (Chapter Ten). Since the Dade County Police Department has refused to investigate, I added the virtual crime scene tape. Someone has suggested the tape should read—**CRIME SCENE   DO NOT INVESTIGATE**

Photo of Adam with the baseball bat is courtesy of the Hollywood Historical Society & Michael Hopkins of Gerlinde Photography, Hollywood, Florida

Category: Nonfiction true-crime book
ISBN: 9781943612321
eBook ISBN: 9781631929861

- Translation Services: German/English translations were done by Sondra Schalk, MA Contact: GermanEnglishTranslationCentral.com
- Germany chapters reviewed and critiqued by Sergeant Pete Altman and David Rodriquez
- First editing by Sharon Eaton: Sharon.23@gmail.com
- Second editing by the team at Content Mastery Guide: http://www.contentMasteryGuide.com
- Third editing: by Joanne Lane with www.FirstEditing.com
- Final editing and proofing by William Greenleaf at Greenleaf Literary Services: Contact: www.GreenleafLiteraryServices.com

Disclaimer:

While every attempt has been made to ensure that the information provided in this book is accurate, the information is from witness statements, FBI records, Hollywood, Florida police records, and Broward County State Attorney's Office records. The author of this book is not responsible for any errors or omissions, or for the results obtained from the use of these public records.

This book contains content which may be disturbing to some readers. Discretion is advised for readers who may be affected by passages which depict acts of cruel violence.

JusticeForAdam.com

On my website at JusticeForAdam.com are some free downloads of records that include:
The three-CD set of the HPD's Adam Walsh case files.
- CD no. 1: contains all information released in 1996.
- CD no. 2: contains information from 1996 to 2008 when the case was closed.
- CD no. 3: audio files (not included).

These are the files Thomas Julin fought for and the HPD wanted no one to see. Now everyone gets to see these free public record files, because it's not about the money. It's about justice for Adam Walsh.

More Free Downloads

- Broward County State Attorney's Office (SAO) Adam Walsh case files.

- Florida Department of Law Enforcement's (FDLE) full negative roll of ninety-eight 35 mm photos used by Detective Joe Matthews to implicate Ottis Toole in Adam Walsh's abduction and murder.

- FBI Jeffrey Dahmer files.

- Extra files and folders.

Dedication

This book is dedicated to Adam and the Walsh family.

Injustice anywhere is a threat to justice everywhere.
_____**Martin Luther King Jr.** _____

Acknowledgements

I owe a great deal of gratitude to Thomas R. Julin of The Hunton & Williams LLP Law Firm, located in the Brickell section of downtown Miami. Tom's willingness to give me free legal advice and a pro bono contract is testament to the type of person he is. Tom's passion for justice and civil law is second to none.

Jay Grelen earned all my respect by spearheading the lawsuit in 1995 and taking on the Hollywood Police Department (HPD). Jay set the precedent and showed the true colors of the HPD. It's not that they didn't want anyone to see information that would interfere with the investigation, as they wanted John Walsh to believe. Rather, they were already in full cover-up mode and did not want anyone to see what an inept farce their investigation really was.

I have more respect than ever for Broward County Circuit Judge Leroy H. Moe. Against vehement opposition, on February 16, 1996, Judge Moe ordered the opening of the police files into the Adam Walsh case. It was the release of these files for public scrutiny that would eventually cause me to realize the full scale and extent of the HPD's incompetence, as well as what I believe to be a misrepresentation of some, if not many, facts in Adam's case.

I would like to thank Bob Norman, a writer for *The New Times, Broward—Palm Beach* edition, and his blog, *"The Daily Pulp"*: *—Bob Norman's Blog*. Bob has been one of the most outspoken writers in exposing the corruption at the HPD. No one can tell the story of their corruption, ineptness, and nepotism like Bob, so with his permission, I include his article "Rotten to the Core: Your One-Stop Shop for Hollywood Police Corruption," dated July 30, 2009.

Dan Christensen, an investigative reporter with more than thirty years of experience and founder of the nonprofit investigative news site *"Broward Bulldog,"* gave me permission to include his article titled; Finkelstein says Satz favors bigshots, police over "everyday citizens." This came out on January 14, 2010. You can view Dan's free online newspaper at browardbulldog.org.

I want to thank Sondra Schalk, MA for helping me complete the chapters on Germany. Sondra has her own translation service. When I asked her to do translations and investigate German search engines and archives, she not only accepted but also made all the difference in the world. Much of the information gathered with respect to the murders in Germany is from her efforts.

I will be forever grateful to David Rodriguez and Billy Joe Capshaw for sharing their stories of what it was like to be Jeffrey Dahmer's roommate in Germany and for helping me understand what Dahmer was like while stationed in Germany. Preston Davis also has all my respect for his service in the army and for sharing much of his story with me.

It would be remiss of me not to give gratitude to all the witnesses in the Adam Walsh case who have been adamantly steadfast in what they witnessed that Monday on July 27, 1981. I am especially thankful to the witnesses who were kind enough to tell me their story and help assemble this puzzle. A good prosecutor once said: "You don't get to choose your witnesses; you have to work with the ones you have." I have met witnesses of every kind. Some immediately invited me into their homes and couldn't wait to tell me their story, while others closed doors on me.

TABLE OF CONTENTS

APPENDIX

PHOTO ABOVE: 1981——This was me at work in the *Miami Herald* pressroom.

INTRODUCTION

My name is Willis Morgan. I was in the Hollywood Mall on July 27, 1981, the day that Adam Walsh went missing. I was compelled to write this book so the true story of the Adam Walsh case could be told, because in spite of what has been written elsewhere I know it hasn't been, at least not until now, because I was there. This is the account of Adam Walsh's abduction and my attempts stretching across decades to find justice for him. As much as this book is a case for Jeffrey Dahmer being Adam's murderer, it is equally a study of how the Hollywood Police Department (HPD) conducted the homicide investigation. This police department has become the greatest ally of America's most notorious serial killer by refusing to consider him a suspect.

The HPD employs 337 police officers and 263 civilian support personnel. They handle an average of 139,000 calls for police services a year. I know some might take issue with my excessive berating of the HPD, so I want to take a moment to make it clear that this book is not a condemnation of every rank-and-file police officer. There are a lot of really good police officers in this police department. My issue is with the homicide detectives involved in this case and the hierarchy that protects them.

I'm trying, in some small way, to make up for what I didn't and couldn't do over three decades ago. That's why I've worked so hard to bring to light these facts and logical deductions. I present the truth of the case using uncalled witnesses and the HPD's own case files, which were sealed for so many years and can now be downloaded for free at JusticeForAdam.com. Right after Adam's abduction, I tried to report to the HPD what I had witnessed at the Hollywood Mall, but they totally rejected everything I said. That was the beginning of my odyssey as a frustrated witness.

Almost everyone knows the story of Jeffrey Dahmer, and there are plenty of books that have been written about him. This book focuses on what all the other books have left out. This is the untold story of Dahmer's service in Germany and his sojourn in South Florida. Many of the books I've read about Dahmer barely mention Germany, and some do not mention his nearly six-month stay in South Florida at all.

It really bothers me whenever I hear Ottis Toole's name mentioned in relation to the Adam Walsh case. I always knew Adam's abductor had to be that guy I encountered on the same day, at the same time, and at the same location where Adam was last seen. I just didn't have a name to put to that face until ten years later, when I saw Jeffrey Dahmer's mug shot and name in the newspaper. Since the Hollywood Police Department closed the Walsh case saying Ottis Toole was guilty, I now have no choice but to dedicate a chapter to Toole's noninvolvement in this case.

During the December 16, 2008, closing conference, Police Chief Chadwick E. Wagner fed the Walsh family and the media more baloney than would fit in any sandwich. Mainstream media outlets accepted the transparently contrived story as the truth without investigating and without even the slightest bit of skepticism. As a consequence, the media ate the sandwich.

The following are just some of the headline stories that ran the day after the closing:

- **Case Closed: Police ID Adam Walsh Killer (ABC News)**
- **Cops Solve '81 Slaying of *AMW* Host John Walsh's Son (NBC News)**
- **Cops: 1981 Adam Walsh Murder Solved (CBS News)**
- **The Murder of Adam Walsh: A 27-Year Mystery Solved (FOX News)**
- **Police ID Killer of 'Most Wanted' Host's Son (USA TODAY)**
- **Adam Walsh Murder Case Closed (*America's Most Wanted*)**
- **Adam Walsh Case Finally Solved (*Newsday*)**

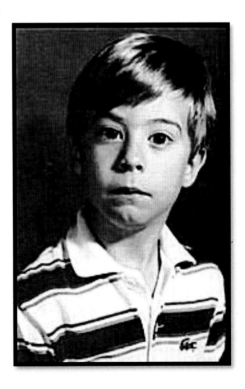

Afterward, I tried to tell the media the true story, but in the gold rush frenzy of media competition, they seemed to be more interested in getting the official story out. Since most got it wrong, my frustration as a witness was exacerbated. Getting the HPD, the State Attorney's Office, and the courts to listen has proven harder than I ever imagined. This, then, is my odyssey as a frustrated witness. And this is Adam's story as much as it is mine.

PHOTO RIGHT: Adam Walsh in his first grade photo. He is wearing the same red and white striped shirt he was abducted in.

CHAPTER ONE
ENCOUNTER IN RADIO SHACK

1964 Postcard by
Florida Natural Color

Courtesy of Bob Hynes
owner of the Mall Barber Shop

PHOTO TOP RIGHT:
The Hollywood Mall's interior, looking north. Sears is on the left over the bridge crossing the moat. The north entrance is straight ahead. Radio Shack is on the right near the end. The wall on the left is covered with gold river-rock panels. The floors are terrazzo. Orb-style light fixtures hang from the ceiling.

RIGHT: Neison clocks on Bourbon Street. To get to the sidewalk café from inside the mall, shoppers would have to walk down Bourbon Street. Photo by Candace Barbot

In 1981, I was working my tenth year at the *Miami Herald*. I worked as the training supervisor in the pressroom. My work days were Wednesday through Saturday, from 7 p.m. to 5:30 a.m. Usually, during the week, I would get to sleep around 6:30 a.m. and get up around 3 p.m., but on my days off—Sundays, Mondays, and Tuesdays—I would get to sleep around midnight. This would give me full days to get personal things done.

Monday, July 27, 1981, was one of those days when I got up early. I didn't have anything scheduled, so I decided to go to Waldenbooks and then have lunch at the German Deli in the Hollywood Mall, or the Sears Mall, as it was called.

This was a regular 310,000-square-foot, fully air conditioned, interior-type suburban mall that opened in October 1964, with Sears taking up 125,000 square feet. It occupied a forty-acre parcel with a total of thirty retail outlets located one and a half miles west of downtown Hollywood. It was the third enclosed mall in the State of Florida.

I'd been going to that mall for years before Adam's abduction and went there many times after. My optometrist, Dr. Sheldon Mayer, was located there. I used to go to the detached Sears Auto shop, Morrison's Cafeteria, the Hollywood Mall Delicatessen (which everyone affectionately called the German Deli), Woolworth's lunch counter, the Waldenbooks store, the Mall Barber Shop, Radio Shack, and of course Sears.

I was not paying attention to the time, but it was around eleven in the morning when I left for the bookstore. I parked in the east parking lot and went into the mall through the east-side food court entrance. I browsed in Waldenbooks for about twenty minutes and left without buying anything. Before heading to the German Deli for lunch, I stopped by Radio Shack, which was located on the same side of the mall as the bookstore.

As I walked into Radio Shack, I headed toward the right-aisle side of the store but stopped at the "red tag sale" table. I picked something up that caught my eye and was looking at it when I noticed someone coming from the north mall entrance and stopping at the entrance to Radio Shack. I looked up and saw a dirty, disheveled young man staring at me. When I first made eye contact with him, he appeared harmless and somewhat goofy.

He gave me a friendly grin and said, "Hi, there. Nice day, isn't it?"

Oh, he wants to talk to someone, I thought. I wasn't interested in conversation. I'd never had someone come up to me in a mall and just try to start a conversation before, and I was caught somewhat off guard. I didn't know what to do, so I did nothing. I didn't answer him, thinking this irritant would just go away.

Standing there with a big, stupid grin on his face, he seemed like a jovial, unintimidating goofball at first. That was, until he realized I wasn't answering him— then things got bizarre. He lost the smirk and started staring at me intently. His physical presence alone wasn't intimidating, but everything else about him began to alarm me. He was staring daggers at me with a dull, empty look of anger in his eyes, as if he were upset about my lack of response.

When I looked back at him, his face morphed into an expression of rage. After staring at each other for what seemed like an eternity—in real time, it was more like ten to fifteen seconds—I then looked back toward the table and the item I had picked up, thinking that if I broke eye contact, he would just go away. I guess he won that stare-down contest.

What I now find interesting is that Dahmer was known at times not to have much eye contact with others. Yet that day, he was intent on staring me down, and instead of leaving, he came into the Radio Shack and stopped about an arm's length from me. Invading my personal space, breath reeking of beer, he then repeated the same line in a very loud tone, "Hi, there! Nice day, isn't it?"

Again, not wanting to start a conversation, I said nothing. I was thinking, *This guy wants someone to talk to really badly! Why is he talking so loud when he's standing right next to me?* At that point, I was no longer interested in the item I had picked up, and to this day, I can't even remember what it was. I was more or less feigning interest because I didn't know what else to do. My real concern was keeping an eye on this weirdo standing next to me with a progressively noticeable and imposing presence of someone obviously disturbed.

He just stood there in an angry posture, as if he were getting ready to do something. This guy was staring me up and down, sizing me up. A feeling came over me that he was tensing up. I started wondering what he was going to do. Because of his posture and the fact that he wouldn't leave, I had the feeling that he wanted to grab my arm. I glanced at his eyes again and shook my head in annoyance. I feared this guy with an empty look in his eyes was going to pull a knife on me and physically attempt to get me to leave the mall. I couldn't help but wonder if he really had a knife or maybe even a gun.

At that point, I thought something was going to happen for sure. I mentally began formulating a plan. I did not want to start a fight, so I decided not to do anything at all. That is, unless he put a hand on me first. I wanted a witness so that I wouldn't be accused of starting the fight if it came to that. I looked over to my right to see where the sales clerk was. I felt very uncomfortable turning my back on this wacko. All I could do to protect myself was to use my left arm as a sort of shield without being too obvious, just in case he tried to stick me while I was looking the other way. I saw the clerk all the way in the back of the store putting some items on a shelf.

I thought about walking to the back of the store, but then thought better of it. I decided to stay put because, if this guy had a weapon, the two of us could end up dead in the back of the store. I didn't want to put the clerk in jeopardy.

Also, I didn't want this guy to see me walk with a bit of a limp because I have a right-leg, above-knee prosthesis that I traded my motorcycle in for back in the summer of 1977. True, I hadn't been to the gym since 1977, but I was no weakling. At 5 feet 10 ½ inches and 188 pounds, I could easily bench 360 pounds before my accident. However, I'm no fool, either. When you have a prosthesis, you can't run, and you can't stand and fight. No matter how macho you want to think you are, you're at a huge disadvantage.

This goofy-looking nutcase had a very dangerous look about him at this point. Just as I turned back around to the table, I saw him abruptly stomp off. He moved as if he were trying to punch holes through the floor with his feet, like a little kid who'd just had his toy taken away.

Whew . . . Man, oh man . . . Wow! What the hell was that?

Whether he saw me first and saw that I walked with a limp, I will never know. I do know one thing for sure: when I read in the paper years later who this guy was and what he did up in Milwaukee, it gave me a lot to think about.

He seemed so intent on being with someone that I knew he would approach someone else, and I wondered what his or her reaction would be. Then I realized that someone might need help. I waited a few seconds to give him a lead and then walked to the Radio Shack entrance. As I looked into the mall, I thought I'd lost him, but then I realized he'd crossed over to the other side of the hall. He was meandering deep into the mall, in complete contrast to the way he'd stomped out of the Radio Shack.

I knew at that point that I would have to remember his face. As I started to follow him through the mall at a safe distance, I made mental notes of his description: dirty blond hair to the collar; yellow, long-sleeved, buttoned-*up* shirt; faded blue jeans; white sneakers; a little taller than me; early twenties; about 170 pounds. The one thing I remember the most is that he had a really dark tan—about as dark as a white guy could get. This was too much to remember, and I thought about going into the German Deli to ask for a pen and paper. I never did go into the deli. I knew if I were to explain to someone why I needed a pen and paper, by the time they gave it to me, that guy would be gone.

Just then he turned into Sears, and I watched as he passed the jewelry counter. Two young women stood behind the counter, one training the other, it appeared. He paid no attention to them, and they took no notice of him. He then passed an elderly couple, probably in their mid to late sixties. He took no notice of them, either, and they had no idea who they had just passed.

This was long before Dahmer gained his reputation as a serial killer.

It was around noon when I saw him walk to the far west side of Sears. He then turned to the right. I walked to the point where he turned and looked to the right and saw him turn into the toy department. I stood near a rack of men's suits for a minute or so, wondering what he was doing in the toy department and why he wasn't coming back out. It crossed my mind that he could be looking at or playing the video games, but I never made the connection of kids being in trouble. My thinking at the time was that he was looking to approach someone in their late teens, twenties or around my age (thirty-four). I also believed, at the time, that he ended up in the toy department only because he couldn't find someone to approach along the way.

Then I realized that, since the toy department was at the end of Sears, he would most likely be coming back my way! Not wanting another confrontation, I decided to leave. On the way back to the food court, I passed the jewelry counter and was going to tell the two women to call the police, but in the end I didn't, because there is no law against being crazy in this country. When I got to the east exit at the food court, I looked around to make sure he hadn't backtracked and followed me. The last thing I wanted was a confrontation in the parking lot. Only when I was sure he wasn't in sight did I go out into the parking lot.

I then went home and tried to forget about that nut in the mall. But that wouldn't last for long. That very same evening, I was in the kitchen making a sandwich. I had the TV in the living room turned to one of the local news shows. That was when I heard the news anchor say there had been a kidnapping in the Hollywood Mall. Then I heard "Sears" and then "toy department." I ran into the living room to watch.

A sudden fear came over me, and a chill ran down my spine. My first thoughts were: *That guy did it. . . He actually did it!* They said the time was around noon, about the same time I saw that guy walk into the toy department. I made another commitment to remember his face and description. I remember thinking that I should get a pad and pen and write everything down, especially his description, but everything by this time was so fresh and vivid in my mind that I thought I would never forget. The kidnapping would become case #81-56073, and I had a deep feeling this guy would be in the news again someday; he was just too crazy not to be. It was a face and an encounter I would never forget.

Of course, not writing everything down was a mistake on my part. A decade later, when I told Detective Jack Hoffman that Dahmer was wearing a yellow button-*up* shirt, I might have been wrong. Another witness said it was an army jacket, and I do believe he was right. When reflecting back, I believe it was an army jacket because I remember thinking he could've had a weapon in his pocket. Years later, when other witnesses and I came forward the Hollywood detectives, as well as the State Attorney's Office and others seemed uninterested and dismissed us because they claimed we were not reliable witnesses. Yet for some reason the witnesses that pointed to Ottis Toole *were* reliable.

In general, witnesses might not be very reliable but I can remember incidents going all the way back to kindergarten. I'm not a psychologist, but I believe a witness directly involved in an incident that becomes a murder is much more reliable. When an incident is so far out of the ordinary, the neurons in the brain get so fired up that the incident becomes pigeonholed into the memory. And so, I will remember that encounter for the rest of my life as if it were yesterday.

Tuesday, the day after the abduction, I mentioned it to my neighbor, Valerie Vickers, who suggested I go to the police. I didn't. When I went to work on Wednesday at 7 p.m., I told some coworkers about the incident in the Sears Mall. Richard Herland suggested I go to the HPD. The next morning, on Thursday, July 30, 1981, around 9 a.m., I went to the HPD across the street from the Sears Mall.

I walked up to the glass window in the lobby and told the receptionist I was there about the kidnapping at the mall. Like an idiot, I started telling her what happened. She stopped me and told me to see Officer Presley. "We have a special desk set up just for information about this case," she told me, as she pointed over to a desk by the elevator in the small main lobby.

I tried to tell the officer what happened, but he didn't seem interested. He only wanted to know if I had seen a tag number. I tried to explain to him that the incident never went out of the mall. He then asked for a description, which I gave him. When I tried to tell him what happened, he said, "Let me ask the questions." He asked all the pertinent questions that seemed to come from a prepared list. He even took some notes. My thinking at the time was that he was on light duty and the HPD had stuck him on a desk. He didn't seem like he wanted to be there.

Officer Presley asked if I had a receipt to show I was in the mall. When I told him I hadn't bought anything, he was curt. He took my name and phone number and said they would call me if they needed me. He was so condescending and arrogant that I walked out of there literally shaking my head, feeling like an idiot for even bothering to go in there.

No one ever called me. At the time, I thought they were not calling me because I had nothing to offer, since I never saw a tag number or vehicle. When I returned to work that evening, Herland asked me if I had gone to the police. He then asked me what they had to say. I was actually reluctant to tell him they just blew me off and that they made me feel I was making the whole thing up, so I told Richard, "They just took my statement," and left it at that.

I would later learn that, at this time in the case, there was total chaos at the police department. The HPD detectives were too inept to handle a case of this magnitude themselves, yet they were too arrogant to ask for outside help. The infighting was intense. Hollywood's lead detective, Detective Jack Hoffman, told Miami Beach's Detective Joe Matthews to butt out when Matthews suggested having one person oversee all the tips that were coming in. According to Adam's father, John Walsh, when the Broward County Sheriff's Office offered to help with the case, they were told to butt out as well. The general feeling at the HPD was that, whenever a break came in the case, the HPD wanted to be the only ones to take the credit for it.

I continued to follow the case in the newspaper. Feeling guilty about leaving Sears, I joined one of the search teams. We formed into small groups and searched undergrowth, residential back yards, and trash bins. We were looking for anything that could belong to Adam, such as his red and white striped shirt, green shorts, yellow sandals, and beige captain's hat. Our team searched from late morning until early evening. Of course, we never found anything.

I remember reading about the Walsh's houseguest, James Campbell. The Hollywood investigators considered him a suspect. They intensively interrogated him for weeks. The story I read said Adam might have been targeted, and only John Walsh and James Campbell knew that Adam and his mother Reve were going to the mall.

Without even seeing a photo of Campbell, I knew he hadn't kidnapped Adam. The person I followed had been meandering through the mall. He had approached me first, so certainly Adam wasn't targeted. If they had charged Campbell, I would've contacted his lawyer and gone to his aid. But they never did charge him.

John Walsh was quite upset with the HPD for concentrating their efforts on his houseguest and letting so many other potential leads slip away with time. As strong as John Walsh's discontent was with the HPD, I think it was even stronger with the media. The media had written about the two-year infidelity of Reve Walsh and claimed she was having an affair with James Campbell. They made allegations of John having ties to the mob. Some even wrote about Reve's attire the day Adam went missing. She was planning to go to the Apollo Gym after Sears, and she was wearing her gym outfit. Reve retorted by saying if she had known that Adam was going to disappear that day, she would've dressed properly for the occasion. John and Reve felt the media was trying to sensationalize their personal tragedy.

Second Encounter

About three weeks after Adam's abduction, I finished my day at the *Miami Herald* at around 4:40 a.m. We would typically finish early in the summer. I lived eighteen miles north, in the first town over the Broward County line, and as I turned onto Bedford Avenue in Hallandale, which is a short dead-end street, I noticed a blue van turning right behind me. I didn't give it a second thought, because similar vehicles were delivering newspapers to homes about this time. But as I pulled up to my home near the end of the street, the blue van pulled up alongside me. I parallel parked in front of my place because my boat was in the driveway. As I got out of my car, the driver rolled down his window, accused me of almost hitting him, and asked if I had insurance. I realized this was no newspaper guy and ignored him.

I didn't make much eye contact, but as I was walking to my door, he kept talking in an extremely assertive manner, repeating that I had almost caused an accident and demanding proof of insurance. I told him, "Almost doesn't count!" But I had no clue what he was talking about. He had totally made it up that I had nearly hit him. The driver then asked me if I was single. I was, but I told him no and went inside. I was in the bedroom emptying my pockets when I decided to check and see if he'd left. I went to the front kitchen window. When I looked out, I could see him sitting on the hood of my neighbor's car wearing dirty jeans and a long-sleeved blue shirt. He was just sitting there staring at my home and my '77 Pontiac Catalina.

I hadn't made the connection to the mall incident yet, so I took my time getting a knife from the kitchen drawer and then changed my mind. I went into the bedroom to get my Smith & Wesson .38 caliber revolver and my .25 caliber Beretta that I kept in my closet safe. I put the Beretta in my right pocket then removed the .38 from its leather case and checked to make sure it was loaded. I then went outside to confront this guy as I wanted to ask him what his problem was, but he was gone. He might have been spooked if he'd seen me looking. And he must have left in a hurry, because as I looked down the street, I didn't see his taillights. It finally dawned on me that it was the same guy I'd encountered in Radio Shack!

I ran back inside to grab my car keys and tried to catch up to him but the van had disappeared into the streets of Hallandale. After frantically driving around for a while, searching every street including the main boulevard, I gave up and went home. I was going to call the police to file a report, except I didn't get the tag number, and given my last attempt to help the police, I decided not to report it. That van was a dull dark blue with no back windows on the driver's side. It appeared to be a late '70s non-extended Dodge. I never did get to see the passenger side or the rear of the vehicle. Years later, when I saw Jeffrey Dahmer's mug shot from an arrest on October 7, 1981, in Bath, Ohio, I was certain this was the guy from the mall as well as the guy with the blue van.

While checking the case files, I noticed someone else had called on August 19, 1981, to report a blue van at a convenience store on SW 8th Avenue in Hallandale. This was only a few blocks from my 1981 address. The caller also said the van and driver matched the suspect in the Adam Walsh abduction. The operator did not take the name of the caller, so I wasn't able to get any more information. Although I can't now recall if it was Wednesday, August 19, 1981, or the morning of Thursday, August 20, that sounds like the correct day and date of my second encounter with the man I now know to be Jeffrey Dahmer.

ABOVE: HPD case files: Roll 1, P. 3145

I never said anything about this second encounter to anyone because I was afraid I would lose credibility. And, believe me, I would've lost credibility. The HPD would've used this against me to portray me as just wanting to inject myself into the case or being unreliable and even crazy in order to further solidify their cover-up. I wasn't even going to mention it here, but I wanted the full truth to be told, even if there are doubters—and there will always be doubters—as the odds of running into Dahmer not once but twice were slim. Then again, there are very few cars on the road at 5 a.m.

Ever since that second encounter, I have debated with myself how I could've handled things differently. The first time, I didn't know for sure something was going to happen. But what was my excuse the second time? If I'd realized this was the same guy, I could've talked with him, offered to go for breakfast, and told him to wait because I needed to change my uniform first while I called the police. They could've blocked off the street. There was only one way in and one way out. I could've even blocked him in with my own car, maybe even shot out his tires. I remember thinking there sure were a lot of crazy people in South Florida, but by the time I realized this was the same crazy person, it was too late and I had let him get away! I will spend the rest of my life regretting this.

Hindsight has allowed me to see with greater clarity than was possible at the time. What I should have done has become obvious. Something else that became obvious was that Dahmer was not only prowling our malls, he was prowling the streets of South Florida at a time when hitchhiking was very common. Also, he wasn't riding around only on his weekends.

Right after Adam was abducted, John Walsh consulted with Broward County medical examiner Dr. Ronald Wright. During this conversation, Dr. Wright first said to John, "You've got to accept the fact that Adam might be dead. I've got four girls up in the Broward County morgue, all homicide victims. . . They range in age from thirteen to sixteen. I believe they were all runaways. A couple of them were tortured very, very badly" (*Tears of Rage*, p. 81).

Knowing that Jeffrey Dahmer was riding around in the blue van trying to pick up people, I wondered if Dahmer could have picked up any hitchhikers in that van. In May 2013, I decided to go to the Broward County Medical Examiner's Office to get the records for any homicides during the time frame when Jeffrey Dahmer was working at Sunshine Subs and had access to the van (June 25 through September 30, 1981). I was told that unless I had a name and exact date for a homicide, they would not be able to help me. Their records were computerized in 1999 and anything before that date required a manual research. They didn't do that for just anyone, and they wouldn't allow anyone to look through their records.

When I explained that some of the homicides might not have names because they could've been runaways, I was told, in that case, they wouldn't be a public record, because only cases that had been solved were considered a public record. They told me I would have to go to the police department. The problem was that the Medical Examiner's Office covered all of Broward County and I didn't know which police department to go to.

Even though there was no evidence that Jeffrey Dahmer committed any of the hitchhiker homicides, he did approach me twice. He also showed up at his job a number of times with bruises and broken eyeglasses, which at the very least should have made him a person of interest, especially in light of his dishonesty.

Jeffrey Dahmer Leaves Florida

In September 1981, out of work and just about out of money, Dahmer called his stepmother, Shari, in Ohio. She told him she wouldn't send any money but would send him a one-way Pan Am plane ticket that would be waiting for him at the airport. Dahmer accepted, and around September 23, 1981, Jeffrey Dahmer was on his way back to Akron, Ohio.

I can only imagine what the people sitting next to him must have thought. Dahmer's dad Lionel said in his 1994 book *A Father's Story* that when the younger Dahmer stepped off the plane at the Cleveland Hopkins Airport, he was plenty drunk and stank. He had a scraggly and unkempt moustache. His clothes were unwashed and covered with stains. The Dahmers then drove the thirty-two miles back to 4480 West Bath Road near Akron, Ohio.

It didn't take long for Dahmer to get into trouble again. On October 7, 1981, or according to *A Father's Story*, about two weeks after he was back in Ohio (which means he left Florida around September 23, 1981, Dahmer was arrested at the Ramada Inn in Bath, Ohio. He staggered into the Maxwell Lounge, a hotel bar, with an open bottle of vodka. When he was asked to leave, he refused. Employees physically removed him to the parking lot and kept him detained until the police arrived. He was charged with disorderly conduct, having an open container, and resisting arrest. He kept insisting, on the way to jail, for the police to stop the car and beat him up. This wasn't much more than two months after he had abducted Adam, but it wouldn't be until 1991 that Lionel would make the connection between his son and Adam.

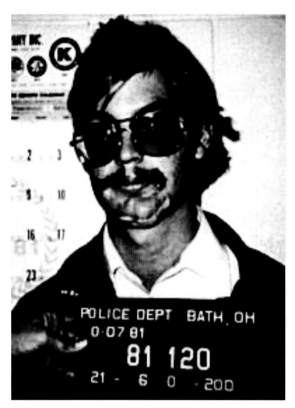

October 7, 1981.

PHOTO LEFT: The mug shot on the left is what Jeffrey Dahmer looked like two months after Adam's abduction and exactly as I remember him sitting on my neighbor's car with his eyeglasses on, minus the chin Band-Aid. Notice that he still has his Florida tan.

PHOTOS BELOW: The mug shots at the bottom of the page is Dahmer one year after Adam's abduction, when he was arrested by Milwaukee police for exposing himself to kids at a Wisconsin state fair. This is the way I remember him when he approached me in Radio Shack without his eyeglasses, except that his hair was longer and he had a dark tan.

August 8, 1982

Milwaukee PD

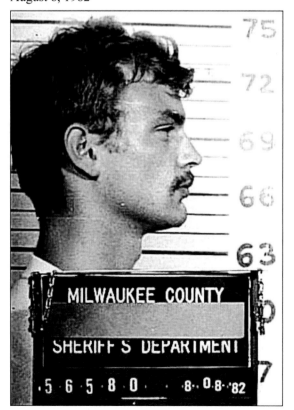

PHOTO RIGHT: This is the north door I had seen Jeffrey Dahmer enter the mall from. Radio Shack was the second store inside, on the left. The Mall Barber Shop is the second store on the right. The German Deli is right after the barber shop.

Photos taken in 2007 by Willis Morgan

ABOVE: This is a photo of the interior north entrance of the Hollywood Mall. Radio Shack was the second store on the right. It has since closed and moved to another location outside of the mall. In 2015 the Hollywood Mall electronics retailer went out of business for good.

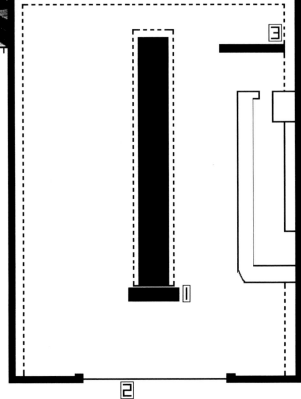

PHOTO RIGHT:
Radio Shack sketch: I made this rendering from memory and it isn't to scale.
1: Me at the "red-tag sale" table.
2: Jeffrey Dahmer at the entrance to the store.
3: Store clerk, in the back of the store behind a four-foot-high partition.

CHAPTER TWO
THE GREEN MACHINE

"When you've done the types of things I've done,
it's easier not to reflect on yourself."
_____*Jeffrey L. Dahmer*_____

Jeffrey Dahmer Goes to College

Back in the fall of 1978, Jeffrey Dahmer did a one-semester stint at Ohio's largest college, Ohio State University (OSU) at Columbus. OSU had open admissions back then. Any Ohio resident who graduated from high school with decent grades could get in. In *A Father's Story*, Lionel wrote that he thought this would be a period of renewed hope for his son.

In the beginning, when Lionel and Shari went to visit, Dahmer showed them around the campus and proudly displayed his dormitory room, number 541, which was in pod 540. That was one of six pods on the fifth floor, located on Cannon Drive in the all-male, lower-half Ross House section of the twenty-four-story Morrill Tower dormitory. The dormitory was isolated between the Olentangy River and the huge Ohio Stadium. To get to the main (east) side of campus, one had to walk through the open intramural athletic fields. It was even farther to North High Street, the off-campus, mile-long strip of bars, shops, eateries, and fast-food carry-outs that bordered the eastern edge of the campus and was the heart of student life.

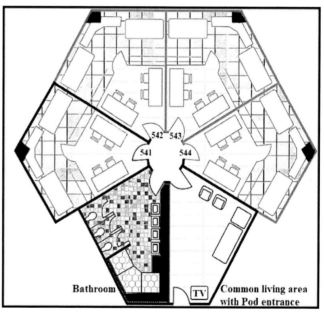

Pod 540 in Morrill Tower, rooms 541/542/543/544

Jeffrey Dahmer seemed proud to be a freshman at college, and he actually appeared happy. He even decorated his area in the bedroom with a photograph of Vice President Walter Mondale, a small picture of his dog, Frisky, and a snakeskin he'd found in the woods around his house, the only one of his many dead animal treasures that was normal enough to keep with him at college, according to *My Friend Dahmer* by John "Derf" Backderf.

It was all an illusion. Early on, Dahmer started dropping out of classes. When he did attend, he would sometimes pour inexpensive Gallo Thunderbird wine in a soda can and bring it with him. His dormitory room was stocked with bottles of Thunderbird and cases of beer. Dahmer kept his section neat and orderly except for all the empty wine bottle trophies lined up along the top of his three-foot-wide closet.

Everyone on his floor considered Dahmer to be weird. He remained a loner and never talked to anyone except when it was necessary. Whenever he would go to the second-floor Traditions Cafeteria, he would eat a solitary lunch. When students went out for a drink, Dahmer wasn't invited.

Dahmer had his own daily routine. He'd walk the three-quarter-mile trek alone across campus to the North High Street bars, where he would spend his weekly allowance from his father. When the bars closed at 2:30 a.m., he'd stagger back to his dorm, climb into his upper bunk, and collapse on his bed until late morning. Then he'd wake up and do it all over again.

One of Dahmer's favorite drinking holes was a dive bar called Bernie's, where he was a regular. It was a small, dark, dingy hole-in-the-wall bar without windows, known for its $1 draft specials and cheap food. Anyone who walked down the stairs to Bernie's was greeted with the fine musk of stale beer and dirty bathrooms. Located at 1896 N. High Street, Bernie's was a short walk from the Morrill Tower across the athletic fields to 17th Avenue, and another half mile east to North High Street.

A total of about twenty of the two hundred students from Dahmer's 1978 senior graduating class at Revere High School in Bath, Ohio, attended OSU. One of those students, Martha Schmidt, once came across him passed out cold on the sidewalk near Bernie's. She recognized Dahmer from high school and tried to revive him out of his drunken stupor. When she was unable to rouse him, she remembered thinking he was gone, so she left him there, according to a *Chicago Tribune* article on July 28, 1991.

As the weather became colder, Dahmer became less willing to leave his dorm. He'd solitarily drink himself into a stupor right in his room, polishing off several bottles of wine every day as he lay sprawled across his upper bunk. Day after day, he'd lie there and listen to the 1967 Beatles song "I Am the Walrus" and sing along, over and over again, out of key.

In November 1978, Dahmer was suspected of stealing money from another student. Dahmer's roommate, Craig Schweiger, told me he'd once invited Jeffrey Gerberick to his room for a little party. Craig knew Gerberick from high school, and by coincidence, they happened to live on the same floor.

After spending some time in the dorm room, Gerberick changed his clothes, and he and Craig went out. When they returned, Gerberick found $120 missing from the pockets of his pants that he'd left in the room. Gerberick called campus police, and Dahmer, the only suspect, was detained and questioned about the theft. Dahmer admitted nothing and didn't crack under questioning. No charges were filed, but students started locking their doors and hiding their belongings. They even threatened Dahmer, but the young Cannon Drive misfit responded only with his trademark blank stare.

Another time, when Dahmer's roommates returned, they found all the furniture stacked up in one corner of the room and pizza tossed all over the walls. It was no wonder they thought he was weird. Dahmer never did give an explanation for his outburst. If they tried to ask him, he'd get angry. Once, he kicked a hole in the tiled bathroom wall. Another time, Craig's watch went missing, and another time his radio was ruined by someone pouring some liquid onto it. Craig had had enough and shifted to neighboring room 542. After Craig moved out, only two students remained there with Dahmer. One, whose name Craig cannot recall, often headed home to the family farm on the weekends. That meant Michael Prochaska, of Cleveland, and Jeffrey Dahmer were the only ones left in that room on weekends.

Dahmer made no effort to control his drinking. The only time he was sober was when his allowance ran out.

He supplemented his allowance by selling his blood twice a week, for $12 a visit, to a local blood bank, Columbus Plasma Corporation, in order to fund his drinking. The blood bank even advertised in *The Lantern*, the student newspaper, telling students they could "save a life and earn $100 a month."

This also gave Dahmer extra money to rent a bicycle. But what goes around comes around, and eventually Dahmer's rented bicycle was stolen. Craig Schweiger told me he didn't steal Dahmer's bike, and no one knows who did.

Other students in Pod 540 became so fed up with Dahmer that they petitioned the resident advisor to have him expelled from Ross House. However, his father had already paid for the room, and nothing could be done. They were told to put up with him until the end of the term.

Dahmer's father and stepmother picked him up in early December, after the autumn semester. Lionel had already received Dahmer's grade report in the mail several days earlier. Dahmer had earned only two hours of college credits after a full quarter, with a 0.45 grade point average, which is a D-. His performance in Administrative Science had been no more than mediocre. He'd failed Introduction to Anthropology. He hadn't completed Greco-Roman History, and he'd dropped out of other courses after only a few weeks. Riflery 1, an introduction to target shooting techniques, was the only course he had attended with regularity. In that, he managed to get a B.

During his entire stay at Ohio State, Jeffrey Dahmer had made no friends. He'd distinguished himself only for drinking prodigious amounts of Thunderbird, a longtime favorite drink of derelicts. On the way home, Dahmer explained that he'd simply found it difficult to get up in the mornings.

Lionel then gave his son an ultimatum, and the options by that time were slim: either get a job or join the armed forces. When the younger Dahmer refused to get a job and stayed drunk most of the time, his father decided to drive him down to the recruiting office in Cleveland, Ohio. If anyone could straighten his son out, it'd be the United States Army. Dahmer's enlistment date was listed as December 29, 1978, at the entry-level rank of E-1/Private. This was for a three-year active-duty enlistment period followed by three years in the Reserves. His Military Occupational Specialty (MOS) title was 95-B (Bravo). That meant he'd signed up to become a military police (MP) officer through the army's delayed-entry program. He went on active duty on January 12, 1979.

According to FBI files, on his application to enlist in the army, Dahmer marked "no" in response to a question regarding engagement in homosexual activity. He listed his only criminal violation as a motor vehicle offense for driving left of the center line on June 18, 1978, near Richfield, Ohio. He never mentioned anything about having a backseat passenger—the one chopped up and stuffed into five garbage bags—Steven Hicks.

Back in 1978, when the police officer who stopped him called for backup, another officer arrived. They checked his driver's license and gave him a field sobriety test. He was made to walk the line and do the finger-to-nose test, which he passed. They questioned why the bags in the back seat smelled so bad, but accepted Dahmer's explanation that it was two-day-old garbage that he hadn't had a chance to dispose of yet. When asked why he was out at 3 a.m., Dahmer explained that his parents had gotten divorced and he was having a hard time staying home alone. He ended up paying a $20 ticket in traffic court.

Private Dahmer

With at least one murder already under his belt, the Buckeye legend flew to the Birmingham International Airport. From there, he boarded one of those green army buses along with other soldiers that had arrived from across the country, for the sixty-five-mile ride east along Interstate 20 to Fort McClellan, also known as Fort Mac.

When Dahmer first arrived for army basic training, he was assigned to the Reception Battalion for initial in-processing. Getting his boots, dress and physical training (PT) uniform issue, paperwork, blood work, vaccines, haircut, identification, and pictures were just a few stations that he had to go through in those first few days. Those days didn't count toward his actual basic training time but were necessary in order to get assigned to a unit and begin basic training. Pvt. Dahmer was assigned to B Company in the 11th Military Police Battalion.

1979 army photo of Jeffrey Dahmer

Fort McClellan was a major training facility that was home to an average population of about 10,000 military personnel, located adjacent to the city of Anniston, Alabama. Dahmer would begin the rigorous physical and mental basic combat training (BCT) to become a soldier. He arrived at boot camp as a sluggish, out-of-shape kid four months shy of his nineteenth birthday. It wouldn't take long before the army would whip him into shape.

Dahmer's eight weeks at boot camp were filled with a regular regimen of physical activities six days a week, except Sundays. But Sundays weren't exactly days off. He still had to wake up and do PT. After breakfast, he'd have the option of going to church. After that, he would've been doing details all day such as picking up trash, cleaning the barracks, or kitchen patrol duty (KP) peeling potatoes and washing pots and pans. During his entire time in basic combat training, Dahmer was remembered as being a very quiet, chubby kid who kept to himself, although he did earn two army badges, one as a marksman with the .45-caliber handgun and another as a sharpshooter with the M-16 assault rifle.

After he completed boot camp, Pvt. Dahmer was ready for the next step—eight weeks of Advanced Individual Training (AIT). He would enter the U.S. Army Military Police Corps School to become a military police officer. Pvt. Dahmer wouldn't have to travel far, because this was a One-Station Unit Training (OSUT) program, which was eight weeks of basic and eight weeks of MP training combined. He was billeted in the same barracks for both basic and MP training, located in the relatively new section of the base that was constructed when the MP school was moved to Fort Mac in 1976.

Dahmer never finished his MP training because, near the end of April and about two weeks before he was to graduate, he "washed out," according to FBI files. Joyce Wiesner, a spokeswoman for the Army Reserve Center in St. Louis, Missouri, wasn't able to say why Dahmer hadn't completed his training, emphasizing that she couldn't release information about disciplinary or medical actions, citing the Privacy Act of 1974.

I was able to find out that, when Dahmer began MP school, the restrictions, especially on weekends, were less enforced. Someone would've had to give up their off time and conduct Charge of Quarters (CQ) duty on weekends, since there had to be someone on duty in the barracks at all times. Other than that, everyone was off on the weekends and could plan on partying. Although it was still hard to drink in the barracks, Dahmer would've had access to alcohol at an on-base club for enlisted men called the 1-2-3 Club, as well as the Base Post Exchange (PX). There was a spot under some trees to the side of the PX where soldiers could sit on the grass and drink without being bothered.

Pvt. Dahmer was regularly reprimanded for drunkenness and for having a total lack of ambition. He managed to get his entire platoon punished with extra physical training. Several times he was beat up for his insubordination. Once a large black private and a large white private took him into the men's room and gave him a beating severe enough to give him a concussion and rupture his left ear. This would cause Dahmer to have earaches for years to come. The physical beating was so bad that he had to be transferred to Fort Benning in Columbus, Georgia, for treatment. After a short recuperation, he returned to Fort Mac.

When I told Billy Joe Capshaw, Dahmer's Germany roommate, about the beating, Billy told me he didn't know about that, though Dahmer frequently would hold his left ear and complain about having an earache and a headache. But Dahmer had never mentioned anything about getting beat up. Billy got it right; it was the left ear.

A military police officer's basic job description is to protect lives and property on army installations by enforcing military laws and regulations as well as controlling traffic, preventing crime, and responding to emergencies. The army apparently decided Pvt. Dahmer wouldn't be very good at general policing activities and security. Around May 7, when he returned from Fort Benning, they reclassified his Military Occupation Specialties (MOS) to 91-B, and on May 11, 1979, Dahmer was transferred to the 5th Army, 232nd Medical Battalion for combat medical aid training at Fort Sam Houston in San Antonio, Texas. Jeffrey Dahmer also mentioned this in his confession to Milwaukee detectives that can viewed at JusticeForAdam.com (Part-1, p. 117).

Without the capacity for empathy, Dahmer trained to save lives on the battlefield. The combat medic is the first line of medical aid. "Medic!" is a cry that has been heard on battlefields for centuries. But now it would be Pvt. Dahmer coming to a wounded soldier's aid. Dahmer underwent his six-week course to become a combat medical specialist, which is the equivalent of a nurse's aide, for the front-line units in the Cold War. The focus of the program was to be able to treat those catastrophic injuries and preventable causes of death at the point of injury and get that soldier back to an aid station at the rear.

His barracks was an open-room setup with twenty to twenty-five soldiers per room, located in an area at Ft. Sam called "down the hill." Those who were specializing in adjunct specialties such as dental, x-ray, dietary, lab, and veterinary medicine were located "up the hill," which was like a really strict college atmosphere. Dentists and doctors also trained there for the Basic Officer Leadership Course (BOLC).

Down the hill was not so much like college, but rather more like light basic training. The process was not really that much fun. At 4:30 a.m. during the week, Dahmer woke up for PT and then breakfast, followed by classes or field training every day starting at around 8 a.m. and going on until around 5:30 p.m. When finished, he ate again, got released for about two hours, and then went to bed at 9:30 p.m. Weekends, when he got them, started out Friday evening with no restrictions on movement. He had to be back before 10 p.m.

Military medical classes are fast but boring, teaching the basics before CPR licensing such as Basic Intravenous Therapy (IV), stop bleeding and transport are just some classes he went through. Putting military into the medical field came with loads of outdoor time and running around. A trainee would go to the field, come back, and then get the heck out of Ft. Sam.

Dahmer might have learned a lesson from that beatdown in MP School, because he managed to complete his medical training course without being caught in a state of alcoholic paralysis, though it didn't stop him from drinking. Halfway up the hill was a bar called the Sam Houston Club. The bar was close enough to the barracks so that the cacophony of bar sounds and music could be heard from the barracks. To Pvt. Dahmer, that sound was like a beacon calling him.

Steven Lampley was transferred to Ft. Sam Houston after basic training for advanced individual training as both a medical specialist and a clinical specialist. He was in the 232nd Medical Battalion at the same time as Dahmer. Every Friday night after classes, Steven and his friend Steve Baker would go to the Sam Houston Club for some beers. Jeffrey Dahmer would also be there. Although Dahmer wasn't in the same classes as Lampley and Baker, they often seemed to end up sitting at the same table with Dahmer, at least on five or six Fridays. Of course, Dahmer could've been going more than just on Fridays.

Steven said he remembered Dahmer as being a gentleman who joined him and his friend for drinks. They described him as quiet, nice, cordial, and friendly with sandy blond hair and aviator glasses. He mostly sat directly across from Lampley and Baker. They had casual conversation, which mostly consisted of how their week was going. Dahmer mostly sat quietly, staring into space. He never initiated a conversation, but if asked a question, he would give a minimal answer. Steve Baker also told me he remembered seeing Dahmer in the mess hall a number of times and even sat with him there. His memory of Dahmer was that he was very squirrelly. He didn't talk much, and when he did, he wouldn't make eye contact.

This is what Steven posted: *A few years after the army, my best friend asked me if I remembered that quiet guy with the sandy blonde hair that had joined us. I, of course, remembered. He asked me if I knew who he was and I responded with 'I didn't remember his name if I had ever known it.' It was then that he told me that person's name was Jeffrey Dahmer. In shock and disbelief, I immediately began researching. Indeed, Jeffrey Dahmer WAS stationed at Ft. Sam Houston at the SAME TIME I was (232nd Medical Battalion for Medical Training at Ft. Sam Houston). When I went back and looked at the photo, I was sure.*

PHOTO LEFT: Private Dahmer on furlough with his father Lionel and his brother David before going to Germany.

When Dahmer completed his training on June 22, 1979, he took a three-week furlough to visit his father. It had been five and a half months since he'd left home. Lionel said in *A Father's Story*, "This new, completely refurbished Jeff was a handsome, broad-shouldered young man who smiled brightly when he stepped off the bus. His hair was close-cropped, his clothes neat and orderly. More important, perhaps, there was not so much as a hint of liquor on his breath." During his three weeks at home, Dahmer raked leaves and did other yard work. When he wasn't working, he'd cook hamburgers and steaks on the grill. When the three weeks were up, his dad took him to the bus station in downtown Akron for the ride to the Cleveland Airport. He then flew to the army reception center in Frankfurt, West Germany, where he was deployed to the 2nd Battalion, 68th Armored Regiment, 8th Infantry Division in Baumholder, West Germany.

Baumholder is home to the largest concentration of U.S. combat soldiers outside the United States, with a population of 13,000 soldiers and family members, and a local population of 4,800 Germans. The American military community coexists with the city of Baumholder, as various housing units and post facilities are located in and around the city. Baumholder is located in west-central Germany, in the state of Rhineland-Palatinate, about sixty-five kilometers north of the French border and about seventy-two kilometers east of Luxembourg.

When Dahmer arrived in Germany with all the signs and symptoms of a budding psychopath, it was still divided. The Berlin Wall would not fall until November 1989. The Cold War would not end until after the collapse of the Soviet Union in 1991.

Pvt. Dahmer Goes to Baumholder

I received the information in this section from Billy Joe Capshaw, David Rodriguez, Preston Davis, and other soldiers stationed with Dahmer, as well as from my own research into FBI files and other records. Sondra Schalk's German language research also helped.

Pvt. Dahmer was billeted in the 8400 Harold D. Smith Headquarters Building. At the entrance to the building, there was a twenty-four-hour Charge of Quarters duty station (CQ desk) where visitors would have to sign in and check back out no later than 10 p.m. Of the fifty or so rooms in the 8400 barracks, three rooms were dedicated to the twenty-one or so medics. Only nine or so lived on base, and the rest lived off base. Rooms 103 and 104 were both eight-man rooms, and across the hall was a two-man room for the sergeants.

Monday through Friday at 6 a.m., all the medics were supposed to fall in formation in front of the building, including soldiers that lived off base. Behind the building was the on-base Sixt car rental agency. However, most on-base facilities were within walking distance of the 8400 barracks.

Dahmer spent his early days mostly as a loner. His room walls had posters of heavy metal bands like Iron Maiden and Black Sabbath, known for songs of death and evil. He stayed in uniform during the week and would frequently lie in bed and listen to his music. With his headphones plugged into a 1970s vintage eight-track tape player, he would drink beer, gin, and vodka until he had drunk himself unconscious. On some weekends, he would revive himself enough to go off base—alone.

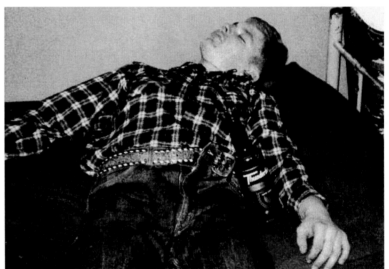

PHOTO RIGHT: Rodriguez planted the bottle next to Dahmer in 1979 as a prop joke for the photo taken by another soldier. This photo is courtesy of David Rodriguez.

Dahmer was known to pour out the contents of soda bottles and refill them with straight vodka. His long-time roommate, Billy Joe Capshaw, said Dahmer frequently mixed martinis in the barracks using shakers, a metal stirrer, martini glasses, flasks, and other bar equipment that he carried in a black briefcase. Billy described it as a "portable cocktail bar" that Dahmer might have purchased from the Post Exchange and used to evade detection from inspections carried out to enforce a ban on liquor in the barracks. According to Dahmer's sergeant, Pete Altman, his portable mini-bar was eventually confiscated. The alcohol policy was one six-pack or one bottle of wine per person. No hard liquor was allowed.

David Rodriguez, who was nineteen at the time, was room commander of room 103. He shared the room with Jeffrey Dahmer for a short period in 1979 until Dahmer was transferred to room 104 because no one wanted him in 103. He described Dahmer as generally personable and as having a sense of humor.

PHOTO RIGHT: David Rodriguez (left) in room 103 with Jeffrey Dahmer in 1979 when Pvt. Dahmer first arrived in Germany. Photo is courtesy of David Rodriguez.

"I could see how he'd lure them in," Rodriguez told me. "He was basically a likable guy, except when he was drinking, he would act different." He would ask Dahmer to do the easiest chores, such as taking out the garbage, but Dahmer was defiant and told Rodriguez to go to hell. Sometimes Rodriguez would have to take out the garbage himself because Dahmer refused to do what he was supposed to do.

Rodriguez remembered Dahmer as being a gin-swilling "wimp" who seemed incapable of the grisly murders in Milwaukee. Dave told me, "He'd be shut out from the rest of the world. Beginning on Friday afternoons, he'd put on his headphones and drink until he passed out, then wake up and start all over again. He was in his own little world." He wouldn't even go to the mess hall for chow. But that was not every weekend. Some weekends Dahmer would disappear from the base, and no one would know where he went. "He was pretty much a loner who never went out with other medics."

Rodriguez was also in charge of the medics' motor pool and said that whenever Dahmer was assigned to the motor pool and Rodriguez would have to show him what to do, Dahmer showed no interest. Instead, Dahmer would give him this cold, icy stare and then find a vehicle to crawl into and fall asleep.

When he gave me the names of other soldiers to contact, the first one I contacted was Preston Davis. Specialist E-4 Davis, who had been at Baumholder since June 1977, was asked by his platoon sergeant in October 1979 to train the new guy who arrived on July 13, 1979. One of Pvt. Dahmer's first assignments was to go on a two-and-a-half-week field exercise with Davis. They went to the Baumholder train station, where Davis showed Dahmer how to load an Armored Personnel Carrier (APC) onto a lorry-rail train and then offload it again near the border of Belgium. They drove around with an armored field artillery battalion, and Davis taught Dahmer how to read a map and set up a field hospital in support of the convoy.

PHOTO RIGHT: Army photo courtesy of Preston Davis.

According to Davis, they never had access to alcohol, and Dahmer was sober during the entire trip. The conversations were mostly army talk. Davis said Dahmer was personable and even likeable during the two-and-a-half-week assignment.

I suspected there was more to Preston's story than he was saying, because he seemed very agitated when talking about Dahmer. I didn't want to press him, but give him Billy Joe Capshaw's phone number when he asked for it. Preston and Billy would become friends, and it was to Billy that Preston would first tell his full story of his encounter with Dahmer—and even then, it would take more than a year. Many soldiers who are "assaulted" won't go public with their story. The shame alone is overwhelming.

One day in June 2011, Preston called me to say he had been assaulted by Jeffrey Dahmer after Jeff gave him a drink that knocked him out. The assault occurred in the APC near the border of Belgium at the end of the two-plus-week assignment.

On February 4, 1980, just two weeks before Billy Joe Capshaw arrived, Preston Davis left Germany for good. But the trauma he went through lives with him to this day. It would be years before Preston came forward and filed for (and was granted) his claim for post-traumatic stress disorder (PTSD).

First Trip to K-Town

One time, when Dahmer admitted that he'd never kissed a girl, a group of soldiers became determined to get him to lose his virginity. Sometime in the afternoon around the end of October 1979, several of them took him to Annabella's Haus (House), a well-known four-story brothel that still looks more like a motel than a brothel. It's located in the Vogelweh section of Kaiserslautern (K-Town) and can be seen from the Autobahn. It has been said that if a soldier can't have fun in K-Town, then there is something wrong with him.

After dragging Jeff in and introducing him to one of the "hostesses," they split up and left him with the girl. What happened next is not known, except that Jeff didn't stay. He snuck out without doing anything. Back at the barracks, when questioned, he said he didn't need a girl.

Over the next fourteen months, a number of women in the area were found strangled, stabbed, and mutilated. On November 2, 1979, one unidentified woman's charred body was found in a field outside Bosenbach, a village about halfway between K-Town and Baumholder. The body had been doused with gasoline, ignited, and burned. The woman was black, between twenty and twenty-three years old, and five feet seven inches tall. She was of slender build and had medium-length, black, curly hair. The Criminal Investigation Division determined she had been murdered on Saturday, October 27, 1979.

Although it is not known for sure, this could've been the same weekend night Dahmer walked out of Annabella's. It is very plausible he could've rented a car and driven around alone in his comfort zone looking for hitchhikers when he passed through the village of Bosenbach on his way back to Baumholder. The fact that it was a weekend makes it even more probable that this could've been something Dahmer did. When questioned by Milwaukee detectives about bodies dismembered and found in Germany during the time he was stationed there, Dahmer stated that he remembered reading in the newspapers in Germany about a black female who was found beheaded and dismembered and left in a field. He then added that it only rang a bell because it was big news at the time. (Dahmer's confession, PART-1, p. 91)

According to the German TV show *Aktenzeichen XY Ungelöst* ("Unsolved Cases"), around midnight, a young couple on the way home from the movies passed by and noticed a suspicious fire. The next day, Sunday, a father and son were searching for chestnuts at the edge of the forest when they saw what they thought was a dead calf, but they never did get too close. It would be almost another week before hikers found the charred body and called the police.

According to *European Stars and Stripes*, a police spokesman said they were "ninety-nine percent" sure the murdered woman was not an American, but American involvement in the slaying had not been ruled out due to the proximity to Baumholder. Bosenbach was popular among Americans who frequented a nearby disco close to where the body was found. This case had German police and American army investigators collaborating but without results.

The American investigators said none of their women were missing. They put up posters and talked to hundreds of servicemen as well as the owners and workers at the club but came up with zero. The victim was presumed to be a young black prostitute who frequented the club scene. She had a suitcase with her that was also set on fire, so she could have been simply looking for a ride. Of the suitcase, only some metal parts survived. Investigators were unable to identify her, and they never could determine a motive, according to *Aktenzeichen XY Ungelöst*. No evidence points to Jeffrey Dahmer being the perpetrator of this murder. Yet, given Dahmer's track record of killings, circumstantial suspicion now is natural.

And then there is what happened on Thanksgiving.

First Thanksgiving

On November 22, 1979, Jeffrey Dahmer and Preston Davis were two of the soldiers that Specialist Carlos Cruz and his wife invited to their home for Thanksgiving dinner. They lived in the village of Birkenfeld, eight miles west of Baumholder. While they were eating dinner, the temperature dropped to sub-zero, and it began snowing heavily. Carlos invited the soldiers to stay over for the night and make their way back to the base in the morning.

All the soldiers accepted except for one. Apparently, Jeffrey Dahmer didn't like the sleeping arrangements. After an argument with Preston Davis around 10:30 p.m., Dahmer walked out the door into the freezing cold night. Preston said they looked for him but gave up after thirty minutes or so and retreated back to the warmth of the house, presuming that Dahmer had found a taxi back to Baumholder. Four hours later, Dahmer knocked on the door. He appeared confused and had lost his glasses.

Preston told me Dahmer's jacket was not cold when he touched it, as would be expected after being out in sub-zero weather for four hours. Cruz also said when he took Dahmer to the kitchen, where he energetically washed his hands his jacket was warm to the touch. Cruz and Davis also noticed blood on his jacket (this was also mentioned in Dahmer's confession, Part 1, p. 107). Then Dahmer sat at the kitchen table and just stared at the table in cold silence. When Cruz asked him where he'd been, Dahmer vaguely replied that he couldn't remember where he had been or what he'd been doing. Dahmer admitted, "I think I did something bad, but I can't talk about it."

Pathological Liar

On July 29, 1991, Milwaukee detectives Dennis Murphy and Patrick Kennedy informed Dahmer during questioning that they had a call from Carlos Cruz, who stated that he had been in Germany with Dahmer and told them about the Thanksgiving dinner. After maintaining that he never stayed overnight anywhere except when he went to Oktoberfest and when he went on temporary assignment to Landstuhl Regional Medical Center, Dahmer stated that he now did remember spending Thanksgiving at Mr. Cruz's residence. Then Dahmer said it was "snowing hard, similar to a blizzard," so he "did not leave the house." He remembered staying there and leaving in the morning, but he did not remember being covered in blood. I suppose Dahmer never expected Carlos Cruz to call the Milwaukee police. These detectives never pressed him on that issue or any of his many other lies. One thing you will notice about Jeffrey Dahmer is that, whenever he was caught in a lie, he simply blamed it on a lapse of memory, his intoxication, or his thought that it was irrelevant. But let there be no question, someone had a very bad night on November 22, 1979.

They say you are only as sick as your secrets, and Jeffrey Dahmer had plenty. They were the kind of secrets that would slowly rob him of his sanity and begin his descent away from humanity. What happened when Dahmer walked out into that cold Thanksgiving night is not known. Even the extensive archive searches in Germany by Sondra Schalk didn't turn up any civilian murders on that night. That leaves the possibility that something could've happened on a military installation. While doing my own research, I came across the following double murder in a twenty-two-page article titled "Sex Scandals in the Gender-Integrated Military," written by Rutgers University history professor William O'Neill. When I contacted Professor O'Neill, he said he'd gotten this information from a book by Linda B. Francke, *Ground Zero: The Gender Wars in the Military.* I ordered a copy of *Ground Zero.* It didn't have much more than what Professor O'Neill's article said, relevant to the Wacshack (lingo for Woman's Air Core barracks), so I called Linda Francke.

> The violence was so intense at a "Wacshack" in Germany in 1979 that one Army woman spent her own money to live off base in an apartment. "I came back from flying one day to find the building locked down and MPs in the hallways," says a combat aviation mechanic known as Dragon Lady. "It turned out two women had been murdered and left in the shower, one strangled, the other impaled on a broomstick. I never went back inside. We weren't even safe in our own building."

ABOVE: Quoted from Professor O'Neill's article.
BELOW: Quoted from *Ground Zero* p. 165.

> The problem was that with more and more women in the service, there was more and more sexual harassment, so much so that it required institutional reform, not just a watch-dog agency. Even women in segregated barracks were not safe. In one particularly gruesome instance in 1979, two Germany-based Army women were murdered in the shower of their barracks, one strangled and the other impaled on a broomstick. At Fort Hood, Texas, rapes were so frequent at one point that gunships of the 6th Air Cavalry flew nightly patrols over the base.[30]

She told me the information came from the female pilots that she met with and interviewed back when she was writing the book. Linda Francke seemed anxious to help me find the Dragon Lady. She even sent out the following message to her many friends and contacts:

I wrote a book some years ago, "Ground Zero: The Gender Wars in the Military," *and spent a lot of time with the aviators in the WMA. One of them was a combat aviation mechanic stationed in Germany in 1979 who was known as* "Dragon Lady." *(She chose to live off base because of two murders in the* "Wacshack"*). I wrote about the murders on p. 165. A guy named Willis Morgan has contacted me about the murders. He is convinced they were committed by the serial killer Geoffrey Dahmer. He would like to speak to the 1979* "Dragon Lady" *or anyone else at the WMA who could shed any light on the case, like which base the Dragon Lady was stationed at. He can be reached by email: //////////////////@////.com or by phone: /-///-///-////. I'm at: //////////////////@////, phone: /-///-///-////.*

The trail may be cold by now, but Willis is determined to keep investigating other murders that Dahmer might have committed but was never charged with.

Thanks

Linda Bird Francke

In the last e-mail I received from Linda, she told me the Dragon Lady had been located by her contacts, but they would have to get permission from her before they could give me her name and phone number. That was the last I heard from Linda. Apparently, the Dragon Lady didn't want to talk.

Since no one is talking, I have no way of even knowing if this double murder happened on Thanksgiving 1979. Even if it was another date, this is something Jeffrey Dahmer was capable of doing, though suspicion is circumstantial.

Bunkmates' Assessment

On August 11, 1991, Robert Dvorchak of the *Associated Press* wrote: " 'He was smart and well read, but he just wanted to slide by,' [said] Michael Masters, who was room commander of room 104. 'He was just goofy. He always had that look about him, that sinisterness. He was on a steady decline in life. He was on a losing skid and didn't know how to pick himself up.' "

In early 1980, Dahmer was transferred to room 104 with Michael Masters, who was quoted by the *New York Times* as saying, "He had an IQ of at least 140 or higher; he read a lot." In fact, Dahmer would spend hours at the library reading books like *Gnomes.* Created by Terry Pratchett, *Gnomes* was about a fictional character, humanlike in appearance, living under the ground. Sometimes he'd bring his portable bar with him to the library.

Masters also said, "Dahmer often became a menace to others living in the barracks. When Dahmer was on his drinking binges, he would get belligerent and moody and had a passion for making obnoxious racist remarks. . . There was often friction between Dahmer and Eric Logan a black soldier from Texas."

David Rodriguez told me that both he and Masters believed someday it would be proved that Dahmer committed some murders while stationed in Germany. However, Michael Masters will never get to see that outcome. His wife Barbara told me he passed away in October 2009.

The Mad Medic

In 1991, Linda Sue Swisher would make the connection to Dahmer and the murders and rapes in Germany. When she saw his photo in the paper, she recognized him instantly. Of all the people who went through the medic refresher program that she taught at the Baumholder Health Clinic, also known as 56th General Hospital, he was the only one she remembered. "He was extremely antisocial." She remembered thinking at the time that he could be a serial rapist.

The snapshot image of him that she remembered most was from one day in class. It was his turn to replace a fake liver in its proper place in a full-sized anatomical medical dummy. "He had this cold, icy, blank stare with no light in his eyes, and he was smiling all the time while replacing it." Linda told me the smile didn't match the cold, icy stare, and that was the only time she ever saw him smile. Most of the time, he did little more than show up. He never paid attention, never asked questions, and didn't pass to the next level.

David Rodriguez said he was in that six-week first aid training class with Dahmer and remembered him not showing any interest in class. "He didn't look like he ever took an interest in the anatomy," he said. Apparently, Dahmer did.

During this time, three males were severely beaten and raped. All three males were short and fairly thin, probably not the type capable of defending themselves. The three rapes happened within a few months of each other, and all while Dahmer was stationed on base. According to Linda, one Hispanic male was so badly sodomized that he had to have a colostomy bag. He would've died had he not been stabilized within thirty minutes from the time he was found. All three had injuries so severe that they had to be transported to the larger hospital in Landstuhl. Linda said she was unable to find out any more information about the men except that all three survived.

In Linda Swisher's own words:

> *In November of 1980, I left Baumholder, West Germany as a medic who had been assigned to the Post Station hospital. The hospital had a refresher training program for medics who had little contact with real ER medical problems. I too looked at the front page and saw a man I had helped to train. Yes, there are cold case crimes from Baumholder, Germany. This post is where Dahmer served as a U.S. Army medic as did Billy Joe Capshaw and where I was in part responsible for teaching ER care skills to other medics. The Army taught basic life support skills to Dahmer and I helped him to learn.*
>
> *The first day I saw Dahmer's picture I knew evil had a face and that I helped to teach him.*

Posted by ColdWarMedic, August 18, 2007, on ABC's *Primetime* blog.

CHAPTER THREE
LIVING WITH JEFF

According to roommate Billy Capshaw in 1980, when Dahmer was housed in room 104, there were only about four men in that room. One of those soldiers was Texan Eric Logan, but he had a girlfriend here and there to hang out with and so wasn't around much on his off time. Nobody wanted to stay in that room with Dahmer. Many nights, soldiers would go out and party without Dahmer, so he would have the room pretty much to himself. They said he went through a kind of Jekyll-and-Hyde transformation, a loner when sober but agitated and loud after a few drinks. David Rodriguez confirmed that even he wasn't always around. He was on temporary duty assignment to Landstuhl Medical Center for three months and did a lot of traveling. In February of 1980, room 104 would get another roommate.

I've known Billy Joe Capshaw since 2008, when true-crime writer Art Harris gave me his phone number. Billy enlisted in the army as a 5'10", overweight, 200-plus-pound new recruit on October 29, 1979. He was barely seventeen years old. He came from a poor background in Arkansas and wanted to help his family financially. After completing basic training, a medical specialist course, and a short furlough he was sent to Frankfurt, West Germany, for processing. A week later, they sent him to Baumholder. On February 24, 1980, Specialist David Goss showed Billy to his room. This was the same room Pvt. Dahmer was in. Goss told Billy that Dahmer would be a good roommate and would show him the ropes. Dahmer then shook hands with Billy and introduced himself as Jeff.

PHOTO RIGHT: Courtesy of Billy Capshaw.

The eight-man room was on the first floor. It had four sets of beds, most with top bunks, though one was used as a couch, as the top bunk was missing. By virtue of seniority, Dahmer made Billy take the bunk above his.

Showing Billy "The Ropes"

Next to Dahmer's bunk was a small, dorm-sized refrigerator with a small freezer compartment that Dahmer used for his ice trays. He would fill the ice trays from a plastic jug of water and use the ice cubes for his mixed drinks. According to Billy, Dahmer bought the refrigerator from another soldier who returned to the States.

During the time Billy and Dahmer were roommates, there were about three "health and welfare" room inspections conducted by the U.S. Air Force with drug-sniffing dogs. On a more regular basis, soldiers had to be prepared for the Inspector General inspections conducted by the platoon sergeant or the first sergeant/commander. Lockers and refrigerators were always checked for cleanliness and hygiene.

Sergeant Pete Altman, who participated in at least two of these inspections, told me that Dahmer's locker was very simple. He had four sets of uniforms, some civilian clothes, and a few *Rolling Stone* magazines. Billy told me that the only civilian clothes Dahmer owned were a blue plaid shirt, a brown plaid shirt, a pair of blue jeans, a pair of brown corduroy pants, a gray cool-weather zip-up sweat shirt, a pair of shoes, a blue bath robe, and a belt.

Billy said, "At first, Jeff seemed to be a likeable person and was a great conversationalist," but it wouldn't take long before Billy became frightened of Dahmer as he began his process of controlling Billy. Dahmer was several years older and several inches taller. In a matter of days, Dahmer had taken complete control over Billy.

During this time, Billy said he was drugged, raped, molested, and physically beaten. Dahmer started by masturbating in front of Billy, and then Dahmer progressed to manhandling Billy. Billy said it got so bad that he had serious plans to kill Dahmer when he was in one of his drunken stupors. Billy's plan was to hit Dahmer over the head with the same metal bedpost Dahmer would beat him with, but Billy could never bring himself to do it.

Dahmer also masturbated in the open shower room and sometimes would get caught by other GIs. He would "get into little scuffles," that he described as "just tussling and stuff, not knock-down, drag-out fights. He wouldn't get violent. He'd just get agitated and loud." He'd then go back to his room and take it out on Billy.

What Happened to Billy?

According to E-6 Specialist Linda Swisher, Billy was a regular visitor to the base dispensary. One time when he was taken to the base hospital, the doctors asked, "What the hell happened to you?" Billy was compelled to say he had an accident, and PFC Dahmer, at his side, vouched for him.

When Billy complained to those in authority, all his attempts to get help were ignored or mocked. He was told that he was a pussy and was not taken seriously. The severity of the physical abuse increased, and Dahmer more than once used the metal bedpost to beat Billy, often hitting him across the joints with the bedpost. This caused the most pain, particularly in his knuckles and shins.

Billy said, "When he'd drink, he'd get real violent with me . . . You could tell in his face that he wasn't joking. It was for real. That's why it bothered me. It was a whole different side. His face was blank. It was kind of like he just wasn't there. I've never seen it on anyone else's face." Once, after being drugged, Billy woke to find himself tied up with a rope and unable to get free. Dahmer choked Billy nearly unconscious and had anal sex with him while he was still tied up. Without a passport, Billy couldn't even go AWOL. It would take years of therapy before Billy could tell his story. "Sometimes he was nice . . . too nice," Billy said. "He would make me lie next to him on his bunk, then grope and caress me like a woman. He would tell me he loved me."

Billy told me of the conversations Dahmer had with him. "He talked about his dad. He wanted to please his dad." However, he never said anything about having a younger brother. "I thought he was an only child." Sometimes he would spend hours reading children's picture books to Billy like *Three Billy Goats Gruff*, a story about a fearsome troll and three goats that needed to cross a bridge to get to greener pastures on the other side of the stream.

At other times, Dahmer would tell boozy W. C. Fields one-liners. For Billy's September 16, 1980, birthday, Dahmer gave Billy a belated birthday card when he returned from Oktoberfest. The card had a beer mug on it and a Fields punch line. Dahmer wrote: "To a fellow guzzler on his 18th birthday." Years later, after Jeffrey Dahmer was captured in Milwaukee, he would come up with his own one-liners:

- To his father after his arrest: "I really screwed up this time."

- "When I was a little kid, I was just like anybody else."

- "It's hard for me to believe that a human being could have done what I've done, but I know that I did it."

- "I couldn't find any meaning in my life when I was out there. I'm sure as hell not going to find it in here [in prison]. This is the grand finale of a life poorly spent."

Whenever Billy went to the mess hall, Dahmer would go with him. When Billy didn't go, Dahmer would bring him something from the mess hall to eat. At least once a week, Dahmer would buy bratwurst, chicken, and schnitzel dinners from a restaurant near the base theater just west of the barracks to share with Billy. Once, Billy got sick afterwards, and he thought Dahmer was spiking his food.

Billy went to the base movie theater with Dahmer three times to see *The Amityville Horror*, *Star Trek: The Motion Picture*, and *Mad Max*. The movies were only a buck, and the popcorn was free. Other than that, Billy would stay on base, in his room, while Dahmer went out on weekends by himself. Billy said one time Dahmer came back to the barracks from a long night out with scratches on his face and arms, and blood on his shirt. Billy thought Dahmer had just gotten into another of his fights, but Billy knew enough not to question Dahmer about what happened, because it would only make him angry. During this same period, a number of young women were mutilated and murdered. Dahmer was not a suspect in these murders until 1991, when he was captured in Milwaukee. Billy said Dahmer always wore his army jacket when he left the base. It had deep pockets for his buck knife that he always carried. Base personnel were all warned to be careful when going off base. One Milwaukee FBI report states that Dahmer himself even said he heard news reports pertaining to the homicides and saw posters but didn't know of specifics concerning the homicides.

One of Dahmer's favorite hangouts was an on-base park called Family Park, located about a half mile northwest of the barracks. The park had picnic tables and two man-made ponds. The army stocked the larger pond with rainbow trout. Families and kids would cast corn-baited hooks in the pond to catch a three-fish limit. Once, to Billy's knowledge, the Army MPs picked Dahmer up there in a drunken state and delivered him back to his room. Dahmer was given a written reprimand. Preston Davis also confirmed that Dahmer was brought back to the barracks from the park by the MPs long before Billy Joe Capshaw arrived in Germany.

One day, Dahmer had two bottles of Paul Masson wine and made Billy go with him to the park. As they sat at a table, Dahmer made Billy drink some wine with him. When Billy saw that Dahmer was starting to act crazy, Billy ran into the woods and hid. It was obvious to Billy that Dahmer had a large knife in his army jacket pocket. Billy said Dahmer ran after him "like a crazy man, like a wild nut." Eventually Dahmer returned to the table, finished off both bottles of wine, and then returned to the barracks. Billy made sure not to return until he was sure Dahmer had passed out.

Second Trip to K-Town

Billy confirmed what others said about Dahmer being a loner. Only once did Billy go off base with Dahmer. David Goss invited them and room commander Michael Masters to K-Town for dinner. They all piled into Dave's beige 1971 Variant Volkswagen Squareback for the one-hour drive. It was early March, when Billy had first arrived on base. He didn't have much money, so Goss paid for Billy's dinner. Dahmer said he was broke as well, and Goss ended up paying for Dahmer's dinner, too. After dinner, they went to the renowned Annabella's House, but Dahmer refused to go inside.

Billy, Michael, and Dave went inside. Michael picked out a nice young hostess for Billy. She was delightful, with long, shining, blond hair and a beautiful clear, soft complexion. When she realized Billy was inexperienced, she was very kind with him. Goss paid for that, as well. They were in Annabella's for only for about thirty minutes. Without a lot of money, that was about all the time the hostesses allotted.

When they had finished their business, they retrieved Dahmer from a nearby bar, even though he was supposed to be broke. On the way back to Baumholder, Billy bragged about the beautiful girl he had been with. Dahmer sat quietly during the entire trip, but when they were in their room together, Dahmer smacked Billy around for having sex.

The Pond Man

German divers pulled the very cold body of a deceased male from the lake in Baumholder Park. When they realized he was an American soldier, they contacted the American authorities. SP6 Linda Sue Swisher was summoned to collect the deceased male from the lakeside. She brought with her some other medics from her refresher class to show them the collection process and how to treat the dead with as much dignity as time allowed. After an army warrant officer signed off as the medical officer to make the formal declaration of death, she sent the body to the morgue at

Landstuhl Medical Center to be examined for the cause of death. One of the medics was elected as an escort. Swisher's job as a licensed practical nurse (MOS 91-C) was only to collect and ship the body, and she did not follow up on the cause of death. Although his identity was not known to her, he was known by the MPs who knew he was missing.

Linda told me she had dubbed him the "Pond Man." She described him as a young, thin, black male and estimated that the bloated body had been in the lake for about three days. She said, "This caused the flesh to have the texture of boiled chicken." According to Linda, he had told people he was going to the lake and hadn't returned.

The Pond Man was never connected to Jeffrey Dahmer. Again, there is no evidence one way or the other to say that Jeffrey Dahmer murdered this guy. However, I still have to wonder, with so much mayhem going on during the time Dahmer was stationed in Baumholder, whether at least some of these murders were the work of the man who would become America's most notorious serial killer. We can never know for sure.

Much of the information about the victims in Germany came from Sondra Schalk, MA, who is a German/English translator and interpreter. Her expertise is not Internet searches, but she has done quite well searching old German newspaper archives and Internet sites that have links to old TV shows such as the German show *Aktenzeichen XY Ungelöst*, which was first aired in 1967. The U.S. version, named *America's Most Wanted*, was conceived by Fox TV in the summer of 1987, and John Walsh was selected as the host of the show.

Christine Ebelshäuser

PHOTO RIGHT: Police file photo of Christine Ebelshäuser

Christine Ebelshäuser, thirty, was found dead on July 31, 1980, at a local club she managed in Pirmasens, located about thirty-one miles southeast of Baumholder. The club was the Europa Movie, an adult movie theater on the outskirts of the pedestrian zone.

Christine usually closed the business up punctually at midnight. The last customer would normally leave around 12:30 to 12:45 in the morning. Christine then tallied up the night's receipts. According to the Criminal Investigation Unit in Pirmasens, there were a total of fourteen guests on the night of her death, six of whom were located and interviewed by police. Two customers were still there at closing time. One was twenty-four-year-old regular Manfred Kölsch from Pirmasens, who went to the Europa Movie several times a week, and the other was a "quiet, young, blond man" sitting alone at a table near the bar, who had never been seen there before.

Investigators found witnesses that heard Manfred Kölsch say good-bye to Christine at the front entrance of the club as he was leaving. It has been determined that Kölsch left the Europa Movie before midnight. That would've left the blond man alone. If that blond man was Dahmer, it would've been very dangerous for her to attempt to close up on him. Investigators at the time said they were anxious to speak to the rest of the patrons of the Europa Movie that evening, especially the young blond man.

Investigators determined that Ebelshäuser was apparently struck by a glass ashtray first and then stabbed twice. She died of the stab wounds. About 1,500 marks (USD $630) were missing from her tallies. The receipts that she intended to give to the owner were lying next to her body. Authorities estimated she was murdered around 12:30 a.m. on Aktenzeichen XY Ungelöst.

According to Billy, about that time, Dahmer came back to the barracks with a fistful of German marks and put the money on the top shelf of his locker. To keep Dahmer from buying so much alcohol, Billy managed to take some of the money and put it in the bedpost of his top double bunk. The post caps were missing, but no one could see inside the post without climbing up on the bunk.

This murder appears to have the telltale signs of Jeffrey Dahmer all over it, and when a re-enactment of this murder was done on German TV, an actor that looked eerily like Jeffrey Dahmer was used.

A similar incident occurred on April 7, 1985. Dahmer went into a bar on South 2nd Street in Milwaukee around 3:15 a.m. The female bartender refused to serve him because he was drunk and abusive. Dahmer demanded to be served and warned that he would shoot her. She called the police, and Dahmer became even more furious. Four police officers were required to take him into custody, where he remained until 1 p.m. the next afternoon. Dahmer was then released on his own recognizance. The charges of disorderly conduct, threat to injure, and city hindering were never brought to court. Had the police not shown up promptly, this incident could've ended up in murder.

Although he might not have had it on him, Dahmer did own a Colt Lawman .357 Magnum with a two-and-a-half-inch barrel. He'd had the gun for about a year before his father discovered it and took it away from him.

Last Train to Düsseldorf

Jeffrey Dahmer admitted to investigators that he went by rail to Munich for Oktoberfest in 1980. Although Oktoberfest officially is a two-week holiday, many of the venues continue celebrating it until the end of October. The "Toller Bomberg," train number 620, went toward Baumholder. It was then necessary to make a transfer at Wiesbaden. The last train left from Munich daily at 3:15 p.m. When Dahmer finally returned to the base, late, the story he gave to Billy was that he got off at the wrong transfer station in Nuremberg and ended up in Neubrücke.

On Saturday, November 1, 1980, twenty-eight-year-old Vesna Nasteva, from Sofia, Bulgaria, boarded the number 620 intercity train at Nuremberg to return to her home just north of Düsseldorf. Vesna got into the second-class compartment, and there she found a place to sit. The train only had a few passengers that day. It would be Vesna's last train ride. It is not known whether her murderer was on the train already or if he boarded at some other station. At 5:01 p.m. the train left the Nuremberg Central Station. Two and a half hours later, the train reached Frankfurt after a stop in Würzburg. At 10:02 p.m. the train departed Cologne for its next destination, Düsseldorf Central Station. Its scheduled arrival time was 10:25 p.m.

PHOTO RIGHT: Police file photo of Vesna Nasteva

Around 10:20, a thirty-three-year-old male passenger heard groaning sounds, and he decided to investigate. A few cabins away, he found himself face to face with a man stabbing his victim like a crazed maniac. The suspect turned around, the bloody knife still in his fist, and pulled the emergency brake above the cabin door. He then ran out into the small corridor. The train came to a screeching halt seven miles before Düsseldorf. There, the unknown male suspect jumped out of the rail car door and disappeared into the dark night.

Vesna was rushed to the Düsseldorf University Clinic by ambulance. Before she died, she described what had happened. An unknown man came into her cabin and sat down. Without any warning, he brutally attacked her with a knife.

The male passenger gave the first description of the suspect whose eyes he'd glimpsed for a second: a young man around twenty years old, about 1.75 meters (5'9") tall, dressed with a blouson (bomber jacket) made of black Nappa leather, black gloves, neck-long slightly greasy hair, and glasses with metal frames. The witness was able to give a facial composite. The knife, meanwhile, was described as having a solid blade, similar to a stiletto. The only thing that didn't fit Dahmer was the height given by the witness. However, the suspect was leaning over his victim instead of standing up straight.

When I told Billy about the description and black jacket, Billy told me the greasy hair could be because Dahmer wouldn't take a shower and had stopped getting haircuts. He also told me that the jacket could've been his. When he received orders to be stationed in Germany, his uncle gave him a size forty-six black leather jacket, knowing it would be cold in Germany.

Only circumstantial evidence again implies that Jeff Dahmer possibly committed this murder, and I mention it only because the timeline fits. The police never questioned Dahmer, of course. In fact, they didn't even bother to take down the names of the passengers. No surprise that the criminal investigation unit had little success with its investigation. The police assumed the suspect escaped by hitchhiking or by taxi. But once again, there will never be a way to prove anything now.

Second Thanksgiving

November 27, 1980, was Dahmer's second Thanksgiving in Germany. Dahmer told Billy that he had arranged to meet a family in an adopt-a-soldier program, where soldiers would spend holidays with German national families. Of course, Dahmer also could've made this up to explain to Billy why he would be gone for three days. According to Billy, when Dahmer returned, he took off his jacket to change into clean clothes. Billy noticed blood on his shirt and pants. In fact Dahmer's shirt had actually stuck to his skin from all the dried blood. Billy said Dahmer then spent a good deal of time washing his clothes.

At this time, the body of twenty-two-year-old Ericka Handschuh was found. Erika lived at home with her parents near Heidelberg. She went to visit her boyfriend around 7:30 p.m., but she would never arrive. Because it was cold, she decided to hitchhike, and three days later her body was found in nearby Bad Kreuznach. She had been killed by strangulation, with multiple stab wounds inflicted after death. It would only take two days for the police to identify her, because her fingerprints were registered with the German Bundeskriminalamt (BKA)—Federal Criminal Police Office—due to a small misdemeanor charge. The police told her parents they were looking for a possible serial offender, because they had five unresolved cases involving young women hitchhiking from Heidelberg. Four of them had been found in the same field near the city of Bad Kreuznach (forty-two miles northwest of Baumholder). Some evidence suggested that all of the cases were connected. Three of the four victims were of a similar age, had multiple stab wounds, and were mutilated. Police believed they were dealing with an unknown subject who wasn't committing murder for the first time. When police interviewed her boyfriend, Klaus, he had reputable witnesses for a solid alibi. Erika was found frozen in the snow on November 30, 1980, three days after the Thanksgiving holiday that Dahmer claimed he'd spent with a German family.

PHOTO RIGHT: Police file photo of Erika Handschuh

When I contacted Sergeant David Goss in Michigan, he confirmed to me there was an adopt-a-soldier program but doubted that Dahmer would've signed up for it. Although it isn't known if Dahmer ever participated in such a program and really spent time with a family, what is known is that Dahmer left the base on the afternoon of November 27, 1980, and returned to the base late Sunday night, November 29, covered in blood. Because of his inability to interact with people, it's most likely that he didn't spend that time with a German family.

These five cases remain in the cold case files to this day. Due to the similarities of mutilation, police also felt these murders could've been committed by the same serial killer who was behind the January 8, 1980, murder and decapitation of thirty-two-year-old Roswitha Schnorrenberg, who lived in the city of Wesel (seventy-eight miles northwest of Baumholder). Police never did find Roswitha's severed head or her hands that had been sliced off at the wrist. (Something Dahmer would become famous for doing a decade later in Milwaukee.)

Dahmer could've driven around Germany trolling for hitchhikers. He had an Ohio driver's license with an expiration date of May 21, 1985. Billy once went through Dahmer's wallet and saw his license. Dahmer also used his father's car a number of times after he returned to Bath, Ohio. He would leave the car at one of the local bars for his father to pick up the next day. Sometimes he couldn't remember where he'd left it, and his father had to search for it (*Massacre in Milwaukee*, page 50, and also, *Milwaukee Massacre*, page 68).

Late in 1981, after Billy was discharged, Dahmer even drove to Hot Springs, Arkansas, to visit Billy. Fortunately for Billy, he wasn't home at the time. Billy's mother and sister met Dahmer. Since Billy was in Little Rock visiting his father, Dahmer returned to Ohio.

Switzerland

Sondra Schalk told me there were several murders that occurred in northern Switzerland during the time Dahmer was stationed at Baumholder. The real kicker was the similarities to the murders committed around Baumholder. Germany, Austria, and Switzerland are the three German-speaking countries in Europe, and many American servicemen would go on weekend trips to Switzerland. From Baumholder to Zurich is only a four-and-a-half-hour drive, closer to Baumholder than most other large cities in Germany such as Berlin and Munich. Crossing the border by train or car back in 1980 was never a problem. Sondra suggested that Dahmer might have gone to Switzerland to commit some of his gruesome crimes, convinced that being in another country would make it more difficult for a connection to be made.

The Beginning of the End

Until March 24, 1981, PFC Dahmer was the subject of numerous actions on the part of military authorities for disobeying orders and alcohol abuse. His file reflects numerous periods of counseling by enlisted personnel and officers regarding his behavior and actions that were a result of his alcohol abuse. Sometimes he would show up to work at the post's medical aid station in improper uniform. When he was sent back to the barracks to get into proper uniform, Dahmer wouldn't show up again. When his superiors looked for him, they would observe his bed wasn't made and his area in the barracks wasn't clean.

When Sergeant Altman, the supervisor in charge, counseled Dahmer about his performance and his abuse of alcohol, the sergeant explained that it was in Dahmer's best interest to leave the army now, while he would receive an honorable discharge. If he continued down the path he was on, he would not only receive disciplinary actions but also could be discharged under less than honorable conditions. Altman even gave him time to think about being discharged prior to making that recommendation to the chain of command. Dahmer agreed with Sergeant Altman that it would be best for him to leave the army on good terms.

On January 29, 1981, PFC Dahmer was clinically evaluated for disobedience, constantly being late for work, aggressive behavior, and alcohol intake. His performance was below the minimum requirement, and his drinking failed to improve with counseling. He was recommended for elimination under honorable conditions, as required under Chapter 9 upon separation. Afterward, Dahmer was given one last chance to rehabilitate himself. On February 5, 1981, Jeffrey Dahmer was forced to enroll in an alcoholic rehabilitation treatment program, but he indicated he wasn't willing to control his alcohol consumption.

On March 23, 1981, Billy Joe Capshaw was hastily given an assignment in the field. Sergeant Pete Altman and another soldier escorted Billy to the motor pool. Billy traveled as a medic with a convoy for more than three days. Billy said, "When I came back on the 27th, that sorry S-O-B [Dahmer] was gone." When the time came for Jeffrey Dahmer to be chaptered out, he didn't want to leave. "I heard that they had to drag him out of there. He didn't want to go."

Statement posted by Sergeant Pete Altman—8/18/07 (*on ABC's* Primetime *blog*):

> *I was Dahmer's supervisor in the Army . . . I am the one who made the recommendation for him to be discharged from the Army due to being a failure in the Army's Drug and Alcohol Program.*

Sergeant Altman said this about Dahmer: "J.D. was not what I would consider normal . . . He could be very vocal when drinking, but he mostly talked about politics, Cold War issues. He was very intelligent. . . He never spoke about home much. He and I had some things in common, which is Ohio. He went to the same amusement parks, visited the same historical spots, etc. Physically J.D. was very normal and mentally seemed to be very sound. . . Obviously, we all know differently now."

As clinical specialist David Goss reflects back, he remembers Dahmer would frequently leave the base in a cab on Friday and not be seen again until Saturday or Sunday. Goss also said it was he who escorted Dahmer to his final flight out of Germany. He told Jeff he knew he could have made it in the army, and the only thing that he was proving by getting out was that he was a loser. Goss recounted Dahmer's parting words as he flared up and started walking toward him. He raised his voice and told Goss, "I may not have made it in the military. That's one thing I'll tell you, Goss, is that I'm not a loser. Some day, you'll hear about me again. You'll see me again, or you'll read about me. But someday, you will hear about me, and you'll know that I'm not a loser."

I don't think that when Jeffrey Dahmer said that, he was talking about his future plans in Miami or Milwaukee. He more likely might have been referring to what he had already done in Germany. He knew what he was capable of.

To say Jeffrey Dahmer never killed while stationed in Germany would appear to be wrong, given the number of local unsolved murders, Dahmer's lack of known whereabouts at and around those times, and eyewitness accounts of Dahmer's condition upon returning to base. Circumstantial evidence would certainly imply that Jeffrey Dahmer might have committed a number of these unsolved murders. Now that Jeffrey Dahmer's greatest secrets are bottled up in an urn we will never fully know what he did on those weekends when he left the base—alone.

Thank You, Private Dahmer, You Are Dismissed!

A very troubled Jeffrey Dahmer left Baumholder under escort to a military plane, which then flew him stateside to Fort Jackson, South Carolina, on March 24, 1981. Under Chapter 9 of the Uniform Code of Military Justice, a directive that deals administratively with alcohol and drug abuse by army personnel, Dahmer would process out and collect his "mustering-out" pay for any money the army owed him, usually for unused leave pay or the like. Two days after leaving Germany, the processing out was complete. On March 26, 1981, after serving two years, two months, and fifteen days, with his honorable discharge certificate and DD-214 form in hand, he was discharged from active duty under honorable conditions.

Jeffrey Dahmer was a civilian again. The army told him he could have an airline travel voucher for a flight anywhere in the United States. Dahmer said he couldn't go home to face his father, so he decided to set up shop in Miami because he was tired of the cold.

Years later, after Billy told his story of being molested by his roommate, he was given a 70 percent medical disability pension, plus a one-time substantial lump sum of money based on his E-4 rank, retroactive from his discharge date of October 29, 1981. On his four-page award-for-money letter, the army simply stated that Billy was "tortured by a roommate." According to Billy, a few years later, the army gave him the full 100 percent disability.

Billy Joe Capshaw's Statement:

I was Jeffrey Dahmer's bunkmate in the U.S. Army stationed in Baumholder, Germany, from February 1980 to the time he was discharged in 1981, when he went to Miami. I believe I know Jeff Dahmer better than anyone else, better even than his father. Jeff tortured, raped, and molested me. I was 17 when it started. I have a 100% disability from the Army in which it says I was tortured by a roommate. I am still in constant pain from the many beatings all over my body he gave me, as well as his attempt to cut out my prostate, after he'd drugged me.

I think Jeff killed Adam Walsh. I don't think his victims were only young men. The military police would bring him back to our room and told me they had found him masturbating in front of children in Family Park in Baumholder. He was arrested in Wisconsin for the same thing. I also found bloody knives in his locker, and once, he came back after a weekend leave with his shirt stuck to his stomach because of dried blood.

There were five mutilation murders nearby in Germany that happened while he was stationed there. Jeff was drinking heavily when I knew him, and was angry at having to leave the Army. When I heard Willis Morgan describe his encounter at the mall, I knew that was Jeff he'd seen. For more information about me, and my treatment for PTSD, please see my psychologist Dr. Eugene Watermann's site, www.survivingjeffreydahmer.com

The Germany timeline relevant to Jeffrey Dahmer's time and disciplinary actions in Germany is at the end of this book.

Setting the Stage

During his interrogations, Jeffrey Dahmer was never honest with investigators about the time he served in Germany. In fact, he never once mentioned his roommate, Billy Joe Capshaw. He should have been a prime suspect in at least some of these murders. We might argue Dahmer's modus operandi (MO), but it cannot be denied that he had the opportunity to commit murder, which in itself is in sharp contrast to what he told investigators in 1991.

I want to be clear: I am not trying to solve any of the murders in Germany. I only want to show that Jeffrey Dahmer had lost track of morality long before his arrival in South Florida. By the time he arrived in Florida, he was already a murderer and quite possibly a serial killer.

In the rush to examine a killer's behavior, even police can become distracted by attaching him to a particular MO, as you will read in the following chapters. In Jeffrey Dahmer's case, he definitely killed animals when he was a young kid in Ohio. He might have murdered women while stationed in Germany, preyed on kids while in South Florida, and murdered mostly gays when he lived in Milwaukee. Dahmer seemed to be an opportunist whose MO reflected his circumstances and times.

CHAPTER FOUR
JEFF GOES TO WORK

"This is America's most famous child murder case, perpetrated by America's most infamous serial killer, investigated by America's most incompetent homicide detectives."
_____*Willis R. Morgan*_____

"I should have gone to college and gone into real estate and got myself an aquarium. That's what I should have done."
_____*Jeffrey L. Dahmer*_____

After a short flight from Columbia Metropolitan Airport to Miami International Airport, Jeffrey Dahmer arrived on March 26, 1981, the same day as his discharge. When he mustered out at an E-3 pay grade with two years' service, his pay rate was $519.60 per month. He would've received twenty-six days pro-rated for his March paycheck. According to his DD-214 form, he had accrued twenty-three days of leave pay. This totaled forty-nine days' pay. Dahmer would've had around $850, plus whatever money he had in his pocket.

Once Dahmer landed in Miami, he found his way to Miami Beach. Not much is known about his first three months in South Florida before he was employed in late June at Sunshine Subs. Most of what I know was what Dahmer told Milwaukee detectives, the FBI, and Hollywood Lead Detective Jack Hoffman in his interviews. According to interview records, Dahmer said he took a room for a week or so, on the beach, overlooking the ocean, at discount summer rates and spent his time drinking. After that, he rented a room just once or twice a week to take a shower. Not being very good at managing his money, he soon ran out and had to become resourceful. He started sleeping on the beach more often and dumpster-diving for food.

According to Dahmer, he was beaten up a couple of times and robbed once (most likely not true) while sleeping on the beach. However, his luck would soon change. While he was having dinner from the dumpster located behind the RK Village Plaza Mall on Collins Avenue in Sunny Isles Beach, he landed a job as a busboy. That job would last for a full three months, and he would be remembered at the sub shop only as Jeff.

I never had the opportunity to speak to Sunshine Subs shop manager Kenneth Haupert Sr. Most of what I know of him comes from my many conversations with true-crime writer Arthur J. Harris, who spoke to Ken a number of times. According to Arthur, fifty-five-year-old Ken was taking out the garbage one day when he saw a young man rummaging through the dumpster collecting slices of pizza to eat. He felt sorry for the guy and asked if he was hungry. The man said yes, so Ken invited him into the pizza and sub shop for a sandwich.

A couple days later, Ken found the man eating out of the dumpster again, and this time Ken asked him if he needed a job. Being the good man Ken was, he hired Dahmer as a busboy, but he also had to mop floors, take out the garbage, clean the bathroom, and do some food preparation.

This was supposed to be a five-day, late morning to early evening job with a Monday through Friday workweek. Instead, Dahmer worked sometimes three or four days in a week, twenty-four to thirty-two hours per week, because he would either be sent home or not show up. His start time was between ten and eleven in the morning. He would finish around four to six in the evening.

Ken paid Dahmer minimum wage in cash plus meals. It might not seem like a lot of money, especially after Ken deducted a little money each week for the $400 deposit he put on a room for Dahmer as well as the eyeglasses Ken had to buy him, but Dahmer also applied for and started collecting unemployment compensation.

Ken said, "Jeff was paid on Friday and never worked weekends." Several weeks after Dahmer started getting paid, he started coming in on Mondays around 10 a.m. totally dirty and disheveled. Ken would refuse to let him work. "He would be sent home, and the next day he would come to work in a little better shape and manage to get through the week." At other times, Dahmer didn't even bother to show up. "The first two to three weeks, he was OK. Then all of a sudden, he came in filthy dirty and drunk." His excuse was that he stayed up all night drinking because he was afraid to sleep on the beach and get "mugged" again. Of course, Ken had no way of knowing his new employee was stealing the company's sister store Mr. Pizza's blue van and using it to troll the streets and malls of South Florida.

According to Ken, sometimes Dahmer would come in all beaten up and scratched, with his glasses broken. "I had to buy him new eyeglasses once and deduct the money from his pay . . . When I would ask him what happened, Jeff would say he was jogging on the beach and fell." At least three times, Dahmer showed up to work with bruises. I speculate that, when Dahmer showed up to work pummeled, he might have committed assaults on hitchhikers that he picked up while driving around in the blue van and not been beaten up at the beach, as he claimed.

In a similar vein, in September of 1990 in Milwaukee, while on probation for second-degree sexual assault and enticing a child for immoral purposes, Dahmer told his probation officer, Donna Chester, that he was mugged for $10 and his bus pass. At a previous meeting, he complained of being sued for $300 by a suburban West Allis hospital for injuries he said he suffered as a victim in a May 27, 1990, mugging. About that time, Dahmer lured a young man (name unknown) to his apartment. Dahmer might have had an altercation with his guest, who escaped after robbing him of $300 and his watch. Naturally, Dahmer never reported this incident to the police. His probation officer advised him to move out of this neighborhood, not realizing Dahmer might have been the one initiating the violence.

Although Jeff Dahmer maintained an unkempt appearance, Ken actually thought he would have a good employee if only he could get Dahmer to clean himself up and get a haircut. To that end, Ken helped Dahmer get an efficiency room at the single-story Bimini Bay Motel, just five blocks north of the sub shop. Ken paid the first month's rent of $400 for the furnished room. He then deducted the money from Dahmer's pay. Dahmer moved in around the first of July, but he didn't keep up the rent and might have lost the room after just one month in early August of 1981, or just about the time Adam's severed head was found. In his 1994 interview with Detective Hoffman, Dahmer described the room as a small motel-type room with a short fridge, bathroom, and TV.

PHOTO ABOVE: 1960 Postcard-Bimini Bay Motel-175th & Collins Avenue-Miami Beach Florida

One day, Ken asked Jeff where he was from and why he never called home. Ken then initiated the first call to Dahmer's father. He asked Jeff for the phone number and dialed it himself. When Lionel got on the phone, Ken handed the phone to Jeff. Dahmer told his father he was working in Miami at a sandwich and pizza place called Sunshine Subs.

Adam's disappearance was one month into Dahmer's nearly three-month tenure at Sunshine Subs, which came to an abrupt end in late September when Dahmer's disheveled appearance, tardiness, and dirty work habits became more than Ken could take. In late September 1981, Ken terminated Jeffrey Dahmer's employment.

Years later, Ken moved to Dewey, Oklahoma, and opened up his own sub shop called Reubens & Subs, across the Oklahoma border in downtown Caney, Kansas. In July 2010, I finally found Ken's business and the phone number. When I called and talked to one of the waitresses, I was told Ken was very ill and would not be in. Several weeks later, on July 18, 2010, Ken passed away at the age of 84.

I was able to talk with Darlene Hill, who was co-owner of the two stores—Sunshine Subs (at which Ken Haupert was manager) and Mr. Pizza. The stores were about ten blocks apart on Collins Avenue, just north of 163rd Street, in Sunny Isles, Florida. Both stores shared three delivery vehicles: two white pickup trucks and one blue Dodge van. The van was used for getting supplies for the two stores and was also used as a backup delivery vehicle. She said all the employees had access to the vehicles: "The keys were always on the desk in the office at Mr. Pizza. Everyone knew where they were." Ken also had a set of keys that he kept in his pocket, though he never used the vehicles much because the sub shop was not a real money maker and didn't do much business in deliveries.

Darlene Hill's statement:

In the late '70s and early '80s, I owned and operated a small sandwich shop on Miami's North Beach, a safe and happy area where my young girls and I could live and work within two blocks. Between this store, which later became Sunshine Subs, and its sister shop, Mr. Pizza, on Collins Avenue, 10 blocks north, we employed Jeffrey Dahmer and many other young people. We did a big business in deliveries, and one of our company delivery vehicles was a blue van.

True crime-writer Art Harris first tracked down Ken Haupert and Darlene Hill in 2002. He also found a number of other employees who worked at the two stores. They confirmed what Darlene said. Darlene also said the blue van belonged to Michel Pelletier, who was the manager and co-owner of Mr. Pizza with Darlene.

Since Adam Walsh was abducted in a blue van, Art told me that he had passed this information to Detective Smith at the HPD in 2003. Smith did a cursory check with the Florida Department of Motor Vehicles and was told the records only went back fourteen years. Because of this, Smith dismissed the blue van as a theory and went no further with it. The HPD has never interviewed Ken or Darlene. Darlene said she used the blue van herself to move her furniture into storage. Then she added, "If there was no blue van, then my furniture must have walked to storage."

If the owner of the stores said she had a blue van, then I don't think it's a theory. The owner of Mr. Pizza and the Sunshine Sub shops should know what kind of vehicle she had, especially when that knowledge was corroborated by a number of employees. Pizza delivery driver Gino Cocco told me Mr. Pizza co-owner Michel Pelletier used the blue van to pick him up at the Fort Lauderdale Airport in 1980. Another employee reported using the blue van to go to Orlando for a weekend.

I found Michel Pelletier, an ex-Montreal police officer, living in Miramar, Florida, located just a few miles west of me. I wanted to see what he remembered about the blue van. I went to visit him, but I was unable to get into his gated community. I did get the security guard at the gatehouse to verify that Pelletier lived there, and I knew I had the right Pelletier because the search site that I used listed his previous address in Sunny Isles.

Years before, Art Harris had contacted Pelletier, but he refused to talk to Art because he "didn't talk to reporters." When Art passed Pelletier's name on to the HPD, they did send a detective to talk to Mr. Pelletier. Nothing came of that interview, and there is nothing in the case files. Art wrote about this in his book *Jeffrey Dahmer's Dirty Secret*, published in 2009. In Art's book, he would rename Michel as "Larry" and Mr. Pizza as "Beach Pizza." My guess is Art did this because he didn't have much good to say about Mr. Pelletier.

I wrote Pelletier a letter explaining who I was and why I wanted to talk to him. I made sure to let him know I was a witness, not a reporter. I sent the letter by regular mail but did not hear back. I waited for a couple of weeks and then sent another letter, this time as registered mail with a return receipt requested. After about three weeks, I received the receipt back, unclaimed.

I made one more attempt to contact him. In March 2011, I went back to the gatehouse and told the guard I was there to visit Mike Pelletier, and I asked if he could give Mike a call to let him know I was there. I just wanted to know if he was home and didn't want to talk to me or if he was out of town. The guard told me that his phone had been disconnected.

After that, I let Mike Pelletier go as a witness. Even if he had talked to me, I'm not sure how much help he would've been anyway. The HPD said that he couldn't remember a blue van but did remember the white pickup trucks, or at least that's what the HPD claims Pelletier said. However, I never was able to speak to Pelletier. Perhaps Pelletier didn't want to associate himself with the blue van that could've been used in such a tragic event. Regardless, Pelletier wasn't talking.

Gino Cocco was nineteen years old in 1981 when he worked for Mr. Pizza. He drove the blue van for pizza and food deliveries. When I talked to Gino, he confirmed the existence of the blue van. Gino told me Mike Pelletier would use it in the mornings to pick up supplies for the two stores. When he returned, Gino would use it for deliveries because, in the season, all three vehicles were needed for deliveries. He described the van as a dark blue, regular-length 1979 Dodge, possibly a Ram, with windows on the back doors. Gino also confirmed the white pickup trucks. He said Pelletier liked the pickup trucks because they were better on gas. Gino also told me that Pelletier had a lot of vehicles over time, but none of them were in his name. Gino didn't have a car, so sometimes he'd take the blue van to Fort Lauderdale to party. According to Gino, Joey Trapasso, another delivery driver, would take the keys from Pelletier and say he would be back in several hours but wouldn't return for several days.

In April of 1981, Gino returned to his native Montreal, Canada. He didn't return to South Florida for nearly a year and a half. Gino wouldn't have met Jeffrey Dahmer, since Dahmer wasn't employed until the end of June 1981. When Gino did return, the blue van was gone and only the white pickup trucks remained. Dahmer was employed with Sunshine Subs during the summer, when business was slow. Mr. Pizza did most of its delivery business during the winter season, when all the ocean-side hotels were full.

Let there be no doubt: Mr. Pizza did have a blue delivery van. Enough witnesses have confirmed it. One of those witnesses was Darlene Hill, Pelletier's ex-wife from a short-lived marriage. I met Darlene in 2007 at Art Harris's apartment. Actually, this was the second time I'd met Darlene. Back around 1981 or 1982, I stopped at Mr. Pizza for two slices of pizza and a Diet Coke. Darlene was there, and I talked to her. It was just small talk. I remember she asked me how the pizza was, and I told her it was great, which it was. Also behind the counter, if my memory is correct, was Michel Pelletier. I recognized him when Gino showed me some old photos of Mr. Pizza.

In 2010, I called Darlene, and she gave me the name of another busboy who worked at the Sunshine Subs shop at the same time as Jeffrey Dahmer. This was Joseph Trapasso. I wanted to ask Joe if he remembered Dahmer and the blue van. I quickly found Joseph's mother, Linda, in New Jersey. She told me Joseph passed away in 1995 of pneumonia. When I explained to Linda why I was looking for Joe, I was surprised to find out how much she knew about the two stores. Linda told me that, in 1981, she was living in a condo at the Salem House on 172nd Street, located between Sunshine Subs and Mr. Pizza. She was friends with Darlene Hill and frequented both shops. Linda also remembered the blue van at Mr. Pizza. She thought it belonged to Mike Pelletier, the manager of Mr. Pizza.

In 1991, Dahmer admitted to the FBI that he had lived in South Florida. The FBI passed this information on to the HPD. The FBI office in Miami informed the HPD that Jeffrey Dahmer was considered a prime suspect in Adam's abduction for a whole host of reasons: Dahmer had a well-documented history of alcohol abuse in Germany as well as in Miami, Adam was decapitated like some of Dahmer's other victims, witness composites placed Dahmer in the mall the day Adam was abducted, and Dahmer fit the profile of someone who would abduct a small child.

When Dahmer was interviewed by the FBI in 1991, he admitted that he frequently took the bus to downtown Miami to go to the Omni Mall to look at and buy knives. The Omni Mall was at least twelve miles from Sunshine Subs and Mr. Pizza. The Hollywood Mall was less than ten miles away.

PHOTO ABOVE: R.K. Sunny Isles Plaza at 18080 Collins Avenue. Mr. Pizza is the second store on the left. Photographer: Peter Andrew Bosch ©1992

When the HPD received information from the FBI about Jeffrey Dahmer being a prime suspect in Adam's abduction, they did their usual cursory check. Another restaurant had replaced Sunshine Subs and a brand-new freestanding Walgreens drug store had replaced the Bimini Bay Motel, located at 17480 Collins Avenue, in 1990. The HPD wouldn't know about the sister store, Mr. Pizza, until Art Harris told them around the end of 2002, but by that time, even that store was gone.

Dahmer told Detective Hoffman in his interview that his boss's name was "Ken Houleb." He even spelled it for Hoffman as H-O-U-L-E-B. Of course, he spelled the name wrong, and the HPD never located Mr. Houleb or anyone else from the sub shop. The HPD then ended their investigation because what was the point of going any further? Dahmer denied killing Adam, and Ottis Toole had confessed.

A Realistic Theory

On July 27, 1981, Dahmer had worked a full month at the Sunshine Subs shop. It was Monday, eight hours before he had to report to work. He had nearly finished drinking up his weekly pay, and he was feeling very lonely and in desperate need of company. At 2 a.m. Miami time (8 a.m. in Germany), Dahmer made a phone call to Billy Joe Capshaw. According to Billy, Dahmer sounded as though he had been drinking and was in need of someone to talk to really badly.

Dahmer talked about his life in Miami. He told Billy that he had a job at a sub shop and a room at the Bimini Bay Motel. He also bragged to Billy that he'd met a girl and had sex with her, as if this were some great accomplishment (and most likely not true). As the call went on and Dahmer started telling Billy how much he missed him, Billy became nauseated, which would later send Billy to the base dispensary. The day of the phone call is supported by army medical records. Billy tried to keep the conversation short because he felt that Dahmer was stalking him by phone. He passed the phone to David Goss, who also talked to Dahmer that day.

Later on, Dahmer also called his father again and told him that he was now living with a woman, an illegal alien who had offered him money to marry her (*A Father's Story*, p. 111). In a conversation with Art Harris, I learned that there actually was a twenty-eight-year-old woman named Julie from Ireland who worked at the sub shop, but she was not illegal. Ken said he didn't think she would've offered to marry Dahmer (also mentioned in Dahmer's confession, Part 2, p. 57).

Later that Monday, although inebriated, Dahmer managed to report to work at around 10 a.m. Ken took one look at him and told him there was no way he was going to work in his sub shop reeking of alcohol and looking as he did. Dahmer was sent home again. Lonely and dejected, Dahmer would have to make the best of his Monday. Dahmer could then have walked the ten blocks north to the sister store, Mr. Pizza. Ken said he wouldn't have given Dahmer the keys to the van because he was always drinking. However, Dahmer probably already knew the keys were in the office at Mr. Pizza. He might have taken the keys to the blue van, or he could've already made a copy, as this wouldn't be the first time he used the van.

He apparently then went on to the Hollywood Mall, at most a twenty-minute drive from Mr. Pizza. Dahmer could've arrived at the mall as early as 11 a.m. Adam was abducted around 12:16 p.m. to 12:30 p.m. at that very same mall. My encounter with him was around noon. The timeline fits.

Monday, Mondays

Monday, August 17, 1981: At 1 p.m., an eleven-year-old boy named German Lebedin was walking home when he noticed a blue van stopped on the west side of the street. German walked past the van and then crossed the street. The van started up and began driving slowly, following him. When the van stopped, the driver got out and came toward German, who ran into his apartment and locked the door. The man started knocking on the door and then started kicking the door for a full ten to fifteen minutes. German called the police.

By the time the police arrived at 1:17 p.m., the man had left. The suspect was a six-foot-tall white male, twenty to twenty-three years old with brown curly hair, a thin build, mustache, and thin face, wearing black sunglasses, a dark-blue, long-sleeved shirt, and blue jeans. The van was dark blue with black bumpers, with no bumper stickers, of unknown make, and with no spare tire, according to the Miami Beach police report, which can be read at JusticeForAdam.com (SAO case files, box 6, file 03, pp. 331-333).

When the Miami Beach Police Department realized the information was very close to the description of the white male suspect and the vehicle in the Adam Walsh homicide, they immediately contacted Detective Ron Hickman at the HPD. They even sent an officer to deliver a hard copy of the report to the HPD, which was left at the complaint desk of the HPD. They noted in their copy of the report that the HPD would probably follow up on it.

In August 2010, I contacted German Lebedin at his workplace in Hallandale. German said a witness had given the description of the suspect, and it would be better if I contacted him. Beyond that, German wasn't much help. He told me he was more concerned about getting away than getting an ID. He didn't know the witness, and too many years had passed so he didn't know the witness's name. I was unable to read it from the HPD's copy of the report, because when it was put onto microfilm, it became blurry. So I went to the Miami Beach Police Department to get the original report copy.

The witness's name was David Gennady Papismedov. In late March 2011, I located David at his North Miami apartment. David said it was so long ago and he was so young that he couldn't recall much. He recognized the police report with his name on it as a witness but couldn't make any positive determination as to whether the suspect matched any of the photos and composites I showed him of Jeffrey Dahmer. The one thing both witnesses remembered was that they were never contacted again by any other agency after the initial police report was made.

The HPD could've had the boys make up a composite to see if it matched the other composites, or they could have shown the boys the other composites and asked them if that was the same man. But no, they were too busy interrogating James Campbell, the house nanny that lived at the Walsh home. Though Miami Beach Police recognized the connection to the Adam Walsh abduction, neither Lead Detective Hoffman, Detective Hickman, nor anyone else from the HPD ever even saw the need to talk to the two boys. The HPD could've called them at the very least, but the only thing the HPD did was file the incident report in their case file.

Monday, July 20, 1981: Denise Smith lived in Miramar, Florida, not far from the Hollywood Mall. She was adamantly positive about whom she encountered at the Hollywood Mall. Denise's thirteen-year-old daughter Lisa received a gift certificate for her July 7, 1981, birthday. On Monday, July 20, exactly one week before the Adam Walsh abduction, Denise took Lisa to the Sears at the Hollywood Mall to buy something for her. Around noon, a young disheveled stranger kept staring at Lisa, who had Down syndrome. She was certain that man was Jeffrey Dahmer. Sensitive about people staring at her daughter, Smith stared him right back. Denise told me, "Some faces you don't forget. He had very distinct eyes with a cold, dead look." Denise also said that, when she saw Dahmer's mug shot in the paper in 1991, "I knew right away that it was him, and I didn't even know he lived in Florida."

She never went to the police because she thought no one would believe her. But after years of it weighing heavy on her mind, one day Denise went to *America's Most Wanted*'s webpage. She got scared and started shaking when she saw the "Report a Crime" page and decided not to write. Another day, she did a Google search and found investigative news reporter Colleen Henry from Milwaukee.

Months earlier, Colleen flew 1,260 miles from Milwaukee, Wisconsin, to Hollywood, Florida, to do a special news investigation for WISN 12 News, Milwaukee. I was one of the witnesses that she interviewed. The interview took place at the Hollywood Mall. It was the first time I was able to show anyone what happened that day on July 27, 1981. She'd flown in when the HPD wouldn't even walk across the street with me. The story, "Did Dahmer Have One More Victim?"

was picked up by the Associated Press and ran nationally on February 5, 2007, on TV, radio, and in print. WISN 12 reported: "As the victims' families faced the horror that was Jeffrey Dahmer, 12 News now knows a subplot was unfolding that police tried to keep from the headlines."

Denise sent Colleen Henry an e-mail. Colleen then passed her name and phone number on to Patrick Fraser, WSVN-TV MIAMI. I was then given her phone number in April 2011. Denise told me she was devastated when they closed the case. "I knew it had to be that guy I encountered, even though it was a week before." She then asked me if it was too late to call the police department. I had to tell her, "Don't even bother." What made Denise's account most believable was that Denise had no way of knowing that Dahmer was getting sent home on Mondays when he would show up to work in a state of disarray. In Denise Smith's own words:

> *I, too, recognized J. Dahmer after he was arrested. After my memory was jogged, I remembered seeing him in the Sears Mall in Hollywood, Florida, one week before Adam was abducted. He was staring quite intensely at my daughter, who is mentally disabled. He only turned his eyes away when he noticed I was staring back at him. Who could forget those eyes! I was in that store one week before Adam's abduction to use a Sears gift certificate given to my daughter, whose birthday is in early July. It seems he liked to hang out at that Sears and stalk certain people.*

It should be noted that, on February 8, 2007, model/actress Anna Nicole Smith died, and suddenly her death dominated the news and preempted Jeffrey Dahmer's abduction of Adam Walsh. The very next day it was no longer a news story.

America's Most Wanted posted the following in response to the media blitz started by Colleen Henry's story as well as Patrick Fraser's story "Did Dahmer Do It?" on 7 News Investigations– WSVN.com Miami, which was also picked up nationally.

America's Most Wanted Statement on Reports of Possible Adam Walsh/Jeffrey Dahmer Connection

2/6/2007

America's Most Wanted has issued the following statement regarding reports on the possibility of a connection between notorious convicted killer Jeffrey Dahmer and the murder of Adam Walsh:

"Despite news stories prompted by the publication of a recent article in a Florida newspaper, *America's Most Wanted* is aware of no credible information connecting Jeffrey Dahmer to the murder of Adam Walsh, the son of *AMW*'s host, John Walsh.

AMW producers and investigators [most likely Joe Matthews] have been aware of rumors of such a connection for years. Several investigations have already discounted this theory. According to the police in Hollywood, Florida, where the abduction of Adam Walsh took place, a potential Dahmer connection was first investigated in 1991, and nothing was found to validate the story. Then, two years ago, when writer Arthur Harris approached the HPD with his theories, a detective was assigned full time to reinvestigate the Dahmer leads and any new information provided by Harris. According to investigators, they found Harris's claims to be totally unsubstantiated.

John Walsh has long stated that he believes Ottis Toole to be responsible for the abduction and murder of six-and-a-half-year-old Adam in July, 1981. However, because the case was never closed, Mr. Walsh feels that any potential new information should be thoroughly investigated, and he is confident that the Broward County District Attorney's Office will continue to do its job.

America's Most Wanted encourages anyone with information on unsolved crimes to come forward in a responsible way, to help victims and their families find justice."

As you will read throughout this book, time and time again, year after year, the HPD would deflect the Jeffrey Dahmer connection to Adam's abduction and murder by assuring everyone that they investigated. But they hadn't, at least not in any meaningful way. And let's not forget that *America's Most Wanted* had a parasitical detective, Joe Matthews, working in a key position as their lead investigator, which made me wonder who had input on the *America's Most Wanted* statement.

On Monday, July 27, in the mall again for the second day in a row, Mia Cockerham saw the same man wearing the same dirty clothes as he had the day before: *"He was really close to the kid, leaning over and talking to him* (referring to Adam). *He leaned down, took his hand—by his fingertips, as he is talking to him."* The little boy looked confused, and she didn't hear him say anything. You will read more about this witness in a later chapter.

When Dahmer's mug shot showed up in all the papers across America in 1991, fifty-five-year-old Vernon Galbraith of Pigeon Forge, Tennessee, called the Knoxville branch of the FBI. According to FBI case file notes, he said he was living in South Florida in the early 1980s. He was in the mall the day Adam was abducted. He said he saw a man that looked like Jeffrey Dahmer propositioning young males at the mall. The man was carrying a camera and taking pictures. His behavior was strange, and Galbraith also described him as a cold-eyed, very disturbed-type person (FBI files, roll 1, p. 156).

The FBI noted in the report that this information was being provided to the FBI's Miami division, which in turn passed the information on to the HPD. There was nothing in the HPD files to show they ever even contacted this witness who passed away in 2002. This incident fits Dahmer's pick-up approach. In Milwaukee, Dahmer was known to go into malls with a camera and ask young boys to pose for photos. According to FBI agent Neil Purtell, more witnesses contacted the FBI to say they had seen someone matching Dahmer's description at the Hollywood Mall, although he refused to identify them. Purtell would only say that a list was compiled, and he had passed their names over to the FBI field office in Miami at the time. This office would've passed their names on to the HPD, but nothing in the Adam Walsh case files shows that any of them were contacted. This makes me wonder whether the Hollywood detectives filed the tips the FBI gave them in the circular file, because so few FBI tips made it into the Adam Walsh case files. Then again, that's why I set up a website, so the case files could be accessed. Maybe some ambitious readers out there will find some clues that I missed.

What was really ironic was that the FBI, who had nothing to hide, redacted their files so heavily that some pages had more lines blotted out than visible text. Conversely, the Hollywood police, who had everything to hide, did very little redaction of their files, which was probably just another one of their blunders. Had they redacted out witnesses' names, I would've been unable to locate them, and the HPD cover up would've remained intact. In addition, several thousand tips were called in to the HPD within the first several days after Adam's abduction. Yet when the case files were released to the public in 1996, only a fraction of those tips remained. I wonder whether some of the tips were so credible and so damaging to the reputation of the HPD, especially Lead Detective Hoffman, that they were expunged.

Although witness and FBI tips were ignored, Detective Hoffman did have time to go gallivanting across the country, interviewing unrealistic suspects like other psychos who confessed to Adam's murder as well as other killers that fit the profile of someone who would abduct and murder a six-year-old boy. This includes the time detectives Jack Hoffman and Bill Wynn went on a first-class, all-expense-paid trip to Las Vegas, staying at the Union Plaza Hotel & Casino while feasting on roasted duckling and shrimp cocktail before Keith Allen Warren's interview.

Warren was arrested on February 2, 1986, for the rape and attempted murder of a fifteen-year-old hitchhiker. Warren slashed Jack Taylor's throat, turned him over, and tried to decapitate him from the back of his neck. Jack was left for dead in a field near Henderson, ten miles south of Las Vegas. He managed to crawl back to the road and was found by a passing motorist. He identified Warren in the investigation. The Clark County police discovered that Warren was living in South Florida in the early 1980s. They contacted the HPD with this information. This was enough for Jack Hoffman to make the connection, especially since it was in the vacation city of Las Vegas. Yet when Dahmer surfaced in Milwaukee, Hoffman said he didn't fit the MO, because Adam was too young. Yet he wasn't too young for Warren to be a suspect, even though Warren couldn't complete his decapitation and Dahmer had many times over.

PHOTO RIGHT: Myself, sitting in front of Pachamamma in 2007. In 1981 this was Sunshine Subs.

Photos taken in 2007

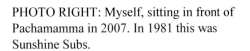

Pachamamma is half Inca and half Spanish.
In Inca: Pacha = Earth,
In Spanish: Mamma = Mother,
thus 'Mother Earth.'

CHAPTER FIVE
MANIC MONDAYS

PHOTO RIGHT: Terry Keaton. Photo courtesy of Terry Keaton

NOTE: For anyone who likes timelines, the date below is exactly two years from the day Jeffrey Dahmer landed in Germany on July 13, 1979.

On Monday, July 13, 1981, two weeks before Adam's abduction, at 11:30 a.m., a ten-year-old boy named Terry Keaton ran from the toy department of Sears in the Twin City Mall of the Lake Park suburb of North Palm Beach. He was yelling, "He's trying to grab me! He's trying to grab me!" He finally took refuge in the boy's clothing section, begging Jane Houvouras and her eleven-year-old son Matt for help.

The suspect stopped dead in his tracks. He made eye contact with Jane and Matt, and then he fled from Sears. Jane then brought Terry to the shoe department, where salesman Barry Colverton paged Terry's mother to come and pick up her son.

When I contacted Barry to see what he remembered, Barry said he recalled a woman bringing Terry to his department. The boy appeared to be upset. The woman said a man was chasing him through the store, but Barry didn't see the suspect.

After Terry's mom, Ginger, picked up her son, she headed into the mall to look for the security office in order to report the incident. On the way, Terry pointed out a man and said, "Mom, that's the man," as they passed a dirty, disheveled young man in the hallway. The guy gave Ginger an icy look that Ginger interpreted to mean, "What are you going to do about it?"

Ginger said because of his "weird, scary eyes," she became so frightened that she grabbed Terry's hand and left the mall without reporting the incident to security. "The man's stare scared me, and I just wanted to get out of there. He's probably the only person who stared at me who I was so totally afraid of. He put the fear of God in me. It stopped me from telling on him."

When Jane Houvouras heard about the abduction of a six-year-old boy in the toy department of the Hollywood Sears, she called the North Palm Beach Police Department on August 10, the same day Adam's severed head was found. On August 12, 1981, North Palm Beach Police Chief John Atwater called the HPD to let them know of the incident at the Twin City Mall. Mrs. Houvouras had already called the HPD on August 11, 1981, and given the Hollywood detectives a description of the suspect: a white male in his mid-twenties, about 5'10", 180 pounds, with dark hair and a full mustache, wearing dark slacks and a blue T-shirt.

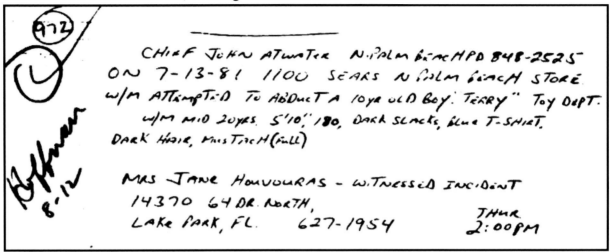

ABOVE: HPD-Adam Walsh case files: Roll #1, page 3124

She and her son Matthew were asked to come to the HPD for an interview. Detective Hoffman then drove them to the Miami Police Department, where sketch artist John Valor drew the composites from both Matt and Jane's descriptions. The next day, they were released to the media, and they ran in the local papers.

I remember seeing them and thinking that whoever made those composites had seen the same guy I saw at the Hollywood Mall. It didn't look exactly like him because the hair was neater but I didn't think I could describe him any better. I was relieved to know the police finally had their composites. The HPD felt this was germane enough to the Adam Walsh case to send two of their finest detectives, Jack Hoffman and Dennis Naylon, to the Twin City Mall to conduct a complete investigation. On August 14, 1981, they asked the Sears manager, Walter Biffle, to make a list of all employees that were working on Monday, July 13, 1981, and they proceeded to interview them. Mr. Biffle was even asked to check with other Sears stores in the state to see if there were any other attempted abductions.

I don't know what qualifies one to become a homicide detective, but these detectives were unfit for that duty as homicide detectives and should have been assigned to a boulevard with a radar gun—nothing more. Despite the fact that the description and composites were a spot-on match with the composite and description given by other witnesses from the Hollywood Mall, Hoffman, an expert at being confused, quickly came to the conclusion that the Twin City Mall incident had nothing to do with the Hollywood Mall incident. A blind man could have seen the connection, yet there is nothing in the record to show that Detective Denis Naylon didn't concur with that discombobulated assessment. This conclusion was made after the Sears security guard Mark Langill suggested over one month after the incident that it could've been him while on security detail, chasing a shoplifter.

It was this conclusion by Jack Hoffman that would steer the investigation in the wrong direction when Ottis Toole confessed in 1983. There is a whole panoply of reasons Toole could have been eliminated as a suspect. The Twin City Mall incident was just one of them because the record shows that Toole was at the Alfa blood bank in Houston, Texas, on June 15, 1981, before going to Wilmington, Delaware, then on to Newport News, Virginia, until he arrived back in Jacksonville, Florida, on the afternoon of July 25, 1981, and not anywhere near the state of Florida on July 13, when the first incident occurred with Terry. For the HPD to now admit a connection between the two incidents would be an admission that they were stumbling half-conscious through the entire time of Adam's murder investigation: a very good reason to cover up facts, not allow anyone to view the case files and perform the greatest magic trick of all—making evidence vanish into thin air.

Even if security guard Langill had resembled one of the composites given by Matthew or Jane Houvouras, this alone shouldn't have been enough to dismiss this lead as not being related to the Hollywood Mall abduction. I don't just say this with the advantage of hindsight; I say this with the advantage of common sense. The HPD just assumed that Terry was shoplifting, when in fact he was only playing with the video games and looking at some fishing lures and you know what happens when you ass-u-me. Langill, a high school football standout from northwest Connecticut, wouldn't have bolted from the store after he cornered and caught his ten-year-old shoplifter. The detectives never even bothered to ask him if he did leave the store.

On February 2, 2010, I contacted Terry's mother, Ginger Keaton. She said the detectives never did talk to Terry as part of the investigation and Terry "was not shoplifting!" She confirmed that Terry was just playing the video games and looking at fishing lures. Ginger went on to tell me that, one day in 1994, Terry was watching the news on TV in the living room when he sat up erect, stared at the TV, and then jumped up shouting, "Mom! That's the guy that tried to grab me in the mall! Oh my God, Mom, I'll never forget that face. That's the guy. That's the guy!" He still has nightmares, she said.

The news story was about Jeffrey Dahmer, when he was clubbed to death by a deranged fellow inmate in Portage, Wisconsin.

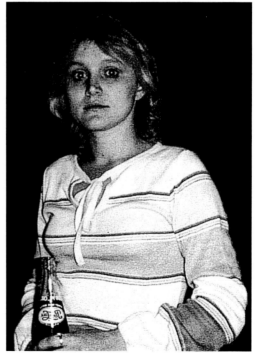

Willis,

I surely hope that the right person will be named in the kidnap and murder of Adam Walsh. I can now say that I could swear in a court of law that the person who attempted the same on my son Terry Keaton was in fact Jeffrey Dahmer. I am stating this based on the eyes in the police photos which I received from you and, more importantly, on the effects and actions that my son had when he saw on the news the death of J. Dahmer

PHOTO RIGHT: Ginger Keaton. Photo courtesy of Ginger

When I asked about Ottis Toole, Ginger responded, "Not even close. I've always said that wasn't him. The person I saw was much younger and had more hair." Thinking that the man she'd seen had also taken Adam, she wondered why John Walsh thought Toole had done it. "Maybe he knows more than I do."

Back in 1981, after Adam's abduction, Ginger and Terry Keaton also called the HPD. Detective Ron Hickman took the phone call and asked Ginger to put Terry on the phone. Terry did most of the talking. He tried to explain to the detective what happened but was brushed off. Detective Hickman asked Terry if he had been touched. When Terry explained, "No, I got away," the detective told him that since he wasn't touched, there was nothing they could do about it. That was the one and only time anyone from the HPD ever talked to him.

When the two detectives went up to the Twin City Mall to do their retroactive investigation, Terry was not part of that investigation, and to this day no one has ever bothered to contact him again. Terry told me that all they had to do was get him to identify the security guard. "I could have told them that wasn't him. He was after me. He was definitely trying to get me." Then Terry added, "My mom's right. I do have nightmares about it to this day." Terry described the man as about six feet, normal build, in pretty good shape, with dirty blond hair, a little long. His age was fairly young, maybe twenty-five. "He wasn't ugly; he looked like an average guy." He didn't wear glasses.

Terry said he was playing the video games and had started looking at some lures in the fishing department when this guy came into the fishing aisle and picked up a lure. He wasn't really looking at it, instead, he kept looking around. "He never said anything to me, and I was starting to feel very uncomfortable with him standing there. I asked him what kind of lure he had. He didn't answer. That's what really freaked me out." The man had this look about him that made Terry want to get out of there. That was when the man started chasing Terry. He then started running and shouting, "He's trying to get me! That guy is trying to get me!" He ran to the first people he saw, and Dahmer was right on Terry's heels all the way to the clothing department. "One hundred percent, my instincts saved my life that day."

In 1991, Terry saw a mug shot of Jeffrey Dahmer in the local newspaper and commented to his mom, "That looks like the guy that tried to grab me in the mall." Not knowing at the time if Dahmer was ever even in South Florida, he brushed it off and forgot about it. In November 1994, when Dahmer's death made national news, Terry realized that was indeed the guy who tried to grab him in the Twin City Mall Sears toy department.

At the time when Detective Hoffman received the calls from Palm Beach, he was zeroed in on the Walsh's houseguest James Campbell as the one and only suspect. And I submit that it was this tunnel vision that might have caused Hoffman's loss of investigative objectivity. This caused him to pursue other genuine leads with little intensity while he concentrated his efforts on James Campbell. Although Campbell passed a polygraph test three times, Hoffman still concentrated on Campbell's lack of an alibi when Adam was abducted. Campbell explained to Hoffman that it was too windy to rent boats at the Golden Strand, so he'd stayed in his cabana.

The HPD detectives thought they knew Campbell's motive: Reve Walsh. James admitted having a two-year affair with Reve. Detective Hoffman believed James wanted to marry Reve, but she would not leave John because of Adam. James was living with the Walshes at the time, and John had asked him to pack up and leave just two weeks before Adam's abduction. Hoffman thought James might have wanted to get rid of Adam. Hoffman suggested to Campbell, "I think Adam was the one that kept John and Reve's marriage strong. And Adam was the person standing between you."

Hoffman was so hell bent on getting a confession that he could be heard all the way down the hall from the interrogation room, yelling at Campbell, "We're going to get you one way or the other. . . You lying piece of [expletive]!" For hours on end, day after day, week after week, Campbell was interrogated. They called him a loser, a live-in dildo, and a family pet, and all the while, they never even bothered to advise him of his Miranda rights. Detective Lieutenant Richard Hynds said they did everything to Campbell short of giving him a beating. "We used some techniques that bordered on violating his civil rights. Well, they didn't border; they flat out violated his civil rights."

After nearly four months, twenty interviews, and multiple polygraph tests, James Campbell was dropped as a suspect. Hoffman was so focused on Campbell that all tips that came in to the HPD at that time that did not point toward James Campbell were dismissed, including the Florida Turnpike witnesses (Chapter Fourteen) and the Twin City Mall attempted abduction.

John Walsh hired Joe Varon, Broward County's top criminal defense attorney, known as the Silver Fox, for James Campbell in order to get the HPD to leave him alone. On the next page is a copy of Varon's two-page letter to Detective Jack Hoffman.

Eventually, they stopped investigating Campbell as a suspect. There's an old saying in the South: "You can't read the label when you're sitting inside the jar." Lead Detective Jack Hoffman and others never were able to figure much of anything out. Stuck on hypotheses, they never went back to revisit all the tips that were passed over. Cold case detective Mark Smith took over the case in August 1994, after Hoffman was forced off. Smith then discounted the love triangle motive, finally saying Campbell was not a suspect.

Police Baffled by Lack of Leads—Search Cut for Adam's Killer

HPD spokesman Fred Barbetta cited the reason for the scale-back in investigating the Adam Walsh case was because they were stumped: "We have nothing to go on. Nothing whatsoever." The investigation was then narrowed down to two investigators: thirty-five-year-old ex-Harlem cop Jack Hoffman and forty-two-year-old devout Catholic Ron Hickman.

VARON AND STAHL, P.A.
ATTORNEYS AND COUNSELLORS

JOSEPH A. VARON
STEADMAN S. STAHL, JR.
J. DAVID BOGENSCHUTZ
H. OOHN WILLIAMS, JR.
HARRY GULKIN

2432 HOLLYWOOD BOULEVARD
HOLLYWOOD, FLORIDA 33020

TELEPHONE 923-1548
FORT LAUDERDALE 523-1488
DIRECT MIAMI TELEPHONE 949-1241

December 2, 1981

Detective Jack Hoffman
Detective H. Hickman
Hollywood Police Department
3250 Hollywood Boulevard
Hollywood, Florida

Re: James Edward Campbell

Gentlemen:

I have been consulted by the above subject who
has retained our office in connection with your investigation
of the Adam Walsh homicide. From what has been explained to
me by my client, it is apparent that each of you have
designated him as a target of your investigation.

I have been informed of the various meetings you
had with Mr. Campbell and the tests that you have submitted
him to, such as polygraph examinations and hypnosis. The
manner and method of these tests and the unusual procedure
employed have created an atmosphere of apprehension. This
is particularly true where I have been informed certain
threats have been made such as "We know you did it, and we
are going to get you one way or the other". If this is true
in any measure, then the time has come to inform you both
that there will be no longer any communication between your
Department and my client, James Edward Campbell.

Any communication you care to make with Mr. Campbell
you must accomplish through this office. I have been informed
that you have continually harassed Mr. Campbell almost on a
daily basis. This seems to be beyond the realm of propriety
and I must ask you both to desist from this practice.

-2-

I appreciate very much the vigor with which you pursue your sworn duty to investigate this terrible offense, but there is a limit to which my client can submit to your continual tests and threats. Should you have any warrant or other process, please advise and I will be glad to submit Mr. Campbell in a spirit of cooperation. On the other hand, if no charges have been made or formalized, then I would appreciate your both staying away from him.

Very truly yours,

Joseph A. Varon

JAV:car
cc: Honorable Sam Martin,
    Chief of Police

On August 13, 1981, psychologist Dr. Mark Reisner of the Los Angeles Police Department offered a psychological profile of the type of person capable of abducting, murdering, and decapitating Adam Walsh. In a memorandum to the HPD, Reisner stated that a profile can only be of a general nature due to the lack of physical evidence. A copy of that memorandum is in the case files (CD-ROM 1, roll 1, pp. 811-812).

SEX: Male.

AGE: 19-35 years of age but more likely in his early to mid-20s.

RACE: Caucasian or Latin. Although with this type of conduct, not interracial.

MENTAL STATUS: Borderline psychopathic/psychotic personality with a tremendous homosexual conflict expressed in violence and rage. Probably a 'loner' and not liked by many people. Individual not likely to brag or talk about this act. Unlikely that he will exhibit any remorse or guilt over act or confess to the abduction or murder.

EDUCATIONAL BACKGROUND: Little formal education.

OCCUPATIONAL SKILLS: Probably has had many unskilled or minimally skilled laboring jobs.

SOCIAL RELATIONS: Identifies with and is attracted to children. Poor relations with both females and males.

CRIMINAL HISTORY: Almost certainly has abducted or attempted to abduct a child in the past. Very likely has been arrested and imprisoned for such acts in the past.

Reisner stated that the decapitation indicated that there had been sexual conduct with the boy. After the abduction, the individual would seek an isolated environment (Chapter Ten) where the individual would maintain control over the boy by employing both deception and physical force.

The HPD should have pinned this memo to their bulletin board. It fit Dahmer almost to a tee, not Toole. Dahmer was apprehended several times in Family Park, while stationed in Germany, for masturbating in front of kids.

On October 2, 2009, I contacted Matthew Houvouras. He told me he and his mom never did believe that security guard story because, "That kid was mortified!" The suspect was observed running from the mall. He had on blue jeans, a long-sleeved shirt, and was dirty. I again wondered why a security guard would stop dead in his tracks after cornering a would-be shoplifter and then bolt from the store. Even after making eye contact with Matt's mom, whom the boy was "clinging to" and begging for help, a security guard would not take off without explaining anything. Matthews confirmed that he and his mom were the ones to give the Twin City Mall composites.

In the meantime, Dahmer would head back south. Still not wanting to give up after his failure at the Twin City Mall, he would make at least one stop along the way, at the Deerfield Beach Post Office.

On August 14, 1981, first thing in the morning, Veronica Jackson went to the Deerfield Beach Police Department to file a report. She said that, when she watched the news on August 13, she observed a composite of a man who was involved in an attempted abduction of a child in West Palm Beach. She stated that, approximately one month earlier, on July 13, she was at the post office located on SE 2nd Avenue and observed a "dark blue van" drive into the parking lot. The subject was looking out of the driver's window at a small, approximately five-year-old, white female child. He then circled around. When he saw the child's mother, he went back out onto SE 2nd Avenue continuing to look at the child. The van then headed southbound on SE 2nd Avenue, and she didn't see it again.

The van was described as a 1978-1979 vehicle of an unknown make, dull dark blue in color and with no windows on the driver's side. There were two doors on the back of the van, both of which had clear windows. The van had an outside mirror on the driver's door and a small square mirror with a triangular mount. Veronica stated in the report that the driver of the van fit the description of the suspect involved in the West Palm Beach case.

Although I was not able to find Veronica, I do give a lot of credence to Veronica's statement because of the relevant timeframe and the fact that vans don't fly. That van would've had to drive the surface roads to the Twin City Mall and back to Sunny Isles. (see map on page 267)

Because the attempted abduction at North Palm Beach (Lake Park) was being cross-referenced to the Adam Walsh murder case, Detective Kramer called the HPD. He talked to Lieutenant Hynes at 9:45 a.m., at which time Hynes spoke with Veronica Jackson. Detective Kramer sent the HPD a hard copy of the police report as well. This report did end up in the HPD case files (roll 1, pp. 3299-3300), but the HPD did not follow up on any more interviews with Veronica. Instead, these detectives drove fifteen miles out into the everglades to a location where a psychic said they would find the rest of Adam's body. Of course, they didn't find anything.

If Hollywood's brightest hadn't been so quick to write off the witnesses at the Twin City Mall and the Hollywood Mall, they might have been able to get more information from them. Even the HPD said, "It wouldn't be from detective work that this case would be solved but from witness statements," but not if you don't listen to them. Witnesses were dismissed because they weren't able to pick Ottis Toole's photo out of a six- photo lineup. Of course, Dahmer's photo wasn't in that lineup.

The old adage, "If you have ten people witness an accident, you will get ten different versions," was as true in this case as in any accident case. There were plenty of witnesses, whom I'll discuss in depth later in this book. The Pottenburghs remember seeing Adam walking around the parking lot and Dahmer retrieving his blue van. Phillip Lohr saw Dahmer carry Adam out of the Sears. I remember him wearing a yellow buttoned-up shirt, while Bill Bowen remembers him wearing a green army jacket, and Jenny Warren remembers him wearing a T-shirt. But the Pottenburghs describe the same blue van as Phillip Lohr, Janice Santamassino, Mia Taylor, and Bill Bowen. My description of Dahmer has always been consistent and matches the description given by the Pottenburghs, Jenny, Janice, and Mary Hagan. Vernon Jones, Phillip, and Jenny all describe Adam to a tee.

I watched a criminology show on TV once. In it this professor was writing on a blackboard and had her back to the class. On her desk was her briefcase. From the back of the class, a strange man walked in, took the briefcase, and ran out of the class. The professor turned around just in time to see the stranger leave the room. She yelled at him to stop and even chased him down the hall. When she returned to the class, she asked her students if they had seen what happened. When the class responded with a resounding yes, she said, "Good, because I'm going to give you a test." She asked the students about the stranger's height, color of his hat, shirt, pants, shoes, etc. Some students saw a red shirt, some green, and some blue. The actual color was a red and blue plaid. The students weren't in full agreement on any of the questions, but when the "stranger" reentered the room, they were a hundred percent positive that it was him.

Without getting too philosophical, I think it goes to show how we as individuals process information, taking into account our past as well as current experiences in our lives. A shoe salesman might zero in on shoes, and a hairdresser might concentrate on hair. The point is witnesses should not be so quickly dismissed on points of differences. Investigators must look at the entire statement and see how much of it matches. When I talked to witnesses in the Adam Walsh case, I could see we were all talking about the same incident.

I don't care what color shirt Dahmer was wearing that day. It doesn't matter if it was an army jacket, yellow button-up, T-shirt, or multi-color. I admit, I could be the one who was wrong about the shirt. I remember one time when I was describing Dahmer's shirt to Hoffman in one of my interviews. I said, "It could have been green." Sometimes I remember it as yellow and sometimes green. Hoffman wasn't having it. He made me feel as if I wanted to change the color in order to inject myself into the case just for attention.

The real problem was that it'd been ten years, and the expression on Dahmer's face and his psychotic eyes overshadowed everything else. More important than the color of a shirt or any other discrepancies in descriptions were Dahmer's actions. Enough witnesses corroborate what I have been saying all along, that Dahmer abducted and murdered Adam Walsh.

Yet, no matter how many witnesses corroborate my statement, years later in 2007, Charles Morton Jr., chief assistant state attorney in Broward County, noted in a letter to the *Miami Herald* that the "new" witness accounts "add intrigue and mystery to Adam Walsh's tragic death—but are problematic. The delayed Dahmer identifications would raise serious legal and moral questions in a potential prosecution of Dahmer."

Mr. Morton needs to get it right. This wasn't "delayed." I went to the police in 1981, 1991, and many other times since then. Morton was just playing his very small part in a much larger culture of corruption by going along with the HPD in their cover-up.

The delayed identifications were due to the HPD's incompetence as well as their attempt to cover up their incompetence by misleading the media and everyone else, including the Walsh family, about facts in Adam's murder. The HPD was responsible for Adam's murder not being solved.

Reve's police statement is interesting. She didn't have her watch on, but she thinks she got to the Sears Mall around 12:15 p.m. This is incorrect, as you will read in a later chapter, Adam was abducted at around this time. She walked Adam hand-in-hand to the toy department as she had done "a hundred times before." Kids were already playing, and Adam was about three deep in the crowd of kids waiting their turn.

She told Adam, "I'll be in the lamp department."

Adam said, "OK, Mommy."

When Reve went back to the toy department, Adam was gone. She tried asking the other kids if they had seen Adam, but they were too busy playing their video games. One Spanish kid pointed toward the door, but it wasn't the north door. He pointed to the west-side garden shop door. Reve thought it was ridiculous that Adam would've gone out the west door. Adam had never done that before. Thinking the kid was just being polite to a grown-up or didn't understand her because he was Spanish, she dismissed his response (*Tears of Rage*, p. 45).

Reve then went to the service counter, got them to page Adam, and ran out into the mall. After running up and down the mall a couple of times, she went back to the toy department. This time Reve said, "All the kids were gone!" Which means Adam was already missing the FIRST time Reve went to retrieve Adam and all the kids were still there. Security guard Kathryn Shaffer must have asked the other kids to leave during the time Reve was searching for Adam in the mall hallway. Only after Reve returned the SECOND time were all the kids gone.

The HPD and Joe Matthews maintained—and still maintain—that Adam was one of the kids the security guard ordered to leave. Not true! Adam was NEVER kicked out! Nor was he ever asked to leave by anyone. You will read more about this when you read the witness statements later in this book.

In order to make a point to Detective Hoffman, I added the glasses and whited out the mustache in one of the Twin City Mall composites because Jeffrey Dahmer had on glasses in his 1978 high school photo. I also tried to make the hair similar to the high school photo. It was a waste of my time, as all my points fell on deaf ears because Jack Hoffman seemed to be resolute in not making the connection.

LEFT: Jeffrey Dahmer
1978 High School photo

RIGHT: Twin City Mall
Composite Comparison

Suspect Composite from Hollywood Mall

Jeffrey Dahmer photo

Suspect Composite from Twin City Mall

Milwaukee mugshot Jeffrey Dahmer

Close-up comparison of mug shot and composite

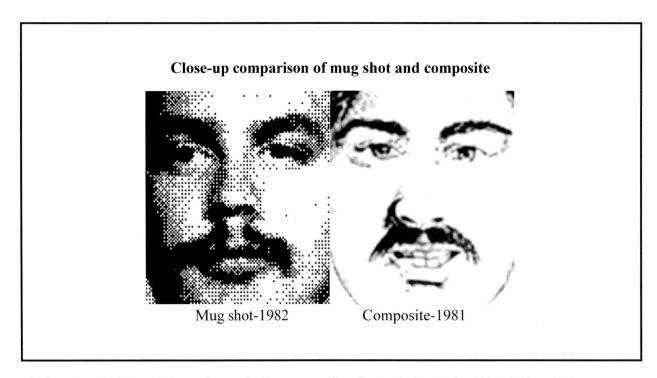

Mug shot-1982

Composite-1981

*Sketch artist John Valor, who made the composites for both the Twin City Mall and The Hollywood Mall, passed away on July 3, 2000.

PHOTO RIGHT: Security guard Mark Langill. Photo courtesy of Bill Langill. Mark was nineteen years old in 1981. He is unable to speak for himself because on April 12, 1985, Mark was attacked with a knife, stabbed, and killed. This photo was given to me by his grandfather, William "Bill" Langill.

Beyond Incompetence

The following is an outrageous quote from Detective Jack Hoffman as to why he dismissed the Twin City Mall incident. Hoffman told the press: "I'd put a lot of faith in that the two incidents were related. But the Houvourases composites didn't match James Campbell."

On August 14, 1981, he reported that the Houvourases agreed that the man they'd seen was the security guard (although they insisted it wasn't). When the facts don't fit the theory, a detective is supposed to change the theory; instead, Hoffman changed the facts to fit his false assumptions and instead of dismissing James Campbell, Hoffman dismissed all the witnesses!

After Detective Hoffman dismissed the Twin City Mall incident and composites, the following article ran in the *Sun Tattler* on August 15, 1981.

Vol. 52-No. 195   Hollywood, Florida Saturday, ©August 15, 1981

Main Walsh lead only false hope

By Lindsey Logan

Hollywood detectives thought they may have had a picture of Adam Walsh's killer. Instead, they had a very accurate drawing of a store security guard.

Hollywood detectives on Friday identified the man that witnesses said tried to abduct a child in the North Palm Beach Sears store two weeks before Adam was abducted. But the man who matched a composite drawing released Thursday was a store security guard trying to prevent a shoplifting, investigators found. With the identification, investigators have lost what they had called their best lead in the Walsh killing.

The full article can be read at JusticeForAdam.com in the SAO case files (box 2, file 5, pp. 149-50).

NOTE: If you believe the July 13, 1981, Twin City Mall lead wasn't a false hope as I and the other witnesses do, then that alone would dismiss Ottis Toole as a suspect in the Hollywood Mall abduction of Adam. Toole didn't arrive back in Florida until July 25, 1981. Neither the stymied Hollywood Police Department nor Joe Matthews was capable of figuring this out.

Hollywood Mall Incident Report:

INCIDENT REPORT
INCIDENT NUMBER: HW-81-056073
POLICE DEPARTMENT-HOLLYWOOD
PAGE: 1

Incident: MISSING PERSON—JUVENILE
Location: 300 HOLLYWOOD MALL
Type of premises: RETAIL
Time & date of incident: 13:55 7/27/1981
Day: MONDAY subjects: 2 vehicles: 0

----------------SUBJECT #1----------------
Status subject: REPORTEE
Name: WALSH, REVE race/sex/dob: W-F 7/24/51
Address: 2801 MCKINLEY STREET phone (res): 921-0434
----------------SUBJECT #2----------------
Status subject: MISSING PERSON - JUVENILE
Name: WALSH ADAM race/sex/dob: W-M 11/14/74
Address: 2801 MCKINLEY STREET phone (res): 921-0434
Height: 3-06 weight: 045 hair: SANDY BL
Eyes: HAZEL build: THIN complex: MEDIUM
Further description: SEE NARRATIVE
------------TEXT------------
JUVENILE WAS LAST SEEN WEARING A RED AND WHITE STRIPED SHIRT WITH
GREEN ADIDAS GYM SHORTS. CREAM COLORED CANVAS CAPTAIN'S HAT WITH
A BLUE RIM AND YELLOW RUBBER SANDALS.

REPORTEE ADVISES THAT THE ABOVE MISSING PERSON WAS LAST SEEN IN THE
TOY DEPARTMENT OF SEARS DEPARTMENT STORE. MISSING PERSON WAS TO
MEET REPORTEE WHEN SHE WAS DONE WITH HER BUSINESS IN ANOTHER PART
OF THE STORE, NAMELY THE LAMP DEPARTMENT. REPORTEE RETURNED TO TOY
DEPT APPROXIMATELY TEN (10) TO FIFTEEN (15) MINUTES AFTER SHE LEFT THE
MISSING PERSON AND THE MISSING PERSON WAS NOT TO BE FOUND. REPORTEE
LOOKED FOR MISSING PERSON FOR APPROXIMATELY FORTY (40) TO FORTY FIVE
(45) MINUTES BEFORE CALLING POLICE.

UPON ARRIVAL, THE UNDERSIGNED OFFICER TOOK INFO FROM THE REPORTEE
AND THEN NOTIFIED NCIC/FCIC AND REPORT WAS TAKEN BY BADGE #617. THE
UNDERSIGNED, REPORTEE, AND THE GRANDMOTHER THEN CONDUCTED A
STORE TO STORE SEARCH OF THE MALL.

NO FURTHER INFORMATION AVAILABLE AT THIS TIME.
REPORTING OFFICER: CSO M DONAHAY
SQD 5 - BADGE: 1334-ENTRY: DDEO24-03:10 07/29/81

CITY OF HOLLYWOOD, FLORIDA
INTER-OFFICE MEMORANDUM

TO: ALL UNITS   DATE: 8/15/81   FILE:

SUBJECT: Homicide, ADAM WALSH

FROM: DETS. R. HICKMAN/J.HOFFMAN   REFERENCES: 81-56073

SUSPECT: W/M mid-20's, 5'10", 200 lbs. stocky
build, medium complexion, dark brown to black hair
over the ears.

Attempted abduction occurred Monday, July 13th, 11:00
AM, Sears, Twin City Mall, North Palm beach.

Suspect was observed by witnesses fleeing from the
store. At the same time the witnesses were approached
by a 10-year old boy, whose first name is believed to
be Terry, who told the witnesses, "That man is trying
to grab me." The boy had been playing in the toy
department at the store when the attempted abduction
occurred. He then ran to the clothing department,
where he approached the witnesses. The boy appeared to
be terrified.

The Hollywood Police Department is attempting to
locate this boy. His identity will be kept secret
after he comes forward. Anyone with information should
contact Det. Jack Hoffman or Ron Hickman at 921-354 or
921- 3362.

Retyped from CD # 1- Page 818/823

CHAPTER SIX
OTTIS TOOLE

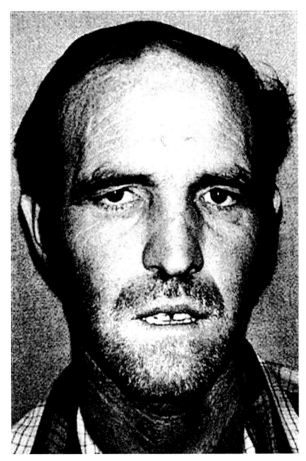

PHOTO LEFT: Toole's 1983 mugshot.

"I just wanted to make the police look stupid."
_____***Ottis Elwood Toole***_____

"No, that's not him."
_____***Willis Russell Morgan***_____

In the fall of 1983, I went to work on the night shift. When I walked into the pressroom office, Monica, the pressroom secretary, came up to me with a newspaper in her hand and asked, "Willis, is this the guy you saw in the mall?" I looked at the photo and told her no.

"Are you sure? Because he said he did it." I looked at the photo again. It was a photo of a creepy, disheveled-looking guy. His name was Ottis Elwood Toole. As I studied the photo, I realized two really big distinctions: The guy I encountered in Radio Shack was in his early twenties, and this Toole character was in his thirties. Also, he had a really high hairline that was certainly in contrast with whom I had seen or any of the suspect composites in Adam's abduction.

I told Monica, "No, that's not him."

Later, when I read the article, I learned that this guy was indeed confessing to Adam's abduction. At the time, I thought the police would figure it out in short order. The fact that he didn't have a blue van should have been enough to eliminate him as a suspect. Little did I know at the time that Detective Matthews would not eliminate him, and years later he would pin Adam's abduction and murder on this sycophantic serial confessor. Police Chief Chadwick Wagner would agree with Matthews's conclusion.

At 9:45 a.m. on the evening of January 4, 1982, two-bit arsonist Ottis Toole set ablaze one of Betty Goodyear's rooming houses, located at 117 2nd Street East in the historical Springfield section of Jacksonville Florida. Eleven tenants were in the wooden rooming house when the fire began. Some of the residents had to jump from the second floor because the fire spread to the hallway and then traveled up the stairs. Twenty-one firefighters fought the blaze for thirty minutes until it was brought under control.

The most severely injured person was sixty-four-year-old George Nicholas Sonnenberg. He was found unconscious on the floor of his room shortly after the fire was put out. Rescue workers desperately tried to revive him, but with third-degree burns covering most of his body, Sonnenberg died a week later.

On January 11, fire marshals ruled the fire an accident. However, Ottis Toole's juvenile companion James Redwine and another juvenile were arrested for an unrelated arson of an unoccupied house on Hubbard Street. They quickly admitted to the Hubbard Street arson. Redwine later told officers that they had also helped Ottis Toole in the Second Street East fire. The once-petty larcener was then arrested for arson and murder without resistance on June 8, 1982.

After his arrest, Toole freely confessed. He said he set the rooming house on fire because he was upset with several of the men who lived there. He took a can of gasoline from the trunk of his car, made his way into a vacant back bedroom of the house, doused the room with fuel, and lit it with a match. In April 1984, Toole was convicted. On August 5, he was sentenced to death in Jacksonville for Sonnenberg's murder.

It wasn't because of any investigative skills that the HPD stumbled onto the seventh-grade dropout. It was a fortuitous fluke, he was already sitting in the Duval County Jail convicted in the fatal arson rap and pressured into confessing to other arsons and murders. If they wanted confessions, he would give them all they could handle. Toole's penchant for numerous storytelling murder confessions earned him a reputation as one of America's most heinous serial killers as well as the reputation as one of the country's worst serial liars.

Confessions are nice, but they still have to match the evidence. None of Toole's confessions matched the physical evidence—including in the Adam Walsh case—until he was helped along.

At 9 p.m. on October 10, 1983, two years after Adam's murder, the movie *Adam*, starring Daniel J. Travanti as John Walsh, aired on NBC. The very next day at 9 a.m., Brevard County detective Steven R. Kindrick telephoned the HPD and said an inmate in the Duval County Jail wanted to talk. When I contacted Kindrick in May 2010, he told me he was in Jacksonville to interview Toole in an unrelated Brevard County case.

Toole thought Kindrick was from Broward County and wanted to talk to him about something. Kindrick said it wasn't his case, so he didn't really know that much about it, and forwarded the information to the HPD. He also told me he met the HPD detectives in Jacksonville. He could not remember their names, but "they were quite arrogant." Kendrick's report would bring Ottis Toole from anonymity to infamy in a matter of days. That report can be read at the end of this chapter.

Hollywood detectives Jack Hoffman and Ron Hickman (Mr. Personality and his sidekick, as they were referred to by their own peers) flew to Jacksonville. When they arrived, other detectives were annoyed by the two HPD detectives. They were wearing their dress suits and were too arrogant to even introduce themselves. "They barely said hello. They were too big for that," said one detective, "and we were only trying to help."

In what would be more of an Abbott and Costello routine, on October 19 and 20, 1983, the two Hollywood detectives had their first crack at the oddly effeminate Toole. They wouldn't need to get cute with the Constitution in order to get to first base with him. No enhanced interrogation techniques were necessary. Ottis Toole waived his counsel per Miranda.

This was too easy. While glancing around in a trance state (which he was in), the somewhat soft-spoken thirty-six-year-old pyromaniac freely obliged these detectives with a complete confession. Toole said he hadn't seen the TV movie, and these detectives believed him.

Then Toole spun his first version of the kidnapping to the Hollywood detectives. He claimed that he and one-eyed cohort Henry Lee Lucus had driven to Fort Lauderdale in the 1971 Cadillac and were in the mall parking lot when they saw Adam "running around, jumping on cars." They snatched the boy from the Sears parking lot and locked the doors on the Cadillac. They then drove to a remote area off the Florida Turnpike, where Toole said Lucas killed Adam using a bayonet to cut off the child's head.

Now that these resolute detectives had their confession, the search for the truth stopped (not that they were doing such a good job anyway) and the focus on Toole began.

At this meeting, Jack Hoffman showed Toole the crime scene photos including photos of the footbridge at mile marker 130 in order to help Toole recollect events. Toole said they buried the body a few miles from where the head was found. Later, detectives couldn't find the body and learned that one-eyed Lucas was locked up in a Maryland prison the day Adam went missing.

PHOTO LEFT:
Det. Jack Hoffman
Badge #0038

PHOTO RIGHT:
Det. Ron Hickman
Badge #0434 holding
up the suspect
composite.

Photos courtesy of
the Hollywood
Historical Society.

Toole then came up with his newest version, saying he snatched the boy by himself and fed the body to alligators in a nearby swamp. During his confession frenzy, Ottis Toole again changed that version and claimed he cremated Adam's torso in an old, gutted-out refrigerator in the backyard of his mother's house and then disposed of the remains at one of Jacksonville's three main dumps.

The police found that his mother's house had burned down in June 1981, before Adam's abduction. They still dug up the whole yard and found nothing, causing Hoffman to actually make an attempt to search all three of the Jacksonville dump yards, since Toole couldn't remember which one it was. Hoffman soon realized what a daunting task it would be. After seeing the immense size of the dump yards, he quickly gave up and settled for just taking some photos. This event is described in the *Investigation Report #26* at the end of this chapter.

Toole's early tall tales had more holes than a pound of Swiss cheese. In one version of his story, Toole claimed he was driving down the road, tossing body parts out the window. Of course, he was helped along with anti-psychotic drugs like Thioridazine (Mellaril), used in the treatment of disorganized and psychotic thinking as well as false perceptions, such as hallucinations or delusions. He was getting 200 mg three times a day and an extra 200 mg at bedtime.

In his first interview with Hoffman, Toole failed to identify Adam on a missing person flier and gave an inaccurate description of Adam's features and clothing. He said Adam was wearing white sneakers, jeans, and mittens, because he'd abducted Adam around the first of the year. Hoffman asked him what direction he went when he left the mall. Toole said he took A1A along the ocean and headed south toward Homestead, which is about sixty miles south of Hollywood.

Whether deliberate or not Hoffman used "suggestive questioning" techniques to skillfully guide Toole to all the correct answers and directions while diligently taking notes. Later, when Hoffman wrote his brilliant summary report, he only listed the correct answers. In the early interviews, when Toole's answers were very wrong, Toole attributed it to being intoxicated. After the fourth interview, Toole started getting the answers to conform to what the detectives wanted. Hoffman even commented to him, "Are you sure you were intoxicated? You're getting all the answers right now."

On October 20, 1983, Toole's 1971 Cadillac was retrieved from Wells Brothers used car lot, and on October 31, it was delivered to the Jacksonville Regional Crime Laboratory. A list of items such as hair samples, carpet cuttings, and vacuum sweepings was collected for further processing

---

TEST RESULTS:

1. Blood samples on carpet were insufficient for further testing.
2. Hair standards from Adam's head did not match any hair samples collected from the Cadillac. **NOTE:** No attempt was ever made by Toole to clean the Cadillac; yet, even after collecting hair samples from the backseat carpet, front carpet, trunk, center console, dashboard, and other locations, not one hair of Adam's was found in that car.

3. Chemical test on the blade edge of the machete demonstrated the presence of a trace of blood in a quantity that was insufficient for further testing.

4. Chemical test for blood on the "canvas sheath" was inconclusive.

NOTE: Not one weapon was ever proven to be used in the murder of Adam Walsh. That is until Detective Sergeant Joe Matthews came along.

After the tests were completed, all items were given to the HPD on February 11, 1984. This has been documented by USPS Postal Return Receipt [#191905] in the SAO case files (box 7, HU-06-98, volume IV, file 18). The package was signed for by someone named Sykes. Also, the HPD acknowledged receiving items in two separate phone calls from the lab. The Jacksonville Police Department suggested the lab mail everything to the HPD, since they were in charge of the Adam Walsh case.

In Joe Matthews's book *Bringing Adam Home: The Abduction That Changed America*, he suggests the Cadillac simply vanished. Not true: The Jacksonville Crime Lab didn't lose the 4,200-pound piece of evidence as others would like you to believe. After the 1971 white Cadillac was fully tested, it was properly returned to Wells Brothers Used Cars, its rightful owners, as required by standard procedure. The car couldn't be sold and was eventually junked.

Years later, while searching the case files, I found a Miami Beach Police report dated Monday, August 17, 1981. It was about an attempted abduction and was hand-delivered to the front desk at the HPD and given to Carol Sykes. I wondered if this could be the same woman I spoke to when I went to the HPD back in 1981. I decided to search for her. I didn't expect much, since she worked for the HPD, but I wanted to at least give her the chance to help. If she also accepted and signed for the evidence sent from the Jacksonville lab by the postal service, she would've been working behind the front desk. Maybe she was that young, tall woman that was behind the front desk in 1981. It was possible she might remember the officer I spoke to at that special desk they set up in the lobby just for this case.

I found her through the Broward County property tax records and PeopleFinders.com. After I knocked on her door, she came out to talk to me. She was not as tall as I remembered. I remembered her to be about five-eight. This woman was only five-six. She was as sweet and nice as could be. We talked for at least thirty minutes. As it turned out, Carol told me she was not the Carol Sykes I was looking for. "There is another Carol Sykes who lives a few blocks west of me," she said. "I know because we both work out at the same gym." She told me she'd never met the other Sykes, and she isn't related. It was just a baffling coincidence, but she knew of her because they asked her at the gym if they were sisters, since they looked so much alike and had the same name. I returned home to get the address of the correct Sykes. It wouldn't take me long to find her. Her full name was Carol Lynne Sykes. She was fifty years old, which meant she would've been twenty back then. I went to her home in Pembroke Pines. I immediately recognized her, but she would neither confirm nor deny it. When I asked her if she remembered Officer Presley at the special desk in the lobby, she simply told me she was a Hollywood police officer and didn't want to talk to me.

From Brilliance to Buffoonery

Although buffoonery would easily attach its name to this police department, The HPD detectives had their fleeting moments of brilliance. While tracking down Toole's timeline to see if he could've been in Hollywood, Florida (332 miles south of Jacksonville), on July 27, 1981, at the time Adam Walsh was abducted, they were actually able to find a police report dated August 1, 1981. Toole filed the report after getting a beat down by his brother Howell at the apartment where he was staying. The landlord at Betty Goodyear's boarding house provided a receipt showing that Toole paid the rent on July 31, 1981. Then the HPD traced Toole to Newport News, Virginia. On July 22, 1981, Ottis Toole was admitted to Riverside Hospital for depression and released on Friday, July 24, at 2:36 p.m. This was eleven days AFTER the Twin City Mall attempted abduction of Terry Keaton and three days BEFORE Adam Walsh's abduction.

Also on July 24, the itinerant Ottis Toole arrived at the Salvation Army in Newport News, Virginia, looking for assistance to get back to Jacksonville. The record shows Toole made a phone call at 3:20 p.m. on Friday, July 24, from the Salvation Army to Southeastern Roofing Company, a past employer of Toole. The call lasted two minutes. The call was placed to verify that he would be reemployed once back in Jacksonville. The Salvation Army required this verification before issuing the check (HPD case files, roll 1, p. 198).

Toole then used his Social Security card as identification in order to receive a $71.95 check for his bus fare to Jacksonville, Florida. The check was made out to "Greyhound Bus." Hoffman even got the canceled check back from the bank, which was also located in box 4 of the SAO files.

Only three relevant buses would arrive in Jacksonville between 6:30 a.m. and 6:55 p.m. on Saturday, July 25. The Salvation Army closed at 4 p.m., so that would mean the check was given to Toole between 3:30 p.m. and 4 p.m. Once Toole had his check, he had to walk three miles from the Salvation Army headquarters to the Newport News Greyhound bus station, where he exchanged the check for a one-way ticket to Jacksonville. At an average walking speed of four mph, it would take approximately thirty-five minutes to get to the bus station. This would put the time of arrival at the Newport News Bus Station at 4:30 p.m. to 5 p.m. Toole stated he waited at the Greyhound bus station for approximately two hours for his bus to arrive.

By my own estimation, that would most likely put Ottis Toole on the 6:30 p.m. bus for an arrival time of 10:25 a.m. on Saturday in Jacksonville, Florida. Ottis Toole claims he arrived in Jacksonville in the afternoon, and that would place him on the 10:50 p.m. departure bus. According to one report in the HPD's case files, Toole left Virginia at 1:20 a.m. and arrived back in Jacksonville at 6:55 p.m. on the 25th. Even if Toole left on an earlier bus, which is most likely, he would still have been carless and penniless. The bus schedule was as follows:

DEPART NEWPORT NEWS	ARRIVE JACKSONVILLE
06:30 p.m.—24th	10:25 p.m.—25th
10:50 p.m.—24th	04:20 p.m.—25th
01:20 p.m.—25th	06:55 p.m.—25th

BELOW: HPD & SAO case file records

This is a fourteen-and-a-half- to twenty-one-hour trip, depending on the stops, which are usually in Richmond, Raleigh, and Fayetteville. Betty Goodyear said she never saw Toole with a car when he stayed there in 1981. "He would get picked up for work by someone named John."

For the fourth time, on October 26, 1983, Hoffman returned to Jacksonville to confront Toole with his findings. Toole admitted he was in Newport News and received some money for a bus ticket. Toole stated that, when he arrived in Jacksonville, sometime on the afternoon of July 25, he was "penniless and starving." He didn't even have money to pay his rent. Ottis Toole might have paid his initial rent with some advance money from the roofing company, according to John Reaves, owner of Southeastern Roofing.

From the downtown Jacksonville bus station, at 10 North Pearl Street, he had to walk several miles to the roofing company located on 2031 East 19th Street. Toole explained to Hoffman, "Those were hard times, you know." He then said he took a job with Southeast Roofing Company, saved up some money to buy a car, and then drove to Fort Lauderdale to abduct Adam, according to the HPD files.

During a moment of clarity, Hoffman explained to Toole in no uncertain terms that, with so little time and money, it would've been impossible for him to go to Hollywood and abduct Adam. Toole then stated, "No. I didn't kill Adam Walsh. If I did, I would be able to show you where the rest of the body is." Despite this impossibility, Hoffman would refuse to accept Toole's recantation because Toole was unable to state his whereabouts on a particular day, two years previously.

This exchange is from the HPD case files (roll 2, pp. 875-876):

Det. Hoffman: Okay, and how did you come up with Adam Walsh's murder? How did you confess to that and tell us some, some ah, facts of the murder that only the police and the medical examiner knew about?

Toole: Maybe like you said I did, I did hear it on television.

Det. Terry: Just tell me the truth, that's all I want to know.

Toole: No, I didn't kill Adam Walsh!

Det. Hoffman: Are you sure, or are you not sure?

Toole: I'm sure I didn't.

Det. Hoffman: How are you sure? What makes you sure you didn't kill Adam Walsh?

Toole: Because if I was really sure, I could come up with his body.

Det. Hoffman: Yeah. If you're sure you didn't kill him, can I speak to somebody here to verify that you were in Jacksonville at the time of his abduction? Are you that sure?

Toole: (No answer)

Det. Hoffman: Are you sure you stayed in Jacksonville all this time when you got back from

Newport News, that you stayed there for a period of time, a few weeks, before you earned some money? Can you be sure of that? Ottis, can you answer that?

Toole: (No answer)

Toole was then left alone with homicide detective Jesse Walter "Buddy" Terry of the Jacksonville Sheriff's Office for a twelve-minute interim. After this time period, Toole then recanted his recantation and stated that he did kill Adam Walsh.

Hoffman then went to Texas to interview Toole's partner in crime, Henry Lee Lucas, who informed Detective Hoffman that Toole would never kill a child, never mind decapitate him, and actually never did anything by himself. Even this information wouldn't stop the HPD's relentless pursuit of Toole. By this time, Toole's one-eyed crimmie had already started singing in Texas. Henry Lee Lucas claimed that police stripped him naked, denied him cigarettes and bedding, held him in a cold cell, and didn't allow him to contact an attorney. After four days of this treatment, Lucas said he decided to confess to other crimes in a desperate bid to improve his treatment. Lucas's lawyer described his client's treatment as "inhumane" and "calculated solely to require the defendant to confess guilt, whether innocent or guilty. Becoming a publicity confessor was the only way for him to get out of his cell." They would bring him to an interview room, sometimes with donuts, muffins, coffee and cigarettes waiting.

A common trick detectives will use is to offer attractive benefits to an inmate if he or she confesses to a homicide, irrespective of culpability. In the old days, they would torture out confessions from suspects. Today, they use a much more humane method, offering a pack of cigarettes, better prison arrangements, field trips, and lots of camaraderie as if they are the best friends of the suspect.

If the suspect needs help with his or her memory—no problem. The solution is simple. All the detectives need to do is drop some inside information about the crime so that the suspect sounds somewhat plausible when he or she parrots back the details. Fortunately, very few police departments resort to this tactic. To the credit of the Hollywood Police Department, they might not have deliberately given Toole leading questions. It is very possible they were simply outwitted by a seventy-four IQ.

On the downside, this tactic would cause detectives to fly in from far-off cities to corroborate the confessions, at taxpayers' expense. Also, it didn't always work. At least not when Detective Hoffman interviewed Jeffrey Dahmer in 1992, even though Hoffman said the homemade muffins he brought with him were really good.

While Lucas toured the country as a star killer looking for evidence of his handiwork for zealous police departments wanting closure, Toole, Henry's illiterate "mass-killing" sidekick, decided he wanted to be his own killer with even more outlandish confessions. He used his half-witted, IQ to outwit police departments across America with an orgy of confessions. They would consider him to be the ultimate one-man crime buster who solved hundreds of cases across America. Cops were jumping up and down, shouting like traders on the stock market floor, clamoring at the chance to interview him. Toole's unique crime-solving technique was to simply confess. He started confessing to crimes from coast to coast.

For three days, Toole ran the Jacksonville Sheriff's Office around to various bogus locations where he said he'd left bodies. No bodies were ever found, because Ottis Toole lied about everything. Unlike the HPD, it would take only three days for the Jacksonville Sheriff's Office to realize there was no veracity or evidentiary value to anything Ottis Toole was saying before they ceased investigating the claims he was making.

Ottis Toole was even flown in the Texas governor's plane to help the good people of Texas solve some crimes languishing in their cold case files. This ruse ended when many police departments that closed cases based on his confessions had to reopen them because his timelines clashed.

As police departments across America quickly dismissed Toole's confessions as nothing more than tall tales, only the HPD would be left. The match between Toole and the HPD was on. It would pit America's dumbest serial confessor against America's dumbest homicide detectives, and all Toole wanted was a steak sub, some smokes, and a field trip to Hollywood, all of which he got. Ottis Toole wallowed in the attention the doting HPD detectives gave him.

Lieutenant Jim Suber

In 1983, Jim Suber was the supervisor in charge of the Jacksonville Homicide Unit and Detective Terry's direct supervisor. Suber describes Terry as Toole's mentor and custodian. Although Toole might have obtained information from news sources, Suber believed Terry was grandstanding and might have also given Toole more information than Toole gave him regarding Adam's murder.

That a detective would involve himself in a case that belonged to another agency in itself was very unusual. Terry might have signed a book deal with Toole, and that might have been a reason to leak information about the case. Terry denied leaking information and said, "The deal was inked in jest," after Toole told him about a number of other book deals he had agreed to. But Terry's superior, Undersheriff John Nelson, felt differently, and Terry was eventually moved to the communications department.

In May 2010, I called Detective Terry at his Middleburg, Florida, home. At first Terry said he was convinced Toole had abducted Adam. When I asked if he knew about any of the witnesses that were in the Hollywood Mall the day Adam was abducted, Terry told me he had no idea. However, Terry was a good listener as I gave him a rundown and the early background including the timeline of Jeffrey Dahmer's stay in South Florida. Terry told me he didn't know about any of that and was very impressed. Terry's last comment to me was, "I will tell you one thing . . . Hoffman is about as dumb a detective as there is."

A Field Trip for Ottis Toole

On October 21, 1983, under tight security, Toole was taken on a field trip by plane to Hollywood, Florida. At 9 a.m. they arrived at Hollywood's North Perry airport and then drove to the Broward Mall in Plantation in order to trip him up. This would not fool Toole. He already knew it had to be a Sears next to the police station, and he told them the Broward Mall didn't look right. Next, they took him to the Hollywood Police Station, and later Toole would go for a day trip along the Florida Turnpike to the spot where Adam's severed head was found. This field trip to Hollywood would be the one and only time Ottis Toole has ever been proven to be in South Florida.

At 4 p.m. when they arrived at the location off the Florida Turnpike, near mile marker 126, just north of Radebaugh Road, they slowed down to twenty miles per hour and asked Toole if he knew where the road was. Only then did Toole point to the dirt road and say, "I think that's it." Later on, detectives would say Toole led them to the road.

Once there, Toole guided them and pointed out great locations for them to search. Eventually, after they couldn't find anything, Hoffman started calling Toole names like son-of-a-bitch, retard and dirty asshole. On a late break, Toole was eating a sandwich while the detectives did all the hard work out in the hot Florida sun. In anger, Hoffman smacked Toole's sandwich from his hand. Toole said, "F--k you," to Hoffman. Toole himself said this only served to irritate him, thus encouraging him to play with these detectives even more. This was in box 2 of the SAO case files (file 2, p. 285) as well as the HPD files and in *Bringing Adam Home*, p. 97.

No remains were ever found, yet the HPD investigators said Toole relayed details that only the killer could know, such as the description of the short footbridge at mile marker 130. Overall, detectives thought Toole did quite well, considering he was trying to recall something from several years earlier, during a time when he was intoxicated. In their reports, detectives would forget to mention all the empty holes he made them dig.

The reports sounded impressive until Detective Mark Smith said in one of his reports, "Toole makes reference to a wooden bridge prior to seeing it at this location; what should be noted, however, is that it appears Toole was shown a picture of this bridge during his initial interview and statement on October 19 and October 20, 1983, in Jacksonville. Also, he led detectives to the location of a dirt road leading to the canal where Adam's severed head was found."

The Florida Turnpike runs mainly north and south, but this seven-mile stretch runs east and west. On the north side of the Florida Pike was an area known as the Fort Drum Marsh Conservation Area, where there's parking on the shoulder area of the turnpike. The little footbridge is no more than thirty or so feet from the road edge. Adam's severed head was seventy-five feet from the established road edge. I have been to that location. The footbridge was visible from the turnpike and that was how I located it. It was at mile marker 130 in 1981. Now, with the extension of the turnpike to Homestead, all the mile markers have moved, and it has changed to mile marker 174.

After searching for Adam's remains at mile marker 126, detectives then drove to the footbridge at mile marker 130. As they approached the mile marker, they slowed down to twenty miles per hour and drove on the shoulder of the turnpike. They asked Toole if he had seen the spot where he disposed of Adam's severed head. Only after Toole saw the footbridge did he say that was the spot (see diagram at the end of Chapter Fourteen, p. 220, as well as two photos on p. 222). My personal turnpike photos can be viewed at JusticeForAdam.com.

PHOTO ABOVE: Detectives dig at a location Ottis Toole points out for them. Photos courtesy of HPD file

PHOTOS BELOW: Ottis Toole at mile marker 126 just north of Radebaugh Road

Back at the HPD parking lot, detectives again asked Toole if he knew where the Sears was. He looked around and pointed to a large Sears sign across the street as if only the real murderer would've known that. The detectives lacked common sense and when they asked how he knew that was the Sears, Toole responded, "Because I know a Sears when I see one!" These cops would turn that statement into an Ottis Toole slogan.

Everything started coming together for these overzealous, under-experienced investigators. That very Friday night, at a dramatic press conference, Hollywood Police Chief Sam Martin told the media what they had been waiting for two years to hear: "We have our suspect in the Adam Walsh case. He knew things only the real killer could have known. The man responsible for Adam Walsh's murder has been located, and he has confessed." Assistant Chief Leroy Hessler then added, "The Toole and Lucas murders make Charles Manson look like Huckleberry Finn." A photo of Ottis Elwood Toole was released to the media. With his quest for criminal notoriety complete, the "one-man crime stopper" would get his first public introduction to America.

John and Reve Walsh expected closure in the case. Not realizing he was surrounded by the misapplication of logic, John addressed the media the following day: "My heart will always be broken for the rest of my life. I miss Adam more now than when he went missing, because the reality hadn't set in at that time." John said he prayed that the criminal justice system would not break down and that Adam would receive justice (*Tears of Rage*, p. 181).

Later, on January 6, 1984, three months after the first confession, Toole recanted his confession and then reconfessed. Then he recanted again and again. He said he wanted to make the police "look stupid," which, after all is said and done, he did. To the HPD's thinking, once Toole confessed, he couldn't take it back. They did everything they could to make his confession stick.

Toole said, "That's just a bunch of garbage I put together." But the HPD operated on the premise that only confessions count; recantations do not. So it was a case of, "Too late, Mr. Toole, you've already confessed!" Eventually, Ottis Toole was diagnosed as a paranoid schizophrenic, and his death sentence was commuted to life in prison. Toole moved away from his next door neighbor on death row, notorious serial killer Ted Bundy, and back into the general population. Bundy… not so lucky.

Ottis Toole Recants

Ottis Toole tried to tell the truth, but no one would listen. The following was cropped from the Adam Walsh case files from January 10, 1984 (HPD case files, roll 2, pp. 1512-13):

Hoffman: Okay, and what is the reason that you are giving us this statement regarding ADAM WALSH?

Toole: Ah, I didn't ah, I didn't kill ADAM WALSH.

Hoffman: You didn't kill ADAM WALSH?

Toole: No.

Hoffman: Can you tell me in your own words why you stuck with your confession all these months now, from the first time I met with you and the numerous interviews that we conducted and also crime scenes that you have taken us to along the turnpike, indicating that you were responsible for the abduction and murder of ADAM WALSH? Can you tell me why you stuck to your story all this time?

Toole: Ah, I was trying to hang HENRY LUCAS at first, but ah, I found out he was in jail and ah, and so I changed it three or four different times. I did.

Hoffman: What was your reason for changing it? Why didn't you come out and say, you know, I was not responsible for the murder of that boy at the time, once you knew that HENRY was in jail up in Virginia or Maryland?

Toole: Well, after I already made the statement, I didn't know if I could change it back or not. That's why I kept telling different stories about it, 'cause I didn't know as anybody would believe it or not. I didn't know how to turn it back around, but I really didn't kill ADAM WALSH.

Hoffman: So, you were kind of scared to retract your confession, then?

Toole: Yeah.

It wasn't that Ottis Toole drove the Hollywood detectives crazy with all his confessions and recantations. It was the detectives that drove Toole crazy by not being willing to listen when he tried to tell the truth and recant. That was one of the reasons he would reconfess.

Henry Lee Lucus said of the confessions in a 1998 interview with The Associated Press, "I'm not some kind of saint, but I do believe I'll go to heaven. And I do believe those who did the killings will be punished by God." He blamed the confessions that he and Ottis made on a steady diet of tranquilizers, steaks, hamburgers, and milkshakes fed to him by investigators, along with crime scene clues he said they repeated back to detectives.

A few weeks after Toole made that first confession, the HPD detectives announced that they no longer considered him a suspect. However, Toole would continue to be an on-again, off-again suspect. In the end, Toole would become a suspect again, not because the HPD thought Toole kidnapped Adam Walsh but because they needed to cover up their own incomprehensible blunders and to give the Walsh family closure. I also suspect that Detective Inspector Joseph M. Matthews craved the credit for solving the case in order to better promote his novel.

Investigative Reporter Patrick Fraser for Fox-WSVN TV in Miami put it best when he told me, "If you give Ottis Toole two Krispy Kreme doughnuts, he would have confessed to nailing Jesus Christ to the cross." I have talked to Pat many times and was on his local news show once. Pat told me he went up to the Florida State Prison at Raiford to interview Ottis Toole. Ottis told him that he confessed to "get out of his cell and to go on a trip to Hollywood."

In his book *Tears of Rage*, John Walsh said, "A lot of sickos had claimed to know something about Adam's murder, some out of revenge, others in a twisted quest for glory. All I knew was what I had learned from my FBI contacts—that whoever had murdered Adam was a psychopath, and that it's usually hard to know whether these guys are telling the truth or completely fabricating it. . . The only way to tell for sure if what these guys are telling you is true is to back it up with some hard, corroborating evidence."

In fact, Toole wasn't the only sicko that tried to take credit for Adam's murder. Others tried but were quickly dismissed when police were able to pin down their locations on July 27, 1981. Most were in jail and just trying to get some extra smokes. Investigators couldn't pin down Toole's location on July 27, 1981, but that doesn't mean Toole did it!

It is—or should be—evidence that separates honesty from lies. John Walsh didn't realize that hard evidence against Toole simply didn't exist. Toole's confessions to coworkers and cellmates were not hard evidence. Toole's lack of an alibi for his whereabouts on the day Adam went missing was not hard evidence. Toole didn't need an alibi since he was the one confessing. He could not prove he was in South Florida or anywhere else on July 27, 1981. Police never charged him while he was alive. Now, with Toole conveniently dead and gone—buried in the prison graveyard—nobody can question him.

Detectives' Verdicts

On January 10, 1984, Captain R.S. Davis, then head of the Hollywood detective division, wrote about the task force findings: "In the three months since Toole had surfaced as a suspect, the six investigators assigned full-time to the case had traveled to Jacksonville, Georgia, Texas, Virginia, and North and South Carolina—at a cost of 3,500 man-hours and $62,000. All persons known to have had contact with Toole during the summer of 1981 have been located and interviewed. Detectives have been unable to uncover any evidence, other than his confessions, linking him with the Walsh homicide." At the end of this chapter is the actual interoffice memorandum with the findings of Captain Steve Davis.

Detective Ron Hickman, one of the original case detectives, said in 2001, "He's as pure as the driven snow. . . I spent a hundred hours with that individual; I'll tell you right now: he didn't do it."

Detective Jack Hoffman also eventually dismissed Toole and has been quoted as saying he would stake his professional career on Ottis Toole not being Adam's abductor. In Hoffman's summary report after an interview he and FBI Special Agent William "Bill" Hagerty conducted with Ottis Toole on October 7, 1991, he wrote, "It is this detective's opinion that Ottis Toole was being truthful and sincere about his noninvolvement in the Adam Walsh homicide." In late October 1984, Hoffman assured reporters that Toole had been "unequivocally eliminated" as a suspect. Finally, after spending all that time and money, Hoffman had it right.

After Jeffrey Dahmer was captured in 1991 and the Toole evidence mysteriously vanished, Hoffman then said that, when they brought Toole to Hollywood, "He didn't know where the hell he was going. He would continually contradict himself on directions and yes or no questions. Detectives would have to keep asking him, 'Which is it, Ottis?' " Below is what Detective Hoffman said in one 1996 report:

NOTES ON INTERVIEW
OFFICER JACK HOFFMAN
5/28/96

Officer Hoffman explained that the suspect OTTIS TOOLE did not direct the investigators to either location. Regarding the decapitation location, Officer Hoffman explained that they had made two or three stops as they traveled north on the Florida Turnpike, and stopped at random locations that remotely could have been the "crime scene" location. Each time, TOOLE did not identify a location. When they stopped at the location on the north side of the RADEBAUGH RD overpass on the turnpike at mile marker 170, TOOLE had not told them to stop there. In fact, they had driven past it and saw the turnoff as they drove by. They stopped and backed up, and after looking about, TOOLE advised that it "could be" the location. Officer Hoffman advises that it was not until this site had been "identified" that any verbal harassing of TOOLE began (SAO case files, box 2, file 3, p. 276).

PHOTO RIGHT: Detective Sergeant "Jim" J.B.
Smith searching through tips for the blue van.
Photo by Maria Rosas, ©August 16, 1981.

In 1984, Lieutenant J. B. Smith concluded,
"My opinion, as is most everyone else
from the city of Hollywood, is that he did
not do this killing . . . The only thing that
we will say for sure is that 3,500 hours and
$62,000 later, we can't confirm anything
he has said. It was probably the most
complete investigation we've ever done to
prove that somebody didn't do it. In fact, it
took us almost a year to prove he didn't do
it."

Even the FBI dismissed Ottis Toole as a suspect in the abduction of Adam Walsh; Bill Hagerty
interviewed Toole and eliminated him. Since the 1970s, Hagerty has been conducting seminars
for law enforcement agencies in advanced criminology. He was conducting one of those
seminars with another instructor, *America's Most Wanted* Detective Joe Matthews, whom Bill
had invited to speak. The conversation turned to the Adam Walsh case. Hagerty explained to
Matthews that Toole said he had not been involved in the Walsh kidnapping. Since he returned
to Jacksonville from Virginia, Toole said he had not left the Jacksonville area. Hagerty then told
Matthews that Toole said the reason he told people otherwise was for his own personal gain: to
get out of jail for a while, eat good food, and get some cigarettes.

After interviewing Ottis Toole about a 1983 Tallahassee murder, Leon County detective Johnny
Miller said, "Toole would often tell law enforcement whatever he thought they wanted to hear.
Toole liked to toy with law enforcement officers and would confess to many crimes, making it
somewhat difficult to determine when he was being truthful. Toole loved being in the limelight
and liked to have media attention." In 2008, Miller wondered why the HPD had now determined
that Toole was Adam's killer. He questioned the motives of the HPD because it didn't appear
that any new evidence had surfaced, according to his statement on WCTV-TV 6 Tallahassee, on
December 18, 2008.

In contrast to all the original detectives, Sergeant Joe Matthews in *Bringing Adam Home*
theorized that Toole's penchant for changing details was a positive: "If no detail were to vary in
a killer's various confessions, then you might worry that you were hearing a tale memorized and
scripted for some hidden purpose."

1987

"The law was playing games with me so I was playing games with them."

_____*Ottis Elwood Toole*_____

After years of chasing blue mystery vans, on December 16, 2008, Hollywood Police Chief Chadwick E. Wagner held a press conference announcing the end of the twenty-seven-year-old investigation. Despite the missing evidence, the waffling confessions, and the questions about where Toole got his information, Chief Wagner said they had more than enough evidence to indict Toole. "The murder mystery has been solved," Wagner said. "If Ottis Toole was alive today, he would be arrested for the abduction and murder of Adam Walsh on July 27, 1981. Investigators past and present believed Toole was guilty."

This was a blatant falsehood in stark contrast to what the original investigators really said, with the exception of Joe Matthews. I personally talked to detective Ron Hickman; he vehemently stated his belief that Toole was not the abductor. The chief apologized to Adam's parents, John and Reve Walsh. He said he regretted that the case had not been closed earlier and attributed that failure, in part, to flaws in his department's investigation. Both police and prosecutors gave credit to retired Miami Beach Homicide Detective Sergeant Joe Matthews in the decision to close the case by exceptional clearance.

Without practical wisdom or the slightest twinge of guilt, shame, responsibility or remorse, Chief Wagner said when announcing the case's closing, "I agreed with the ultimate conclusion of this independent investigation (Matthews Report) that Ottis Toole was the perpetrator of this crime." When I asked for the Matthews Report on which the case was closed, suddenly, it went from a "neatly and skillfully put-together report" to nothing more than a regurgitation of Wagner's already completed investigation. If that's so, the chief got it backwards. He should have said that the Matthews Report was in complete agreement with his already completed investigation.

Besides, if the chief did his own investigation, where was his report? How could he conduct an investigation on such a high-profile case without an investigative report? Even more puzzling was how he managed to do it without ever calling any of the witnesses. And how did he close a case without a closing report? The answer is that the chief used the Matthews Report as other than that there were no reports from the HPD. We only know the case was closed.

Chief Wagner said the investigation had always focused on Toole and added that the case was strong enough for the police to have charged him before his death. However, Chief Sam Martin had tried to indict Toole in the mid-1980s but was turned down for lack of any proof linking Toole to Adam's murder. Honestly, if Ottis Toole were alive and they had tried to indict him, I would've come to his aid in the same way I would've gone to James Campbell's aid.

Long on Drama—Short on Substance

While Adam's closing event was short on substance, it was long on drama and compassion for the Walsh family. Wagner acknowledged that evidence was destroyed (deliberately expunged would be more accurate) and apologized to the Walshes for investigative mistakes. The family were then ushered out of the room before taking questions from the media.

Detective Smith sat behind Wagner to the far right during this conference. For many years, Smith was "the keeper of the files" on the Adam Walsh case. When the media tried to ask him a question about the case, he just thumbed toward the chief as if he were trying to say Wagner was the one that was implicating Toole, so ask him the difficult questions.

As leader of the pack, the chief jumped in to save his top minion: "This closing was not the result of any new discovery, but rather the accumulation of all the circumstantial evidence over the years." Chief Wagner then added, "What was there was everything that was in front of our face for years. Police had a vast amount of circumstantial evidence to prosecute Toole before his death in 1996 . . . from confessions, to sightings, to witness interviews. It's all there." Then his tongue became muted as he declined further questions from the media and walked off.

Although Smith refused to answer media questions, I guess he is not much of a Dahmer believer either, because when I tried to tell him what happened, he dismissed me with, "Yeah right." He was just the kind of man they would want as the keeper of the files. You know the old adage: "There's no future in being right when your boss is wrong." I guess that was why he was promoted to assistant to the chief just in time for his retirement. That would keep his mouth shut. But the problem for them was, it wouldn't keep *mine* shut!

I read all the Ottis Toole statements, interviews, confessions, and recantations which were nothing more than pages and pages of rambling, nonsensical gobbledygook. For every guess that he came close to getting right, another ten were outrageously wrong. At first, Toole said Adam's head was cut off with a bayonet, but he later changed and refined his story to a machete in order to conform to what the detectives were saying. He also said in his first statement that Adam was wearing blue jeans, a blue shirt, white sneakers, and mittens. Remember, Toole said he abducted the boy in early January. The actual description from Adam's incident report reads as follows:

12:30 HRS—7/27/1981

Missing from the Sears toy department at the above time. Has not showed up at home, 2810 McKinley St. Not located in the Hollywood Mall. W/M, 6 YRS., ADAM WALSH, 45 LBS., 3-1/2 FT. TALL, SANDY BLOND HAIR, RED-AND-WHITE STRIPED SHIRT, GREEN SHORTS, CREAM-COLORED CAP, YELLOW SANDALS, HAZEL EYES, THIN BUILD.

In one of Detective Hoffman's supplement reports at a time when he was trying to implicate Toole, Hoffman listed all the admissions of Ottis Toole's method of murdering Adam Walsh and compared them against Broward County medical examiner Dr. Ronald Wright's findings as to how the victim was murdered. Matthews might have used reports like this, reporting only the correct answers, in order to close the Adam Walsh case.

The following can be located on the HPD CD (Adam Walsh case files, roll 1, p. 752):

1: Toole states: He placed the child, unconscious, facedown to chop his head off.

1: Dr. Wright's findings: The victim was decapitated lying face down.

2: Toole states: He chopped the head off close to the skull.

2: Dr. Wright's findings: The victim's head was chopped off close to the skull.

3: Toole states: He admitted to having hit the victim in the face with a closed fist.

3: Dr. Wright's findings: The victim received blows to the face around the eyes and had a fracture to his nose.

4: Toole states: He choked the child into unconsciousness. And the child never woke.

4: Dr. Wright's findings: He believes the child was dead before the decapitation.

5: Toole states: He chopped the head off in four to five blows.

5: Dr. Wright's findings: The head was severed in five blows.

6: Toole admits: Using a machete on the victim when chopping off the head.

6: Dr. Wright's findings: The instrument used was probably a machete-type tool.

7: Toole states: He used a two-hand hold on the machete.

7: Dr. Wright's findings: The perpetrator must have used two hands on the machete for the necessary force.

8: Toole is right-handed.

8: Dr. Wright's findings: The perpetrator had to be right-handed and was probably decapitating the victim from the victim's right side.

It should be noted: A Luminol test was conducted on the interior of the vehicle, which Ottis Toole states he used, with positive results of blood evidence found in the interior of the vehicle. Blood was found on the front floor at the driver's feet. Blood was found on the floor in the left rear of the car and on the floor along the driver's seat.

>Two of the reasons the HPD gave for Ottis Toole being the abductor of Adam are:
>
>**1:** Toole knew the type of weapon used.
>
>**2:** Toole knew how many blows it took to decapitate Adam's head.

According to the medical examiner, Adam's head was decapitated by five chops to the back of the neck with an approximately five-and-a-half-inch machete-type weapon. In his October 19, 1983, interview with Detective Jack Hoffman and Detective Ron Hickman of the HPD and Detective Buddy Terry of the Jacksonville Police Department, Toole started off with an eighteen-inch bayonet that morphed into a five-and-a-half-inch machete with a little help from detective Jack Hoffman. Hoffman would also help Toole get close to the number five in order to match how many times the medical examiner said it took to decapitate Adam. Toole first started with two to three times, then three to four times, then less than ten times. He was up to a dozen before he started running out of digits and stumbled on the digit five. When Hoffman wrote his *Interview Summary Report* on November 6, 1983, he would do his best to only mention the most correct answers.

The following are excerpts of the Ottis Toole interviews, quoted from the Adam Walsh case files. Let's start with the back of the head.

Q: HOFFMAN / A: TOOLE

Q: But you're a hundred percent positive in your own mind that that child was lying face down when his head was decapitated?

A: Well, the kid could have been turned all kind of ways.

(HPD case files, roll 2, p. 668, Oct. 24, 1983)

Bayonet or machete?

Q: Okay. Now, while you're traveling northbound on this roadway, did anything occur in the car between yourself and the child or between Henry and the child? [Henry Lee Lucas—Toole's partner].

A: Well, Henry says find somewheres and turn off. We turn off and got on a, like a, we went down a dirt road down there and ah, and ah, he said he couldn't hold the kid and so ah, he got the f***ing bayonet out of the car and ah, I held the f***ing kid and Henry chopped the f***ing kid's head off.

Q: With the bayonet?

A: With the bayonet.

Q: What kind of bayonet are we talking about? When you say bayonet, are you talking about . . .

A: Bayonet is a big knife about like that. [For the record, he is holding his fingers eighteen inches apart].

Q: You're saying almost eighteen inches long?

A: Yeah.

Q: Similar to, like, a machete?

A: Yeah, like a machete.

(HPD case files, roll 2, p. 638, Oct. 24, 1983)

The number of chops

When Detective Hoffman first asked Toole how many times it took to chop off Adam's head, Toole responded, "Two or three." Hoffman then asked if it could've been more than two or three. Toole responded, "Three or four." Could it have been ten, Hoffman asked. "It don't take ten fuckin' times to chop a little fuckin' kid's head off," Toole responded.

The following are some of those interview statements quoted directly from the Adam Walsh case files. How any of them equals five, I will never know.

Q: Okay. All right, while you held him down and Henry chopped the child's head off, do you recall how many blows to the head it took to decapitate the child?

A: I think maybe 'bout three or four times. If you catch somebody just right, shit, you can chop the head off in two or three times, you know.

(HPD case files, roll 2, p. 639, Oct. 24, 1983)

Q: How many times did it take you to chop his head off? To sever his head?

A: I'd say about four, about four times.

(HPD case files, roll 2, p. 709, Oct. 24, 1983)

Q: Okay, now what did you do?

A: I kept chopping, and I chopped him more than one time, you know. I coulda chopped [him] four or five times, a half a dozen times.

(HPD case files, roll 2, p. 778, Oct. 24, 1983)

Q: Okay. How many times did you strike him in the head, the neck area, with the machete? How many times did you chop?

A: Quite a few times.

Q: Quite a few times. Do you remember how many is quite a bit?

A: I'd say between a half a dozen times and a dozen times.

Q: In your earlier statement you told us last week, it was between four and five times.

A: Well, that could be.

Q: Now a half a dozen times?

A: It could. It could have been in 'tween, in 'tween that—nine . . . I chopped his head off.

(HPD case files, roll 2, p. 912, Oct. 24, 1983)

On October 27, 1983, Public Defender Elton H. Schwarz was assigned to defend Ottis Toole regarding the criminal charges pending against him in Jacksonville. A letter was sent out to law enforcement agencies notifying them of his representation of Ottis Toole, who was indigent, and requesting that no contact be made with regard to the taking of a statement or other criminal investigative procedures without first notifying him so that he might effectuate Toole's privilege against self-incrimination and his right to effective assistance of counsel. The Schwarz letter can be read at the end of this chapter.

The following statements are quoted from Hoffman's supplement report from the HPD CD (Adam Walsh case files, roll 1, pp. 168-69, Nov. 6, 1983).

OTTIS was questioned as to how he knew it was a Sears store, and he replied, "Cause I know a Sears when I see a Sears."

OTTIS stated he was intoxicated when the Adam Walsh Abduction occurred.

OTTIS stated it took three to four blows to chop the child's head off and the child was lying face down.

OTTIS stated the boy was a pretty-looking kid. The weapon described was a machete.

OTTIS stated that Henry told him to turn off the road because he couldn't hold on to the kid anymore.

On page 171, Hoffman wrote:

Ottis states the child was unconscious due to OTTIS having hit him so many times in the face and stomach. He states he removed the unconscious child from the front seat of the vehicle and carried him to an area close to where he parked the car, then laying the child facedown, chopped his head off with the machete. OTTIS states he used two hands to hold the machete and it took four to five chops to sever the head, and chopped the head off with blows that were close to the head.

NOTE: With all this trauma going on inside Toole's car, there should have been at least one hair of Adam's found in that car.

When Chief Wagner took over on November 3, 2007, as the new police chief, without any efforts at using due diligence, he vowed to close the Adam Walsh case. And close it he did. John and Reve were there and gave a heartfelt speech. "For twenty-seven years, we have been asking ourselves who would take a six-year-old boy and murder him and decapitate him. We needed to know [who]. Today we know. The not knowing has been a torture, but now that journey is over. It is only fitting that it ends here at this police department."

The HPD homicide detectives, along with Joe Matthews, sat to the right of the Walshes without moral conscience, knowing the perpetrator wasn't Ottis Toole. I was there, too. This was a travesty of justice from its inception to its closing. This would be the second time they officially named Toole as Adam's killer. Of course, the first was when they took him on that field trip to Hollywood. Due to a lack of direct evidence then, the police were forced to back off. They would have to wait for Toole to die before they could posthumously charge him again and close their problematic case convicting a dead man without a legal trial through what is known as the *mis*use of "exceptional clearance." That way their convenient pet suspect, Ottis Toole would no longer be able to recant. Destroying constitutional protections without presenting any old or new evidence, Hollywood Police Chief Chadwick E. Wagner tried and convicted Ottis Toole on national TV. Whether he was guilty or not seemed to be irrelevant, these HPD thugs in uniform predicated their false premise solely on the fact that it had to be somebody—so it might as well have been Ottis. Ever since the closing, Wagner has declined interviews.

The following is the statement in full of Police Chief Chadwick Wagner on the resolution of the twenty-seven-year-old investigation into the murder of Adam Walsh:

Good afternoon, everyone. I am here today to discuss and bring some closure to the Adam Walsh abduction and homicide investigation that began over twenty-seven years ago.

Approximately twelve years have lapsed since the Adam Walsh files were disclosed for inspection. Although I did not necessarily agree with the court decision to disclose the investigative files, our Agency has continued to investigate leads and interview potential witnesses during the years since.

This police department has spared no expense during this period, including sending detectives to destinations throughout the country, in the furtherance of any new information regarding the abduction and death of Adam Walsh.

Since my appointment to police chief nearly one year ago, I have approved dispatching our detectives to location(s) outside of Florida to conduct interviews.

Our continuing investigation during the past twelve years has only recommitted our focus upon Ottis Toole.

Through a lengthy process of exclusion over the entire investigative period of twenty-seven years, the direction of this investigation has always continued to focus upon Ottis Toole as the perpetrator of this horrific crime.

During my tenure with the Hollywood Police Department, I have served as a homicide investigator, among other investigative assignments. Prior to this year, I never actually had the opportunity to review the entire Adam Walsh investigation. I did observe the investigation handled by others in the department and admittedly realized, even years ago, that this investigation had flaws. This fact was confirmed when I recently had the opportunity to digest the entire investigative file. Nevertheless, in the first few months into my appointment as police chief, I committed as a priority to resolve and conclude this investigation. I believe the Walshes are entitled to this level of commitment.

As I referenced earlier, I made it my priority upon my selection as chief of police to review the investigative direction of the Adam Walsh case and contact John and Reve Walsh personally.

My reason for contacting them directly was twofold: to indicate my intention of reviewing the direction of this investigation and to apologize for investigative mistakes that transpired during the early years of this investigation. Although I was not a member of the Hollywood Police Department when this tragedy occurred in 1981, I am nevertheless a parent who can only imagine the pain the Walshes have endured through the years without the satisfaction of closure in this investigation. It is inherently my responsibility on behalf of this police agency to express remorse to the Walshes and indicate to them the emphasis we have placed on this continuing investigation regardless of the initial investigative difficulties.

Having analyzed and reviewed the Adam Walsh investigative file several times during the last year, I had the opportunity to meet retired Miami Beach homicide detective Joe Matthews, who has been involved in this case since the inception, and who had conducted an independent review and investigation of this case.

Consistent with the opinions of investigators past and present, I agreed with the ultimate conclusion of this independent investigation that Ottis Toole was the perpetrator of this crime. With the acknowledgment that our investigation placed Ottis Toole in Hollywood, Florida, at or near the time of Adam's abduction, along with the multiple confessions countered by several subsequent recantations, our agency has devoted an inordinate amount of time seeking leads to other potential perpetrators, rather than emphasizing Ottis Toole as our primary suspect.

One common denominator remains, following an additional twelve years of investigating leads and interviewing potential witnesses after the court-ordered disclosure of the investigative files: that the pedophile and convicted murderer Ottis Toole has continued to be our only real suspect. As we know, Ottis Toole is deceased, and formal legal action is not possible, nor is it something that the Walsh family is seeking. However, in the interest of justice, the Hollywood Police Department is announcing today that it is our determination and conclusion that Ottis Toole was the abductor and murderer of Adam Walsh. This conclusion is one that is based on a vast amount of circumstantial evidence.

Therefore, it is my decision, as Chief of the City of Hollywood Police Department, in consultation with investigators past and present, to exceptionally clear this investigation with the conclusion that if Ottis Toole was alive today, he would be arrested for the abduction and murder of Adam Walsh on July 27, 1981.

This decision is predicated upon thorough discussions with the Broward County State Attorney's Office as well as the Walsh family. I sincerely hope that John and Reve Walsh realize some closure with this decision.

This was posted by John Walsh on his *America's Most Wanted* website:

There are two agencies we would like to thank for never giving up: the Broward County State Attorney's office—in particular, Assistant State Attorney Chuck Morton—and the Hollywood Police Department, and specifically, the courage of Chief Chad Wagner for moving this case to its conclusion.

Secondly, former Miami Beach Police homicide detective Joe Matthews, who worked this case tirelessly for 27 years and developed so much of the crucial evidence to close this case.

The decision to close the case was also supported by Charles Morton Jr., the chief assistant at the Broward state attorney's office.

Except for the HPD latching onto Ottis Toole's confession, Ottis Toole would never have been a suspect. Jeffrey Dahmer was a legitimate suspect. The FBI suspected him. Dahmer's own father suspected him. Even John Walsh suspected Dahmer until he was befriended by retired detective Joe Matthews, who convinced John that Toole was guilty.

"I believe Ottis Toole killed Adam,
I believe that Toole is in Hell right now,
and I believe that he died a horrible death in prison."

_____ ***John Edward Walsh*** _____

Blame It on the Dead Guy

For the Hollywood police chief, this closing was a catastrophic success. This time, Ottis Toole had no say in being accused, and he had no family that would come to his aid. In fact, his family didn't claim his body after his death, so he was buried in the prison cemetery.

RIGHT PHOTO: Ottis Toole.
From Miami-Dade police files, 1983

Instead of just reading from superficially scripted lines, Chief Wagner should have explained why he thought Ottis Toole killed Adam. Rather, he said, "There was no new evidence against Toole that made police name him as the killer." And the media accepted that.

I might not have made a lot of friends in law enforcement or the media, but I state the facts as they are. The time is always right to do what is right, but Chief Wagner allowed Joe Matthews to bamboozle him into doing what was wrong. Chief Wagner said he was big enough to admit past mistakes and correct them. Instead, his greatest accomplishment during his tenure as police chief will go down in history as being one of the worst ever incompetent bungles of our time.

Matthews, in his own condescending way, trashed the chief and the entire department in his book *Bringing Adam Home* when he said, "If anyone chooses to assume that it was Chad Wagner and his men who'd finally put two and two together, that was okay, too. Wagner was, in my eyes, deserving of plenty of credit. There were surely many of his own men who would have preferred that he simply do as all his predecessors had done. But Chad Wagner was a stand-up cop." Matthews would go on to refer to the HPD as not being able to add two and two, and credit himself with solving the case.

So what was the chief going to do now? Well, nothing. He couldn't do anything without admitting yet another mistake, and a big one at that. So he now had no choice but to continue going along with Matthews's closure right up until the day when he was suddenly forced out of the department in 2013.

To all other homicide detectives, I would like to say: Never hand-pick your witnesses by selecting only the ones that fit your own personal scenarios and suspicions and dismiss all the rest. That will only doom your investigation right from the start. Most of the early supplement reports made by Detective Hoffman are worthless because they are only a summary of what Hoffman wanted the outcome to be, not the actual facts. Fortunately for Hoffman, he finally got it right; it wasn't Ottis Toole.

Also, even if you do mess up a case really badly, never, ever cover up. It might catch up to you. Chief Wagner did his best to charge the wrong person with a murder and then managed to get the State Attorney's Office to back him up; something that calls into question every other person that has been charged and convicted by these departments. The chief himself said, through his attorney that he was quite upset at Matthews for getting him into this situation, but I find it hard to have pity on the chief after I was threatened with arrest by his department (Chapter Thirteen) in the hopes that I would disappear as a witness.

FBI Agent Neil Purtell once told me, "The cover-up can be worse than the crime." Certainly, all the players involved in the closing of this case are the worst of the worst; they are the criminals we pay to arrest the criminals we don't pay. And the media? Nearly all the media would accept Wagner's closure with few or no questions.

Vindication of Ottis Toole

There are those who believe, or want to believe, that Ottis Toole was responsible for the abduction and murder of Adam. Some have been led to their belief as a result of inaccurate or partially presented evidence. There are also those who have fitted the evidence together—either in their own minds or in actuality—to apparently prove that Ottis Toole was the perpetrator.

I have painstakingly gone through each and every page of the case files, sifting through and weighing the evidence. I have also talked in person with numerous witnesses. As a result of being a witness myself, I know Ottis Toole didn't commit this particular crime. I have a problem with facts that don't fit, with witnesses not being called or used, with bungled investigations, and with cover-ups after the fact. Also, I can't discount the fact that I saw someone I know to be Jeffrey Dahmer walk into the toy department about the same time Adam was abducted.

I have made and will continue to make what I believe is a compelling case for why Toole did *not* murder Adam and for who I believe *did*—Jeffrey Dahmer. I know I've been outspoken at times, but I'm very sure about what I witnessed. I've been as objective as I can be after years of being involved, researching and writing this book.

I'm not a professional writer, but rather am simply presenting evidence from the case files, any or all of which I invite anyone to look at, download or save from my website:

JusticeForAdam.com

Readers can form their own opinions and conclusions. Even if you don't believe that Jeffrey Dahmer murdered Adam, hopefully you will at least agree that it wasn't Ottis Toole.

Toole's timeline relevant to the Adam Walsh case can be read at the end of this book.

On the following pages are copies of reports from the Adam Walsh case files.

The two-page *Kindrick Case Report* that started the Toole line of inquiry:

BREVARD COUNTY SHERIFF'S DEPARTMENT
TITUSVILLE, FLORIDA 32780

Page - 1 of 2

CASE REPORT

MO.	DAY	YEAR	TIME REPORTED:	OFFENSE		UCR CODE:	CASE REPORT NUMBER:
10	23	1983	12:20 P.M.	A.O.A. - Duval County			83-55309

MO.	DAY	YEAR	TIME: OCCURRED	TO	MO.	DAY	YEAR	TIME:	LOCATION: Jacksonville, Florida Duval County Sheriff's Office
10	10	83	12:02 P.M.						

NAME: c XX w☐ v☐	ADDRESS:	R	S	A	PX: (H)____
Buddy Terry	Duval County Sheriff's Office				(W) 904-633-4202

NAME: c☐ w☐ v☐	ADDRESS:	R	S	A	PX: (H)____ (W)____

NAME: c☐ w☐ v☐	ADDRESS:	R	S	A	PX: (H)____ (W)____

SUSPECT SECTION

NAME: SU ☒ WD☐ AR☐ MP☐ MJ☐	ALIAS/NICKNAME:	R	S	A	DOB:
Ottis Elwood Toole		W	M	36	3-5-47

HGT.: 6'	WGT.: 170	HAIR: Brn	EYES: Brn	SCHOOL/OCCUPATION:	PLACE OF BIRTH:

ADDRESS: Duval County Jail, Jacksonville, Fl.   POSSIBLE DESTINATION/AREAS FREQUENTED/CHARGE(S)

NAME: SU☐ WD☐ AR☐ MP☐ MJ☐	ALIAS/NICKNAME:	R	S	A	DOB:

HGT	WGT.	HAIR:	EYES:	SCHOOL/OCCUPATION:	PLACE OF BIRTH:

ADDRESS: POSSIBLE DESTINATION/AREAS FREQUENTED/CHARGE(S):

NAME: SU☐ WD☐ AR☐ MP☐ MJ☐	ALIAS/NICKNAME:	R	S	A	DOB:

HGT.:	WGT.:	HAIR:	EYES:	SCHOOL/OCCUPATION:	PLACE OF BIRTH:

ADDRESS: POSSIBLE DESTINATION/AREAS FREQUENTED/CHARGE(S):

VEHICLES

☐ USED IN CRIME ☐ CONFISCATED ☐ OTHER
☐ HOLD ☐ PROCESSED ☐ TOWED ☐ RELEASED ON SCENE

YEAR:	MAKE:	MODEL:	STYLE:	COLOR:	LICENSE NUMBER:	STATE LIC.:	YEAR LICENSE:

VEHICLE IDENTIFICATION NUMBER:	IDENTIFYING CHARACTERISTICS:	INSURANCE COMPANY:

VALUE STOLEN:	VALUE RECOVERED:	WRECKER SERVICE:	LEIN HOLDER:	PAYMENTS CURRENT? YES☐ NO☐

PROPERTY

ITEM	QTY.	PROPERTY DESCRIPTION (MAKE, MODEL, BRAND, TYPE, COLOR, CALIBER, ETC.)	SERIAL NUMBER OR V.I.N.	VALUE STOLEN	VALUE RECOVERED

CASE STATUS

☐ PENDING
☒ CLEARED NON-ARREST ☐ ADULT
☐ UNFOUNDED ☐ CLEARED ARREST ☐ JUVENILE
☐ REQUEST CAPIAS ☐ EXCEPTIONALLY CLEARED

REPORTING OFFICER SIGNATURE/ID No.: S.R. Kindrick _Kindrick_ 85.

REPORT APPROVED BY/ID No.: _____ 66

REFERRED TO/ID No.:

REVIEWED BY/ID No.:

SD 425 (Rev 5/83)

Page - 2 -

CR #83-55309
Agent S.R. Kindrick
October 24, 1983

On October 10, 1983, Reporting Agent responded to Jacksonville
and met with AGENT BUDDY TERRY. AGENT TERRY introduced Reporting
Agent to OTTIS ELWOOD TOOLE, W/M, DOB 3-5-47. TOOLE is an inmate
at the County Jail, who has been charged with numerous murders
throughout the Southeastern United States.

TOOLE waived his rights and spoke with Reporting Agent freely.
Reporting Agent taped an interview, starting at 11:32 A.M. and
lasting for approximately thirty (30) minutes. Shortly after
Reporting Agent stopped the recording, TOOLE started a
conversation regarding Ft. Lauderdale. As Reporting Agent was
putting away the recorder, TOOLE asked "Are you from Ft.
Lauderdale?" Reporting Agent said, "No." TOOLE, "Are you sure?"
Reporting Agent, "Ottis for the last hour we have been talking
about Cocoa, Cocoa Beach, and Rockledge. I introduced myself as
an investigator from Brevard County." Reporting Agent then
inquired of TOOLE. "You expecting someone from Ft. Lauderdale?"
TOOLE, "Yeah, yeah I am.". Reporting Agent asked, "You get into
something there?" TOOLE, "Yeah, I did."

Note should be made, TOOLE confessed to Reporting Agent about
being present and/or taking part in what he believed to be
approximately sixty five (65) murders. During this time, TOOLE
was calm and produced an image of two people talking about the
weather. During the brief conversation about Ft. Lauderdale,
TOOLE completely changed. He held the sides of his chair,
shifted from side to side, and started looking into the floor,
which is something he didn't do before.

Reporting Agent felt due to TOOLE'S obvious nervousness about Ft.
Lauderdale, it would be best not to pursue the matter, but to
have AGENT TERRY do so. At the conclusion of the conversation,
Reporting Agent met with AGENT TERRY and advised him about the
conversation and TOOLE'S body language. Reporting Agent also
brought up the ADAM WALSH death. Reporting Agent felt for a man
to admit involvement in sixty five (65) murders, but get upset
about Ft. Lauderdale, it had to be something appalling.

Reporting Agent contacted DETECTIVE JACK HOFFMAN from Hollywood
Police Department on October 11, 1983 and advised him about the
situation and referred him to AGENT TERRY.

Case closed.

Sworn To And Subscribed
Before Me This 25TH Day
Of Oct.   19 83

AGENT S.R. KINDRICK

Diane R. Clarke

NOTARY PUBLIC, STATE OF FLORIDA AT LARGE
MY COMMISSION EXPIRES MARCH 22, 1986
BONDED THRU MUROSKI-ASHTON, INC.

002446

The two-page *Philip Mundy Investigative Assignment*:

March 2, 1998

Investigative Assignment #96-02-262

INVESTIGATIVE REPORT #26

TO: **RALPH J. RAY, JR.**
               Chief Assistant State Attorney

FROM: **PHILIP J. MUNDY**
               Investigator

SUBJ: **City of Jacksonville Landfill - 1981**

RE: **Homicide Investigation of Adam Walsh**

****

On November 19, 1983 Ottis TOOLE told Det. J. HOFFMAN that he had not disposed of Adam Walsh's body near the Florida Turnpike but rather had returned with it to Jacksonville. He now claimed that he burned the body in the back yard of his mother's home, having placed the body in a junked refrigerator and then not being able to completely disintegrate the body put the remains in a blanket. He claims he then put the blanket and body in the trunk of the Cadillac. TOOLE also mentions that he watered down the blanket while in the trunk because it was still smoldering. The next day, July 28, 1981, he drove to the City of Jacksonville landfill and disposed of the remains. In addition, TOOLE told Det. HOFFMAN that the trunk liner was saturated and had evidence of blood and so he disposed of that material there as well.

Research revealed that Det. HOFFMAN did obtain the names of three City of Jacksonville employees who worked at the landfill on the date in question. The results of his inquiry could not be found in the report, although it is recalled that in discussing this case with Det. HOFFMAN he indicated they did investigate the possibility of a search of the landfill but that it would have been an impossibility.

On January 14, 1998 Mr. Dennis BEDWELL was contacted by telephone. Mr. BEDWELL in July, 1981 was in a supervisory position and knowledgeable of the operations of the City of Jacksonville landfill project.

Mr. BEDWELL explained that he had been questioned by a number of police investigators back in 1983, including Hollywood P.D., although he did not recall any names. He reiterated what he told them which was that the landfill was open to private citizens who paid one dollar for using the site. When the vehicles of private citizens came in they were weighed and then weighed again when they exited. The difference in the weight being of course what was dumped.

Investigative Assignment #96-02-262
Page Two

INVESTIGATIVE REPORT #26

There was no record kept of vehicles entering the premises either by type, tag number, or driver, as the only concern the city had was the amount of tonnage being dumped, which Mr. BEDWELL says at that time was between four to five hundred tons per day.

Mr. BEDWELL recalled that the police did come to him with the weight of a vehicle (Faye McNett's Cadillac) and with the date they were concerned with. He remembers researching the weight receipts for that day and it is his recollection that there were several vehicles of the same weight on the day in question.

The police also questioned Mr. BEDWELL as to where vehicles were dumping on the day they were concerned with. Mr. BEDWELL could only give them a general area, and by this time, 1983, there would have been a depth of about sixty feet to reach 1982 dumping material. Obviously excavation of the site was not feasible.

INV. PHILIP J. MUNDY

cc: Det. John Kerns, Hollywood P.D.

Captain Davis's two-page inter-office memorandum:

CITY OF HOLLYWOOD, FLORIDA

INTER-OFFICE MEMORANDUM

TO: LeRoy R. Hessler
Assistant Police Chief

FROM: Captain R. S. Davis
Commander
Detective Division

DATE: January 10, 1984   FILE: DB-84-01

SUBJECT: Adam Walsh Homicide

REFERENCES: Case #81-56073

Since Ottis Toole's confession on October 19, 1983, six (6) investigators have been assigned, full time, to the Adam Walsh case. Approximately 3,500 man hours and $62,000.00 have been expended during the investigation of Toole as a suspect in the homicide of Adam Walsh.

The investigation has led detectives to Texas, Virginia, North Carolina, South Carolina, Georgia and the Jacksonville area. All persons known to have had contact with Toole during the Summer of 1981 have been located and interviewed.

Detectives were able to trace Ottis Toole's movements during the latter part of July 1981. It was substantiated that Ottis Toole departed Newport News, Virginia on July 24, 1981 en route to, and arriving in, Jacksonville on July 25, 1981 at 10:30 A.M. It was further learned that he rented a room in the Jacksonville area on July 31, 1981. Investigators are unable to positively account for Toole's whereabouts, between July 26, 1981 and July 31, 1981, a five (5) day period, being the time during which Adam Walsh was abducted and murdered.

A vehicle, a 1971 Cadillac, once owned by Toole, was sent to F.D.L.E. in Tallahassee for technical processing. The only evidence located in the vehicle was a positive luminal test indicating blood was present inside the car. The test could not specify if the blood was human or other. All further tests for fiber, fingerprints and hair specimens were negative in linking this vehicle with the Walsh murder.

A suspect murder weapon was located in the Jacksonville area. This weapon was examined by the Florida Department of Law Enforcement and the Dade County Crime Lab. No evidence was found on the weapon which would aid in this investigation.

During this investigation, Toole has recanted his confession several times. Toole has not been eliminated as a suspect, however, detectives have been unable to uncover any evidence, other than his confession, linking him with the Walsh homicide. It is felt that there is insufficient evidence at this time to file criminal charges against Ottis Toole.

CSI-03

CITY OF HOLLYWOOD, FLORIDA

INTER-OFFICE MEMORANDUM

TO:	LeRoy R. Hessler Assistant Police Chief	**DATE:** January 10, 1984	**FILE:**
		SUBJECT: Adam Walsh Homicide	
FROM:	Captain R. S. Davis Commander Detective Division	**REFERENCES:** 81-56073	

Since October 19, 1983, detectives have been investigating Ottis Toole's connection with the Adam Walsh Homicide.

At this point in the investigation, it has been determined that "MAYBE HE DID AND MAYBE HE DIDN'T."

Investigation is continuing..........

RSD/ab

CSI-03

Letter from the offices of Elton Schwarz:

LAW OFFICES OF

ELTON H. SCHWARZ

PUBLIC DEFENDER

NINETEENTH JUDICIAL CIRCUIT OF FLORIDA

MARTIN COUNTY OFFICE:
(MAIN OFFICE)
SUITE 215, COURTHOUSE ANNEX
P. O. BOX 2314
STUART, FLORIDA 33495-2314
(305) 283-6760 EXT. 380

DIRECT LINES TO MAIN OFFICE:
(305) 287-2966 (STUART)
(305) 464-8564 (FORT PIERCE)
(305) 562-1515 (VERO BEACH)
(813) 763-7979 (OKEECHOBEE)

REPLY TO: ___Stuart___

October 28, 1983

Chief of Police
Hollywood Police Department
3250 Hollywood Boulevard
Hollywood, Florida 33021

Re: Otis Toole

Dear Sir:

This letter is to advise you that our office has reason to believe that the above-mentioned individual is indigent and entitled to the services of the Public Defender's office of this Circuit for representation regarding the criminal charges pending against him. Under Rule 3.111(c)(4)(i), Florida Rules of Criminal Procedure, this individual is entitled to the services of the Public Defender in his pending charges.

Pursuant to that Rule, and in order to effectuate his rights under the Fifth and Sixth Amendments to the Constitution of the United States and the Declaration of Rights of the State of Florida, I am requesting that no contact be made with this individual with regard to the taking of a statement or other criminal investigative procedures without first notifying me so that I may represent him effectively in this charge.

Again, I am making this request in order to effectuate his privilege against self-incrimination, as guaranteed by the Fifth Amendment to the United States Constitution, and his right to effective assistance of counsel, as guaranteed by the Sixth Amendment to the United States Constitution, both Amendments being applied to the several states by the Fourteenth Amendment to the Constitution of the United States.

Thank you **very** much for your consideration of this individual's request.

Very truly yours,

Elton H. Schwarz
Public Defender

EHS:kmg

RECEIVED
OCT 31 1983
CHIEF OF POLICE

INDIAN RIVER COUNTY OFFICE:
COURTHOUSE ANNEX
2145 14TH AVENUE
VERO BEACH, FLORIDA 32960
(305) 562-7074
305-567-8000 EXT. 545

ST. LUCIE COUNTY OFFICE:
111 ATLANTIC AVENUE
FORT PIERCE, FLORIDA 33450
(305) 465-6086

OKEECHOBEE COUNTY OFFICE:
SUITE 400
501 N.W. FIFTH AVENUE
OKEECHOBEE, FLORIDA 33472
(813) 763-7977

003238

THE JOHN WALSH STATEMENT

Here is the full statement John and Reve Walsh that was posted on *America's Most Wanted* following the closing of the Adam Walsh case naming Ottis Toole as the murderer:

(Also compare this December 16, 2008 statement to what John said in 2006, at the bottom of page 199 of this book).

It has been more than 27 years since our son Adam was abducted from a Hollywood, Fla., mall, then murdered. The situation that we have endured since then is beyond a parent's worst nightmare. Despite an ongoing, 27-year investigation, our son's murder case has remained open—until now.

Although Adam's killer never served one day in prison for destroying our son's life and almost ruining ours, nor will he ever because he died in prison serving time for an unrelated murder, we are satisfied that the main suspect in Adam's murder—Ottis Toole—has now been positively identified and that this chapter in our lives is now closed.

There are two agencies we would like to thank for never giving up: the Broward County State Attorney's office—in particular, assistant State Attorney Chuck Morton—and the Hollywood Police Department, and specifically, the courage of Chief Chad Wagner for moving this case to its conclusion.

We want to express our deepest gratitude to two men who worked with us all these years, pro bono, to get justice for Adam and give us some answers: Kelly Hancock, former Broward County state attorney prosecutor and now prominent private attorney with the law firm of Krupnick, Campbell, Malone, Buser, Slama, Hancock, Liberman and McKelly.

From the beginning, Kelly Hancock worked within the criminal justice system to make sure that Adam's case did not fall through the cracks and to ensure that there was a resolution for Adam and our family.

Secondly, former Miami Beach Police homicide detective Joe Matthews, who worked this case tirelessly for 27 years and developed so much of the crucial evidence to close this case.

From all of the evidence presented to us, we agree with the conclusion shared by the key investigators that it is clear and irrefutable that Ottis Toole was the abductor and killer of our son Adam.

We can now move forward knowing positively who killed our beautiful little boy. We, along with our children, Meghan, Callahan, and Hayden, pray for the thousands of parents of murdered and still-missing children. We continue to fight for their safety, and to make sure that no child—especially Adam—died in vain.

John & Reve Walsh
Hollywood, Fla.

The Adam Walsh case chronology can be read at the end of this book.

CHAPTER SEVEN
JEFFREY DAHMER

"This is him! This is the guy I saw in the mall!"
_____ ***Willis Russell Morgan*** _____

July 23, 1991 Mug shot of Jeffrey Dahmer

I'm not sure exactly what night it was, but I think it must have been Wednesday, July 24, 1991. I was in the pressroom office, and the papers started coming in for paper check. We had papers from six presses lined up on a long counter. We started going through the papers together. When I turned a page somewhere in the "A" section, I stopped. I saw a small mug shot and got an immediate flashback.

I started freaking out. "This is him! This is the guy I saw in the mall!" I said, somewhat loudly. I became so flushed with adrenaline that I tuned out everything around me and zoomed in on that mug shot. That guy I thought I might see in the news someday was in the paper. This was him.

I barely noted the voices around me saying, "Willis, what are you talking about?" and, "Calm down." I was about as calm as I was going to get. I remembered that face, and I was positive this was him. I could hardly function the rest of the night. I drank one cup of coffee after another and kept looking at that mug shot.

The article said nothing about the person being in South Florida, yet I knew he had been. The article said nothing about a connection with Adam Walsh, yet I knew he had one. The article was only about the horror in an apartment in Milwaukee, yet I knew without doubt he was the one involved in that abduction.

Later on in the night, in the final edition, an updated story came out and said the person had been living in Miami Beach in 1981. That was all the confirmation I needed. It turned out to be quite a night for me and I needed another cup of coffee.

The very next morning, I went back to the HPD, newspaper in hand. I was referred to a detective on the third floor. The detective I spoke with told me Detective Hoffman was on that case but was on vacation. He took my name, phone number, short statement, and told me Hoffman would call me when he returned. It took three months for Hoffman to call me.

In the meantime, I called the *Miami Herald* library and asked them to find the composite that ran in the paper back in 1981. This was a pay service, but since I was an employee, they sent it to my in-house mailbox in the pressroom at no cost. I was told any further information I needed would be at no charge so long as I used the in-house mailbox.

October 23, 1991: Detective Hoffman did call me back and asked me to come in. When I went to see him, he asked why I was coming in now and hadn't in 1981. Incredulously, I exclaimed, "But I did come in, in '81." I showed him the following 1981 suspect composite and the 1982 mug shot of Jeffrey Dahmer.

Twin City Mall Composite   **Milwaukee Police Booking Photo**

Jeffrey Dahmer: August 1981   **Jeffrey Dahmer: August 1982**

Detective Hoffman's response was, "I don't see it; they look nothing alike." I was flabbergasted! No one else had said that.

I did not realize the composite I had wasn't even from the Hollywood Mall. Only after the Hollywood Police closed the case in 2008 and I got a copy of the case files on CD-ROM would I realize this composite was from the Twin City Mall, which was sixty miles north of the Hollywood Mall, when Dahmer attempted to abduct another boy from another Sears.

I must've missed that article. Back in 1981, I was working a ten-hour-day, four-day work week and didn't read the paper on my days off. What I do remember is that, when I saw that composite in the paper in August 1981, I was relieved, thinking the HPD finally had the right composite. I don't remember reading anything about another mall.

Remember, however, that Hoffman had investigated the Twin City Mall incident back in 1981 and completely dismissed it as having anything to do with the Adam Walsh abduction, even though it was in a Sears, in the toy department, on a Monday at about the same time of the day, and the suspect description and composite matched the Hollywood composite [p. 58].

In the Adam Walsh case, witnesses did remarkably well at creating a composite likeness of the suspect, considering that a law enforcement facial composite sketch is a graphical representation of an eyewitness's memory of a face, after the fact, as recorded during an intense consultation session by a composite artist who has never seen the suspect. Despite the incredible technological leaps made in investigative work, the forensic art of composite sketching still relies on the basic elements of drawing skill, interviewing ability, and the spoken word, which is then transformed into the features of a suspect. Composites can be one of the most crucial investigative tools in law enforcement, although not necessarily a perfect likeness.

Once Jeffrey Dahmer was captured and his photo and mug shot were in the national news, almost all the witnesses I talked to said Dahmer was the person they were trying to describe. The sketch artist even did a great job trying of capturing that lifeless, dead, dull look in Dahmer's eyes.

However, when I told Hoffman that whoever gave that composite saw the same person I saw and that the 1981 composite matched the 1982 mug shot of Jeffrey Dahmer, he was loath to accept the likeness and refused to get excited enough to accept Dahmer as a possible suspect.

Hoffman then asked me to wait and left the room. When he returned, he asked me, "If you came in in 1981, where is your taped statement?" I told him I didn't make a taped statement and explained to him that Officer Presley took some notes and said they would call me back, but no one ever did. I thought I had nothing more to offer, so I never came back. Hoffman told me to wait a minute and then left the room again for a good twenty minutes.

When he returned, he told me, "We never had an Officer Presley."

I explained, "Well, you had one back then. He was in full uniform at the desk in the lobby. You don't know who you had working here?"

I remember the name, of course. Anyone who was part of my generation wouldn't forget a name like Presley. He wasn't anything like the six-foot pop and country rocker. I remember he was a little guy that looked to be a regular police officer in the standard black uniform.

Hoffman wasn't exactly giving me a good first impression as a homicide detective, but I had no idea he might have personal reasons for not wanting to solve this case. Looking back with hindsight, I would now bet he never even checked for an Officer Presley. Now I'm left to think Hoffman might have just gone to the break room for twenty minutes in the hope I'd leave and not come back—I actually almost did.

In my opinion, it was probably about that time that Hoffman's dots started lining up and he realized he'd messed up miserably in 1981. Also, it was likely around that time that the Adam Walsh case files suspiciously dropped to just over seven thousand pages and the Ottis Toole evidence grew legs and walked off. Of course, that is just speculation on my part. I have no way of knowing exactly what transpired, but I know that officers claimed the case files ran approximately ten thousand pages and that the Ottis Toole evidence did vanish by their own admission.

Hoffman asked me to come back in for a taped statement and kept in touch with me. When I went home, I called the *Herald* library again and asked them to send me some composites (before capture) and mug shots (after capture) of other serial killers so that I could compare them. I made some copies to show Hoffman. Included was the composite and mug shot of Jeffrey Dahmer.

When I gave them to Hoffman, he looked at them and, with his usual condescending, flippant tone, asked, "What is this?"

I tried to explain to him that since he didn't think the composite and the mug shot of Dahmer looked alike, I wanted to show him that they looked just as much alike, if not more so, than other serial killers like Richard Ramirez. He grumbled as he tossed them on his desk, as if he were totally disinterested. The way he tossed them gave me the impression that my trying to help was annoying him. He must have disposed of them right after I left because, years later when I got a copy of the case files, I never saw them in the files. But I do get to include them here at the end of this chapter.

One of the drawings I saw in the HPD case files was Dahmer's high school photo, along with the 1981 composite that ran in the newspapers. I added glasses to the composite and removed the mustache with white-out. My purpose was to show Hoffman that the high school photo and composite were the same person. Again, Hoffman said they looked nothing alike, [see p. 57].

One day, Hoffman called me to say he was going up to interview Jeffrey Dahmer. I offered to go to Wisconsin with him and even pay my own way, but I was shot down with, "Well, that's not going to happen!" I had a sinking feeling he was going to blow that interview.

Before Detective Hoffman went to interview Jeffrey Dahmer, I had already had several interviews with the detective. In my first interview, when I told him about following Dahmer until he walked into the Sears toy department, his sarcastic response was, "Well, what are you doing following someone around?"

I want to be clear about one thing: this was the one and only time I ever followed anyone around. I just knew someone might need help. I thought maybe this guy would approach someone like me. I was prepared for words to be exchanged and possibly a shoving match or a fight. I was not prepared for the abduction of a six-year-old child.

In that same interview, I told Detective Hoffman where Dahmer had parked his vehicle. Not that I saw the vehicle, but I did see the door he came into the mall from. My thinking was that you park by the door you enter from. I asked him to just check with the other witnesses. "I'm sure they will tell you the vehicle was retrieved from near the north entrance of the mall." Hoffman just gave me a strange blank look and never replied. Years later, I found out that other witnesses (the Pottenburghs and Bill Bowen) had indeed said the suspect had retrieved his vehicle (a blue van) from the exact spot I said he would've parked. I remember thinking Hoffman knew something but didn't want to tell me. It was as if Hoffman deliberately and purposely didn't want to put the puzzle together (see diagram on page 243 of this book).

Another time, I asked Hoffman to come to the mall so that I could show him what happened. His response was (and I should add, in a quite nasty tone), "I'm not going over to that mall!" I was thinking Hoffman didn't believe me, so I then asked him to at least let me take a polygraph test. Hoffman responded sarcastically again: "We don't give polygraph tests." Later on, when I read the case files, I found that they gave everyone polygraphs. They even gave the Walsh family and everyone in close proximity to them polygraphs. Well, they polygraphed everyone except Ottis Toole in 1983 and Jeffrey Dahmer after 1991, but then again, they didn't need to—the killer's word was good enough for Jack Hoffman.

One time, Hoffman told me something that was so strange that it took years for me to realize the purpose behind it. He said, "That mall is a known gay hangout. Gays hang out there to pick up other gays. That could have been any gay in South Florida" (referring to my encounter). My thinking at the time was that the police should know that because their station was right across the street. Maybe they were getting a lot of complaints about gay activity, although I'd never heard of such a thing.

It was years later that I finally realized Hoffman was just trying to deter me from insisting that I was at that mall. I was just slow in catching on and kept going back to him, and that was before he even went up to Wisconsin for that infamous Jeffrey Dahmer interview.

Another time, Hoffman told me he believed me but, "South Florida has so many crazy people, so it could have been any crazy person in South Florida."

So first it was a gay person, then a crazy person. This was ridiculous as I knew it was Jeffrey Dahmer and not anyone else. That encounter I had was not something I would forget or get wrong. Why did Hoffman not want to even consider Dahmer as a possible suspect? Why was he doing his level best to get me to disappear as a witness? I had no answer. I only knew it was Dahmer. At the time, I was thinking Hoffman didn't grasp anything I told him.

Now I believe it was more likely he didn't want any witnesses to come forward, because he had gone into full cover-up mode from the very first day I spoke to him and showed him that Twin City Mall composite. I was convinced there was no hope for this case with this detective at the lead.

As it turned out, that interview with Dahmer would be a one-time calamity. When Detective Hoffman returned from his interview with Dahmer, he called me at home and told me he was eliminating Dahmer as a suspect. I told him, "That's not possible. You can't do that. I am sure beyond a doubt; it was him. I was face-to-face with him."

Hoffman told me Dahmer had looked him straight in the eye and said he didn't do it. And he added, "You know what? I believe him." Then Hoffman stated that it was his opinion that Dahmer was telling the truth and was being totally cooperative throughout the interview. This was in spite of the fact that Dahmer's own father learned a long time ago not to believe anything his son said. Newspapers, including the *Herald*, then printed articles saying Jeffrey Dahmer had been eliminated as a suspect in Adam's murder.

Great! Now I had to put up with several coworkers joking with me whenever other serial killers would make it into the *Herald*. They would ask me things like, "Willis, did you see this guy, too?"

Detective Hoffman told me, "Dahmer was working ten hours a day, seven days a week, and never took any days off." Hoffman continued to parrot Dahmer: "Every once in a while they would just give him a day off. He didn't know where the mall was, and he was sleeping on the beach. He was drunk all the time, and besides, he didn't have a vehicle to pick anyone up with. Dahmer told me he wanted to come to Florida because he knows Florida has the death penalty, and he doesn't want to live. Besides," Hoffman added, "that little kid doesn't fit his MO."

I blurted out to Hoffman, "I guess someone forgot to tell Dahmer he had an MO to stick to."

If guilt was based on a suspect's confession our prisons would be empty and our morgues full. Yet Hoffman insisted, "If Jeffrey Dahmer committed the Adam Walsh homicide, he would have confessed to this crime."

This detective preferred taking the word of an untreatable sociopath who kept a barrel full of torsos in his bedroom and stashed severed heads in his refrigerator over my word, even though FBI Agent Bill Hagerty, who interviewed Ottis Toole, said Toole didn't do it, and FBI Agent Neil Purtell, who interviewed Jeffrey Dahmer, said Dahmer could've done it. Dahmer's own father had called *America's Most Wanted* soon after his son was captured to tell them that Jeffrey Dahmer was a pedophile and that he thought his son could be responsible for Adam's abduction.

On July 8, 1981, Hollywood Police lieutenant Richard Hynds described Adam's murderer as a "dangerous psychopath" who would kill again. At the time, Hynds didn't know it, but he had described Jeffrey Dahmer perfectly. Yet, in 1992, Detective Hoffman completely dismissed Dahmer.

I was forced to think Hoffman just didn't want Dahmer to be a suspect, so he would make Dahmer's word instrumental in deciding he wasn't Adam's killer. Something was really starting to stink in Hollywood. Little by little, it became more and more apparent that this police department didn't want witnesses

Also read Dahmer's confession at JusticeForAdam.com, Part 1, p. 91.

In 1991, John Walsh called Detective Hoffman and told him, "Dahmer's a pedophile, and his own father is saying that he was in South Florida at the time Adam was abducted." Some time later, John called Hoffman back and asked when he was going to talk to Dahmer. Hoffman told John that he would think about it.

In the meantime, the FBI called John to tell him that Dahmer's lawyer had quit and they could get the HPD right in. The FBI asked John, "Where the hell is this detective? Why the hell hasn't someone been up here to investigate it?" John himself said the FBI had some serious doubts about the abilities of the HPD investigator who seemed less than enthusiastic about pursuing the interrogation. It would take thirteen months for Jack Hoffman to get up to the Columbia Correctional Facility in Portage, Wisconsin.

In 1992, Purtell had to convince John Walsh to get Hoffman to go. That's when John wrote a letter to Michael Satz at the Broward County State Attorney's Office. In that letter, Walsh referred to me and Bill Bowen as "two credible witnesses" and added, "Many people have forgotten that Jeffrey Dahmer started out as a pedophile, kidnapper, and torturer of young boys. He certainly fits the profile of someone who might be capable of murdering a beautiful six-year-old boy.

Walsh was so moved by the Dahmer link that he made a remarkable request. He asked Satz to write a letter stating that Florida wouldn't seek the death penalty. The death penalty never needed to be waived. There was more than enough evidence to indict and convict Dahmer. He could've been extradited back to Florida without a promissory letter.

"I just wanted closure. I knew he'd never get out of prison," John said. "I want to know if Jeffrey Dahmer was the man who killed my son."

Once John had his letter, he called Hoffman back. This time Hoffman told John, "The HPD has already spent thousands of dollars on Adam's case, and there isn't any money in the budget for that kind of trip."

Then John informed him, "You know what? I'm making a pretty good living on TV these days. I'll pay your way to go talk to Dahmer."

With his back to the wall after using up all his excuses, Detective Jack Hoffman finally relented. After more than a year of the FBI and John Walsh prodding him, he finally went up to Wisconsin on August 13, 1992. The trip would be a bust.

Hoffman did that August interview—over homemade muffins—but the interview wasn't a genuine effort to get at the truth. He had with him that promissory letter to waive the death penalty. He never pressed Dahmer on any issue, and he never offered the concession on the death penalty to Dahmer as John Walsh requested, possibly out of fear that Dahmer just might accept. Hoffman himself said he would only offer it if he found it necessary. Since Dahmer denied murdering Adam, Hoffman apparently didn't find the need to offer it—except, that was the whole idea of offering it.

At the very most, the State of Florida should have only offered to reduce Jeffrey Dahmer's charges . . . from 2,000 volts to 1,000. I know I'm being sarcastic, but the HPD turned the case into a joke first. Hoffman pitched only softball questions and talked mostly of Dahmer's life growing up. Whenever Hoffman got bored, he'd simply comment on how great the muffins were, which he had brought with him, and asked Jeff Dahmer if he wanted another. Hoffman accepted everything the deranged, sociopathic, pathological liar said at face value.

I read the transcripts of that August 13, 1992, interview. There were many inconsistencies. June, July and August was the middle of South Florida's humid, subtropical rainy season. Surely Hoffman could've asked if Dahmer had ever taken shelter from the rain and where. Dahmer told Detective Hoffman he was working all those ungodly hours, seven days a week, yet he was always broke and always drunk. Hoffman accepted that, even though Dahmer said at another point in the interview that he was off on weekends.

Surely some of what Dahmer said should have raised some red flags. He couldn't be broke and drunk all the time when he was working all the time, because he would've had no time to spend his money. At one point, Dahmer admitted to having a room at the time Adam was abducted, but at another point in the interview, he said he had no place to bring anyone. Then he caught himself and added, "no place acceptable." Yet his Milwaukee apartment was acceptable? Dahmer even said that he watched the news about the abduction on TV in his room.

The following are actual interview excerpts quoted from HPD files. The full interview can be found in the SAO case files (box 6, volume IV, p. 313).

Q: HOFFMAN / **A:** DAHMER

Q: At what time did you find housing for yourself when you got this job at Sunshine?

A: I . . . I built up enough bank account to get housing sometime in May. . . and I had a one-room, uh, place at the Bimini Bay. It's a motel-type setup.

Q: Is that on Miami Beach also?

A: Right on Collins Avenue. It was about, uh . . . maybe a third of a mile from where I worked. I could walk there. And I just had one room. Small, short fridge, bathroom . . . TV.

NOTE: It was after he was hired in late June that Ken got him that room.

Q: Sometime last year, on two separate occasions, I had two independent witnesses [Bill Bowen and me] that came forward and came up to Hollywood Police Department to meet with me. And, uh . . . one. . .

A: I remember lying in a hotel room—that was one of the times I had a hotel room—and I remember seeing on the news that, that, you know, missing boy Adam Walsh . . .

Q: I asked this gentleman [me], I said, "What was the encounter that you are speaking about?" And he said, "Well, I was, uh, at this store inside the mall" . . . And, uh, the person that he believed to be you . . .

A: Uh huh.

Q: Came up to him and tried to pick him up, had conversation, asked him, "Isn't it a beautiful day outside?" and started following this gentleman. He got a little leery and he continued to walk through the mall, and you followed him, and eventually he lost you somewhere inside the Sears Mall.

A: Uh huh.

Q: That's my purpose for being here. You at no time were in Sears? Or ever in Hollywood, Florida?

A: Absolutely not, and I wasn't, I wasn't . . . I didn't have the . . . a place to go back with anyone, where I felt comfortable with, anyway. I remember sitting after work one night right on Collins Avenue, and there was this guy from Canada, and, uh . . . he tried to pick me up . . . which is a switch. . . And I didn't want anything to do with him, 'cause my place was a mess and I just didn't feel like going back. So I wasn't into picking up people or starting relationships with anyone then.

Q: Then this gentleman [Bill Bowen] that came in from out of state had spoken to us. He also, after seeing accounts of you on the news and also in the newspaper, he brought down this newspaper from Alabama with him . . . and he said that he remembered that he parked his vehicle in the parking lot and [as] he was approaching the store, he saw some child apparently having a problem with a male.

A: Uh huh.

Q: He described the male, you know, similar to you . . . And the one . . .

A: Coincidence.

Q: Excuse me?

A: What a coincidence, huh?

Q: And, uh, the thing that stuck out in his mind is that here it was the middle of July, and this gentleman was wearing an Army fatigue jacket.

A: What year was this supposed to be?

Q: '81, when you were down there.

A: Oh, '81, down in Alabama . . . The only time I was in Alabama . . .

Q: No, not Alabama . . . Hollywood, Florida. He came down from Alabama to tell me about this incident while he was living in Hollywood, Florida.

A: Oh, I see. All right.

Q: And he said that the boy was saying, "I don't want to go. I don't want to go," and this man was struggling with him and eventually threw him into a vehicle.

A: Uh huh.

Q: And the vehicle took off. I said, "Did you see this gentleman's face and everything?" All he said [was], "I saw his profile," because he saw you from an angle. I said, "Well, who do you believe it to be?" and he said, "I saw this article on the news and I saw the newspaper, and I got a flashback, and I believe it to be Jeffrey."

A: Uh huh.

Q: I said, "Well, we'll have to follow this up."

A: Right.

Q: And, uh . . . now we want to know if you had anything to do with the abduction of Adam Walsh.

A: I didn't. You heard all the false leads about I supposedly had done something to some women in Germany. That was proven to be just bunk.

Q: No, I didn't hear that . . .

A: And people said they seen me in Arizona and in California. . . Never been there. . .

Q: You pretty much kept to yourself?

A: Uh huh. Too busy working.

Q: And you say at that time you were also having a problem with alcohol?

A: Uh huh.

Q: That stems from . . .

A: All the excess, yeah.

Q: Was that every day?

A: Not every day, 'cause I'd have to work, but on the weekends, and it got worse towards the end because I ended up drinking up on my bank account. And that's why I moved back to . . .

Q: What was your bank at?

A: The highest it was at was about, uh . . . a little over a thousand.

Q: OK, a thousand. And what bank, do you remember?

A: The bank that was right next to the sub shop, and I don't know the name of that anymore. But I was working, uh . . . every day, almost every day. Once in a while, I'd get one day off on the weekend. I'd be working ten, twelve shift . . . uh, days from morning to night. . . And, uh . . . didn't leave any time for recreation at all.

NOTE: Notice how Dahmer's response to a question does nothing to address the question. He is very good at deflecting questions.

Dahmer's denial, retyped from the end of his interview (HPD case files, roll 1, p. 2658):

Dahmer: OK, thanks for the muffins . . .

Hoffman: And I appreciate your candidness with us, and, uh . . . just to reiterate my main purpose of coming here for, you know, the investigation of Adam Walsh, and [for you to] go on record to say that you had nothing to do with it.

Dahmer: Nothing to do with it.

Hoffman: That murder or kidnapping.

Dahmer: I heard it on the news, but I had nothing to do with it, no.

Hoffman: And if you did have something to do with it, you would . . . [Dahmer reaches for another muffin]. You want another one? You would admit to it.

Dahmer: Uh . . . right. Yeah. Uh, yeah, I guess I will take one more.

Hoffman: Susan will be happy that you liked her muffins . . . [INTERVIEW CONCLUDED]

Hoffman bungled that interview. The question is, was it deliberate? When Dahmer told his father about that interview with a detective from the Hollywood, Florida, police department, his father hired a Philadelphia lawyer, since Dahmer's trial was over and he no longer had his attorney, Gerald P. Boyle, to protect him. It was the Philadelphia lawyer who refused to let Dahmer talk to any investigators from the state of Florida and initiated the following back-and-forth bantering letters between himself and the HPD. Also included is the response letter from Joel Cantor, attorney for the HPD.

LAW OFFICES

MOZENTER & MOZENTER

SUITE 700

1411 WALNUT STREET

PHILADELPHIA, PENNSYLVANIA 19102

(215) 568-4630
—
FAX: (215) 568-2145

ROBERT B. MOZENTER
JOYCE S. MOZENTER *

*ALSO MEMBER NJ BAR

NEW JERSEY OFFICE
20 KINGS HIGHWAY WEST
HADDONFIELD, NJ 08033
(609) 795-6700

August 18, 1992

Detective Jack Hoffman
Hollywood Police Department
3250 Hollywood Boulevard
Hollywood, Florida 33021

Re: Jeffrey Dahmer

Dear Detective Hoffman:

Please be advised that I represent the above mentioned individual who is currently serving seventeen consecutive life sentences at the Columbia Correctional Institution in Portage, Wisconsin.

It has been brought to my attention by my client and his family that you visited him and questioned him concerning an open homicide which apparently took place in 1981 in Florida. I am advising you that you are not to speak to my client without an attorney present, either myself or Steven J. Eisenberg, Esquire of Madison, Wisconsin. It was also brought to my attention that you taped your interview with my client. I am respectfully requesting that you forward this conversation to me at the above address, or I will take the appropriate legal action to retrieve this tape. I am surprised that an experienced police officer would attempt to interrogate a suspect without either warning him of his Constitutional Rights against self-incrimination or contacting his attorney prior to any questioning. I am requesting a complete explanation of your conduct within ten (10) days.

Very truly yours,

ROBERT B. MOZENTER

RBM/jas
cc: Steven J. Eisenberg, Esquire

004897

CITY of HOLLYWOOD, FLORIDA

POLICE DEPARTMENT · 3250 HOLLYWOOD BOULEVARD · ZIP 33021-6967

August 26, 1992

RICHARD H. WITT
Police Chief

Robert B. Mozenter, Esquire
Mozenter & Mozenter
Suite 700
1411 Walnut Street
Philadelphia, Pennsylvania 19102

Re: Jeffrey Dahmer

Dear Mr. Mozenter:

In response to your correspondence addressed to Detective Hoffman
dated August 18, 1992, please be advised that Detective Hoffman
interviewed the above-referenced subject on August 13, 1992,
regarding any possible involvement in the disappearance and death
of Adam Walsh during the summer of 1981. Adam Walsh was kidnapped
from the Hollywood, Florida area in July of 1981 and his body was
subsequently discovered in the Fort Pierce area of Florida.
Following Jeffrey Dahmer's arrest, Milwaukee Police informed the
Hollywood Police Department that Dahmer resided in the South
Florida area during the period in which Adam Walsh was kidnapped
and murdered.

According to several recent United States Supreme Court cases, you
have absolutely no standing to assert Mr. Dahmer's fifth or sixth
amendment privileges regarding unrelated incidents for which he has
not been charged. It is well established that Mr. Dahmer must
personally invoke his fifth and sixth amendment privileges in order
to prohibit interview contact by law enforcement. Aside from this,
we have additionally discovered that you are not defense counsel
for Mr. Dahmer and even if we were to question him regarding his
involvement in the multiple homicides that took place in Milwaukee,
Mr. Gerald Boyle and not yourself would be contacted regarding a
possible interview.

I am very disappointed that you have to resort to derrogatory and
idle threats in your correspondence to Detective Hoffman.
Detective Hoffman is an experienced detective who obviously is far
better versed in the laws regarding police interviews than you

004894

Robert B. Mozenter, Esquire
August 26, 1992
Page 2

appear to be. If you wish to be provided with cases names or citations regarding police contact of incarcerated suspects on unrelated charges, I will be more than happy to send you this information.

Very truly yours,

Joel D. Cantor
Police Legal Advisor

JDC:cw

CC: Detective Jackie Hoffman

LAW OFFICES

MOZENTER & MOZENTER

ROBERT B. MOZENTER
JOYCE S. MOZENTER

ALSO MEMBER NJ BAR

SUITE 700
1411 WALNUT STREET
PHILADELPHIA, PENNSYLVANIA 19102
—
(215) 568-4630
—
FAX: (215) 568-2145

NEW JERSEY OFFICE
20 KINGS HIGHWAY WEST
HADDONFIELD, NJ 08033
(609) 795-6700

September 2, 1992

Joel D. Canto
Police Legal Advisor
c/o Police Department
3250 Hollywood Boulevard
Hollywood, Florida 33021-6967

RE: JEFFREY DAHMER

Dear Mr. Canto:

I have received your letter of August 26, 1992. Please be advised that I represent Jeffrey Dahmer not Gerald Boyle. If you had contacted Gerald Boyle prior to your seeing my client, you would have known that I am his attorney.

Please do not tell me what my client's constitutional rights are. I am respectfully requesting that you forward to me immediately, the tape that you obtained from my client. You are to cease and desist from interviewing my client with regard to any homicide or any other crime without first contacting and consulting my office.

I assure you that I have not threatened you in any way, but I have made promises that I will take the appropriate legal action if I do not receive these tapes.

Very truly yours,

ROBERT B. MOZENTER

RBM/jas
cc: Steven Eisenberg, Esquire
Shari Dahmer

004896

Dahmer was more lucky than brilliant. He admitted to detectives that he was in Florida. He had no choice. His father sent him that plane ticket back to Ohio from Florida. His father even called *America's Most Wanted* to tell them he thought his son had something to do with Adam's murder. *America's Most Wanted* forwarded this information to the HPD, but it didn't interest them. At the same time, the Milwaukee prosecutors did their best to keep the Adam connection quiet. They were afraid it might prejudice the jury for the Milwaukee trial.

When Dahmer told Florida detective Jack Hoffman that he'd lived in the Bimini Bay Motel and that he worked at Sunshine Subs, he had no way of knowing they had both closed. Had the sub shop still been there, the Hollywood detectives might have been able to track down employees. They might have found out that Dahmer had not been forthcoming to them about his hours of employment. They would've known he wasn't the open and honest person that defense attorney Gerry Boyle and a lot of other people were making him out to be. Why did anyone in the media ask Boyle about Dahmer's honesty, anyway? He was a defense lawyer, not a psychiatrist. You should never ask a defense lawyer about the integrity of his client!

Jeffrey Dahmer didn't always lie, but he didn't always tell the truth, either. With Dahmer, it was hard to know when to believe him. For example, when he said he was collecting unemployment while living in Miami, I believe him. When he said he went to the Omni Mall in downtown Miami to buy knives, I also feel that could be true. However, when he claimed he never went to the Hollywood Mall, that was an overt lie. He was there the day Adam was abducted, because I met him there in Radio Shack.

On *Anderson Cooper 360*, on February 4, 2007, Forensic psychiatrist and profiler Dr. Park Dietz said he didn't believe that Jeffrey Dahmer murdered Adam Walsh. Dr. Dietz seemed to think that children who had not yet reached puberty held no interest for Dahmer. However, Dahmer was arrested in Milwaukee in 1982 for exposing himself to a crowd of twenty-five women and children, and in 1986 for masturbating in front of two twelve-year-old boys. He initially admitted the offense but quickly changed his story and claimed he had merely been urinating. He was still charged with indecent exposure. He was again arrested and charged on September 27, 1988, for sexual exploitation of a child and enticing a child for immoral purposes. Moreover, one of his confirmed murder victims was only fourteen years old.

Jeffrey Dahmer once said he hated no one. If Dahmer lived in an Irish neighborhood, there would be a lot of dead Irishmen, and Dr. Dietz could say Irishmen were his MO. If he lived in an Asian neighborhood, there would be dead Asians. Dahmer's killings reflected the times and neighborhoods he lived in. One thing is for sure: Dahmer would've killed, no matter what neighborhood he lived in. He just had an uncontrollable urge to kill.

When Dietz testified at Dahmer trial, the build-up to him just showing up in the court room was kind of like a rock star coming to town. He was the lead consultant to the FBI on serial killers. Yet on *Anderson Cooper 360*, Dietz claimed Adam didn't fit Dahmer's MO. Never mind that the book on criminal-profiling had to be rewritten after Ted Bundy was captured in 1974 and again in 2002 when the District of Columbia (DC) snipers were captured. The DC sniper was supposed to be an "angry white redneck," remember? As it turned out, they were a couple of black Jamaicans, one mentor and one student assassin. So even though other MO's were found to be flawed, at the time of this writing Dr. Dietz still asserted Adam didn't fit Dahmer's MO.

Dr. Dietz seemed to completely ignore the fact that his subject was a convicted child molester who served time for that 1988 incident. Dr. Dietz actually watched pornographic videos with this child molester and let Dahmer control the remote so that Dahmer could start and stop the tape to show Dr. Dietz exactly what type of men appealed to him. Men with muscular shoulders and lean waists were Dahmer's supposed preferred prey.

The problem with Dr. Dietz's analysis is that it was based on Jeffrey Dahmer's integrity. Dahmer wasn't honest to investigators about his time in Germany, South Florida, or even Milwaukee, so why would he be honest to Dr. Dietz?

True crime writer Art Harris, who was also on *Anderson Cooper 360*, pointed out that, in 1981, witness Willis Morgan was a man with a muscular physique. Harris depicted my build at the time as akin to a Chippendales dancer. Harris believed that Dahmer was angry that I had rejected his advances and kidnapped Adam as a substitute for what he couldn't have. Dr. Dietz rejected this theory, saying that Dahmer's MO was seduction. Dahmer was probably unable to overpower the men that he murdered. Instead, he lured them to his apartment, where he drugged and murdered them.

Jeffrey Dahmer might not have been able to overpower me, but he would've been able to overpower a six-year-old. In retrospect, for all I know, maybe Dahmer's intent was to talk me into going back to his room at the Bimini Bay Motel and offer me some drinks.

So, Dahmer got one up on the doctor. He fooled Dr. Deitz the same way he had fooled many others who were gullible enough to believe he was open and honest. What Harris said might have had more validity, except the part about the Chippendales dancers. The only thing that bothers me more than that Chippendales reference is when Art (and others) refer to me as one of his witnesses. I've had to remind Art that I am not his witness: I am Adam's witness.

Jeffrey Dahmer - Dismissed as a Suspect

Back in Florida, when the HPD investigators found both the Sunshine Subs shop at 17040 Collins Avenue [see map on page 267] and the Bimini Bay Motel at 17534 Collins Avenue gone, they ended their search. It was much easier to believe Dahmer than to investigate further.

They were all spent out from wasting their time, effort, and money on Toole. That investigation had cost them nearly $70,000. Why run up another tab like that again? Plus, it would make them look like fools if it were known that they chased the wrong suspect for so many years and spent all that taxpayer money on him. The fact that Ottis Toole takes up nearly half of the HPD's voluminous Adam Walsh case files is testament to their incredible incompetence. The HPD wouldn't stand for their detectives, smugly dressed in their crisp, sharp starched suits and pretty ties, looking stupid. It was better to cover up.

Even though Dahmer had a propensity for violence as evidenced by his crimes, Jack Hoffman made up his written report, concluding that Dahmer was telling the truth. Hoffman informed John Walsh that there was no reason to believe that Jeffrey Dahmer had in any way been involved in Adam's murder and that Dahmer was both cooperative and candid during the interview (*Tears of Rage*, p. 209). Yes, he'd killed all those victims. Yes, he'd lobotomized one of them (actually more than one) and kept him alive that way for days. Yes, he'd dismembered and cannibalized his victims. But no, he didn't kill Adam Walsh. Not wanting to believe a drunken cannibal could be responsible, John Walsh believed him and tossed the theory out the window before examining it in any detail.

In dismissing Dahmer as Adam Walsh's killer, Detective Hoffman and his cronies point to the fact that all of Dahmer's victims were older boys. Yet, the people we entrust to solve murder cases at the HPD now seem to ignore the fact that Ottis Toole's only real, proven victim was sixty-four years old and even that was most likely an arson accident. Toole never harmed a boy of any age, nor did Toole ever decapitate anyone.

After my last August 20, 1992, conversation with Jack Hoffman, I knew more than ever this case would never get solved with this detective at the helm.

In 1992, right after Jack Hoffman told me he was dismissing Dahmer, I went to Patrick May, the reporter at the *Miami Herald* who was covering the Adam Walsh case. I wanted to give my paper the first crack at the story. I was under the impression that he could call down to the pressroom and check my credibility. That didn't happen. Pat told me, "Adam didn't fit Dahmer's MO." He wasn't interested in anything I had to say and that was that.

I then went to several TV stations, during a time when anyone could walk right into the lobby and ask for a reporter and they would come out and talk to you. One of the TV stations I went to was Fox TV on the Normandy Causeway in Miami. Local news anchor Ileana Bravo came out to the lobby. She was just as beautiful as she was on TV; only now she was standing in front of me, talking to me. This was about as close to a date as I was ever going to get with her. Then, I had to remind myself why I was there. I explained to her about the case and gave her a whole portfolio of information. She promised me she would look into it and get back to me.

I even wrote to John Walsh at *America's Most Wanted*. I bought several books about Jeffrey Dahmer and wrote to the authors, care of the book publishers. My thinking was, if they took the time to do research and write a book, they would listen to me. No one ever responded. I didn't know what else to do. No one was listening. I felt as if I were standing on a mountain top yelling, "IT WAS JEFFREY DAHMER!" but no one could hear me. Ileana did call me back a few days later and told me she had called the HPD and talked to Detective Hoffman. She said Hoffman told her Dahmer had been eliminated as a suspect and she could do nothing with the information I had given her.

Now I knew why no one was getting back to me. Who were they going to believe, me or the HPD? I gave up. What else could I do? I tried putting the Adam Walsh case behind me and moving on with my life. John Walsh continued his crusade for justice with his show *America's Most Wanted*.

One night, *America's Most Wanted* did a segment about a boy who was kidnapped from a mall. John came on and said in an angry tone, "I can relate to this next segment because I, myself, had my son kidnapped from a mall, and not one witness came forward," as he shook his angry finger into the camera.

Needless to say, I was incensed. I called *America's Most Wanted*. I told the young girl who answered the phone what I had heard John say about his son and explained that I was at the Hollywood mall when Adam was kidnapped.

"OK, thank you, sir," she said in a tone that really meant goodbye.

I replied, "Thank you for what? I didn't say anything yet."

"Thank you for the information," she said, and then I got a dial tone. I couldn't help thinking that she had been trained to weed out the weirdoes and I had just gotten weeded out!

I called back and insisted on speaking to a supervisor this time. The supervisor told me she would pass on my information, and someone would call me back. No one ever did. I gave up on that show after I called a few more times and got the same treatment. I continued to write and even sent a portfolio full of information, all to no avail. I did see the very first letter I wrote to John Walsh, after Dahmer was dismissed as a suspect by the HPD, in the Adam Walsh case files. John had forwarded it to the HPD and asked them to look into it. Of course, they never did.

Several years later, in August 1994, I read in the *Miami Herald* that Detective Hoffman was off the case. A new "hotshot" detective that was "really good at solving cold cases" was taking over. His name was Mark Smith. I figured I had a chance to get someone to listen to me, so I called the HPD and asked for Detective Smith. When I tried to tell Smith what happened, he all but called me a liar. He didn't want to listen to anything I had to say.

He dismissed me with a sarcastic tone of voice, saying, "Yeah, right . . . yeah, right," when I tried to tell him what happened. That call never went far because he wouldn't allow me to say much of anything. I was dismissed without him hearing what I had to say.

Not long after Smith dismissed me outright, he compiled a report titled *The Abduction and Murder of Adam Walsh*. After he rejected what I had to say, he had the temerity to include me in a section of his report, subtitled *Jeffrey Dahmer Living in South Florida*. The full report can be located on the HPD CD-2, titled "Mark Smith's Report," in PDF format at JusticeForAdam.com.

True crime writer Art Harris once tried to set up a meeting with the State Attorney's Office, himself, and Detective Smith. But when Smith heard I was also going to be there, he insinuated to Harris that he didn't want to be there with me, and that meeting never materialized. To this day, Smith has refused to meet with me and give me an interview. Yet he goes around and tells the media that he has interviewed me, which is an absolutely blatant and overt lie. Like his predecessor, Detective Smith simply didn't want to make the connection to Jeffrey Dahmer.

I now wonder what Smith knew that could've been so damaging to the HPD. We might never know the full extent of their cover-up. Although some of what they might be covering up is included in this book, much more could've been removed from the Adam Walsh case files. Like Jeffrey Dahmer, don't ever expect these cops to be truthful.

Also, I have wondered if the Milwaukee police might have been interested in not linking Dahmer to other murders because they had their own share of major blunders. The Milwaukee police wanted to limit Dahmer's murder count only to the seventeen that he confessed to and was charged with. One of the murders that the Milwaukee P.D. didn't want to connect to Dahmer was the murder of Dean Vaughn, who lived in the same building as Dahmer, which I will discuss later.

Smith said in his report that, although the Milwaukee Police dismissed Dahmer's connection to Adam's abduction, Detective Hoffman went to Milwaukee for an "in-depth interview" anyway and lists what Hoffman learned. The truth is Hoffman learned only what Dahmer told him and even I knew Dahmer wasn't to be trusted. Only in this case does a serial killer get to lie and have the police cover for him.

At the end of this chapter, I have included the page in Smith's report that refers to me. According to his *Fifth Supplement Report*, on February 6, 1996, Smith went to the Florida State Prison to interview Ottis Toole. Toole said he would only speak to Smith off state property. When asked why he wished to speak off state property, Toole stated that he would make it worth the effort.

The interview took place in a department of corrections van approximately one mile from the state prison. Toole hesitated frequently and had to be urged to speak his mind. Then Toole rewarded Smith with a brand new, never before heard, version of events stating that his brother Howell kidnapped and murdered Adam and told him about it. Smith, being the hotshot cold case detective that he was, let Toole know that he didn't believe him. Toole then stated that nothing he confessed to about the Adam Walsh case was the truth, and he had no involvement in the case.

Toole did make it worth the effort . . . *his* effort that is. He got to go for a ride that most of us take for granted. I'm sure he also got to share a good laugh with all his fellow inmates. And for lunch he most likely had a steak sub. Nice going, Toole!

The following is what the FBI had to say about Jeffrey Dahmer being a suspect in the Adam Walsh case in a memorandum dated November 14, 1991, to the Milwaukee Police Department, from page 148 of the FBI case files:

> *What is known from the previous investigation conducted by the Hollywood, Florida, Police Department involving the abduction of ADAM WALSH is that JEFFREY DAHMER closely resembles the description of the person who abducted this young child. Furthermore, the decapitation and disposal of the torso of ADAM WALSH is again the type of behavior that DAHMER had previously exhibited in OHIO and continued to exhibit in Milwaukee with his victims, specifically the decapitation and disposal of the torso. In ADAM WALSH'S instance, the only item of evidence that was recovered and which led to his identification was his head.*
>
> *The research conducted on people such as DAHMER indicates that they can control their compulsions, but that under stress or pressure, they will most likely revert back to the behavior that gives them the most satisfaction, which is the abducting, killing and the sexual gratification they can obtain from complete control of their victim. DAHMER found himself in Miami, certainly the ingredients that would put him as a prime suspect in the ADAM WALSH killing.*

FBI Agent Neil Purtell immediately contacted Hollywood police. He said, "You've got to look at this, because this guy is someone who was living in your area, and he had already killed prior to coming into your area." Purtell had already contacted the Milwaukee Police Department with his conclusion. At a meeting at the Milwaukee Police Department, it was decided not to push this area of interview with Dahmer but rather to continue to seek his cooperation and assistance in identifying his victims.

This would be the top priority of the task force. The Milwaukee Police expressed concern that the scope of this investigation must not be leaked prior to their trial, since it could make jury selection, as well as Dahmer's cooperation, much more difficult. In this process, they had little or no concern for Adam's justice, and their brothers in uniform at the HPD would happily follow suit, because in many ways, these two police departments were as alike as two green peas in a pod.

In a memorandum from the Milwaukee State Attorney's Office to the Milwaukee Police Department dated July 31, 1991, they observed that Dahmer admitted to adult homosexual homicides but hadn't furnished any information involving child molestation or child homicides, although he had three arrests in the city of Milwaukee from 1981 to 1987 involving crimes against children. The memorandum goes on to say the subject's desire to cooperate on adult homicides might be an effort on his part to accept responsibility for the adult homicides and not raise the question of other illegal acts involving children that he was responsible for. Perhaps Dahmer was concerned about violence while incarcerated if, in fact, it was learned that he was also responsible for the deaths of children.

This is from the interview with Jeffrey Dahmer: (retyped from Dahmer's interview, Part-2, p. 1)

NARRATIVE:

On Tuesday, July 30, 1991, I, Detective KENNEDY along with Detective Dennis MURPHY, while interviewing the suspect Jeffrey DAHMER in an interview room of the CIB (Criminal Investigation Bureau), were accompanied by Attorney Wendy PATRIKAS when the following questions regarding possible inquiries into other connections of the above offenses were given to Mr. DAHMER.

At this time, I questioned him regarding the fact that information was received from out of state jurisdictions that in 1981 we received information that a man fitting his description was in the Hollywood Mall which is located in Hollywood, Florida and that this white male fitting his description apparently attempted to pick up an individual and that this individual making this report states that this was the same day that the victim, Adam WALSH, was last seen and then later found decapitated with body parts missing.

Regarding this inquiry, the subject Jeffrey Dahmer states he admits that he was in Florida during the time that Adam WALSH offense occurred. He states he realized this because of the news media at the time; however, he denies any part in the offense regarding Adam WALSH and states that he was never at any time in Hollywood, Florida or the Hollywood Mall.

Yet, not much more than a month later, Milwaukee Chief of Police Philip Arreola sent the following letter to the HPD, dated Wednesday, September 11, 1991:

Department of Police

Philip Arreola
Chief of Police

Wednesday, September 11, 1991

Hollywood Police Department
3250 Hollywood Blvd.
Hollywood, FL 33021

Dear Detective HOFFMAN:

We have reviewed your inquiry regarding homicide suspect, JEFFREY DAHMER. We can advise you that DAHMER has been questioned regarding your inquiry, and at present, we have no way of connecting him to your incident. Enclosed are photos, prints and a brief history of the suspect DAHMER.

Sincerely,

PHILIP ARREOLA
CHIEF OF POLICE

DONALD F. DOMAGALSKI
CAPTAIN OF POLICE

PA/DFD/pmj

004929

Chief Arreola had nothing more than Dahmer's word (or maybe not even this) to base his belief there was no connection between the Adam Walsh incident and Jeffrey Dahmer. He had no witness statements from Florida. He also had no Florida composites and no Florida timelines for Dahmer. That told me one thing about Chief Arreola: he didn't want to make Dahmer a bigger monster than he already was as that would only serve to make his police department look worse than it already did, if that were even possible.

Of course, Arreola could make the argument that he couldn't make a connection because he didn't have any documents. If so, he could've attempted to source them. It can't be denied that the chief did his best to play down Dahmer's role in Adam's abduction and murder. To this day, the Milwaukee P.D. continues to play down Jeffrey Dahmer's role through spokeswoman Anne E. Schwartz, who continues to dish out their spin, saying Dahmer doesn't fit the profile of someone that would murder Adam.

In Hollywood, Florida, the Dahmer cover-up started the day Jeffrey Dahmer made national news for his crimes in Milwaukee, and I, Bill Bowen, and others went back to the HPD as witnesses they didn't want to hear from.

<u>On the following pages are:</u>

1: July 25, 1991: Jeffery Dahmer's initial confession, part one, page 91 of 243 pages (this is the page relevant to his time in Germany and Florida).

2: July 31, 1991: Tip from *America's Most Wanted* to the HPD.

3: The composites vs. mug shots that I gave to Detective Hoffman that never made it into the case files.

4: Although my mug shot comparison wasn't used and I was told the composite looked nothing like the mug shot of Jeffrey Dahmer, someone had the foresight to make their own comparison (HPD case files, roll 1, p. 2735).

5: October 2, 1991: My two-page letter to author Don Davis, in the care of St. Martin's Paperbacks.

6: August 6, 1992: John Walsh's two-page letter to the State Attorney's Office

7: August 7, 1992: Detective Hoffman's three-page letter to the State Attorney's Office

8: August 10, 1992: Two-page letter from the State Attorney's Office to Detective Hoffman at the HPD.

9: August 11, 1992: Letter from the State Attorney's Office to John Walsh.

10: Detective Mark Smith, *The Abduction and Murder of Adam Walsh*, "Jeffrey Dahmer Living in South Florida in July 1981," p. 32.

NOTE: My 1991 taped interview with Detective Hoffman can be viewed on the HPD CD (roll 1, p. 2705). A better copy is on the SAO CD (box 6, p. 373). When the tape was transcribed to text, some errors crept in. For example, it was *Waldenbooks* that I went to, not Walgreens. The best copy of Jeffrey Dahmer's interview with Detective Hoffman can be viewed on the SAO CD (box 6, p. 313). All records are available for free at JusticeForAdam.com.

PD15-8 5-89 SUPPLEMENT REPORT   MILWAUKEE POLICE DEPARTMENT

INCIDENT SUPPLEMENT ☑	PAGE 2 of 4	DATE OF REPORT 7-25-91	INCIDENT/ACCIDENT #
ACCIDENT SUPPLEMENT ☐		
JUVENILE SUPPLEMENT ☐		

INCIDENT INFORMATION

INCIDENT   HOMICIDE (STABBING)

VICTIM   LACY, Oliver

DATE OF INCIDENT/ACCIDENT   7-23-91

LOCATION OF INCIDENT/ACCIDENT (Address)   924 N. 25th St. #213

JUVENILE LAST NAME   FIRST   MID   DATE OF BIRTH

☐ DETAINED ☐ ORDERED TO MCCC ☐ OTHER

QUAN | TYPE OF PROPERTY | DESCRIPTION | SERIAL # | CODE # | VALUE

He goes on the state that after leaving home in Bath, OH to join the Armed Forces, that while in the Army, he was stationed in Germany. When asked why his behavior of cutting up animals and killing and dismembering of human beings did not occur while he was in the Army, he stated that he believes the reason he did not kill or dismember any one while he was serving his tour of duty in Germany, was because he enjoyed the structure of the Army. He stated that during the entire tour of duty, he lived on base and was in a dorm with three other men. Although he did not have any homosexual or heterosexual relationships while he was in Germany, or in the Army, he did satisfy his urge for sexual excitement by masturbation. He stated that he enjoyed the Army and wished that he could have finished his entire tour of duty, however, his abuse of alcohol made that impossible as the Army decided to let him go six months before his tour of duty was up.

When questioned about bodies dismembered and found in Germany during the time he was there, Jeffrey said that he remembers reading in the newspapers in Germany about a black female who was found beheaded and dismembered and left in a field. He related that this was big news at the time, and this is the only reason why it rings a bell with him. He emphatically denied being involved in any of those homicides and indicated that he is not at all interested in females, either sexually or for the purpose of dismembering. He stated that he is only interested in having a relationship with men.

Jeffrey stated that when he was released from the Army, he stated that he was tired of the cold winters that he had endured in Germany and when he was growing up in Ohio, and with the voucher given to him by the Army, he could go anywhere in the United States that he wished, so he stated that he took a voucher for Miami, FL, because he thought it would be nice with the warm weather all the time. He indicated that the entire time that he was in Miami, FL, he did not engage in any homosexual activity, nor did he kill or dismember anyone while he was down there. He stated that he was continually busy trying to make ends meet financially while in Miami, and this is the reason why he had no time to engage in this activity.

Jeffrey stated that he, at one time was actually living on the beach because of lack of funds, and this was eventually the reason why he moved back to the Midwest, so that family members could help support him until he got established.

REPORTING OFFICER   2472   SEC   5   PAGE

PAYROLL #   36

LOC CODE

SUPERVISOR SIGNATURE

July 31, 1991

STF Productions, Inc.

5151 Wisconsin Avenue, N.W.

Washington, D.C. 20016

Telephone (202) 895-3100

Fax (202) 895-3096

A subsidiary of

Fox Television Stations Inc.

Det. Jack Hoffman
Hollywood Florida Police Dept.
3250 Hollywood Blvd.
Hollywood, FL 33021

Dear Det. Hoffman:

The message bellow was taken from our hotline.

Mr. Morgan claims to have been approached by Dahmar, or someone
resembling him, in the Hollywood mall 10 years ago the
same day Adam was abducted. He says he went to the
police at that time, but they did not believe him. He also
claims Dahmar, or again someone fitting his description,
tried to pick him up, but he rejected his advances.

Please call if you have any questions. Thank you.

Sincerely,

Karen M. Tate

COMPOSITES and MUG SHOTS
BEFORE CAPTURE and AFTER CAPTURE

THE MAKING OF A COMPOSITE

America's Most Wanted once had a composite test to test your skills on making a composite. It started with you looking at a face for ten seconds. Then you had to create a composite of that face from memory. First, you had to select a facial outline from the four that were given and then the eyebrows, eyes, nose, mouth, and hair style. When finished, you were given a score. It's not easy to get it 100 percent correct. The point is, just because you don't get everything correct does not mean you are wrong.

After the following four suspects were captured, it became clear that the witnesses that gave the composites were trying to describe that suspect, even if the composite wasn't a perfect likeness.

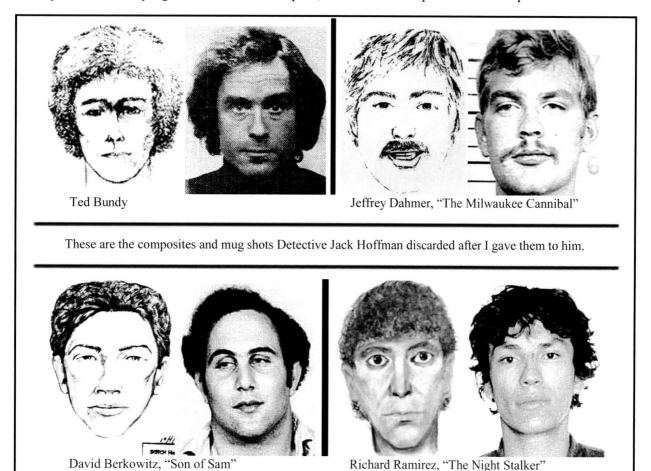

Ted Bundy

Jeffrey Dahmer, "The Milwaukee Cannibal"

These are the composites and mug shots Detective Jack Hoffman discarded after I gave them to him.

David Berkowitz, "Son of Sam"

Richard Ramirez, "The Night Stalker"

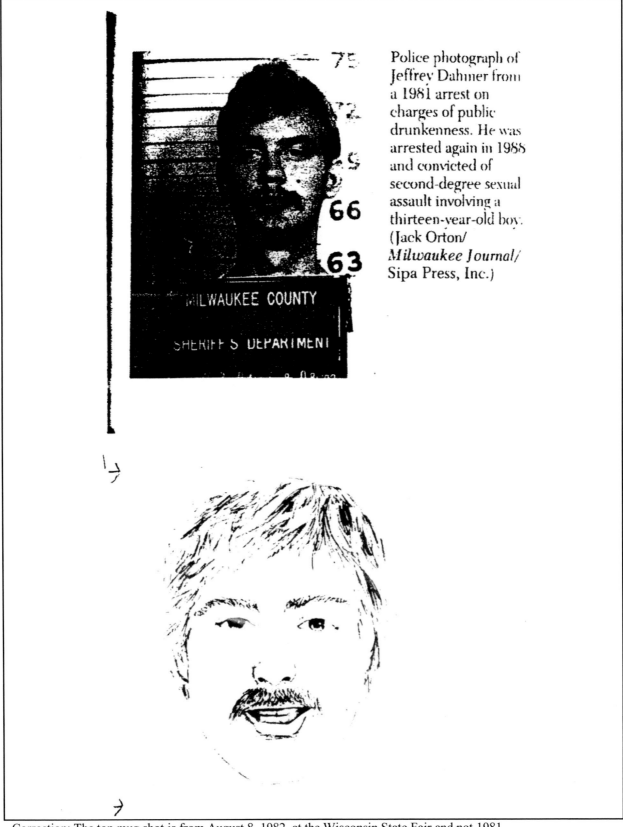

Police photograph of Jeffrey Dahmer from a 1981 arrest on charges of public drunkenness. He was arrested again in 1988 and convicted of second-degree sexual assault involving a thirteen-year-old boy. (Jack Orton/ *Milwaukee Journal/* Sipa Press, Inc.)

MILWAUKEE COUNTY

SHERIFF'S DEPARTMENT

Correction: The top mug shot is from August 8, 1982, at the Wisconsin State Fair and not 1981.
This page was copied from the HPD case files

Oct. 2, 1991

Willis Morgan
128 Bedford Ave.
Hallandale, FL 33009
U.S.A.

(1)

First I want to thank you for the informative book "The Milwaukee Murders" but I should add I'm writing this letter out of frustration more then anything else. I just can't seem to get anyone to beleave me.

On the 27th of July 1981 I went to radio Shack in the Hollywood Mall in South Florida. While looking at some items marked red tag sale a young tall man approched me and said "Hi their, nice day isn't it? I looked him square in the face but never answered him. After a few tense moments of him staring at me I looked around for some help but being a slow Monday afternoon I was alone. Then just as suddenly he turned and left.

I knew he was intent on picking someone up and out of curiosity as to what their reaction would be, I followed him down the Mall - keeping my distence.

Sure enough when he turned into Sears, I could see by the way he was looking around that he was looking for someone to approach but Sears was as slow as the rest of the mall. Before I knew it we were at the far end of Sears when he turned to the right toward

004899

②

The toy department.
I didn't follow him into the toy dept. because I was afraid he would turn around and come back toward me so I left.
Anyway that evening I heard on the news about a 6 year old boy being Kidnapped from the toy dept. at Sears.
The next day I went to the Hollywood Police Dept. The officer I talked to was as inept as they come and the only thing he wanted to Know was if I seen a tag number or if I actually seen this man grab the*boy. When I said no, he dismissed me with "we have your Statement, If we need to Contact you, we will!" But they never have.
I have always made it a point to remember the face of that young man and Ten years After, I have a name to go with it after Jeffrey Dahmer had his photo on the front page of The Miami Herald.

*The boys name is Adam Walsh and his head was found two weeks later decapated!!

Thanks for your time and please follow through on this.
Willis

Phone #(305) 458-4598

VIA OVERNIGHT MAIL

August 6, 1992

STF Productions, Inc.

5151 Wisconsin Avenue, N.W.

Washington, D.C. 20016

Telephone (202) 895-3100

Fax (202) 895-3096

A subsidiary of

Fox Television Stations Inc.

Mr. Michael Satz
State Attorney - 17th Judicial Circuit
201 South East 6th Street
Ft. Lauderdale, FL 33301

Dear Michael:

I have been speaking on and off to Jack Hoffman, the lead investigator in my son Adam's murder case, for several months about the need of the Hollywood police to speak to Jeffrey Dahmer concerning Adam's case.

It is my understanding that Dahmer's father came forward and said that his son had mustered out of the Army and was hanging around the Hollywood Florida area at the time of Adam's death. I also understand two credible witnesses have come forward placing Dahmer inside and outside the Hollywood mall the day of Adam's abduction.

I had hoped the Hollywood police could talk to Dahmer during the early stages of his case, but it is my understanding that Dahmer's defense attorney prevented any law enforcement agency with an unresolved case to talk to Dahmer if the state the case was from, was a death penalty state. I believe the FBI's assisting Jack Hoffman in getting access to Dahmer.

I have discussed the situation with my wife Reve, and we both concur that it is acceptable for you to offer whatever concessions you deem necessary in order for the Hollywood police to question Dahmer.

We are not vigilantes nor are we obsessed with vengeance, but after ten years of heartache and the nightmare of wondering why and who took Adam and if they would ever strike again against our family or our two beautiful new children, we need to know something. I know Dahmer will never get out of prison and I believe he will receive justice in the next life as well. At least knowing whether he did it or not would be some consolation.

Mr. Satz - State Attorney
August 6, 1992
Page 2

Many people in the criminal justice system and the
public have forgotten that Jeffrey Dahmer started out
as a pedophile, kidnapper, and torturer of young boys
and committed the ultimate travesty to a family. After
being released on parole for the kidnapping and
molestation of the youngest son in the family, in an
act of cold blooded brutal revenge, he kidnapped,
tortured, and murdered the other son in that family.
He certainly fits the profile of someone who might be
capable of murdering a beautiful six-year-old boy.

You have our confidence, and I know you will proceed
full speed ahead.

If I can be of assistance with any law enforcement
agency please don't hesitate to call me or my
assistant, Karen Tate, at 202/895-3092.

Respectively submitted,

John Walsh

JW:kt

cc: Jack Hoffman, Hollywood Police Department

CITY of HOLLYWOOD, FLORIDA

POLICE DEPARTMENT • **3250 HOLLYWOOD BOULEVARD** • **ZIP 33021-6967**

RICHARD H. WITT
Police Chief

August 7, 1992

Mr. Michael Satz
State Attorney
201 S.E. 6 Street
Ft. Lauderdale, Fl. 33301

Dear Mr. Satz:

As you know the Hollywood Police Department has been actively investigating the abduction/homicide of Adam Walsh since July 27, 1981. Over the years this agency has pursued numerous leads and interviewed many potential suspects. As of this date no individuals have been charged in this murder case.

On July 22, 1991 the Milwaukee Police Department arrested Jeffrey Dahmer, charging him with 11 counts of homicide. After Jeffrey Dahmer's arrest, he received national media coverage.

The Milwaukee Police along with the Federal Bureau of Investigation profiled Jeffrey Dahmer as a serial murderer responsible for more than 17 deaths over 10 or more years.

As a result of this background investigation of Jeffrey Dahmer, it was revealed that Dahmer was discharged from the Military, March 26, 1981. Mr. Dahmer then flew to Miami, Florida. Jeffrey Dahmer lived in South Florida for 5 months, leaving September 1981 returning to Bath, Ohio.

After Dahmer's arrest, Gerald Boyle was assigned as the attorney of record. Mr. Dahmer continued speaking with the Milwaukee Police about the murders he committed. When outside agencies wanted to speak with Jeffrey Dahmer confirming unresolved homicides, his attorney Gerald Boyle would not allow police departments whose state had the death penalty to speak with Mr. Dahmer. Since Jeffrey Dahmer's convictions for murder, he is no longer represented by council. Mr. Dahmer has no other cases pending against him.

On July 30, 1991 William Bowen drove to Hollywood, Florida from Birmingham, Alabama at his own expense. Mr. Bowen advised this detective that he has been following the Jeffrey Dahmer case through the media. After seeing Jeffrey Dahmer both on television and in the newspapers, he recalled an incident which he witnessed on July 27, 1981 at the Hollywood Mall. Mr. Bowen said he was living in Hollywood at the time.

Mr. Bowen was parking his vehicle on the west side of the Sears Store. After he exited from his vehicle, he witnessed a W/M early 20's who was wearing an army fatigue jacket struggling with a small child. The child was saying "no I'm not going, no I don't want to go". The W/M then threw the child into a van that was parked in the fire lane next to Sears. The van then sped off. When Mr. Bowen learned of the abduction of Adam Walsh, he said he gave this information to a police officer. Mr. Bowen then moved back to Alabama and thought this case was eventually resolved.

On July 28, 1991 Mr. Bowen was reading the Birmingham News which had written that Jeffrey Dahmer may be a suspect in the Adam Walsh murder. When Mr. Bowen saw the photograph of Dahmer, he got a flashback that the W/M he saw forcing a child into a van back on July 27, 1981 may have been Jeffrey Dahmer. See attached statement.

On October 23, 1991 this detective met with Willis Morgan at police headquarters. Mr. Morgan informed this detective that he saw the photograph of Jeffrey Dahmer in the Miami Herald on July 28, 1991. After viewing Jeffrey Dahmer's photograph, Mr. Morgan recalled having contact with this subject back on Monday, July 27, 1981 at the Hollywood Mall.

Mr. Morgan stated that this subject attempted to pick him up. Mr. Morgan walked away from this subject and proceeded to the Sears Store where he lost this subject. Mr. Morgan said this W/M appeared to be in his early 20's.

That evening while watching the 11:00 O'Clock news, Mr. Morgan learned of the kidnapping of Adam Walsh. Mr. Morgan reported his incident to a uniformed police officer. According to Mr. Morgan, he is positive that the person he had contact with at the Hollywood Mall was Jeffrey Dahmer. See attached statement.

This detective has been corresponding with Special Agent Neil Purtell of the Federal Bureau of Investigation. Agent Purtell has been conducting numerous interviews with Jeffrey Dahmer in his prison facility in Madison, Wisconsin. Agent Purtell having knowledge of the two aforementioned witnesses, and the knowledge that Jeffrey Dahmer was in the South Florida area for 5 months at the time of Adam Walsh's kidnapping and murder, he feels it would be extremely important that I interview Jeffrey Dahmer.

I have been in constant contact with John Walsh regarding his son's murder for the past 11 years. Mr. Walsh was informed at the beginning, after Jeffrey Dahmer's arrest that he was in the South Florida area when Adam was kidnapped.

Mr. Walsh was advised at the time that Mr. Dahmer's attorney did not want any police agencies whose state had the death penalty to speak with his client. After speaking with his wife Reve, John Walsh informed this detective that he personally had no objections if the State Attorney's Office waived the death penalty for Jeffrey Dahmer in order for this agency to interview him.

Mr. Walsh has conveyed his feelings in a letter recently mailed to your office. I am requesting at this time that your office draw up a letter to Jeffrey Dahmer or a representative of his that the State of Florida would not pursue the death penalty should Mr. Dahmer make admissions regarding the death of Adam Walsh. I would need this letter as soon as possible to take with me when I go and interview Jeffrey Dahmer sometime next week. It may not be necessary to reveal this letter to Mr. Dahmer when I interview him unless he brings up the death penalty for the State of Florida.

Sincerely,

Detective J. Hoffman
Homicide Unit
HOLLYWOOD POLICE DEPARTMENT

MICHAEL J. SATZ
STATE ATTORNEY
SEVENTEENTH JUDICIAL CIRCUIT OF FLORIDA

BROWARD COUNTY COURTHOUSE
FORT LAUDERDALE, FLORIDA 33301-3360
PHONE (305) 357-6955

August 10, 1992

Richard Witt, Chief
Hollywood Police Dept.
3250 Hollywood Boulevard
Hollywood, Fl 33021

Attention: Detective Jack Hoffman, Homicide Unit

Dear Detective Hoffman:

This will acknowledge receipt of your letter under date August 7,
1992, wherein you expressed your intention to interview Jeffrey Dahmer
in Milwaukee, Wisconsin concerning any involvement he may have had in
the disappearance and/or homicide of Adam Walsh, which occurred at the
Hollywood Mall, in Hollywood, Florida on July 27, 1981.   This will
also acknowledge the enclosures with your letter consisting of the FBI
memorandum; the Milwaukee Police Department's supplemental report; the
transcribed statements of William Bowen and Willis Russell Morgan and
the copy of the letter that you had received dated August 6, 1992 from
John Walsh.

Upon examining all these enclosures together with a reading of your
letter combined with our personal conversations regarding this
matter, we understand that it may be necessary for this office to make
a definitive statement regarding whether or not we would seek the
death penalty against Mr. Dahmer should he be prosecuted in this
jurisdiction for Murder in the First Degree, in connection with the
death of Adam Walsh.

The purpose for this letter therefore, is to notify you and anyone
else who may read this letter that should Mr. Dahmer be prosecuted for
the offense of First Degree Murder in connection with the homicide of
Adam Walsh, this office agrees and will be bound by this letter, that

001957

Richard Witt, Chief   -2-   August 10 1992

the sentence of death would not be sought for punishment should he be convicted for this offense. Mr. Dahmer, however, will be exposed to any other punishment provided by law except death, should he be convicted of First Degree Murder in connection with the death of Adam Walsh.

Sincerely,

RALPH J. RAY, JR.
Chief Assistant State Attorney

RJR,Jr:pa

cc: Michael J. Satz
     State Attorney

cc: Richard Witt, Chief
     Hollywood Police Dept.

State Attorney

SEVENTEENTH JUDICIAL CIRCUIT OF FLORIDA
SUITE 600 BROWARD COUNTY COURTHOUSE
FORT LAUDERDALE, FLORIDA 33301
TELEPHONE (305) 765-4100

MICHAEL J. SATZ
STATE ATTORNEY

August 11, 1992

Mr. John Walsh
c/o America's Most Wanted
STF Productions, Inc.
5151 Wisconsin Avenue, N.W.
Washington, D.C. 20016

Dear Mr. Walsh:

This office has been notified by Detective Jack Hoffman of
the Hollywood Police Department that Jeffrey Dahmer may be
willing to speak to members of the Hollywood Police
Department concerning the murder of your son Adam, if the
State of Florida would not seek the death penalty if he was
charged and convicted of the first degree murder of Adam.

I have received your letter stating that in light of
Dahmer's demands, you, therefore, request that this office
not seek the death penalty, should Dahmer be charged and
convicted of the first degree murder of Adam.

This office has therefore communicated in writing to
Detective Hoffman that we would not seek the sentence of
death, should Jeffrey Dahmer be charged and convicted of the
homicide of your son Adam. I am enclosing a copy of this
letter for your perusal and your files.

It is my sincere hope that one day the person who committed
this horrible crime that has caused such great pain to your
family and to all those who loved Adam will be brought to
justice.

Should you have any questions, please do not hesitate to
contact me in that regard.

Yours very truly,

MICHAEL J. SATZ
State Attorney

MJS:jh
Enclosure: as noted

Page 33 of Detective Smith's report

Interestingly, after seeing a picture of Dahmer in a Miami Herald article in July of 1991, Willis Morgan, 44, of Hallandale, Florida claimed to have seen Dahmer at the Radio Shack store in the Hollywood Mall on the day of Adam's disappearance. According to Morgan, after the man he believed to be Dahmer conversed with him in Radio Shack, Morgan went into Sears and did not see him again. As a result of these developments, Hollywood investigators called Detective Joseph Nowicki of the Homicide Unit of the Milwaukee, Wisconsin Police Department. After discussing the statements of Bowens and Morgan, Hollywood detectives requested Milwaukee police question Dahmer in reference to the Walsh case. Though Dahmer denied any involvement to Milwaukee police, Hollywood detectives flew to the Columbia Correction Facility in Milwaukee on August 12th to interview him in-depth.

Detectives learned Dahmer was discharged from the Army March 26th, 1981 and flew from South Carolina to Miami on that date. He rented a room for a week at a Miami Beach hotel before running out of money and resorting to sleeping on the beach and in various public places. He landed a job at Sunshine Subs in Miami Beach in April, rented a room at nearby Bimini Motel and left Florida in September 1981. Apparently this entire time Dahmer relied exclusively on public transportation. In the course of the Dahmer interview he stated he was not involved in the abduction or murder of Adam Walsh, he was not a pedophile and if he had committed the murder he would admit it because he would welcome the death penalty as an alternative to rotting in prison.

CHAPTER EIGHT
AMERICA'S FAVORITE
NONFICTIONAL CANNIBAL

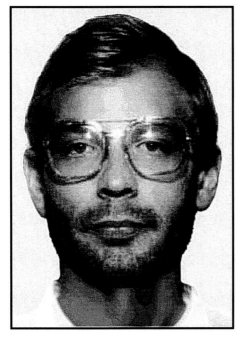

"I made my fantasy life more powerful than my real one."
"I carried it too far, that's for sure."
_____***Jeffrey L. Dahmer***_____

PHOTO LEFT: Mug shot of Jeffrey Dahmer, July 25, 1991.
Milwaukee Sheriff's Department.

Jeffrey Dahmer and the Chocolate Factory

Jeffrey Dahmer was hired on January 14, 1985, by the Ambrosia Chocolate Company, located at 1109 North 5th Street, Milwaukee, in a three-story brick mill building built in 1907, which was demolished in 1993 and is now an empty lot. As one of 380 employees, he worked the graveyard shift as a reclusive laborer and chocolate mixer in the manufacturing department at the rate of $8.25 per hour, taking home $288 to $364 per week, depending on how many hours he worked. His hours were from 11 p.m. until 7 a.m., from Sunday to Friday.

On September 26, 1988, Dahmer left his grandmother's house and moved into his new apartment, number 204 at 808 North 24th Street, Milwaukee, in order to be closer to his job. On the very first day in his new apartment, he met thirteen-year-old Somsack Sinthasomphone on 25th Street and offered him $50 to pose for some pictures. Somsack accepted, and they walked the one block back to his apartment. Once in the apartment, Dahmer gave him a cup of coffee and proceeded to molest him in a way Somsack found strangely threatening. He jumped up, grabbed his school bag, and ran for the door. Fortunately for Somsack, the spiked cup of coffee hadn't had time to kick in yet.

"Wait!" Dahmer said. "Don't forget your $50, and don't tell anyone, OK?"

Somsack went straight home. Two hours later, he became very ill and could barely stand. When his father took him to the hospital, he was diagnosed as suffering from the effects of a drug overdose. The police were summoned. Somsack told the police everything and then took them to the apartment on 24th Street. Police identified the tenant and his place of work.

The very next day, they went straight to the chocolate factory to confront Jeffrey Dahmer. Dahmer was put into handcuffs and embarrassed in front of his coworkers as he was arrested for second degree sexual assault and enticing a child for immoral purposes. Now everyone at work knew he was a homosexual and a child molester (Brian Masters, *The Shrine of Jeffrey Dahmer*, pp. 100-101).

While he was awaiting sentencing, he was ordered to move back into his grandmother's house. In March 1989, while living with his grandmother, he murdered Anthony Sears. Dahmer soaked the skull in a bucket of acetone and then spray-painted it granite before placing it in a one-square-foot wooden lockbox with a metal rim. To keep the skull away from his father's prying eyes he took the box to work and stashed it in his yellow-painted work locker, number 214.

On May 23, 1989, Dahmer was ordered to undergo psychiatric treatment. Three psychologists examined him and concurred that Dahmer was manipulative, resistant and evasive. Hospitalization and intensive treatment were recommended. Yet, he was ordered by the court to serve only one year in the Milwaukee House of Correction with work release privileges followed by four years' probation.

In 1990, both his psychiatrist and parole officer said he was ready to live on his own again. On May 13, 1990, Dahmer moved into apartment 213 on North 25th Street. Anthony's skull remained cooped up in Dahmer's work locker the entire time until he could bring him back to the new Oxford apartment. By this time, he had gotten a raise to $8.75 per hour.

One day, around 10:30 p.m., when Dahmer was walking to West Highland Avenue to catch a bus for the ten-minute, one-and-a-half-mile ride east to the chocolate factory, Oxford Apartments resident manager Sopa Princewill happened to be walking back to the Oxford building. As he passed Dahmer walking down 25th Street in his blue work uniform, Sopa said, "Oh, I see you work the graveyard shift." Dahmer responded, "Everyone has one foot in the grave." A strange response, Sopa told me, but the full implication wouldn't sink in until months later.

On April 7, 1991, Dahmer murdered and dismembered nineteen-year-old Errol Lindsey. Again, he kept the skull as a trophy. Because he didn't want his newfound friend to feel lonely, he brought the spray-painted skull to work with him and placed it in his work locker for three weeks. Dahmer would frequently take breaks to go visit Errol.

Dahmer rarely socialized with other coworkers. He was perceived as being aloof yet polite. When he ate lunch in the break room, he sat alone and ate his meat topped with what he called his "special gravy," but he would refuse to let anyone have a taste.

The Milwaukee Cannibal

Ten years after Adam's abduction, Jeffrey Dahmer would become infamous and tagged by the media with titles like "The Milwaukee Cannibal," "The Butcher of Milwaukee," and "The Milwaukee Monster."

Jeffrey Dahmer showed up at the Grand Avenue Mall in his blue work suit with the name "Jeffrey" embroidered over his left pocket. He approached Tracy Edwards and asked if Tracy wanted to go to a party. When Tracy accepted, Dahmer smooth-talked him into going back to his apartment by saying he needed to change his clothes. Tracy Edwards had no way of knowing that stepping into Dahmer's apartment was like stepping into psychotic quicksand.

"Damn, what's that *stink*?" Tracy nearly gagged and suggested just grabbing a beer and getting the heck out of there.

"That sounds good to me. I can barely stand the smell myself," Dahmer replied.

He hurriedly gave Tracy his special rum and Coke cocktail spiked with 125 mg of crushed Halcion® that had been prescribed to Dahmer at the West Allis Memorial Hospital. While waiting for the Halcion to kick in, Dahmer used the false pretext that it would take him another minute to change before they could leave.

DIAGRAM RIGHT: Oxford apartment #213

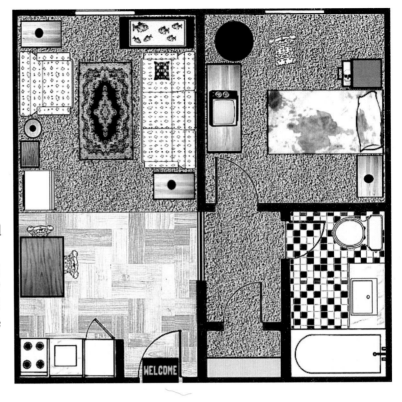

Dahmer kept saying, "Finish your rum and Coke," but when he asked Tracy if he was high yet, Tracy became suspicious and stopped drinking after only a sip. When Tracy made remarks again about getting ready to head out, Dahmer became very agitated. Before Tracy realized what hit him, he had a handcuff on one wrist. Dahmer stuck a large hunting knife with a blue plastic handle and a very sharp blade under Tracy's armpit, right under his heart.

"If you don't do what I say, I'm going to kill you. I've done this before. I can kill you," Dahmer snapped his fingers, "just like that!"

Dahmer struggled with the five-foot-seven, 160-pound wiry fireplug while trying to handcuff him. He first slapped a handcuff on Tracy's left wrist and then tried to force his right arm behind him so that he could handcuff it, too. Ultimately, Dahmer failed to cuff Tracy's wrists together.

Dahmer never hit Tracy but just kept asking, "C'mon, c'mon, let me get your other arm."

In Tracy's own words, "Dahmer was trying to sweet-talk me into my own murder."

With a blade that felt hot as fire, Dahmer ordered the bleeding Tracy into the bedroom. It would be another four hours of hell before Tracy would finally escape.

The bedroom was dark except for a lone light in the corner and a videotape of *The Exorcist* playing on the TV. Dahmer pointed at the television and told Tracy, "This was the best movie ever made." The dingy gray walls were plastered with nude pictures of men in all types of disgusting sexual poses.

Dahmer now looked nothing like the man Tracy had met at the mall. His face had contorted into something demonic. Tracy could tell by the crazed, dead, dull look in his eyes that he had killed before. In the bedroom, Tracy recognized that pungent odor as the smell of death. The smell, the sound of the TV, and Dahmer's muttering were all getting to him. He felt disoriented and queasy. He started to vomit.

"Don't be sick. I'll take care of you," Dahmer whispered to him.

Tracy was forced to sit down on Dahmer's twin-size, dingy bed that was covered in sheets stained brown with blood. Dahmer sat down next to him. Next to the bed was a small two-drawer filing cabinet. Dahmer reached over and pulled open one of the drawers. Inside was a human skull of someone who'd tried to leave. Dahmer rubbed the top of the skull while he stared into Tracy's eyes.

As if he were talking to a woman, Dahmer told Tracy he was beautiful. Then Dahmer started stroking Tracy while saying, "I'll let you go if you just let me put your other hand in the handcuff so that I can take some nude pictures of you. Let me be more in control. Let me take some nude pictures of you, then I'll let you go."

Tracy tried to reason with Dahmer. "You got to trust me. I'm not going to leave you. I'm going to stay with you."

But Dahmer wasn't buying it. As he put the sharp knife right in Tracy's groin and pushed steadily on it, Dahmer said, "You're persistent, aren't you? You're real good—but you're going to stay with me forever." Every so often, Dahmer would open the file drawer and rub the skull. Then he pulled some Polaroid pictures of dead men out of the file cabinet. The bodies in the photos were decomposed. "You'll look real good this way. You'll look better than they did."

He ordered Tracy to lie down on the bed as he lowered himself slowly down on top of Tracy with his ear to his chest. He said he wanted to hear Tracy's heartbeat. Then he told Tracy that he wanted to eat it.

"Let's have a beer," Tracy suggested.

Dahmer agreed. Dragging Tracy with him by the end of the handcuff, Dahmer led the way to the refrigerator and got two beers. They then went to the living room and sat down on the small couch, real comfortable-like. Dahmer started weaving back and forth, not saying anything, just humming in a low tone as if he were in a trance.

Tracy wasn't about to go back in that bedroom again. All the windows in the apartment were blocked. There was no way to get out except the front door. Tracy told Dahmer he had to go to the bathroom. Dahmer let him get up from the couch by himself, and Tracy shot for the door. As he got to the door and turned the deadbolt, it clicked open. Just then, Dahmer grabbed hold of his arm. Tracy turned and hit Dahmer flush in the face with his fist and kicked him backward. Dahmer reeled, and Tracy never looked back.

Tracy Edwards could hear a drunken, sobbing Dahmer yelling in desperation far behind him as he ran out of the building. "Please . . . Don't leave!" This was according to Denny Johnson's interview with Tracy Edwards titled, "The One That Got Away."

Dahmer's Downfall

It was a sweltering Monday, just before the midnight hour on July 22, 1991 (five days short of a decade after Adam's abduction). Two veteran Milwaukee police officers on patrol turned onto North 25th Street in the seedy west side of town replete with slums teeming with drug dealers and transients. Officers Robert Rauth and Rolf Mueller saw a dazed black man with a single handcuff dangling from his wrist running from the well-maintained building with two sturdy flagpoles proudly jutting skyward at 924 North 25th Street. The man flagged them down.

When they asked what he was doing, Tracy Edwards yelled, "There's a guy in there trying to kill me!" Tracy then started to pour out a tale about his four hours of hell: watching *The Exorcist* and being threatened with a knife by this weird dude who lured him into his apartment. As Tracy gasped and pointed toward the Oxford Building, he told the officers that the man lived in apartment 213. Edwards didn't want to press charges. He just wanted the handcuffs removed.

The officers tried removing the cuffs so that Edwards could be on his way, but the officers carried police-issue Smith & Wesson handcuffs, and their keys wouldn't fit the off-brand cuffs on Edwards's wrist. The only way to get the cuffs off would be to get the key from the man in apartment 213. They asked Tracy to accompany them in order to identify the man. Still shaking in fear, Tracy agreed, although reluctantly.

When the officers walked down the blue carpeted hallway on the second floor toward apartment 213, they became more aware of the putrid stench that became pungent to the point of being unbearable. They pounded on Dahmer's door. Without time to think up a cogent story, Dahmer opened the door. As the officers stepped inside, the stink became overwhelming. Nothing could've prepared them for their experience with the real-life Hannibal Lecter from *The Silence of the Lambs*.

The Strange Life of Jeffrey Dahmer

Although Dahmer was intoxicated and his breath reeked of beer, his $395-per-month furnished apartment was neat, and Dahmer acted friendly. The officers asked what the cause of the horrible stench was, but Dahmer didn't reply. When Dahmer was asked about the keys to the cuffs, he tried to stall for time and sort of pointed toward the bedroom. Actually, he'd never had the keys. His method of removing them was to simply slice off the hands.

As Officer Mueller went into the bedroom to look for the key, Dahmer attempted to pass him as if he wanted to retrieve the key himself. Officer Rauth ordered him to "back off." Dahmer then just sat down on the sofa. With an ashen face and a blank look in his eyes, Dahmer asked them if he could drink a beer and smoke a cigarette. Soon it would all be over.

Officer Rauth continued to question Dahmer, but he wasn't saying much as he sat there in his alcohol-induced stupor. While Mueller was checking the rancid, fly-infested bedroom, he saw a Polaroid camera lying on the bed ready for instant action and photographs depicting nude men engaged in homosexual acts. Other photos were of mangled corpses in various stages of mutilation and postmortem dismemberment.

Mueller knew the photos had been taken in the same bedroom where he now stood. He walked into the living room to show them to his partner, uttering the words, "These are for real."

When Dahmer saw that Mueller was holding several of his Polaroids, he leapt up from the sofa. Screaming like a terrified animal, he fought the officers with fierce resistance. They quickly overpowered him, cuffed his hands behind his back, and called for backup. As Dahmer lay pinned on the floor beneath Rauth, he turned his head toward the officers and muttered, "For what I did, I should be dead."

Back in the kitchen, there were pots and pans on the stove with disgusting gunk in them. Officer Mueller then looked in the refrigerator. He shrieked at the face on the bottom shelf that stared out at him, and then slammed the door shut. "There's a f***ing head in the refrigerator!"

Next to Oliver Lacy's week-old, decomposing severed head were a jar of mustard and a box of Arm & Hammer baking soda working overtime.

Dahmer wasn't able to smooth-talk his way out of this one, and soon a cadre of police officers and detectives showed up. Dahmer was shackled at the ankles and wrists for his perp walk. After about forty minutes, he was escorted out the front door by four police officers, two in front of him and two behind him, as he did the shackle shuffle while meowing like a cat all the way to the paddy wagon.

By that time, a crowd had gathered. John Batchelor, who lived in apartment 212, said Dahmer looked like a geek that had gone nuts. Randy Jones from apartment 103 said Dahmer was hollering like a wild animal. When police asked the media not to film or take pictures of the suspect being escorted out of the building, one onlooker yelled, "If that was a black guy they'd allow them to have the cameras down his throat."

Police then took Dahmer to the station and booked him on suspicion of homicide. When they asked him if he was glad it was all over, Dahmer responded, "No, I like my lifestyle." The very next day, his probation was revoked due to numerous violations. On July 25, 1991 Dahmer's bail was set at $1 million.

* *

WARNING: This next section deals with Jeffrey Dahmer's depravations and isn't for the faint-hearted. Shocking truths are mentioned and that truth is graphic. Though quite likely to be distressing, it is a necessary look into the psychology of someone who killed for company.

* *

PHOTO ABOVE: Jeffrey Dahmer dressed in his "suicide watch" outfit without his glasses on.
Booking photos courtesy of Milwaukee Police Department, July 24, 1991.

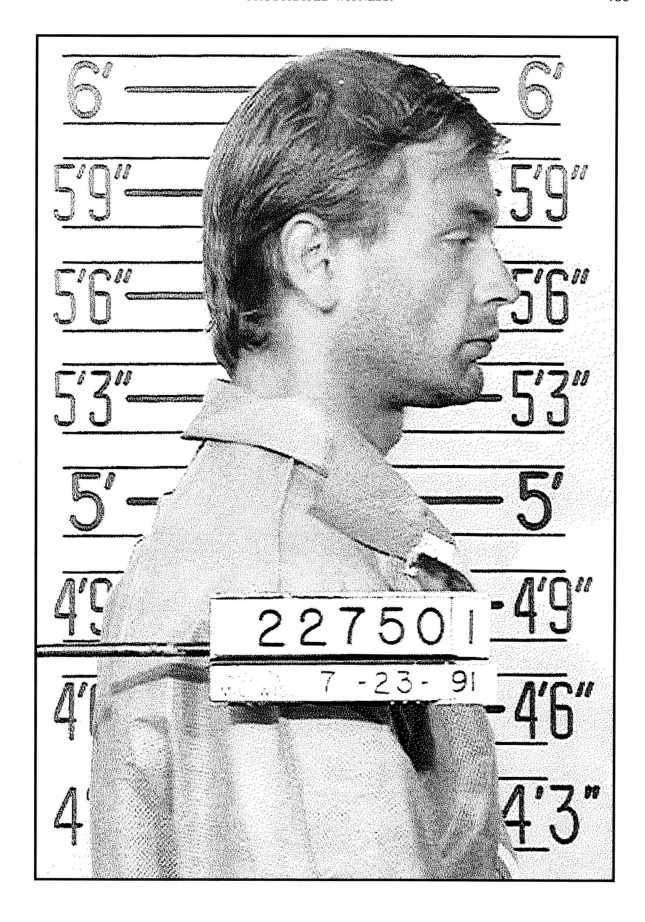

Zombies and Souvenirs

"I trained myself to view people as objects of potential pleasure instead of people."

_____*Jeffrey L. Dahmer*_____

Jeffrey Dahmer was a painfully insecure, alcohol-dependent loner who hated to be alone. He would rather have dead company than to allow a young man to leave. Most serial killers stop once their victims are dead, but that was when Jeff Dahmer came to life. He enjoyed sex with corpses. Kinky to the extreme, he would cut open the abdomen and have sex with the viscera of his victims, often masturbating and ejaculating before photographing and dismembering them.

Police began to inventory Dahmer's ghoulish apartment. Inside the freezer compartment, police discovered arms and other body parts, wrapped in plastic bags. One bag turned out to be Oliver Lacy's heart, which Dahmer told police he saved "to eat later." He ate the heart of another victim after smothering it with salt, pepper, and A-1 Steak Sauce, which "tasted kind of spongy." During his interview with police, he claimed he "ate only the people he really liked."

An array of miscellaneous body parts, bones, and several male torsos were floating in a blue fifty-seven-gallon plastic barrel of hydrochloric acid. In a separate free-standing, waist-high freezer, investigators determined that three plastic bags, tied with plastic twisters, contained the heads of Matt Turner, Jeremiah Weinberger, and Joseph Bradenhoft. A filing cabinet contained a skeleton, a dried scalp, male genitalia, and various photographs of his victims as well as three granite spray-painted skulls. Dahmer would later say he painted them to imitate plastic lab models, and he saved them as an "expression of affection" so their lives "would not be a total loss."

PHOTO LEFT: The 57-gallon blue plastic drum taken from Jeffrey Dahmer's bedroom was found to contain human torsos.

PHOTO RIGHT: In the living room next to the dining table was the lift-top freezer in which three human heads and a torso were discovered.

File photos from the Milwaukee Police Department.

In the back of the bedroom closet was a metal stockpot that contained decomposed hands and a penis. Inside a box on the shelf above the kettle were two more skulls. Also in the closet were more remnants of past friendships "gone bad" in containers of ethyl alcohol or chloroform, some glass jars that held male genitalia preserved in formaldehyde, and Polaroid photos taken by Dahmer at various stages of his victims' deaths and dismemberments. One showed a man's head, with the flesh still intact, lying in a sink. Other photos showed severed heads and human remains such as hands, feet, and penises of dismembered victims.

Dahmer had conducted experiments trying to create living zombies, but that hadn't worked out so well. He drilled 3/8-inch holes in the frontal lobe area of his victims' brains while they were still alive, and then used a turkey-basting needle to inject diluted muriatic acid that he bought at

Ace Hardware into the frontal lobe. Dahmer commented, "I wanted to see if it was possible to make—again, it sounds really gross—uh, zombies, people that would not have a will of their own, but would follow my instructions without resistance. So after that, I started using the drilling technique."

Dahmer's Sadistic Phone Calls

Don't believe Dahmer's claim that he always sedated his victims because he didn't want to hurt anyone. Dahmer was heartless and uncaring about his victims' pain and suffering. Serial killers have no moral emotions such as compassion or sympathy. He sedated them only to give himself his preferred advantage.

According to the *Milwaukee Sentinel*, July 30, 1991, the family of one of Dahmer's known victims, Ernest Miller, received several macabre phone calls two weeks after they had reported Ernest missing on Sept 2, 1990. Corrine Miller, Ernest's grandmother, said her husband received a telephone call from someone moaning and groaning, saying in a faint voice, "Help me, help me, help me!" The family received another call from someone simply making groaning noises and then gagging and choking noises as if in pain. The caller then hung up. That could've been Dahmer, putting the phone to Ernest Miller so that his family could hear the pain of his death.

Carolyn Smith, sister of Eddie Smith, another confirmed victim of Jeffrey Dahmer, said she received a strange late-night phone call from a male who sounded Caucasian in March of 1991, after her brother went missing the previous June. The caller said, "Don't even bother looking for your brother anymore." When Carolyn Smith asked why not, the man replied, "Because he's dead, I killed him." Smith called Milwaukee police to report the phone call. That was when she found out the missing persons report had never been filed. The police department's attitude was, "Well, he's an adult. There's nothing we can do."

Konerak Sinthasomphone's family said they received a phone call a few days after their son went missing. The man said, "Konerak is in danger right now." Milwaukee detectives, however, maintain Dahmer never admitted that he called the families of any of his victims.

Dahmer's Arrest Record

When Milwaukee police did a background check on Jeffrey Dahmer for priors, they learned that he was no stranger to law enforcement:

October 7, 1981: Arrested for public drunkenness in Bath, Ohio.

August 7, 1982: Arrested in Milwaukee for lascivious behavior.

September 8, 1986: Arrested in Milwaukee when he deliberately exposed himself while urinating in front of a group of children.

April 23, 1988: Drugged a man in West Allis, Wisconsin, and attempted to rob him. That charge was dropped for lack of evidence.

September 27, 1988: Arrested and charged with exploitation of a child and second-degree assault of thirteen-year-old Somsack Sinthasomphone.

From 1982 until 1990, when Dahmer was living with his grandmother in the West Allis suburb of Milwaukee, he was arrested twice for indecent exposure, once in 1982 and again in 1986. He also admitted to killing three men while living at his grandmother's house.

During this time, there were many unsolved cases, such as the murder of Eric Hansen, a sixteen-year-old high school dropout from the Milwaukee suburb of Saint Francis. He was a regular in the Milwaukee gay bars and made money working as a male prostitute. On October 4, 1983, his slashed and decapitated remains were found twenty-four miles south of Milwaukee in Kenosha County Petrifying Springs Park near Racine. Eric's head and portions of his hands (a brutal Dahmer signature, as good as a calling card) were never found.

He was last seen alive in the Uptown section of Chicago, a place Dahmer frequented. In fact, four of Dahmer's known victims were from Chicago and had accompanied him back to his Milwaukee apartment. It is very possible Dahmer could've met Eric in Chicago, and they were on the way back to Milwaukee when something went wrong and they ended up at the popular park. No one was ever charged for that crime.

The Hansen case was among twenty-four murders of young males in Illinois and Indiana from 1982 to 1984. There are also a dozen unsolved strangulations and mutilations of young men in Ohio that have baffled investigators since 1985.

On July 21, 1986, the body of nineteen-year-old David Hadaway, who worked at a downtown Columbus Sears store, was found in a dumpster in Columbus, Ohio. Remember, this was the city of Dahmer's alma mater. Hadaway was sliced down the center from his chest to just above the navel. His genitals were cut off and never found.

Dahmer never admitted to either of the abovementioned murders, and since he was being so cooperative, the Milwaukee police never pressed him. Knowing Dahmer to be a prolific liar, there was a very good possibility he could've committed other murders that he never admitted to. I know of at least one that he never admitted to—that of Adam Walsh.

It wasn't until after Dahmer's capture in Milwaukee that the German police made the connection to a number of mutilation murders that occurred during the time Dahmer was stationed there. Dahmer denied having any contact with local authorities while in Germany and further denied any homosexual activities while in Germany. He also denied ever having traveled to any location to meet with homosexuals and had no correspondence with anyone residing in Germany after his return to the United States.

Willi Fundermann, spokesman for das Bundeskriminalamt (BKA), Germany's federal police, said Dahmer was being checked in connection with a number of unresolved killings, but not much came of that retrospective investigation. Hermann Hillebrand, chief district attorney in Bad Kreuznach, would be the one to oversee the investigations. Hillebrand said his office began examining five unresolved slayings that occurred near the army base where Dahmer served on active duty between July 1979 and March 1981. The investigations would be hampered by a lack of German civil records. Madeleine Dwoiakowski, a spokeswoman for the Baumholder community, was unable to find any police background records for Dahmer. She said, depending on the nature of charges, most records were kept no longer than one to three years.

Honest Jeff

Jeffrey Dahmer, in a statement released through his attorney Gerald Boyle, said, "I have told the police everything I have done relative to the homicides." He maintained, "I have not committed any such crimes anywhere in the world other than this state, except I have admitted an incident in Ohio. I have not committed any homicide in any foreign country or in any other state. I have been totally cooperative and would have admitted other crimes if I did them. I did not. Hopefully, this will serve to put rumors to rest." Boyle added that Dahmer wouldn't make any further comments.

Of course, Dahmer would also refuse to take a polygraph test, a telltale sign of having something to hide. Like the good defense lawyer that he was, Boyle had no qualms about propping his client up on a pedestal, no matter how nefarious the client. Even Nancy Grace let Mr. Boyle have it when he was on her show talking about the Adam Walsh case and spouting off about how honest Dahmer was.

Boyle said, "He was very honest. By that, I mean, he seemed to unload everything." Then Mr. Boyle added, "I don't see any reason he wouldn't have said that he killed the boy. But of course, that was not his profile. Young boys was not his profile."

"But he's a serial killer!" Nancy yelled back before dismissing him. At least someone in the media had a little common sense.

During Jeffrey Dahmer's interviews, conducted by Milwaukee detectives Patrick Kennedy[1] and Dennis Murphy, he was asked if he ever owned a gun. Dahmer stated emphatically, "No, never." But in a later interview, after it was discovered that he did indeed own a gun, he was confronted with a receipt from Don Stricker Guns Inc., located at 2465 S. 84th Street, Milwaukee. The receipt showed that Jeffrey L. Dahmer purchased a Colt Lawman .357 Magnum revolver for $350, with the serial number 20301U, dated January 23, 1982. The receipt had his signature on it. Dahmer relented and admitted he did own a gun but only used it for target shooting. When asked why he had lied in an earlier interview, Dahmer stated that he didn't think it was relevant to the murders (Jeffrey Dahmer's Interview, Part 2, pp. 55-56).

The bottom line was he lied! Why would Dahmer deny owning a gun? Could it be that he used it? Detectives accepted this lie from Dahmer the same way they accepted all of Dahmer's other lies. That is what happens when homicide detectives are in such awe of the suspect they are supposed to be investigating that they end up having more respect for the suspect than the murdered victims they were supposed to be helping. They never interrogated him. They only interviewed him, and when they escorted Dahmer down the hallway, other detectives would move up against the wall to give wide berth to the Milwaukee cannibal.

Years earlier, when Dahmer's father found out about the gun, he confronted his son about it. Dahmer tried that "target practice" line on Lionel. He didn't buy it for one minute and told the younger Dahmer, "You don't buy a two-inch-barrel gun for target practice." Lionel then confiscated Dahmer's gun.

---

[1] Sadly, on April 13, 2013, Detective Patrick Kennedy had a heart attack when he was aged fifty-nine years and suddenly passed away.

What really bothered me was seeing Detective Murphy doing interviews with the media and saying how honest Dahmer was. Please, give me a break. Lying about why he bought a gun was only one example of his lies. Only after Dahmer was confronted with his lie did he tell the truth, hardly the definition of being "truthful and honest."

In the Adam Walsh case, Dahmer also lied but for a myriad of reasons that he was never confronted about. Adam Walsh fell between the cracks of justice because neither the Milwaukee or Hollywood police departments wanted to get to the truth

Dahmer's father hired Gerald Boyle again to represent his most famous client as he did in 1988, when Dahmer was arrested for molesting, drugging, fondling, and photographing then thirteen-year-old Somsack Sinthasomphone, brother of later victim Konerak. Dahmer pleaded guilty to second-degree sexual assault and enticing a child for immoral purposes. At the sentencing, the prosecutor, assistant district attorney Gale Shelton, said it was "a miracle" that the boy escaped from Dahmer and asked the judge to give him a long prison term.

In a bid for his freedom, Dahmer told the judge, "This enticing a child was the climax of my idiocy . . . I don't know what in the world I was thinking when I did it. . . I offer no defense." He added, "What I did was deplorable. The world has enough misery in it without my adding more to it . . . It will never happen again." A marvelous performance by a true psychopath!

For effect, Boyle then asked for a more lenient sentence, saying, "We don't have a multiple offender here." Of course, Mr. Boyle had no way of knowing that his client had already killed five men, one of them just two months earlier.

The judge fell for it, and Jeffrey Dahmer received the more lenient sentence. Despite a letter from Dahmer's father urging the judge not to release his son, dated May 24, 1989, Milwaukee Circuit Judge William Gardner released Dahmer on five years' probation and ordered him to serve a one-year term at the Community Correction Center on a work release program that would allow him to continue working third shift at the Ambrosia Chocolate Company. Dahmer was required to register as a sex offender. Mr. Boyle had done a brilliant and stupendous job of representing America's most famous cannibal.

Of course, this next time around, Mr. Boyle wouldn't get his disingenuous client off so easily. A totally different strategy would have to be used. The goal would be to keep the third-shift chocolate mixer away from states with capital punishment, Florida being one of them.

Jeffrey Dahmer blamed no one for what he did. He would accept all the blame. He told everyone that he and he alone was responsible for all the murders. As it turned out, this was a great strategy. It made Dahmer appear to be forthcoming and honest.

Dahmer told Nancy Glass in a February 8, 1993, *Inside Edition* interview. "The person to blame is sitting right across from you. That's the only person. Not parents, not society, not pornography. I mean, those are just excuses."

Gerald P. Boyle quoted Dahmer as saying, "This is my fault. There is a time to be honest, and I want to be honest." Boyle reiterated that Dahmer just wanted to end it. He just wanted to give the police a full and complete statement of his crimes. He said he had no one to blame but himself: not the system, not the courts, not the probation officer

In 2011, Boyle conceded to Colleen Henry, WISN 12 NEWS, and Milwaukee that Dahmer fooled him early on. Boyle said, "I would've bet the farm that Dahmer wasn't capable of hurting anybody." After Dahmer's final capture, Boyle maintained that Dahmer was being very open and honest saying, "I think Dahmer would have graciously told the coppers if he'd done anything to that boy." He referred to Adam without the decency of even mentioning him by name—a defense attorney's way of minimizing the connection to his client.

When I talked to FBI Agent Neil Purtell, he said two German investigators came to the U.S, but they never did get to interview Jeffrey Dahmer. There is nothing in the FBI files to show that they did—not that they would've gotten anything from him, anyway.

The Germans did go to Arkansas to interview Billy Joe Capshaw, but nothing much came of that interview. Billy said he had such shame and guilt about what Dahmer had done to him that he didn't tell investigators the full extent of what happened. He described Dahmer as somewhat of an ordinary guy when he was sober and admitted only to the physical abuse when Dahmer was drinking. "When he'd drink, he'd get real violent with me," Billy told the investigators.

After the German investigators completed their investigation, they returned to Germany, dismissing Jeffrey Dahmer as a suspect. After all, the German investigators concluded, he admitted to all his murders in the U.S., so why would he deny the ones in Germany?

To the Milwaukee and Hollywood police, Dahmer said that, in the army, he hadn't time or opportunity for sex because he was busy and living among a group of men.

Just because Dahmer admitted to investigators that he'd murdered Steven Hicks, suddenly he became a credible serial killer to some profilers but not to all: two of the few that got it right were Dr. George Palermo and FBI profiler, Agent Neil Purtell. Dr. Palermo was Dahmer's court-appointed psychiatrist (the real psychiatrist that everyone seems to ignore) and was the first mental health expert in Dahmer's trial to testify that he was sane and criminally responsible when he committed murder.

"I don't believe his behavior was sexually motivated," the psychiatrist said. "I believe Jeffrey Dahmer killed his victims because he hated homosexuality." Dr. Palermo also said that Dahmer had lied for years and still lied to that day. "He lied to the judge in 1989," when Dahmer was sentenced for sexual assault. "He lied to his lawyer. He lied to many doctors to get the [sleeping] pills. It is my feeling he has embellished a great deal in the things he has said he did." Dr. Palermo then added, "There is no way Dahmer could have gone ten years without killing."

Agent Neil Purtell was assigned to the Dahmer case. He interviewed Jeffrey Dahmer about the Adam Walsh case after his Wisconsin convictions. He came to a different conclusion. He thought Dahmer tacitly admitted killing Adam. Purtell said that Dahmer, in between denials, gave him what he considers near confessions. Once, for instance, Dahmer told him: "Whoever killed him couldn't live in a prison anywhere in America." The implication was Dahmer wouldn't confess because he would be killed vigilante-style in prison for the crime. Then he told Purtell after another denial, "You know, Florida is a death penalty state."

Neil Purtell: "I said, 'Jeffrey, tell me the truth.' He looked away and said, 'Honest to God, Neil, I didn't do Adam.'" Purtell said his years of experience told him Dahmer was lying about not murdering Adam Walsh. He told Dahmer to leave God out of it. Then Purtell added, "It smelled.

All the right smells were there. That's the way I looked at it." When he asked Dahmer to take a polygraph, he quickly refused. "My impression was that he admitted it." Purtell called the HPD to let them know of the link between Jeffrey Dahmer and the Adam Walsh case. Of course, Purtell had no way of knowing that, for good reason, the HPD had no interest in making the connection.

Neil Purtell also said, "In interviewing [Dahmer], I believe he's more than a possible suspect. He's much higher than that. He's probably responsible, in my mind. . . It was by design that the Adam Walsh case was kept under wraps." He meant that the Milwaukee Police Department suppressed the scope of the investigation until after the trial in Milwaukee to keep jurors unbiased and to ensure Dahmer's cooperation.

The Charming Monster—Monday, May 27, 1991

In Milwaukee, Dahmer's trial had been aggravated by friction between the police, the minority community, and the homosexual community. The public charged that the police were insensitive, because their behavior was inexcusable on Monday, May 27, 1991, when a fourteen-year-old Laotian boy, in a "zombieatic," trance-like state, managed to escape Dahmer's cannibal habitat (also mentioned in Jeffrey Dahmer's confession, Part 1, pp. 111–113).

Dahmer had let his guard down. Not realizing his zombie experiment didn't completely work, Dahmer had left the apartment. He went to Gare-Bear's bar and drank until near closing time. As a shy social outcast, he would typically sit alone at the end of the bar and talk with nobody, but when he did talk, he would use one-liners like, "Hi, I'm Jeff. I like the way you dance," or "You're the nicest guy I've met in Milwaukee." These lines were not all that dissimilar to the one-liner approach he used on me in Radio Shack on Monday, July 27, 1981.

After leaving the bar, he started walking eastbound on West State Street. That was when he observed his nude zombie at 25th and State streets, sitting on the curb.

It was just before 2 a.m. when cousins Sandra Smith, 17, and Nicole Childress, 18, who lived in the building next to Dahmer's, called 911 to report an incoherent Asian boy running around "buck-naked." He was bleeding from the head and rectum. Even though it appeared he couldn't speak English, it was obvious to the girls that he was frightened of the white man who had showed up and was trying to get him to return to his apartment. Both girls stood their ground and refused to return the boy to the man until the police arrived.

Soon, three of Milwaukee's finest showed up. Speaking in genteel tones, Dahmer explained to officers John A. Balcerzac, Joseph T. Gabrish, and Richard Porubcan that he and his friend lived together and had been drinking Jack Daniel's. He said his friend was his nineteen-year-old lover who was his houseguest, and the incident was nothing more than a homosexual domestic dispute. "He likes to get drunk and run down the street," Dahmer told the cops. When one of the officers asked him what the boy's name was, Dahmer stuttered, "Well, his name is, well, uh, his name is John Hmong." That was good enough for the officers.

The fire department had shown up even before the police. Paramedics put a blanket around the naked, dazed, and bleeding child. They cared for him until the police ordered them to move on.

The officers did escort the boy back to Dahmer's apartment and looked at Dahmer's photo ID but never ran a background check, which would've told them the calm, soft-spoken man was a convicted child molester who was still on probation.

The unfortunate Laotian boy was Konerak Sinthasomphone. He sat quietly on the sofa unable to talk intelligently, though his family said he spoke good English, while Dahmer showed the officers some Polaroid photos that Dahmer had taken earlier of his houseguest sitting on the same sofa dressed only in his black bikini briefs. That was all the confirmation the officers needed. The officers also missed the fly-infested, decomposing corpse of Tony Hughes that had been on the bed for the past three days.

The officers decided the only treatment "John" needed was Dahmer-care. They didn't know the boy's real name was Konerak Sinthasomphone and he was only fourteen years old. The smooth-talking cannibal, Jeffrey Dahmer, simply apologized that his lover had caused a disturbance and promised it wouldn't happen again. The officers left the stinking apartment with Dahmer's "brain-drilled zombie" still sitting quietly on the sofa, unable to speak.

KONERAK SINTHASOMPHONE TIMELINE

Sunday, May 26, 1991: Konerak goes missing.

Monday, May 27, 1991: Not knowing his identity, police return Konerak to Jeffrey Dahmer's care.

Tuesday, May 28, 1991: Konerak's family notifies police to report him as missing.

Thursday, May 30, 1991: Sandra Smith's mother calls the Milwaukee Police after she reads a newspaper article about the disappearance of a Laotian boy named Konerak Sinthasomphone, who looked just like the boy her daughter saw trying to escape from Dahmer. The Milwaukee P.D. never bothered to send anyone to talk with her. That is, until a couple of months later (Monday, July 22, 1991) when all hell broke loose.

Thursday, May 30, 1991: Jeffrey Dahmer makes a disturbing phone call to Konerak's family. Police tell them there is nothing they can do.

Neighborhood residents have charged that, because the women who reported the boy's plight were black, the investigating officers didn't react aggressively. Smith said, "We tried to give the policemen our names, but they just told us to butt out. I couldn't understand why they didn't want our names." Childress tried to intervene when the police returned Konerak but was told to "get lost" or she would be arrested and taken downtown.

After the boy was returned to Dahmer's apartment, the officers had a good laugh about the whole matter and made jokes about the need to be deloused over their police radio. The recording was made public after Dahmer was arrested. If the officers had looked a little closer, they would've noticed the 3/8-inch hole in Konerak's head, oozing with blood and brain matter. In the meantime, Dahmer again injected muriatic acid into Sinthasomphone's brain. This second injection proved fatal. On Monday, May 27, 1991, Dahmer had to straddle the two bodies in the tub to take a shower before going to work. The following day, May 28, Dahmer took a day's leave from work to devote himself to the dismemberment of the bodies of Sinthasomphone and Hughes.

The Shame of Milwaukee

John Balcerzak and Joseph Gabrish were fired from the Milwaukee Police Department by Chief Philip Arreola, but only after their actions were widely publicized. The officers appealed their termination. Even though their incompetence led to four more victims after they returned Konerak, both officers were reinstated with full back pay and were named officers of the year by the police union. Balcerzak would go on to be elected president of the Milwaukee Police Association in May 2005.

Dahmer's Murder Count:

On the record, Jeffrey Dahmer's official murder count was seventeen. That was what the Milwaukee police want everyone to believe. The real count will never be known.

Forty-one-year-old Aaron Vickers wanted to visit a friend and was dropped off at the three story, beige cinder-block low-rise Oxford Apartments at his request by his mother, Bernice, on June 10, 1991. Since then, he hasn't picked up his disability check, and to this day, nobody has seen him. Aaron's mother said, "My heart dropped in the bottom of my stomach when I heard what happened here. . . Either he's not able to talk or he's dead. If he could talk, he'd call his mama." He disappeared just forty-two days before Dahmer's arrest.

The notion that Dahmer confessed to all his murders is false. Let's not forget about twenty-eight-year-old Dean Vaughn. On May 3, 1991, Dean was found murdered at the Oxford Apartments, one floor above Dahmer, in apartment 308. His mom, Lesley, rented the apartment for Dean to help him live on his own. Dahmer might have gone to Dean's apartment with a six-pack of beer. After they drank a beer together, Dahmer might have murdered Dean. I came to this conclusion because the Nigerian building manager and Oxford resident Sopakriba "Sopa" Atanga Princewill told me that on December 27, 1990, Dahmer tried to do the same thing to him.

Dean was drugged, strangled, and sodomized. He was found on his bed with his pants pulled down to his ankles, an MO that fit Dahmer to a tee. Everyone in the building became a suspect because police were sure it had to be someone within the forty-nine units of the Oxford building. When I talked to manager Sopa Princewill, he told me the building had a locked entrance door. Residents needed a key to get in. Visitors had to use the intercom system to call an apartment so that they could be buzzed in. Every door was knocked on and all the residents were interviewed, including the only white man, Jeffrey Dahmer.

According to a neighbor, Vernell Bass, Dahmer was known to go to Dean's apartment, and Vernell told me himself that he had seen Dean going into Dahmer's apartment at least once.

When investigators went into Dahmer's apartment to inquire if he knew anything about the murder upstairs, Dahmer feared he might be caught, not for Vaughn's murder but for the dead body on his rancid, blood-soaked bed. Investigators asked if they could look around. Dahmer told them they could look all they wanted, but they never did go into the bedroom (FBI files, roll 2, p. 11). Dahmer denied having anything to do with the murder and said he didn't really know the man. This is also mentioned in Jeffrey Dahmer's confession, Part 1, pp. 71-72.

To this day, Vaughn is listed in the Milwaukee Police cold case files. The following message is posted on the Milwaukee Police website, as if they are really interested in solving this case:

Anyone with information is asked to call Milwaukee Police Cold Case Hotline at 414-935-1212. Please mention you saw the profile of the case on the Milwaukee Police Department's Web site under "Cold Case Unit."

Milwaukee Police <u>COLD CASE</u> File
Dean M. Vaughn
Occurred: May 3, 1991
Dean Vaughn was strangled in his apartment at 924 N. 25th Street at about 12:30 am. File photo, Milwaukee P.D.

Less than three months later, while Milwaukee police were still investigating this murder, Jeffrey Dahmer was arrested for mass murders committed in his own apartment, where he had been living with permission from the probation department, since May 14, 1990. Yet Dahmer was never charged with Dean Vaughn's murder, and nothing ever came of Vickers's disappearance.

The record shows Vaughn was sodomized so surely there must be crime scene evidence. The police must have found the suspect's DNA. They should have checked Dahmer for a match. If the MPD weren't too incompetent to make the connection, then this was a cover-up that would make the HPD proud. As with the HPD and their refusal to make the connection between Dahmer and little Adam Walsh, I remain certain the MPD didn't want to make the connection between Dahmer and Dean Vaughn. Detectives might have feared that making the connection would've only added fuel to the raging anger in the minority communities, who were out in large numbers protesting against police racism and insensitivity toward minorities after it was learned that police gave favoritism to a white Dahmer over the word of the two black women.

The bottom line is that no one is infallible. We all make mistakes. However, how we deal with those mistakes is what distinguishes us. Unfortunately, the Milwaukee detectives and the detectives in Hollywood weren't fighting for truth, justice, and the American way like America's favorite superhero; rather, they appeared to be working from the same rule book when it came to conducting homicide investigations involving Jeffrey Dahmer. Their credo seemed to be, "When you mess up, never fess up." Maybe they didn't want the public to know they were in Dahmer's apartment twice before he was arrested, not counting all the times the cops were there for the apartment break-ins that occurred soon after the white man moved in. Everyone in the building was questioned about them, including Dahmer. The management even hired off-duty police officers to patrol the property, but Sopa told me that only lasted several weeks because it was too expensive.

Another time, a resident called to complain about the smell, but the police kicked the wrong door open—apartment 207, down the hall. The police thought someone had died in that apartment. The lingering odor of death permeated the building so thoroughly that the police missed by four apartments, although, to their credit, they were on the right floor. In the meantime, Dahmer heard the commotion in the hallway, and with the fear of being caught, he feverishly dismantled the dead body in his bathtub. The police never did knock on Dahmer's door that time, but Dahmer had to have been an anxious wreck. The police were in that building a number of times, all because of Jeffrey Dahmer.

After Dahmer's arrest, the MPD was accused of gross negligence. They might have been afraid of public outrage for not saving Konerak Sinthasomphone or stopping Dahmer, not once, not twice, but at least three times!

When police executed a search warrant on Dahmer's first apartment on North 24th Street for molesting Konerak's brother, Somsack, Dahmer had the skull of twenty-two-year-old Richard Guerrero in his bedroom drawer. The police missed it. Also, police searched his work locker and found Anthony, but they thought the skull was a fake and left it. At that time, they were looking for evidence of a child molester, not a murderer (FBI files, roll 2, p. 10).

Sopa Princewill believes he might have been a prime target of Dahmer's Drug, Strangle, Sex, Mutilate Routine (DSSM) as well. In his book, aptly named *The Prime Target*, Sopa says Dahmer might have made at least three attempts to murder him. On one of Sopa's stench inspections of Dahmer's apartment, Dahmer apologized and explained the smell away as $150 worth of meat spoiling in his refrigerator, showing Princewill what appeared to be steaks. Dahmer then showed him the empty fifty-seven-gallon blue barrel with the black lid in the bedroom. When Dahmer opened the lid, the vapor from what was putrefying flesh and industrial chemicals nearly knocked Sopa to the floor. Sopa insisted Dahmer immediately get rid of it. He would be back in an hour to check. A short time later, Dahmer went to the office to bring Sopa to the dumpster and showed Sopa that he did get rid of the vat (also mentioned in Dahmer's interview, Part 2, pp. 88-89).

However, when Dahmer was arrested, his blue vat was there on national television being removed by a crew in biohazard suits. Obviously, he'd retrieved it. What was he thinking? If Tracy Edwards hadn't brought him down, eventually the stink would have! And if the stink hadn't brought him down, he would've been in trouble when the August rent was due, because on July 7, 1991, Dahmer was fired from the Ambrosia Chocolate Company for chronic absenteeism, and he was already two months behind on rent.

The putrid odor from apartment 213 was so strong that residents were pulling their refrigerators and stoves away from the walls looking for dead rats. Everyone in the building was talking about it. In fact the stench could be smelled blocks away. The entire neighborhood stank! One time, when the dump truck compacted garbage from the Oxford Apartments huge green steel dumpster, a large bag burst and a brownish-red, smelly sludge oozed from the truck as it made its rounds, spreading the stink throughout the neighborhood. Residents in the area couldn't discern where the stink was emanating from. One resident a block away moved, saying that the neighborhood was the armpit of Milwaukee.

Back in the Dahmer building, Pamela Bass, who lived across the hallway in apartment 214, knocked on Dahmer's door. He wouldn't answer, so she passed notes under his door. In the meantime, she would stuff towels under her own door to keep the odor out. Sometimes the smell disappeared, but when it returned, it returned with a vengeance strong enough to choke a maggot. One time, she stopped Dahmer in the hallway and said, "Jeff, something in your house is really stinking. You ought to do something about it. I don't see how you can stand it." Occasionally, Dahmer would go to Pam's apartment to watch TV or sit at the kitchen table and have a cup of coffee, and talk sports with her husband, Vernell. Once, he even brought Pam a beef sandwich, although now Pam has to live with the thought that she might have eaten "someone's body part." Pam also tried to tell the police that she thought Dahmer killed "Stringbean." That's what everyone called Dean Vaughn, she told me.

I also called Pam's ex-husband, Vernell. Vern told me that he and his ex-wife would hear sawing noises, all hours of the day and night. "I thought he was building bookcases or something. Then, when the buzzing stopped, I heard him yelling, 'Mother f--er! I told you, goddamn it!' It seemed strange because I didn't hear anyone respond or talk, except for him." Vernell also penned his own book, *Across the Hall*, a firsthand account of what it was like living across the hall from America's most nefarious real-life cannibal.

Dahmer's remedy to Pamela's stink complaints was to pay $56 for a fifty-seven-gallon vat. In a sort of do-it-yourself home project, he marinated the torsos of his "companions" that wanted to leave in muriatic acid until they turned into a smelly, slimy sludge that he would flush down the toilet. Dahmer had become so well adjusted to his insane world that he couldn't comprehend that this created even more of a stink. Nanetta Lowery, who lived in apartment 313 directly above Dahmer, was moved to another apartment because of her constant complaints to the manager.

Aaron Whitehead, who lived in apartment 113 directly below Dahmer, said around July 19, 1991, he woke up from his sleep to hear pounding and scuffling. "I heard what sounded like a kid. . . He was crying as if his mother had just walloped him [most likely Joseph Bradehoft]. I heard a big falling sound. . . as if he was being hurt." The thumping sounds were so loud and furious that he thought someone was going to crash through his ceiling. After ten minutes, it stopped, but then came the sound of a buzz saw, and then the water ran all night. The sounds were so constant that Aaron grew used to it. He thought someone was having a really bad relationship or friendship and forever getting into fights.

Yet when Dahmer was interviewed, he said he was not into torture and was very compassionate. "I didn't want hurt anyone . . . I carried it too far, that's for sure," Dahmer told police. He had drugged Bradehoft, and only while he was passed out, he slipped a leather strap around his throat and strangled him to death. He never mentioned anything about Bradehoft fighting for his life. Maybe it can be argued whether Jeffrey Dahmer had an assaultive personality, but it can't be denied that he could put up a good fight when he had to.

Although Vaughn was the only resident murder victim in the building, Dahmer would have no problems killing in his own building and not worrying about the consequences. Sopa told me one time he walked up on an argument between Dahmer and a black male who lived in apartment 215 next to Dahmer. The black male might have rebuffed Dahmer's advances and threatened to shoot Dahmer. Had he accepted the invitation, he would likely have been another victim.

Another time, one week before his arrest, Dahmer propositioned twenty-year-old Douglas Jackson who lived downstairs on the first floor. Douglas wasn't about to accept Dahmer's offer to come up to his apartment for some beer, because a number of times he had observed Dahmer hanging out next to the dumpster in the back of the building, drinking a beer and "acting weird." There would be a lot of cats at Dahmer's feet, following him around all over the place. "Those cats would go crazy trying to jump up and get into the dumpster at his garbage. . . I'm talking twenty-some cats!" Sometimes the dog in the rear of the neighboring building would bark at all hours of the night. When Dahmer went to his apartment, he didn't just walk in. He would crack the door and squeeze in, and he did that all the time. When Doug's girlfriend overheard Dahmer's overture, she came out and pulled Doug back into the apartment and told him he would be crazy to go into the apartment of that weird white guy. One neighbor, Henry Barnett, said, "He never looked you in the eye; he always looked down."

Everyone knew Dahmer, the one weird white guy who always wore the same dirty jeans and the only tenant in the building who consistently turned down management's offer of free carpet cleaning and insect spraying. It was this same weird guy that was spotted standing outside the gay bars at a bus stop for hours on end, which was common practice among male prostitutes seeking customers. Yes, this was the kind of weird madman it would take to murder and decapitate a six-year-old boy.

Jeffrey Dahmer was out of control, and thankfully, it was just a matter of time before he would be arrested. His capture was inevitable. On May 27, 1991, the day after Konerak was murdered, a resident brought to Sopa's attention that the rear exit door was smeared with blood. No one realized it was likely from Konerak until after Dahmer's arrest.

One time Sopa found whole, large, fresh, complete bones with the cartilage still on the ends. They were on a slope near the back of the building. Most likely, the cats were spreading the bones around. Wanting to keep the property neat and clean, Sopa told me he collected and disposed of the bones in the dumpster. He realized the bones were most likely human only after Dahmer's arrest. When Dahmer was arrested, some of the residents found human bones. A reporter described one of them to be a "human shoulder bone." When the police were informed, the residents were told, "Throw them away! They're everywhere." One resident, Kellene Buckett was declined when she tried to hand police a bucketful of bones.

Dahmer's Life Sentence

Milwaukee—famed for its beer, cheese, chocolate, and sausages—has a Summerfest and a Winterfest for three weeks every year. Now on January 30, 1992, this predominantly German city on a Great Lake also had a "Dahmerfest."

Dahmer's prosecution was a total slam-dunk. They just don't get any slam-dunkier. The only possible snag facing prosecutors was the issue of whether Dahmer was too crazy to stand trial. Milwaukee district attorney Michael McCann told a packed courtroom in his closing statements that, "Jeffrey Dahmer was a master manipulator and deceiver who knew exactly what he was doing every step of the way. Ladies and gentlemen, he's fooled a lot of people. Please don't let this murderous killer fool you." Then he went on to say that it would appear Jeffrey Dahmer's ejaculations meant more to him than the life of another person.

The defense dragged up Dahmer's childhood. He had enjoyed killing and torturing small animals as a kid. They argued that bodies were piling up so fast in Dahmer's apartment that he was showering with two or three (actually only two) corpses in his tub which clearly showed he was nuts. They then pointed out that Dahmer's persistent attempts to create a zombie sex slave by drilling into his living victims' heads and injecting muriatic acid into the hole wasn't exactly the work of a sane man.

Dahmer's Verdict

Honesty is the best policy, but insanity is the best defense! But according to the jury Dahmer was neither honest nor insane. After a two-week voyeuristic trial, on February 17, 1992, Dahmer's insanity plea was rejected by the jury, and since capital punishment had been illegal in the Badger State since 1853, he was sentenced to fifteen consecutive life sentences, for a minimum of 936 years. It took them just five hours to find him guilty, but definitely sane, on all of the murder counts he was charged with.

The jury was then forced to make a decision on the insanity defense based on listening to crazy-sounding arguments pushed to logical absurdities by dubiously conflicting expert witnesses who argued diagnoses and definitions of psychosis, paranoia, intact thought process, and other concepts as they elaborated on explanations for why Dahmer's killings were not sadistic:

"The drugging was done to satisfy his sexual need for a not fully cooperative partner."

"The drilling enterprise . . . was not sadistic . . . it was a realistic attempt to disable, but not to kill . . . "

"The killing was the unintended consequence of the drilling . . . the taking-of-life issue . . . "

"Death was an unintended by-product of his efforts to create a zombie."

"Dismembering was a disposal problem . . . "

"The disemboweling was the most efficient way of handling all the remains, which only served an administrative function."

Juror Karl Stahle said, "his whole conduct showed he was a con artist . . . He had just one thing on his mind—to satisfy his ego and to satisfy himself." It does make me wonder what it could possibly mean to be insane. Whatever Dahmer's motives, I hardly think we should take the word of a disorganized killer who was a walking jumble of personality disorders, yet smart enough to give the appearance of cooperation. The "smart con artist," as another juror called him, had been lying and covering his ass for years. Only the truly mad can make us believe that they are sane.

On May 16, 1992, a consecutive life sentence was added for the murder of Steven Hicks. Dahmer was sent off to the funny farm at 2925 Columbia Drive in Portage, Wisconsin, to become inmate number 177252.

End of the Road

Dahmer's apology ran four typewritten pages: "Your Honor, it is now over. This has never been a case of trying to get free. I didn't ever want freedom. Frankly, I wanted death for myself. This was a case to tell the world that I did what I did, but not for reasons of hate. I hated no one. I knew I was sick or evil or both. Now I believe I was sick. The doctors have told me about my sickness, and now I have some peace. I know how much harm I have caused . . . Thank God there will be no more harm that I can do. I believe that only the Lord Jesus Christ can save me from my sins . . . I ask for no consideration."

Prison Time: Over 900 Years to Go

For the first year, Dahmer was separated from the general prison population. For his own safety, he was kept isolated in an eight-by-ten-foot, single-bunked, windowless cell as many as twenty-three hours of every day in the ninety-six-cell Special Management Unit (SMU unit), now called Unit Number Six. Whenever he wasn't in his cell, he was forced to wear shackles. This section of the prison houses prisoners with adjustment and mental difficulties. Without his muriatic acid and tools of the trade, in early 1993, officials at the Columbia Correctional Institute considered inmate number 177252 to be a model prisoner who had adjusted well to prison life. He was a self-proclaimed born-again Christian who was very subdued and shuffled around like a little old man. Dahmer himself said he needed to get out of solitary confinement because it was driving him crazy. Officials decided to allow him to mix with other prisoners in the SMU and his privileges were expanded. Dahmer kept mostly to himself in cell 648. He was allowed fifteen magazines, thirty books, a Bible, four newspapers, two phone calls, and three guests a week, plus a television and a radio in his cell. Gradually, he was permitted to have some contact with other inmates and permitted to attend classes and work, although he was regarded as an oddity, even among the odd.

Dahmer would try to break the monotony of his hopeless situation by joking with guards, "I have over nine hundred years to go!" Or he would say, "I bite" and then laugh as they passed his cell. One time, he put a sign on the wall of his cell "Cannibals Anonymous Meeting Tonight." When they served meatloaf he would shape it to resemble limbs and drizzle on packets of ketchup as blood. Prison spokesman Joseph Scislowicz said, "He had a very interesting sense of humor."

Death of a Madman

Dahmer was attacked twice in prison, the first time on July 23, 1994. After attending a church service in the prison chapel, an inmate, jealous over Dahmer's celebrity status, attempted to slash his throat with a razor blade attached to a toothbrush. Dahmer escaped the incident with superficial wounds. In his next attack, he wouldn't be so lucky. A few weeks later, an informant warned prison officials that Christopher Scarver was planning to kill Dahmer, but that tip was ignored.

At the time, Dahmer had been a janitor for about three weeks. He handed out towels in the shower and worked on cleaning detail. His pay was twenty-four cents an hour. On November 28, 1994, after a breakfast of a hardboiled egg, toast, cereal, and coffee, at 7:50 a.m., a guard escorted three inmates—Christopher Scarver, who was black, and Jeffrey Dahmer and Jesse Anderson, who were both white—to the gym for cleaning detail and inexplicably left them alone.

Dahmer started cleaning the staff bathroom adjoining a basketball court. Anderson cleaned the staff locker room. Twenty-five-year-old fellow inmate from Milwaukee, Scarver, went into the weight room. He took a twenty-inch, 5-pound steel bar from a lat machine and went into the men's room, where he proceeded to beat Dahmer beyond recognition with the metal bar before smashing Dahmer's head against the floor and wall.

Then Scarver went to the locker room, less than a hundred feet away, and bludgeoned Anderson, thirty-seven, who was serving a life sentence for stabbing and bludgeoning his wife, Barbara, to death on April 21, 1992. Anderson's case drew wide attention because of his false claim that two black men had attacked him and his wife in the parking lot of the Northridge Mall as they left

TGI Friday's. Dahmer's death was especially gruesome compared to Anderson's. Scarver caught Dahmer as he tried to run. According to Scarver, Dahmer put up little resistance as he murmured his last words, "I don't care if I live or die. Go ahead and kill me." And Scarver obliged. Scarver was a violent, delusional schizophrenic who believed that he was the son of God. He had been convicted of the first-degree murder of a former coworker at the Wisconsin Conservation Corps during a robbery and was serving a life sentence ("The Final Victim," *People*, Dec. 12, 1994).

After attacking Dahmer and Anderson, Scarver calmly walked back to his cell. When he was asked why he wasn't working, he told the guard, "God told me to do it. You will hear about it on the six o'clock news. Jesse Anderson and Jeffrey Dahmer are dead."

The guard went to check and found that Anderson had his skull crushed with a metal bar and was lying in a pool of blood. He would die several days later at the University of Wisconsin Hospital in Madison when doctors removed him from life support. Dahmer died in the ambulance of severe head trauma from two major blows to the head before reaching the Divine Savior Hospital in Portage. Jeffrey Dahmer was pronounced dead at 9:11 a.m. Scarver was escorted to the forty-eight single-bunked DS-1 cells (Disciplinary Segregation unit), better known as "the hole."

Rita Isbell, the sister of one of Dahmer's last victims, Errol Lindsey, 19, said she always knew that this day would come. For the past two years, she had been getting telephone calls from men identifying themselves as prison inmates, offering condolences and promises that Dahmer would be "taken care of." The last call had come about six months before his death. According to *The New York Times* on November 29, 1994, Ms. Isbell quoted the caller as saying, "You don't know me. . . I'm up here with Jeffrey Dahmer. Don't worry. We'll take care of it."

A blue-ribbon panel investigated Dahmer's murder. During psychiatric examinations, Scarver expressed hostility toward whites. When asked by a psychiatrist whether he thought his own sentence was just, Scarver replied, "Nothing white people do is just." Yet the panel concluded "Scarver acted alone." He was "not part of a conspiracy." Scarver found "Dahmer and Anderson unfit to live." And the attack was "not racially motivated." The reason Scarver gave for killing Dahmer was that he was tired of him taunting others with his sick sense of humor, "Some people who are in prison are repentant — but he was not one of them," Scarver claimed. It would take sixteen years for Scarver to work his way out of maximum solitary confinement. On November 8, 2010, Scarver was released back into the general prison population of the federal prison at Florence, Colorado, where he was sent shortly after that 1994 event.

Jeffrey Lionel Dahmer: (May 21, 1960 — November 28, 1994)

I remember the day I read about Dahmer's demise in the *Herald*. I was totally devastated and disgusted. It had always been my thinking that someday, somehow, some way, someone would get him to confess to Adam's murder. If enough evidence came forward, maybe then they would even extradite him back to Florida to stand trial for Adam's murder. That would never happen now. Jeffrey Dahmer took his biggest secret with him, and as retired FBI Agent Neil Purtell once said, there are always secrets.

Upon learning of his death, Dahmer's mother Joyce Flint responded angrily to the media, "Now is everybody happy? Now that he's bludgeoned to death, is that good enough for everyone?" After subsequent legal proceedings, Dahmer's remains were cremated and divided in half between his mother Joyce and his father Lionel since they were divorced.

CHAPTER NINE
THE FIRST LAWSUIT
1995—1996
AND A CALL FROM ART HARRIS

In December of 1979, Miami police officers pursued motorcyclist Arthur McDuffie in a high-speed chase. When the police finally stopped him, they removed his helmet and then beat him to death with their batons. After the officers were acquitted, one of the worst riots in the history of the U.S. broke out. By the time the rioting ceased three days later, over 850 people had been arrested, and at least nineteen had died. Property damage was estimated at around $100 million. Between April 15 and October 31, 1980, there was the Mariel boatlift when thousands of Cuban "Marielitos" came to Miami. In the 1970s and '80s, the "cocaine cowboys" were engaged in drug trafficking, contract killings, and gangland shootouts and were responsible for many murders in Miami from 1979 to 1980.

Then there was the abduction of Adam Walsh that shook the nation. The investigation was so inept that the HPD would fight with every available resource they had to keep the public from viewing the record, because they knew it would reveal embarrassing details about their investigation and cover-up. Within six months of Adam's abduction, John Walsh had openly criticized the police. In one interview, Walsh lambasted the HPD and characterized the officers as lazy and incompetent: "They were bumbling and stumbling along. . . They were afraid to ask for help."

Yet when a lawsuit was initiated in 1995, George Terwilliger, a Washington attorney for the Walsh family, protested opening the HPD files. "They [the Walsh family] don't want anything to happen that could compromise further investigation and any potential prosecution." Hollywood police managed to change John Walsh's mind to take their side. John Walsh believed the HPD when they said the scrutiny could compromise the case. However, Judge Leroy H. Moe of the Seventeenth Judicial Circuit Court, one of the most experienced and knowledgeable members of the Broward County bench, and Thomas Julin, attorney for Jay Grelen and the *Mobile Press Register*, Alabama, did not.

In 1995, Jay Grelen, a reporter for the *Mobile Press Register*, was investigating the Adam Walsh abduction for a series of stories. Although there was no local connection to Alabama, Grelen managed to talk his news editors into letting him spend several months on the Adam Walsh case. He requested on January 31, 1995, for the HPD to make public all of its investigative files. Jay

Grelen thought the HPD would be grateful for the *Mobile Press Register's* extended help and that the HPD, as well as John Walsh, would cooperate with him.

Jay was wrong on both counts. John Walsh refused to speak to Grelen, despite his repeated attempts to contact him. This may have been because, by this time, John had put all his trust in the new detective on the case, Mark Smith, and the HPD to solve his son's murder, and they didn't want outside help.

Hollywood Police Chief Richard Witt wanted to release the files without having to go to court. He would have no problem abiding by Judge Moe's order when the time came. The homicide detectives, however, didn't want anyone to see those files, and they fought Witt until they got their way. The department refused Grelen's request, contending that the records were part of an active criminal investigation, which constitutes intelligence information exempt from the disclosure requirements of the Florida public records law (Chapter 119 of the Florida Statutes).

The original plaintiffs, the Mobile Press Register Inc. and Jay Grelen, represented by Thomas Julin of Steel, Hector, & Davis of Miami, commenced action on May 18, 1995, against the HPD by asking the court to issue an order to allow them immediate access to the case files. The case number is 95-06324 and can be read in full from the State Attorney CD-ROM files (box 3, file 1, starting on page 18, and files 5 and 6).

At the first hearing on June 12, 1995, the Fort Lauderdale Sun-Sentinel Inc. and the Palm Beach Post Inc. joined the lawsuit as party plaintiffs. Circuit Judge Leroy Moe heard from representatives of the defendant, the HPD, who in the past had steadfastly refused to comply with public information laws. The HPD testified that the investigation was in fact a cold case, but that it recently had been reassigned to Detective Mark Smith, a cold case specialist.

The Cover-Up

When Detective Mark Smith first took over the Adam Walsh cold case, he wrote a three-page interoffice memorandum dated August 16, 1994. This is what Smith had to say about the case: "Due to the amount of time since this incident, it would be virtually impossible to set out and try to establish new suspects or motives" (HPD case files, roll 1, p. 2840). However, now that the HPD was being sued for the case files, Smith suddenly found new suspects …

PHOTO RIGHT: HPD photo of Detective Mark Smith, Badge #1163.

The Despicable Mr. Smith and a Police Department Fraught with Corruption

In a desperate effort to keep the files sealed, defendant Smith claimed he had uncovered new leads and was investigating a new suspect in the slaying of Adam Walsh. Smith told Judge Moe, under oath, that he had identified the suspect within the past six months although he was unwilling to name the suspect. I contend that Smith didn't name the suspect because he had no suspect.

Obviously, looking back now, I know there never was any new suspect. This was nothing more than a smoke screen and a ploy to stall for time. Apparently, it would appear, Detective Smith had no problems telling his distortions of reality to the Walsh family, the media, and even to the judge under oath. He even added that he was also examining one or two other possibilities for suspects during his so-called ten-month review of the case file.
(SAO case files, box 1, pp. 30-34)

Walsh believed him and remained hopeful there would be an arrest on the horizon. John was told there had been some "impressive developments" in the case, though no one seemed to be able to describe those developments.

For these cops to give the Walsh family hope and solicit their help in stymieing any real hope for justice in their son's murder was atrocious and about as repugnant as it gets. This was all part of the HPD's ongoing cover-up of what leads were followed and what leads were abandoned. What should be noted is that Ottis Toole wasn't named as a suspect at this time because he had long since been eliminated.

Thomas Julin wasn't buying it. Neither was Judge Moe, who found it hard to believe the police didn't want to jeopardize their fruitless fifteen-year search. He must have figured out the HPD had ulterior motives for not wanting anyone to view their records. He advised the defendant police department that it would be provided a reasonable opportunity to pursue leads under investigation, but that it would not be permitted to withhold public access to the files indefinitely. Moe allowed the files to remain confidential so Smith could have time to follow up on his so-called leads. The newspapers would be able to renew their request for full disclosure in several weeks, allowing Smith time to question his new suspects.

Thomas Julin said, "We'll be back!"

True to his words, on September 26, 1995, Julin, again representing the *Mobile Press Register* and Grelen, was back. He renewed their request for access to the police investigative files. This time, the big guns in town joined the lawsuit. The *Miami Herald* joined on the side of the plaintiffs, and the fight was on.

Representing the plaintiffs, the *Mobile Press Register*, Jay Grelen, and the *Palm Beach Post* were Thomas Julin, Edward Mulins, Marc Heimowitz, and Martin Reeder Jr. The *Sun-Sentinel* was represented by Kathleen Pellegrino. The *Miami Herald* was represented by Jerold Budney. Representing the defendant, the HPD, was Joel Cantor.

A Defense of Egregious Misconduct

Judge Moe heard the argument on that motion on October 18, 1995. The defendant, the HPD, argued that the investigation was continuing and that an arrest or prosecution "may result." Julin argued that it was laughable to claim that, after fourteen years, police would suddenly arrest a suspect if only they were given another week or two. The Walsh case had remained unsolved for fourteen years, and a press examination of the case might produce new leads.

No evidence was offered by the HPD that Detective Smith had come any closer to securing an arrest or prosecution, even though he had been afforded more than four months to reinvestigate the case. The only clues offered by the HPD seemed more like riddles toward the identity of a new suspect. Surely this was proof that they never had any suspects. Detective Smith tried to fool the judge with a lie and failed, but he still had John Walsh in his corner. In order to prevent the files from being released to the public, the Hollywood police would stoop to an all-time low. Taking advantage of John and Reve's need for closure, they asked the Walshes to remain silent on their son's case, convincing them not to request that the files be unsealed as they were on the verge of solving the case.

Shortly before the records were to be made public, Charles Morton, a prosecutor from the State Attorney's Office, and John Walsh intervened and asked the court to reconsider its disclosure order.

NOTE: At the end of this chapter is George Terwilliger's (together with Michael Christiansen representing the Walshes) February 2, 1996, letter to the Broward County State Attorney's Office, imploring Chief Assistant State Attorney Ralph Ray to do what he could to prevent the Adam Walsh case files from being opened.

The State Attorney's Office filed eleventh-hour motions to block the release, saying it would be premature to release the case files. They claimed that on January 26, 1996, the HPD had delivered its files for review, and the state attorney was evaluating the files. The matter would be presented to a grand jury in the spring if Judge Moe would stay his discovery order.

First, the State Attorney's Office hadn't done anything for fifteen years, yet now, suddenly, they wanted to get involved. If procrastination were a legitimate argument, the State Attorney's Office could keep public records sealed for eternity. Actually, all they wanted to do was come to the aid of their symbiotic friends at the HPD, because these departments are like biscuits and butter.

Reve wanted to address the court but Judge Moe said he wouldn't allow emotion to fill his courtroom, and she could communicate only through her attorney. Judge Moe then cast aside their protests and instructed Hollywood Police Chief Richard Witt to open the file. Moe told the chief, "I expect full, complete compliance with the substance and wording of the order." He allowed the Hollywood police until 12 p.m. on February 16, 1996, to make all of the records sought by the *Mobile Press Register* and Grelen public. This lawsuit is in the SAO case files (box 3, file 1, starting on page 14, plus files 3-6) and available for free download from the website JusticeForAdam.com.

Fifteen years of secrecy was long enough. Judge Moe saw through Smith and the State Attorney's Office, declined their request and noted that the offer didn't "show a good faith anticipation that a prosecution will be commenced in the foreseeable future. Rather, it simply reflects a desire to maintain the confidentiality of investigative records." He also noted that, "Mr. Walsh's interest in ensuring that the efforts of law enforcement officials are not impaired by a premature release is certainly understandable, but his concerns do not supply the evidence that the court requires to conclude that the records at issue are part of an active investigation."

Moe sided with the newspapers, who argued that, with no arrest in sight, the time had come for public disclosure. Again, Judge Moe reiterated his ruling from October 1995 that the police had until February 16, 1996, to investigate new leads before releasing the records. At another hearing, Judge Moe rejected motions made by the Broward County State Attorney's Office and the Walshes seeking to keep the documents closed.

The public records law exempts records of an active criminal investigation, meaning one progressing in good faith or in which an arrest or prosecution is reasonably anticipated in the foreseeable future. However the police had yet to identify a suspect and consequently the HPD released all of its investigative records, which consisted of three rolls of microfilm. Roll 1 and roll 2 equal 7,472 pages of material, and roll 3 has 632 pages of photos for a total of 8,104 pages, available at a cost of $225 per copy.

After the secret, yellowing files were released, John Walsh said, "We are gravely wounded and bitterly disappointed that a judge in Florida has decided that a newspaper's demand to see the police file in our son's case is more important than finding his killer. Now, details previously known only to the police and the killer will be known to all—making it almost impossible to find out who the real murderer is."

In 1981, John Walsh went to the newspapers, seeking publicity for Adam. He knew then that public scrutiny might help. It isn't a question of the media claiming privileges that go beyond the rights of the public, but rather of the media playing their role in the public's right to be informed.

Several weeks after the HPD released its investigative records, columnist Fred Grimm of the *Miami Herald* wrote, "Ottis Toole's ghastly lies do nothing to shed light on the enduring mystery of little Adam Walsh. The only mystery left unsolved was how any cop, without supporting evidence, could have believed Ottis Toole."

It comes as no surprise that, in John Walsh's book *Tears of Rage*, which was on the *New York Times* best seller list for two weeks straight, much of his rage was directed at police officers in Hollywood, who for fifteen years unsuccessfully investigated the kidnapping and slaying of his son, Adam. "I'm afraid that in their ineptitude they've let the real killer get away," John lamented.

Walsh struggled to regain happiness in his personal life and channeled his rage into success by carving a prominent niche as a crime fighter and an advocate of children's and victims' rights. "We're past trying to hold on to one sad tragedy," John Walsh wrote. "Let's not stay stuck on this little gap-toothed face wearing a baseball cap. It's not just about our son anymore. It's about a lot of people's kids."

What prompted John to write his book *Tears of Rage* wasn't simply his sense that his account could benefit others, but also his anger over the release of his son's case files. In February 1996, the confidential case file was opened to the public. "Newspapers were looking to get into the case—not to solve it," Walsh said. "But because I was well known on television, and they were looking to dig up stuff, they used the haughty guise of First Amendment rights."

Displeased with the outcome, the attorney for the Walsh family, George Terwilliger complained that "the media forced the issue" and said, "What you saw in court. . . was a contest between justice for a six-year-old boy who was brutally murdered and the insatiable appetite of the media for these files. Justice lost."

Mr. Terwilliger Got It All Wrong

This was a contest between justice and a brutally incompetent police department that had run amuck with corruption, and this time justice won! The release of these files eventually enabled me to expose the Hollywood Police for all the blatant lies they told, including misleading the Walsh family about details in Adam's abduction. Certainly, Adam would never get justice through the investigative efforts of the Hollywood Police Department, because the HPD never seemed to care about justice for Adam. If Mr. Terwilliger thinks justice *was* lost, the only justice lost was through the efforts of the HPD.

CHAPTER 119, FLORIDA STATUTES
119.01 Florida state policy on public records
(1) It is the policy of the state of Florida that all state, county, and municipal records are open for personal inspection and copying by any person. Providing access to public records is a duty of each agency.

What part of this statute did the HPD not understand? The HPD's willingness to subvert Florida's "sunshine law" is testament to the wisdom of the law. Jay Grelen had every right to view the files. Had it not been for the HPD doing its best to circumvent the laws of the State of Florida, Grelen wouldn't have had to get four newspapers and a half-dozen attorneys to file suit. This is why we need to keep rogue police departments like the HPD on a very short leash. If the media doesn't fight these battles, who will? Who will let the public know the truth?

We live in a democracy in which the supreme power is vested in the people and exercised by the people directly or indirectly, and not the other way around. The taxpayers pay for the services of law enforcement. That gives us the right to have access to official records, and in Florida, the expectation that the public's business will be done in public is confirmed by our open records law.

I have no way of knowing if John Walsh ever read the case files, but he did say the files showed that Ottis Elwood Toole was the prime suspect. John argued that the police were reluctant to pursue the case against Toole after his first confession in 1983. He wrote that the police had committed a grave error by playing tough with the suspect: "As everyone knew, hardball didn't work with Toole; you had to coax him." Although unsuccessful, Walsh even asked Chief Richard Witt to "make a loud, clear, unequivocal statement that Ottis Toole is the prime suspect and it's only because of a lack of evidence or prosecutorial discretion that Toole has not yet been prosecuted and probably won't be." John Walsh is entitled to his beliefs surrounding Toole and the "lost" evidence, but a victim's family does not have the right to select the suspect. This is called vigilantism, something John Walsh has always said he was against.

Judge Moe referred in his decision to the legal protections that guarantee public access, and he rightly ordered the release of the investigative files. In April 2010, I called Judge Moe to let him know how right his decision was. It was Judge Moe's decision to release the case files that ultimately allowed the truth to be revealed and give the Walsh family the real justice they deserve versus Joe Matthews's and the HPD's diabolical cover-up version of events.

When this ruling came out, my first thought was that I would be getting phone calls from the newspapers. But that didn't happen. I couldn't understand why they went through all that effort to sue and then not even look at the files! Surely if they had looked, they would see my statements and give me a call. When that call never came, I was left to think that those newspapers were just concerned about their First Amendment rights.

A Call from Art Harris

Finally, on November 4, 2002, I received a call from someone who was inquiring about the Adam Walsh case. He said his name was Art Harris. My first response was, "Art, you won't believe this, but have I got a story to tell you!" I went on to tell him about my encounter with Jeffrey Dahmer in Radio Shack. I told the story as I had told it so many times over the years to anyone who would listen but Art stopped me and asked if he could interview me in person.

He was at my apartment within the hour. When I told Art the reasons I was given by Detective Hoffman for eliminating Dahmer as a suspect, Art told me that all those reasons were part of the record. Art then asked me if I had a photo of myself from 1981. I went through a box of old photos and found one from that time and gave him a copy.

Art actually had read all seven thousand-plus pages of the Adam Walsh case files. Then he told me that none of what Hoffman said about Jeffrey Dahmer was true. Art had found Darlene Hill, the owner of Sunshine Subs and Ken Haupert Sr., the manager.

PHOTO Right: My photo from 1981.

Listed below in regular type are the reasons Detective Hoffman gave for discarding Dahmer as a suspect. In italics are the reasons why Jeffrey Dahmer should be the prime suspect.

1: Jack Hoffman said to me, "Jeffrey looked me straight in the eye and said he didn't do it. . . and you know what, I believe him."

Jeffrey had been known to look other police officers and even his own father in the eye and lie.

2: Adam didn't fit his MO.

Adam was decapitated like in other murders Dahmer committed.

3: He (JD) had nothing to lose and was open and honest.

Jeffrey Dahmer was not open and honest. Most of what he said has since been found to be false.

4: He was always broke.

How could he be broke if he was apparently working all those hours?

5: Florida has capital punishment. J.D. would like to come to Florida because he doesn't want to live the rest of his life in prison, but he can't confess to something he didn't do.

When FBI agent Neil Purtell asked Dahmer if he kidnapped Adam, Dahmer's response was, "Neil, you know if anyone confesses to Adam, he will not survive in prison." Agent Purtell has said he took this as a near confession (about as close a confession as anyone can now get).

6: He was working ten hours a day, seven days per week, and never took any days off. So he would never have had time. Jack Hoffman also said, "Every once in a while they would just give him a day off."

The man that hired Dahmer has since been found by Art Harris, and he said that's not true. Dahmer only worked part-time as a busboy. He never worked weekends and was constantly being sent home for coming in disheveled.

NOTE: I know for sure that at least on one day Dahmer wasn't working—the day I saw him at the Hollywood Mall on Monday, July 27, 1981.

7: He had no vehicle.

This is true. However, Dahmer didn't mention in his interview with Detective Hoffman that the Mr. Pizza restaurant had a blue van as one of its three delivery vehicles.

8: He was drinking heavily and sleeping on the beach.

Drinking heavily is true. Sleeping on the beach? Sometimes, but not always.

9: He didn't know where the mall was.

One thing is for sure: he was at the Hollywood Sears Mall on Monday, July 27, 1981. Also witnesses place him at that mall at least two other times before Adam was abducted.

Another reason used to dismiss Jeffrey Dahmer as a suspect was because he told Detective Hoffman he didn't have any place to bring someone. But what about *the meter room*? I discuss the meter room in depth in the following chapter.

George Terwilliger's three-page letter to the Broward County Chief Assistant State Attorney's Office

SENT BY: XEROX Telecopier 7017; 2- 2-96 ; 5:21PM ;   2028571737→   305 831 6171;# 4

McGuireWoods
Battle&Boothe LLP

The Army and Navy Club Building
1627 Eye Street, N.W.
Washington, DC 20006-4007
Telephone/TDD (202) 857-1700 • Fax (202) 857-1737

February 2, 1996

VIA FACSIMILE

Ralph J. Ray, Jr.
Chief Assistant States Attorney
Broward County States Attorney's Office
201 SE 6th Street
Ft. Lauderdale, Florida 33301

RE: **Adam Walsh investigation**

Dear Mr. Ray:

As you know, I am friend and counsel to John and Reve Walsh, the parents of the deceased in the referenced matter. We sincerely appreciate your meeting with us on January 30, 1996, and our subsequent opportunities to talk by telephone.

The purpose of our meeting was simple and straight forward: Mr. & Mrs. Walsh wanted to tell you personally of their concern and alarm that the actions of Chief Witt and the Hollywood Police Department in opening the investigative file concerning Adam's death would be the functional equivalent of closing the case - without there having been an adequate opportunity for your office to consider further investigation and/or prosecution. At that meeting, you agreed with us that there was further investigation to be done and that opening the file at this time could both irreparably harm further investigative efforts and curtail the possibility of a prosecution.

As an outgrowth of our meeting, we were given to understand that you would make the views of your office known to Judge Moe to prevent the gross miscarriage of justice that would result from the premature closure of the investigation through the opening of the files. As you know, the Fourth District Court of Appeal, in Riviera Beach vs. Barfield, 642 So. 2d 1135 (Fla. App. 4 Dist.1994), held that the underlying purpose of the exemption for certain criminal investigative information from the requirements of the Sunshine Act is to "prevent premature public disclosure of criminal investigative information since disclosure could impede an on-going investigation or allow a suspect to avoid apprehension or escape detection." In the en banc opinion in the Barfield case (639 So. 2d 1012), the Court referenced existing authority which establishes that: "There is no fixed time limit for naming suspects or making arrests other than the applicable statute of limitations" (at 639 So. 2d 1015). In addition, the Court also quoted, with emphasis, the following: "The fact that the investigators might not yet have decided upon a suspect does not necessarily imply that the investigation fails to meet the statutory requirements

ALEXANDRIA · BALTIMORE · BRUSSELS · CHARLOTTESVILLE · JACKSONVILLE · NORFOLK · RICHMOND · TYSONS CORNER · WASHINGTON, DC · ZÜRICH

Ralph J. Ray, Jr.
Feburary 2, 1996
Page 2

of good faith and anticipation of prosecution in the foreseeable future." (639 So. 2d 1015-16).
The Barfield court itself then stated:

> "This decision indicates the police, so long as they are acting in good faith,
> should be given substantial leeway in conducting an ongoing investigation even
> where there may be no immediate prospect of an arrest or prosecution." 639 So.
> 2d 1016.

After an extensive discussion of the history and rationale for the investigative exemption from
the Act, the Court rendered this significant and relevant holding:

> "Thus, we interpret the definition of active to mean that, even though there is no
> immediate anticipation of an arrest, so long as the investigation is proceeding in
> good faith and the State Attorney or grand jury will reach a determination in the
> foreseeable future, the requested information is not subject to disclosure. Put
> differently, we construe the phrase "anticipation of an arrest or prosecution" to
> mean that an arrest or prosecution may result, not that it must." (639 So 2d 1017)
> (emphasis in original).

As I know you agree, under this standard, disclosure of the investigative file in the Adam
Walsh matter is premature and not mandated by the requirements of the Sunshine Act as
interpreted by Florida's courts. The Police Department has told both your office and us that
there is a primary suspect in the case, more investigation to be done and other leads that may
require further investigation. We agree that it is incumbent upon your office to see that the
requirements of Florida law are met in criminal investigative matters within your jurisdiction.
We are only asking you to do the right thing for the right reasons. As Mr. Walsh so poignantly
told you personally, he fully understands that at some appropriate point, the entire investigative
file will be opened to public scrutiny and he has no fear of that event occurring - except that it
may occur prematurely to the irreparable detriment of the investigation into the murder of his
first born son.

Mr. and Mrs. Walsh, along with those supporting them, are doing everything they can
to make their views known and to prevent this unnecessary event from becoming one more sorry
aspect in the handling of the investigation of Adam's death.

Mr. and Mrs. Walsh have great faith in your office and your dedication to assuring that
those guilty of crimes do not escape punishment. We implore you in the strongest possible
terms to use all lawful tools at your disposal to preserve the integrity of this investigation and
the file that contains the results of investigation until such time as your office has had the
opportunity to fully review and consider the matter and take any further action that you deem
appropriate. John and Reve will provide whatever support they can to this effort. As we have

Ralph J. Ray, Jr.
Feburary 2, 1996
Page 3

discussed, if you believe a letter, affidavit or other involvement by the Walshes will aid your effort to pursue the investigation, we will provide it.

Please contact me if there is any further information needed or anything further that we can do to assist your office in this regard.

Sincerely yours,

George J. Terwilliger, III

cc: Mr. and Mrs. John Walsh

CHAPTER TEN
THE METER ROOM

Entrance to the meter room.
Photos taken by me in 2007.

Interior—trapdoor in the center leads to crawl space.

"That room is just a room."
_____Detective Joe Matthews_____

Adam Walsh was not Jeffrey Dahmer's only Florida murder. In April 2007, in a conversation with Art Harris, Ken Haupert, manager of the Sunshine Sub Shop, said about ten days after Dahmer started working, he had him take the garbage out to the dumpster around 5:30 p.m., just before Dahmer got off work. When Dahmer returned he told Ken in a very matter-of-fact, flat, unemotional tone, "By the way, Ken, you have a dead man by the dumpster." When Ken went out to check, sure enough, there was a man lying dead next to the dumpster. Ken called the police. That date was recorded on the police report as July 7, 1981 (twenty days before Adam's abduction). That would mean Dahmer had to have been hired around June 27, 1981, a month before Adam's abduction.

Art called me and asked me if I would pick up the police report at the Miami-Dade Metro Records Department. I couldn't help but point out the name on the report to the woman behind the counter, and she repeated it in an audible tone, "Jeffrey Dahmer?" At that, someone else in the lobby said, "Jeffrey Dahmer? Who said 'Jeffrey Dahmer'?" His was a well-known name that was etched in the psyche of almost everyone in Miami and across the U.S.

It was a three-page report. When I read it, the first thing I noticed was that everything in the police report was all about what "Mr. Jeffrey Dahmer" had said. According to Mr. Dahmer, the dead man went by the name of Bobby. When the police ran Bobby's fingerprints through the FBI Identification Division, they were able to get identification because Bobby had a history of ten arrests from Homestead to Miami, from 1972 to 1979, for loitering and prowling, trespassing, and disorderly intoxication. Several of the arrests listed his name as Robert Janda, which means Dahmer really did know him as Bobby. The actual name on the July 7 police report is Janda Bohumil. The police asked Ken who found the body. They then interviewed Jeffrey Dahmer.

The police report read, "According to Mr. Jeffrey Dahmer the victim was an old derelict living at the rear of his business in the meter room—the victim was always walking around on Collins Ave. and had been complaining of ill health lately. The victim was found by Mr. Dahmer face down . . ."

In 2007, I contacted Officer R. Nazario, who wrote that police report. He said he remembered that incident, but he couldn't recall Jeffrey Dahmer, who was just another of many witnesses he had interviewed over the years. He did remember the dead guy. "He was only sixteen inches high." Incredulous, I asked, sixteen inches? He replied, "Yeah, he was in the prone position. He was in full rigor mortis. The reason I remember him is because he was covered in ants."

No one knew who Jeffrey Dahmer was back then. As far as the police were concerned, he was just a witness, although he did elevate himself from busboy to cook on the police report and listed the sub shop as his home address. Maybe Dahmer was afraid the police would show up at his room at the Bimini Bay Motel and start poking around.

After a cursory examination, the medical examiner listed the cause of death as chronic ethanolism (chronic alcoholism), but later would question that finding. The probable manner of death was listed as natural, even though the police officer wrote on the report: *Rigor mortis: FULL—Body heat: COLD—Decomposition: SLIGHT*. What the medical examiner might have done was to just parrot the police report, which just parroted Dahmer.

According to Art Harris, Dahmer later confessed to his boss that he had been stepping over the body for three days to get to the dumpster, which would explain why the body was covered in ants and in full rigor mortis, a stiffening of the muscles that usually starts to take place at around three hours after someone is dead, with full rigor mortis occurring at about twelve hours after death.

I can only wonder why Ken never bothered to say anything about Dahmer stepping over this guy. There is no way Dahmer could've been stepping over the dead guy for three days next to the dumpster without someone noticing him. This confession lends credence to the theory that Bobby might have been murdered in the meter room. The alley behind the sub shop was a well-trafficked area, at least in the daytime. All the stores in that mall would have to take their garbage to that dumpster. Someone would've found Bobby before the ants.

It seemed that Dahmer knew the man well, so I wondered why he would tell his boss in such a matter-of-fact tone about a dead man near the dumpster as if he didn't. Art agreed that Dahmer could've murdered Bobby, but he insisted this was a dumpster feud over food scraps. It took me some time to convince him this was no dumpster feud. Dahmer had been employed for ten days, so he wouldn't have been dumpster diving any longer. After reading the police report, it became obvious: this was definitely a meter room feud. The smelly old derelict was even too much for Dahmer, so he was evicted—Jeffrey Dahmer-style. Now, twenty days before Adam's abduction, Dahmer had the meter room all to himself. The only thing he needed would be some company. This was also an example of how a murder could take place outside of a serial killer's so-called MO.

They say dead men don't talk. But this dead man talked a lot. From this police report, I found what I believe to be Adam's murder scene. Bobby would be Jeff's oldest suspected victim, at fifty-four, and Adam his youngest, at six. Both victims were murdered in that meter room. Steven Hicks, the Germany murders, and the meter room murders were Jeffrey Dahmer's introductory performances, a sort of prelude for what was to come in Milwaukee.

One fact that really stood out to me was that there was only one shoe on Bobby's body. The police found the other shoe in the meter room. Why was that important? I started thinking that maybe Dahmer murdered the derelict in the meter room and dragged him to the dumpster when he took the garbage out. So I went to look for myself.

The meter room was unlocked, and the door was ajar. After I looked around, the sudden goose bumps on my arms told me this was the place Dahmer had brought Adam. I had good reason to believe this. I knew without doubt that Dahmer was the guy I encountered in Radio Shack and followed to the Sears toy department. He had to be the one that abducted Adam. I just couldn't imagine earlier where he could've brought Adam. Now I knew! I needed help. I went home to get my camera and returned to take some photos.

Now retired, I went back to the old *Miami Herald* building downtown. Due to security changes, I couldn't get in the building. A reporter had to come down from the fifth-floor newsroom to speak to me in the lobby. Sergio Bustos said the *Miami Herald* wasn't interested in doing stories about Jeffrey Dahmer. "That's old news," he told me and was uninterested in anything I said or showed him, including the police report with Jeffrey Dahmer's name all over it.

I then went to the FBI again. Even after I told them how corrupt the Hollywood police were, they told me to go to the HPD with their usual song and dance routine: "This is a local case, and we don't get involved in local cases." I told Art Harris about my instinct. Art said I was "way off." It took me all of three days to convince him that this was the place Dahmer took Adam after the abduction. I even drove to Art's apartment and showed him the photos. Unbeknownst to me, Art then contacted ABC *Primetime* and presented this story as if he'd figured it out himself. After showing the police report to *Primetime*, Art described his discovery this way: "I'm tracking the path to Jeffrey Dahmer. And figurative doors are opening. And then a literal door opens: the door to that meter room. I'm thinking. . . this is where it happened." When *Primetime* went to the meter room to film a TV show, Art called me and asked me to stay away because "it would not look good if a witness was doing the investigating."

Primetime hired Jan Johnson, a well-known licensed pathologist (crime scene investigator) retired from the Florida Department of Law Enforcement (FDLE). With permission from the RK Village Plaza Mall manager, Daniel Katz, they removed piles of junk, revealing a trap door near the center of the room. PVC pipes, old toilets, and shopping carts filled with more junk were all removed. When they were done, Jan, who specializes in blood spatter patterns, went into the meter room. With a special blue light, she found blood spatter on a back wall that was trying to tell its own story. She said the pattern was "indicative of homicidal chopping." She even described how the homicide occurred. The high-velocity blood spatter, indicative of violence, was going in an upward pattern. "Something traumatic had to have happened down near the floor," she said. With a phenolphthalein field kit, she performed a presumptive blood test on a sample that tested positive for blood. She also took swabs of blood back to the lab for mitochondrial DNA testing, but the samples were too degraded to get a DNA profile. Also next to the spattered wall were a sledgehammer and an axe. Could one of those have been the murder weapon? According to Art Harris, small wads of duct tape were on the floor.

Although the management at RK Village Plaza had allowed ABC initial access to that room, they denied them further permission to do a more complete examination and take more blood samples from which, it was hoped, a DNA profile could still be made that might then be compared to hair samples of Adam's that were kept all these years by the Broward Medical Examiner's Office. That might have stopped ABC *Primetime*, but it did nothing to stop me.

Forensic science begins at the crime scene so after the blood spatter was found and described as being indicative of a homicide, I expected that room would be roped off with yellow crime scene tape and descended on by a cavalcade of homicide detectives and media trucks with satellite dishes lined up like planes at LaGuardia. It never happened. Even if that blood spatter wasn't Adam's, it is likely that someone died a traumatic death in that meter room. Also, the blood spatter hadn't belonged to that man Bobby, as he had no blood on him.

When the sun started rising while *Primetime* was filming, the mall manager requested that everyone leave. My guess was he didn't want clients and store patrons to see all the cameras and commotion, so he told *Primetime* to wrap it up, and his maintenance people put everything back. They might have moved the axe and sledge hammer, not realizing their possible significance. The next day, I managed to get back into the meter room, under the presumption that nothing I did was illegal unless I got caught. I took more photos and retrieved the sledgehammer and axe, which had been moved next to the entrance door.

In a conversation with Art, I told him that I had gone back to the meter room. Right away, Art asked me if I had taken the axe. When I didn't answer, he looked at me and said, "Willis, please. . . please tell me you didn't take the axe; let the police handle this." It took me a good three months before I admitted to him that I took the axe. I also explained to him that if I hadn't taken it, it would've been gone as someone had cleaned out that meter room. That at least kept him quiet and stopped him from being upset.

Over the years, Art has continually misread the HPD. He would go to them thinking they would really do a legitimate investigation. I have always been perplexed as well as angered by Art's naiveté about letting the "police handle this," but then I guess he had not been stonewalled like I had been.

One of the photos at the beginning of this chapter shows a trap door in the middle of the room. When I went down into the crawl space below, the first thing I noticed was how still, damp, and hot the air was. That was in the summer—the same time of year Adam would've been there—and it was so hot and humid that I could hardly breathe. Thinking Adam might have had his hands, feet, and mouth bound with duct tape, I wondered how long he could've survived in that crawl space!

I found a blanket spread out in there. Next to the blanket were two black thirty-two-gallon heavy-duty garbage bags with red drawstrings. In the folds of the blanket, I found a size thirty-four belt. In a conversation with Billy Joe Capshaw, I asked him what size belt Dahmer wore and he told me it was size thirty-four.

Although there is no way to know if this was Dahmer's belt, I do believe Dahmer was utilizing the meter room as well as the crawl space. I don't think anyone else would go down into that crawl space to sleep. It was too damp and dingy down there. And for sure, no one would have had a need for garbage bags in a crawl space. That is, unless someone wanted to get rid of something. Remember Steven Hicks? He was chopped up in the crawl space under his parents' house. In Milwaukee, Dahmer would also put chopped-up bodies in garbage bags and deposit them in the dumpster behind the Oxford Apartments building.

I realized Dahmer had to have put this blanket in the crawl space at the time Adam was abducted and left it there after Adam either succumbed to the crawl space or was killed by Dahmer. Then I wondered if Dahmer brought the blanket to the crawl space before kidnapping Adam. He had been trying to abduct a small child for at least two weeks, including on Sunday, July 26, 1981, the very day before Adam was abducted. You will read about this in witness Mia (Cockerham) Taylor's statement later on in this book. The blanket might have also come from the Bimini Bay Motel. I tried to put the thought of Dahmer hurriedly getting off work and going down into that crawl space to be with his newfound friend out of my mind. Adam wouldn't have survived more than a day or so.

Afterward, Dahmer might have taken his decapitated trophy back to his apartment at the Bimini Bay Motel, as suggested by Billy Joe Capshaw, and kept it in the refrigerator until early August, when he was apparently evicted for nonpayment of rent. Dahmer could've used the garbage bags to get rid of the body. The two bags I found might have been left over from this. It is even plausible that Dahmer put the bags with Adam's remains in the dumpster right outside the meter room. Alternatively, Dahmer might have gotten rid of Adam's remains on August 4, 1981, when two of the four turnpike witnesses saw him at that location (chapter fourteen).

He could've gone back to the turnpike location on August 7, when he was forced to get rid of his severed trophy, and was seen by the other two witnesses. Adam's severed head was found on August 10, 1981, at mile marker 130 off the Florida Turnpike. The only reason the HPD never found the rest of Adam's remains might be because they were being led around by the wrong suspect to all the wrong locations.

The meter room crime scene was located in Sunny Isles, Florida, so I decided to go to the Sunny Isles Police Department where I talked to one of the few nice detectives I have met. He listened to everything I had to say, but in the end, he told me their department was very small and they didn't have a homicide unit: "Even when we have a traffic fatality, we have to call Miami-Dade Metro." He then told me, "I'll tell you what I'm going to do for you; I'm going to get you an appointment with Miami Metro." He left the room to make a phone call.

When he returned, he asked me if I knew Art Harris. I knew enough not to say so, because Art wasn't well liked by the police for snooping into their files and making demands for records. They had portrayed him as someone only interested in writing a book. I responded by only saying that I knew of him. The detective left the room again, and when he returned for the second time, he told me, "Listen, Willis, I wasn't able to get you that appointment. But I can tell you one thing, you will never get any department in the state of Florida to step on the toes of another department."

The next day, I decided to call the Miami Metro homicide unit myself. I talked to their cold case detective in charge, Sergeant Charles "Buck" McCully. His response was, "What crime scene? There is no crime scene." I told him of Jan Johnson's description of the blood spatter. His response was to yell, "Jan Johnson! She is worthless! Do you hear me? Worthless!"

I asked him, "If she's so worthless, why is she the one that trains your police department?"

He answered with another question. "Did she tell you about the bird?"

"What bird?" I asked.

"You see, she didn't tell you about the bird. The bird flew into the wall," he hollered back. "I sent one of my best detectives over there, and he said the bird flew into the wall."

After McCully suggested a bird caused that entire blood spatter, I responded, "Well, he must not know what he's doing. That doesn't explain how the spatter pattern is described as being indicative of a homicide by Johnson unless that bird was murdered."

"Ed Carmody is one of my best detectives; he has twenty-eight years' experience. Besides, how do you know anything is left?" It was as if he was suggesting the crime scene was cleaned up.

That last sarcastic comment spoke volumes. It was the way he said it! I knew something was very wrong, and sure enough when I went back to the meter room I found it was now dead-bolted and had plywood screwed onto the inside of the door vent. I managed to get in, anyway. I was shocked but not at all surprised to see that someone had cleaned up the crime scene.

After looking closer, I noticed that the blood spatter was still on the back wall—it had been missed and I fortunately knew right where to look. It wasn't easy to see, especially since the lighting was so poor. The blanket was still in the crawl space. I assumed Miami Metro Police called the fire department to get it declared a fire hazard, be cleared of all junk and cleaned for inspection. Eventually, the door was replaced with a steel door and lock guard covering the deadbolt lock and they put up a security camera pointing right at the door. A photo of the new door can also be seen on my website at JusticeForAdam.com in the photo album.

I went back to conduct my own crime scene investigation (CSI)—not that I know anything about CSI, but someone had to do it. I retrieved the blanket and chipped some spatter patterns from the wall. The wall was a cement block structure (CBS) that was mortared. This made it easy to chip out samples.

I called Art to ask if he had seen a dead bird in the meter room. He said yes. "There was a small bird several inches long." All that blood from a little Tweety bird? Sorry, I couldn't buy that and besides, as Art emphasized, the bird had no blood on it. It was also located on the opposite side of the room from the blood-spattered wall. The idea that a small bird could have caused a high velocity-impact blood spatter pattern was ridiculous. I propose that Detective McCully knew that. The most the HPD was willing to do was to suggest two pit bulls could have been fighting in that room.

I called several labs to inquire about the collection process. I first sent twenty blood specimen samples to Orchid Cellmark Lab in Dallas, Texas. When they came up with nothing, I started thinking that most of these labs do a lot of work for police departments so maybe they didn't want to find anything. I'm not saying that was so, but I couldn't help but think that. I then hand-delivered the unused returned samples plus additional samples I collected to DNA Labs International Inc. in Deerfield Beach, Florida. When I walked into the lobby, the first thing I noticed was all the recognition plaques on the walls from police departments all over the country. This time, I made up a case. I kept only the relevant information the same, such as the victim's age, the age of the samples, and the environmental condition the samples were found in. I replaced Adam's name with "victim." For the case history, I made up a story. I even changed the location, far away from Hollywood and Sunny Isles, Florida.

Yet, it would be all for nothing. I even drove to the lab to talk to them in person, and I believed the good doctor when she told me she really did her best. I knew I wouldn't get any help from Dr. Joshua Perper at the Broward County Medical Examiner's Office, so I had another plan. If I could've gotten a DNA profile from the meter room blood specimen collection, I was prepared to get some public domain garbage from Reve Walsh's Vero Beach home when it was put out for curbside pickup. But my first plan would have been to contact Reve and ask for her assistance. However, without a DNA profile from the meter room, that never came to fruition.

I spent hundreds of dollars trying to get a sequence analysis of mitochondrial and nuclear DNA from the evidence samples, but to no avail. Time and humidity had degraded the blood specimens, and the lime in the mortared wall had done the rest.

Decades Later, New Clues in a Cold Case
Could Jeffrey Dahmer Be to Blame for Adam Walsh's Murder?

The ABC *Primetime* show aired on August 13, 2007
ABC *PRIMETIME* CAST

PHOTO LEFT TO RIGHT: Me and Bill Bowen and ABC *Primetime* producer Geoff Martz and true-crime writer Art Harris.
Photo taken with my camera in 2007

The *Primetime* show aired regarding the meter room behind the sub shop where Jeffrey Dahmer worked. Geoff Martz was the producer of that show, and Chris Cuomo was the narrator. They stayed at the Diplomat Hotel in Hollywood, Florida, on the 34th floor. When they filmed the show, I realized why Art Harris didn't want me there. As I said, the meter room was presented as if Art had figured this out by himself, and it was my feeling that he didn't want to share the credit with anyone.

I was told this was to be a one-hour episode. They tried to contact John Walsh, but John declined to talk to them and referred them to his "longtime friend" Joe Matthews. Joe did everything he could to get *Primetime* to cancel the show. He told them he had new evidence proving that it was Ottis Toole, and he would reveal that proof on an upcoming episode of *America's Most Wanted* "this fall" in 2007. He even told producer Geoff Martz that he would make a fool of himself if he went ahead with the show.

I believe Matthews succeeded in getting *Primetime* to water down their show. The segment on Adam Walsh went from one hour to about twenty minutes, and Matthews even managed to get a platform for a short speech on the show explaining to Cuomo that it was Toole who murdered Adam. When asked about the meter room, Matthews responded that he was not buying the Dahmer theory. "That room is just a room. What if . . .? That's your whole theory? Everything is based on what if this, what if that. You can't investigate a case based on what-ifs." The episode of *America's Most Wanted* that Matthews was talking about never did air.

Only when I read Matthews's book *Bringing Adam Home* would I learn what Matthews's smoking gun was. Although all the Toole evidence in the HPD evidence room mysteriously disappeared, Matthews was somehow able to find an undeveloped negative roll of 35 mm film from the FDLE. One image was that of a piece of carpet from Toole's white Cadillac. When Matthews looked at it, he was astonished to see "the outline of a familiar young boy's face, a negative, pressed into floorboard carpeting . . ." (*Bringing Adam Home*, p. 273). Also see the FDLE photos on pp. 302 and 303 of this book as well as at JusticeForAdam.com.

Matthews claimed he even purchased carpet samples and mannequin heads. He rushed home and spent the next several weeks trying to duplicate the image that he compared to the Shroud of Turin, yet he never revealed the end result of that test. In another negative, Matthews saw an image of a pair of shoe prints "firmly planted on the driver's floorboards. . . At long last, here was physical evidence tying Ottis Toole to the crime" (*Bringing Adam Home,* p. 255). Matthews put himself in good company: this was something former Los Angeles chief medical examiner Thomas Noguchi ("Coroner to the Stars," who inspired the 1976-1983 TV series *Quincy*) would've done. Only, Matthews was no Noguchi.

Ironically, a week later, Art Harris and I were on a local clear channel communications radio show called *The Footy Show* on News Radio 610 WIOD Miami. We talked about the case, the police report, and the meter room, and then *Footy* started taking calls from the public. Joe Matthews somehow managed to be the very first caller. He told *Footy*, on air, that he was one of the original detectives on the Adam Walsh case, and there was no validity to anything I was saying. He then went on to say that he was going to reveal the smoking gun, proving it was Ottis Toole that abducted Adam Walsh, in an upcoming show on *America's Most Wanted. Footy* asked Matthews if he wanted to talk to me directly, but Matthews refused. *Footy* immediately went to a break and told me the segment was over. I never did get to take any calls, and I never had a chance to refute anything Matthews said.

There Is a Crime Scene (But No One Seems to Care)

The best of the *Primetime* interviews was with Captain Mark Smith. When Detective Smith was shown Bobby's July 7, 1981, police report, Smith admitted he had never seen it before: "That's ironic, but it means nothing. It only adds intrigue." Smith asserted, "Bottom line, Dahmer already said he didn't do it."

Saddled with the Herculean task of deflecting the investigation away from Jeffrey Dahmer, Smith then questioned the importance of the blue van sightings, telling Chris Cuomo that a family had come forward to say it was them having an altercation in the parking lot. However, Smith couldn't recall who that family was, nor could he provide any records or paperwork of this family. There was nothing about this family altercation in the seven-thousand-plus-page case file.

Primetime then contacted retired detective Jack Hoffman, the original lead detective in the Adam Walsh case, and asked him if he knew of any family having an altercation in the parking lot. Jack Hoffman was unable to recall the existence of this family and then declined further comment.

Another Call to Sergeant McCully

In April 2011, I decided to call Sergeant McCully back to find out if he had ever made out a police report for that meter room. At first, he didn't remember me, but when I explained who I was, he remembered both me and the meter room. When I asked him if he had made out a report, he said no. I reminded him that he had sent Detective Ed Carmody over there and asked if Detective Carmody had made out a report.

"Why do you need it?" he asked.

"It should be a public record, and I would like to read it," I explained.

"Listen, Sport . . . "

I had to correct him that my name was Willis. "I don't call you by any name other than your given name, and I would appreciate it if you would do the same, sir."

He said, "This is an open homicide, and that report is not available."

"In 2007, you told me this *wasn't* a homicide," I reminded him. "Which is it, homicide or not a homicide?"

"OK, if that report is available, I'll get back to you," he said.

By this time I was pretty sick and tired of detectives getting away with mistreating members of the public and giving us the runaround when it suited them. I wasn't going to sit by my phone and wait for that call. As expected, Sergeant McCully never called me back.

Claudia Reigada at Miami-Dade records did a record search, but without a case number or much information to go on, she could only search by Ed Carmody's name. She came up with only three homicide reports that were made by him for 2007, none of them related to the meter room.

After I told Art Harris about this non-report, he also sent the following e-mail to Sergeant McCully:

From: Arthur Jay Harris
To: ///////////@mdpd.com
Subject: 2007 incident in meter room behind 170/Collins
Date: Mon, 4 Apr 2011 15:17:16 -0400

Sgt. McCully,

I spoke this morning with Willis Morgan, who said he'd just talked with you. He asked if Det. Ed Carmody had ever written a police report around June 2007 about the blood in the meter room in the 170th Street shopping center on Collins Avenue, which ABC News and I had discovered and spoken to you about at the time. Willis said you told him that Carmody had written a report but it would not be available to him because it was an unsolved homicide case.

Is that correct, that your department considers this incident as an unsolved homicide? If so, I did not know that.

And if so, with the understanding that the case file would not be a public record at this time, could you at least give me a case file number and any other releasable acknowledged facts about it?

I spoke this afternoon with Claudia Reigada of your department, who searched homicide records by computer log but could not find any such report of an incident that was written by Det. Carmody in either 2007 or 2008. She suggested I ask you directly, and supplied me with your email address.

Thank you, Art Harris

2015: Art is still waiting for an answer.

The medical examiner's report for Bobby:

Metropolitan Dade County
OFFICE OF THE MEDICAL EXAMINER
1050 N.W. 19th Street
Miami, Florida 33136

CASE NO. 81-1976 A

Jaida Bohumil   DOB 12/3/25

NAME OF DECEASED -Unknown-Remains-   AGE 55   RACE White   SEX Male

ADDRESS L/K.A - 1970 - 250 NW 187 St., Rural, Dade. Fla.

PLACE OF DEATH Rear Parking Lot :
17040 Collins Ave., Rural, Dade, Fla.

TIME AND DATE DEATH:
FOUND 6:00PM 7/7/81
OCCURRED _____ MED. INVESTIGATOR _____
PRONOUNCED _____

INVESTIGATING AGENCY (PSD # 230242-B)   POLICE INVESTIGATOR Det. R. Nazario
jeb

HISTORY According to initial police investigation, the deceased was a known derelict in the area and most of the time, he lived in an old meter room in the rear of a business. He was always seen walking around on Collins Ave. and had been complaining lately of ill health. This date, he was found lying face down in the gravel directly south of the meter room, expired. He was only known as " Bobby " .

POSITIVE I-D was made by fingerprints.

PRIMARY CAUSE OF DEATH Chronic ethanolism

DUE TO: _____

DUE TO: _____

CONT. CAUSE OF DEATH _____

TOXICOLOGICAL FINDINGS _____

PROBABLE MANNER OF DEATH Natural   ONSET OF TERMINAL EVENT Parking Lot

AUTOPSY / EXAMINED 7/8/81   BY Charles V. Wetli, M.D.
(DATE)

FUNERAL DIRECTOR Fla. Mort.

REMOVED BY _____ DATE _____ TIME _____

(OVER)

This is the police report from July 7, 1981.

PUBLIC SAFETY DEPT. DADE COUNTY, FLORIDA — NATURAL DEATH INVESTIGATION CONTINUATION/SUPPLEMENTARY

ME 7'P - RP   11421 — 63   CASE NO. 2302428

VICTIM'S NAME: Bothumil [deceased] JANDA   AGE 55   SEX M   RACE W   ADDRESS TRANSIENT   RES. PHONE UNK   SOC. SEC. NO. 127-28-7652

OCCUPATION: COOK   EMPLOYER: N/A   VEHICLE (MAKE, YEAR, LIC. TAG): N/A   VEH. STORED AT: N/A

PLACE OF DEATH: 12040 Collins Ave   DEATH OCCURRED: UNKNOWN   IN THE PRESENCE OF (ADDRESS): N/A

FOUND DEAD (DATE & TIME): 7-7-81 6P   BY WHOM (ADDRESS): Jeffrey Dahmer 17040 A. Collins Ave   IDENTIFIED BY (ADDRESS): Fingerprints ID 133803

DATE & TIME VIEWED: 7-7-81 7:35P   TYPE OF PREMISES: Rear Parking Lot & Driveway   WEATHER CONDITION: Hot   ADDRESS OF OCCURRENCE: 12040 Collins Ave

HISTORY (WHAT HAPPENED PRIOR TO DEATH):
According to Mr. Jeffrey Dahmer the victim was an old derelict living at the rear of his business in the meter room. The victim was always seen walking around on Collins Ave and had been complaining of ill health. The victim was discovered by Mr. Dahmer face down directly south of the meter room on the gravel. The victim was known "Bobby" possibly Tanosky (phonetic).

CLOTHING WORN: Reddish Tank Shirt & Grn Work Pants   White/Grn Female Shoes

POSITION OF BODY: Prone N/S Axis Head South   with an elec. cord as belt directly behind

LIVIDITY: ☐ YES ☒ NO ☒ CONSISTENT   RIGOR MORTIS: FULL   BODY HEAT: COLD   DECOMPOSITION: SLIGHT   12040 Collins Ave Munchkins

TRANSPORTED BY: N/A   DR. WHO ATTENDED: N/A   TRAUMA: N/A   MEDICATION TAKEN PRIOR TO DEATH: N/A   INFORMATION US from Grover

HOSPITAL TAKEN TO: N/A

MEDICAL HISTORY: UNK

NEXT OF KIN: Deceased UNK   RELATION: Mother and Father   PHONE NO. / ADDRESS: NOTIFIED (DATE & TIME): N/A

M.E. WHO INDUCTED AUTOPSY (DATE): Dr. C. Wetli 7-7-81   RESULTS: CHRONIC ETHANOLISM

PROPERTY DISPOSITION: NONE HANDLED

REPORTING OFFICER'S NAME: R. NAZARIO   RADIO NO. 620   BADGE NO. 1414   DISTRICT: NE   GRID: 245

DISPATCHED BY, DATE & TIME: Lt. Werner 7-7-81 6:30P
PREPARED BY (SIGN): Richard Mena
APPROVED BY, DATE:

PUBLIC SAFETY DEPT.
DADE COUNTY, FLORIDA - CONTINUATION

Page	Type of Report, Continued	Offense - Incident	Victim Name	☐ Missing Person ☐ Runaway	Case No.
212	OI	DECEASED PERSON	☒ UNKNOWN		23-0242-13

Remarks Continued:

ON THE ABOVE DATE & TIMES, THIS UNIT WAS DISPATCHED TO
THE ABOVE ADDRESS OF OCCURRENCE, UPON ARRIVAL, THIS UNIT MET WITH
ABOVE REPORTER/DISCOVERER WHO ADVISED THIS UNIT OF THE FOLLOWING.
ON THIS DATE AT APPROX. 605PM, REPORTER WAS AT THE REAR OF
THE ADDRESS OF OCCURRENCE DUMPING TRASH. AS REPORTER STOOD AT THE
REAR OF THE BLDG, REPORTER OBSERVED THE BODY OF A WHITE MALE
LYING ON THE GROUND OUTSIDE THE METER ROOM WHICH IS LOCATED ON
THE SOUTH SIDE OF THE BLDG. POLICE WERE NOTIFIED AT THIS TIME.
AS THIS UNIT ARRIVED, THIS UNIT OBSERVED THAT VICTIM (NAME UNKNOWN)
WAS APPARENTLY DECEASED AS RIGOR MORTIS HAD ALREADY SET IN. AT
THIS POINT, THIS UNIT NOTIFIED D.B. SHIFT COMMANDER AND SECURED
SCENE. VICTIM APPEARS TO BE A DERELICT WHO HAS BEEN LIVING IN
THE ABOVE MENTIONED METER ROOM. PERSONAL EFFECTS INCLUDING A BLUE
TRACK SHOE WHICH MATCHES THE ONE THAT VICTIM WAS WEARING WERE
LOCATED INSIDE METER ROOM. HOMICIDE DETECTIVE NAZARIO (UNIT #620)
RESPONDED TO THE SCENE. SGT GOODMAN WAS ADVISED OF INCIDENT,
BLUE COPIES TO UNIT #620

Reporting Officer's Name (Print)	Badge No.	District	Grid
SANTILLIPS PJ	2123	6	542

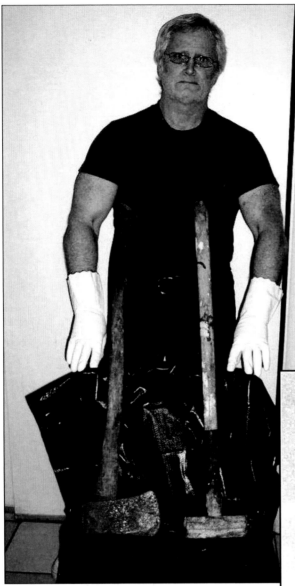

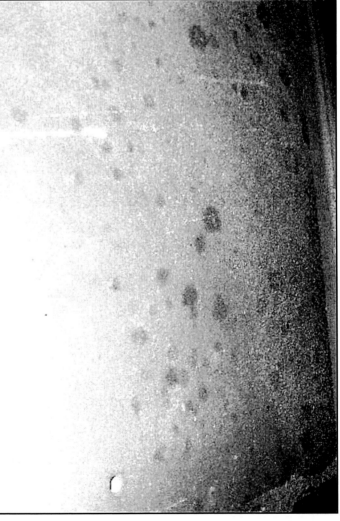

PHOTO LEFT: These are what I believe to be possible murder weapons that were found in the meter room next to the wall with the blood spatter. The axe blade is 4-3/8" wide. Photos by me in 2007.

What makes the axe a plausible murder weapon is that it was found next to the spattered wall. The cast-off blood spatter was in a high-velocity pattern indicative of a chopping motion on the floor.

PHOTO RIGHT: The blood spatter that was found on the back wall of the meter room.

The trapdoor after the meter room was cleaned. The cardboard box, tool box, and plastic bags are mine.
Photos taken by me in 2007

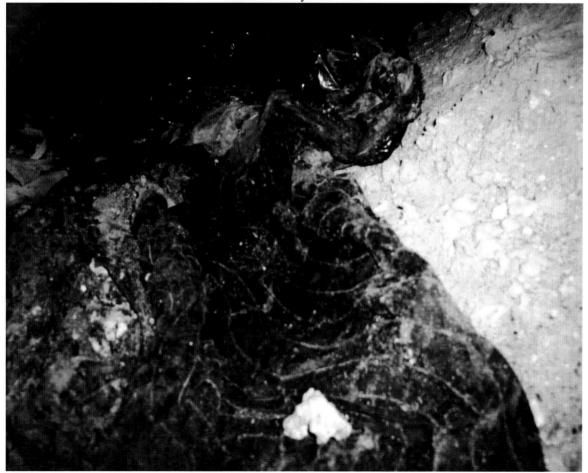

The crawl space under the trapdoor: this is where I believe Adam spent his last days. The black garbage bags at the top might have been left over from when Dahmer disposed of Adam's remains. One side of the blanket is burgundy in color, and the other side is gray. NOTE: The color photos can be seen at JusticeForAdam.com

Bottom: What could be Jeffrey Dahmer's belt with an oxidized buckle found in the folds of the blanket. This photo was taken in 2007 before I gave it to Jan Johnson.

PHOTO ABOVE: The alley behind the sub shop. Photo by me in 2007. Dahmer was found eating out of a smaller version of this dumpster, although the pod is the same. The asphalt was gravel in 1981. Bobby, the derelict, was found on the far side of the dumpster. The meter room is to the right, under the stairwell.

PHOTO ABOVE: Door 17040, behind the dumpster, was the back door to Sunshine Subs. Photo by me in 2007.

CHAPTER ELEVEN
ART HARRIS
AND THE PROZAC KID

PHOTO RIGHT: True crime writer Art Harris
Photo by me in 2007

Over the years, my relationship with Art Harris would become more and more strained. When I first met Art, I told him about the composite I saw in the *Miami Herald* several weeks after Adam's abduction. I explained to him that whoever gave that composite had seen the same guy I saw. Art asked me not to ever tell anyone about that composite: "They found that person. It was the owner of a store chasing a shoplifter. . . You will make a fool of yourself." So I never said anything, not because I believed what Art said but because I just didn't want to make things more confusing.

After the Adam Walsh case was closed on December 16, 2008, when I got my own copy of the case files, I realized right away that it was no store owner. A supplementary report by Detective Jack Hoffman said it was a security guard. But it wasn't a security guard, either. I contacted the witnesses that gave that composite. It came from another mall, sixty miles north of the Hollywood Mall, in the toy department of another Sears, on another Monday, July 13, 1981, just two weeks before Adam's abduction. And the witnesses at that mall said it was no security guard.

When I asked Art where he got his information about that composite being a store owner or security guard, he told me it was from Hoffman. Art's ability to think critically has consistently been inadequate, because I have told him so many times not to trust the HPD. It's the one place you never want to get your information from. Art then told me it was really the Fort Lauderdale

Sun-Sentinel. That made me even angrier. The *Sun-Sentinel* just parroted what the HPD said. I then told him about the witnesses I had found from the Twin City Mall. I gave him their phone numbers, and he called them. Then he went to the media again as if he'd discovered this all by himself. Articles in the papers would never credit me. They gave Art all the credit and would refer to me only as one of Art's witnesses.

One day, when I asked Art why he was taking all the credit, his response was, "I get my information from all sources." It was one thing to get your information from "all sources," but Art was taking credit for things he wasn't able to figure out, which was deceptive.

In the meantime, I also discovered two truck drivers who had witnessed the blue van at the location where Adam's severed head was found. I wanted to keep this to myself and not let anyone know. However, Art called me one day extremely excited. He told me he was keeping information from me because he wasn't sure what my reaction would be. Then he told me, "I found Adam. He's alive!" I immediately thought he'd lost all touch with reality. I then told him about the two truck drivers in an attempt to bring him back to the real world but I held back from giving him their phone numbers. I would only give their phone numbers to David Smiley of the *Miami Herald* who was doing an investigation into the case that ran on Sunday, March 28, 2010. The headline was:

MURDER REVISITED

WHO REALLY KILLED ADAM WALSH?
MAYBE IT WAS OTTIS TOOLE,
AS POLICE SAY. BUT MORE SIGNS SEEM TO
POINT TO JEFFREY DAHMER
BY DAVID SMILEY AND ARTHUR JAY HARRIS

When John South of the *National Enquirer* wrote a two-page article for the April 19, 2010, edition, I wasn't mentioned. I knew I wouldn't be because of what I had told Dave Smiley. I asked Dave if Art had told him about the kid Art had found (and who, apparently, was on Prozac). Dave told me yes. Dave and Art, I believe, might have formed a friendship and coauthored the *Herald* article, and I think Dave could've told Art some negative things I had said about him. I'm not sure exactly what transpired, but it was right after my conversation with Dave that Art called and told me I had been minimized in the *Herald* article, and then he added with a hint of sarcasm, "And you have been eliminated from the *National Enquirer* article."

However, my main goal was to get Dave not to print anything about the guy I dubbed the Prozac Kid, since he'd refused to come forward and publicly announce himself. And I didn't call him "kid" on the basis of his chronological years but on his immaturity. Obviously, he would say his age was the same as Adam's would be.

When Art first told me about the Prozac Kid, I told him to ask that kid why he had called a true crime writer and not the FBI. Art then asked me to look at the eyes and the cheeks of photos the kid had sent him and said, "He has Adam's eyes." At that point I reminded Art about the severed head that was found.

Also, I asked Art to ask this kid questions that weren't common knowledge and might not have been in the papers, such as where Reve stopped before going to the Sears Mall (St. Mark's

Lutheran Church to pay Adam's $90 tuition). Art did and got back to me. This kid said what I thought he might, that he was too young to remember.

I did my best to get Art not to tell the story about this kid on Prozac to anyone. I was too late. Art had already told Jan Johnson. Art even sent her pubic hairs that he'd had the Prozac Kid send him to be tested. He never did get a DNA match, but that wouldn't stop him from believing in the kid who explained the failure of his DNA matching Reve's on the torture Dahmer had inflicted.

Art wanted me to talk to this guy myself, on a conference call, so that I would become a believer. I thought this was a good idea, so I told Art, "Let me have just five minutes with him, and I'll expose him for what he is," After that Art changed his mind. I don't know why, but I guess he was afraid I would scare the kid off. Anyway, the kid's story got so bizarre that I have a hard time telling it. I have an even harder time understanding how anyone could believe such nonsense.

According to Art, this kid was kidnapped by Jeffrey Dahmer, who then took him to a house in North Miami where Ottis Toole was keeping watch over other kidnapped kids between the ages of four to seven. The Prozac Kid also said he'd seen Ted Bundy at this house, even though Bundy was already on death row in Florida. Ottis Toole held him until he could be sold. They both took turns watching the kids. If this were true, someone like Toole would've mentioned Dahmer as his accomplice in at least one of his confessions. Toole didn't, because in 1983, when Toole confessed, just like the rest of us, he'd never heard of Jeffrey Dahmer.

The kid said that one day Dahmer and Toole took a head from one of the buckets filled with heads that they kept on ice at this house and threw it into that canal off the Florida Turnpike at mile marker 130. It was supposed to mislead the police, who would think it was Adam and call off the search.

The story went on from there. I wouldn't mention this guy's name even if I knew it. For all the mental problems this kid might have, some of this story could be nothing more than a sick, deplorable prank he pulled on Art Harris. The *Globe* ran the story on April 19, 2010, with lots of photos and a front-page header:

NEW BOMBSHELL EVIDENCE
JOHN WALSH—KIDNAP SON ALIVE!
Just like Jaycee Dugard

Afterward, Art denied he had anything to do with that article and didn't write it. Too late, though—the *Globe* even credited him for it—although it didn't really matter who actually wrote the article because he told the *Globe*, "It all points to the possibility Adam could still be alive." Art's 'Adam' must have been on the floor doubled over with laughter when his story got into the tabloids.

If this was meant to give the Walshes hope, that was despicable. If it was for a quick buck or just a chance to get in the tabloids, that would be shameful.

As for senior reporter Jordan Rodack of the *Globe*, I met him in 2007 when the police report with Dahmer's name on it was discovered. When I tried to get Rodack to do an article, he told me he wouldn't do anything without Art. Using questionable sources like Art Harris and printing ridiculous stories as if they are facts are two of the reasons tabloids have so little credibility.

Even Joe Matthews would mock that *Globe* article, and it became fodder for his book *Bringing Adam Home*. Matthews said, "The article theorized that Adam Walsh was still alive somewhere, even providing a computer-generated rendition of what he would look like as an adult so that readers could keep an eye out for him." For a change, Matthews was right. That *Globe* article was abhorrent. Yet when the *National Examiner* did a legitimate story about the Adam Walsh case, it went pretty much ignored. Back in its February 26, 2007, edition, this was the header:

ADAM WALSH MURDER SOLVED!
Jeffrey Dahmer did it—new claim

Witnesses link crazed cannibal killer to little boy's murder
(referring to Bill Bowen and myself)

In 2003, the Bode Technology Group Inc. did a mitochondrial DNA test, testing several teeth from the mandible of the severed head against swabs submitted by Reve Walsh. The result was consistent with a maternal match for Reve. The head belonged to Adam. Their four-page report can be read at the end of this chapter and is also located in the SAO case files at JusticeForAdam.com (box 1, file 23, pp. 75-78).

On March 10, 2011, I was granted access by Lieutenant Scott Pardon of the Hollywood police records department to look at the case files. I'd seen the photos of Adam from the location where his severed head was found. One full-color, eight-by-ten-inch photo of Adam's severed head on a white towel, after it had been cleaned up, left me with no doubt that lamentably Adam was dead. Forget about DNA and dental records; there is no question that it was Adam Walsh. Beyond a doubt, it looked exactly like him with his eyes closed.

By the way, that eight-by-ten photo in itself should have been enough to eliminate Ottis Toole as a suspect because the record states that Toole went back to Jacksonville the same day he abducted Adam, whereas with so little decomposition that head could not have been in the water for two weeks. Of course, the truth was that Toole was in Jacksonville the entire time.

Lieutenant Pardon, while observing me, made a comment revealing his abilities as a homicide detective. He said he had already read all the files but "couldn't make heads or tails of them."

In June of 2013, Art called me and apologized for not keeping me updated on his ongoing investigation into Adam's abduction. He then told me that his new book, proclaiming that Adam was alive, was now in paperback. Art said he hadn't wanted to say anything about it until now because he was aware of my strong objection to his conclusion.

Jeffrey Dahmer's Dirty Secret —Book Two: Finding the Victim

Adam was still alive, and the body identified as Adam Walsh was not him, claimed Art Harris. The following is an excerpt from Art's book:

A FRIEND REQUEST ON FACEBOOK

"I THOUGHT YOU MIGHT BE INTERESTED to know that J. Dahmer did kidnap me . . . I have to give you credence outright for laying most of the blame on the man behind my own abduction."

It was signed, "Sincerely, Adam J. Walsh."

For a week, I listened to the story of the man who said he was Adam Walsh.

So much of everything else in the story had turned out contrary to what the police, and the Walshes, had insisted upon. How could I dismiss this, just on its face?

The man said Dahmer had kept him for possibly a month. He let him hear the news about the discovery of Adam, dead. After that, Dahmer tortured him horribly and left him near-dead himself. Unconscious, he had been rescued but didn't know the details. Another family took him in and raised him with their surname.

The man did not sound like he was pranking me. He was clearly sincere. The question was, was he self-deluded? Could I possibly verify anything he had and would continue to tell me? It seemed impossible. The easy response would have been a quick dismissive one, had I chosen it . . .

On July 2, 2013, Art called me again to tell me that the *Globe* was doing another story about his theory of Adam being alive. Their front page on July 15, 2013 read:

Author's bombshell claim:
JOHN WALSH'S KIDNAPPED SON IS ALIVE!

The inside story had a double-page header that read:

Investigator's SHOCKING claim 32 years after abduction that HORRIFIED America:
ADAM WALSH IS ALIVE
— AND I'VE MET HIM!

The article included a large photo of Art Harris, of course, along with the cover of his new book. In his greed to sell his book, he might've become an opportunist at the price of hurting the Walsh family (and himself). His new book was filled with unfounded, gruesome details that the *Globe* article alluded to, such as the claim that Jeffrey Dahmer and Ottis Toole together had planned to "sell the children on 'the flesh market,' for slaves, prostitutes and for their organs."

Art claimed the house where Ottis and Dahmer kept the children was eventually raided by a so-called SWAT team, and all the kids were rescued. He also said the Prozac Kid, who thought he was Adam, was now living as an adult in South Florida with a Latin accent that he'd got from the family that took him in. Harris admitted there were no news reports of the raid, and 'Adam' was unconscious at the time of rescue and didn't remember any details. To this day, Harris thinks the Prozac Kid is Adam.

I don't know when it was that the Prozac Kid first contacted Art Harris, but I received a call from someone I'm sure was the same caller that pranked Harris. This caller told me he was at the mall the day Adam was abducted. In the story he told me, he claimed he was abducted by Ottis Toole in his white Cadillac but managed to escape by jumping out of the car as they headed for Hollywood Boulevard. He then ran back to the mall, and Jeffrey Dahmer offered to help him. When he climbed into the blue van, he saw a young boy in the back seat that he later knew to be Adam. They then went to the mall across the street from the Hollywood Mall and went down the alley to the meter room.

Nice try. It was obvious this caller had done his homework, although not nearly well enough. He knew my phone number, my e-mail address, and a lot about the case, but the mall he was referring to was more than eight miles away, not across the street. When I suggested that he call Art Harris, he quietly hung up and never called again.

After that conversation, I did get the following e-mail from this caller that could have been the same person who contacted Art Harris. Even if this isn't the same person (and most likely is not), it just goes to show there are plenty of people out there with an unstable personality disorder that are willing to spoof someone by using some of the same cold reading techniques psychics and fortunetellers use.

From: William_____ *(last name redacted)*
Sent: Friday, December 03, 2010 2:45 PM
To: /////////@////.com
Subject: 1981

Willis,

Thanks for listening the other day (and not calling the men in the white coats on me. he he). I know I talked your ear off and I know what I spoke of had to sound absurd (but it was true; at least I believe it is true). If you ever need to talk, I will return the favor and listen to you.

I have considered your suggestion that I take a polygraph or something and record events. Still on the fence about that, not because of the cost, but because I sort of want to fade back into anonymity; I would like to just bury all these memories and forget them. But then that might be selfish of me.

I don't know. I'm going to put things aside for now, think about it later.

Thanks, *Bill*

The Bode Technology Group, Inc.
7364 Steel Mill Dr.
Springfield, VA. 22150
Phone 703-644-1200

Mitochondrial DNA Case Report
August 7, 2003

To:

Dr. George Duncan
Broward County Sheriff's Office
201 SE 6th Street, Room 1799
Ft. Lauderdale, FL 33301

TBTG Case #: 2M03-074
Agency Case #: Hollywood PD
81-56073

List of Evidence received on March 27, 2003:

TBTG #	Agency ID	Description
2M03-074-01	1F97	Labeled as "Mandible with 11 teeth – mandible broken in (3) pieces from Adam Walsh"

List of Evidence received on July 25, 2003:

TBTG #	Agency ID	Description
2M03-074-02	81-56073	Labeled as "Oral swabs of Reve Walsh"

ANALYSIS AND RESULTS:

Two teeth from evidence item 2M03-074-01 were processed for mitochondrial DNA (mtDNA) typing. Reference item 2M03-074-02 was also processed for mtDNA typing.

MtDNA is found in subcellular organelles called mitochondria. A specific, noncoding region of the mitochondrial genome called the D-loop is known to have variability within the human population, particularly in two segments of the D-loop that are called Hypervariable Regions 1 and 2. Multiple copies of this region of mtDNA are generated using the polymerase chain reaction (PCR). The base composition, or sequence, is then determined using automated DNA sequencing.

The mtDNA profile obtained for evidence item 2M03-074-01 was compared to the corresponding mtDNA profile obtained for reference item 2M03-074-02.

TBTG Case #: 2M03-074   August 7, 2003

The mtDNA profile of evidence item 2M03-074-01 matches the mtDNA profile of reference item 2M03-074-02.

The DNA profiles reported in this case were determined by procedures that have been validated according to standards established by the Scientific Working Group on DNA Analysis Methods (SWGDAM) and adopted as Federal Standards.

See **Table 1** for a summary of mtDNA profiles reported for each sample.

CONCLUSION:

Based on the mtDNA results, the individual associated with evidence item 2M03-074-01 is consistent with being a maternal relative (e.g. a son) of Reve Walsh (2M03-074-02). These results support the identification of these remains as Adam Walsh.

The mtDNA population database of the Scientific Working Group on DNA Analysis Methods (SWGDAM) has been searched for the mtDNA sequences obtained from evidence item 2M03-074-01 and known reference of Reve Walsh (2M03-074-02). The number of observations of these mtDNA sequences in the SWGDAM database are as follows:

TBTG Sample No.	African Database	Caucasian Database	Hispanic Database	Asian Database	Native American Database	Total No. of Observations in combined Population SWGDAM Database
2M03-074-01	0 in 1305	0 in 1674	0 in 686	0 in 848	0 in 326	0 in 4839
2M03-074-02	0 in 1305	0 in 1674	0 in 686	0 in 848	0 in 326	0 in 4839

The remaining evidence for this case will be returned to the Hollywood, Florida Police Department.

Report is submitted by:

Faith Love Patterson, MSFS
DNA Analyst 2

Shelley Johnson, MFS
Senior Forensic DNA Analyst

Charity A. Holland, MPH
Forensic Technical Leader

Mitchell M. Holland, PhD
Senior Vice President, Laboratory Director

Page 2 of 4

000448

TBTG Case #: 2M03-074   August 7, 2003

Table 1: Summary of Mitochondrial DNA Results

TBTG Sample #	Hypervariable Region I	Hypervariable Region II
01 Teeth from Mandible	*Confirmed Region: 15998-16390* *16209 C*	*Confirmed Region: 35-361* *263 G* *315.1 C*
02 Reve Walsh	*Confirmed Region: 16009-16390* *16209 C*	*Confirmed Region:35-361* *263 G* *315.1 C*

TBTG Case #: 2M03-074

August 7, 2003

INTERPRETATION KEY

The following notations may apply:

a. Transition or transversion polymorphisms as compared to a standard sequence (Anderson, et al. 1981. *Nature* 290:457-465) are designated by the appropriate letter (base).

b. A deletion is designated by a "D."

c. An insertion is designated a ".1" for a one base insertion, and a ".2" for a two base insertion.

>   Note: Polycytosine stretches are often difficult to interpret. A possible cause may be the presence of a mixture of length variants in the mtDNA of an individual. A predominant length species is often apparent; however, the frequency of a particular length species cannot be determined accurately and may vary between maternal relatives. The sequence reported for Hypervariable Region 1 represents the first 10 cytosines observed, beginning at position 16184. The sequence reported for Hypervariable Region 2 represents the number of cytosines present in the predominant base sequence. When no predominant base sequence is observed, the insertions that could not be confirmed are designated by a "N."

d. A position that could not be confirmed is designated by a "N."

CHAPTER TWELVE
ROTTEN TO THE CORE
YOUR ONE-STOP SHOP FOR CORRUPTION

Richard H. "Dick" Witt was the Hollywood police chief from January 16, 1986, to May 1, 1996. Chief Witt blew the whistle on corrupt hiring practices at his own agency. According to one July 25, 2007, *Sun-Sentinel* article, the chief had started to address the problem of corruption, but in an election year, the city of Hollywood wanted to keep the scandal quiet and out of the state attorney's hands with a toned-down internal investigation.

Chief Witt said that, from 1990 to 1995, qualified candidates at the HPD were consistently passed over in favor of unsuitable ones and many friends or relatives of high-ranking city cops were given jobs. After an independent investigation was conducted, the situation was said to be even worse than reported by the chief.

Rotten Apples

The HPD had become a bastion of corruption and backroom dealing. Officers got away with just about anything without consequences. For decades, the HPD had been embroiled in scandal. To this day, they refuse to accept Jeffrey Dahmer as a suspect and all the while the Broward state attorney Michael J. Satz's office has done nothing. All of this made it impossible to get justice for Adam Walsh.

Even the "rotten apple theory" doesn't apply to this police department. According to the theory, corruption is the work of a few dishonest, immoral police officers. However, this theory fails to explain why so many rotten apples have been concentrated in the HPD and not others.

After Chief Witt exposed the HPD's dirty brotherhood and submitted his findings to the Broward County State Attorney's Office on March 21, 1996, he was promptly terminated. As he packed up to leave, Chief Witt told a *Sun-Sentinel* reporter, "Killing the messenger is a custom that goes back to ancient times. Just say I'm leaving for health reasons—the city manager is sick of me."

Following his termination as chief of police, Witt filed suit against the city of Hollywood on two counts: for wrongful termination in violation of an employment contract and for a violation of Florida's Whistle-blower's Act. After several appeals and cross appeals, the case was settled for$300,000.

In 2010, I called Chief Witt. His wife Betty answered the phone and told me he'd passed away on July 23, 2007. I told her I just wanted to let her know what a great chief Richard was. We talked about the Adam Walsh case and the corruption that was still going on in the department. Betty told me that Richard was always strong in his convictions, and that was what she loved about him so much. She thanked me for the call, and that call made me feel good as well.

Corruption at the HPD eventually garnered the attention of the feds. The big bust in Hollywood came on February 27, 2007, after Joaquin "Jack" Garcia posed as a Gambino capo (a captain in the mafia) known to the unsuspecting HPD as Big Jack. According to Garcia, the FBI would've netted many more bad cops, but when the FBI confided in Hollywood Police Chief James Scarberry, the chief leaked information about the investigation to his commanders, who in turn passed it on to the officers being investigated. Garcia relayed his amazing story in his book *Making Jack Falcone*. In this book the six-foot-four, four-hundred-pound FBI undercover agent Garcia said, "What was amazing to me is that it was so easy to get cops to look the other way, to guard trucks for us, no questions asked. I'd never seen anything like it. . . The corruption is systemic throughout the whole [Hollywood] police department. We've heard from numerous sources just how corrupt these guys are." Garcia railed against transgressions ranging from officers turning a blind eye to blatant criminal activity to automatically deducting twenty percent off their checks at local restaurants. These cops had no problems giving the mob uniformed protection for $38 per hour. Garcia and other undercover agents made sure the cops knew what they were doing.

Sergeant Kevin Companion told Garcia, "I've got plenty of guys who'll come on board, but they don't want to know what they're transporting and that it's stolen."

Garcia straightened him out. "That's not okay. I don't want guys suddenly getting religion on me. If they're in, they've got to be in all the way."

Kevin even demanded to know why he wasn't making more money for his efforts. Jack told Kevin that if he wanted to make more money, he would have to "touch powder"—mob lingo for escorting heroin to warehouses and then on to New York. Kevin's eyes lit up at this and he said, "Escort it? No problem. We could do that."

The pay was $8,000 per run. They were paid off at Garcia's hotel room in view of a hidden video camera. This wasn't entrapment but law enforcement, FBI style. What these cops should've done was make an arrest. They had no idea they were setting themselves up for a decade of jail time.

One time, Garcia made what was an obvious drug deal right in front of the chief of police and three of his captains at Mama Mia Italian Restaurant, a popular downtown Hollywood trattoria. The sad part of this story is that it almost defies belief. We trust police departments to protect us from the criminal element, but the HPD seemed to wallow in the criminal element with its greed, arrogance, and power.

For his efforts, Sergeant Kevin Companion received fourteen years. Detective Thomas Simcox received just over eleven years. Officer Stephen Harrison received a nine-year term. And Sergeant Jeff Courtney also received nine years. Thanks to Chief Scarberry, many others were saved from the FBI sting operation.

The Hollywood Florida Police Department

3250 Hollywood Boulevard, Hollywood, Florida 33021

Chadwick E. Wagner

A Message from the

Chief of Police

In order to be recognized as a "Leading Force in Professional Law Enforcement," the Hollywood Police Department realizes our foundation is built on integrity, accountability and efficiency. These core values are accentuated by our ability to impartially evaluate the services we provide to the community. Governed by Florida State Statutes, the Internal Affairs Unit is authorized by the Office of the Chief of Police to thoroughly investigate allegations against Members of the Hollywood Police department.

Mission

The Hollywood Police department continues to be recognized as a Leading Force in Professional Law enforcement. Our purpose is to enhance the quality of life for every individual in the City of Hollywood.

Our foundation is built on integrity. We take pride in our organization and the community we serve. We are accountable to ourselves and the community we serve.

We are accountable to ourselves and the community while providing service with courtesy, compassion and empathy. We are committed to providing the highest quality of service to the community by always performing at our personal best. We are committed to continued progressive policing in partnership with our community.

The text and photo above are from the official site of the HPD, Florida.

The following article by Bob Norman ran in the *Broward New Times*:

Rotten to the Core: Your One-Stop Shop for Hollywood Police Corruption

http://blogs.browardpalmbeach.com

By Bob Norman

Thursday, Jul. 30, 2009 @ 8:54AM

This latest Hollywood police scandal is only the most recent black spot on what I believe can now safely be considered the worst police department in America. The Hollywood department has been plagued with scandal for years, so I thought I'd develop a post that links past stories involving the department's corruption.

This is a work in progress and won't be easy; I may need your help with links. Don't hesitate to send them along. And understand while you're reading this that it represents a failure of leadership from the commission down. I believe it largely reflects the horrid legacy of former Hollywood Mayor Mara Giulianti and many more lackluster commissioners who kowtowed to the rogue force in exchange for police backing in their campaigns.

Also understand that while the corruption in Hollywood's force is systemic and deep, there are still a lot of good cops in Hollywood despite it.

We must start with the HPD's bungling of one of the most notorious crimes in American history: the Adam Walsh abduction and murder in 1981. Investigators botched evidence and ignored witnesses, ending almost any hope of cleanly solving the case. Most famously, Hollywood police investigators actually managed to lose a suspect's car they had in storage and other key evidence. Last year, the department pinned the murder on a dead sociopath, Ottis Toole, who probably didn't do it (though Walsh's dad, America's Most Wanted*'s John Walsh, is sold on the idea). Credible witnesses have more recently strongly pointed the finger at none other than Jeffrey Dahmer, but again, the police investigation of that cannibal's possible involvement has been fatally flawed. Local author Arthur Jay Harris' book on the compelling case against Dahmer in the Walsh murder,* Jeffrey Dahmer's Dirty Little Secret, *was published earlier this month.*

In the 1990s, the department passed over qualified job candidates for unsuitable ones, many of them friends and relatives of Hollywood cops. The sham was revealed by former Hollywood Police Chief Richard Witt, who tried to fight the culture of corruption in the department and was run out of town for it. From an article by former New Times writer Trevor Aaronson, who did a great deal of investigation into the department:

> *During the five-year period, Hollywood hired officers with psychological problems, criminal records, and troubled pasts that should have excluded them from police work. Some cops had been rejected by as many as nine law enforcement agencies before they*

were allowed to patrol the city's streets. Of 59 offered employment by Hollywood at the time, 42 were found to have psychological or background problems that the city did not address, according to a probe by former Fort Myers Police Chief Donna Hansen.

"People that need to be dismissed will be dismissed," Mayor Mara Giulianti told the Sun-Sentinel *at the time.*

It never happened.

Lt. Jeff Marano: That's all that needs to be said right now, and people who have been following the department already know about it.

Female officer Cyndi Commela Ruiz gets pushed out of the force after testifying in a departmental harassment suit involving police officer Kevin Companion and high-ranking Hollywood police brass Louis Granteed. She says she was intimidated and told that she could "never leave the brotherhood of silence." From Aaronson's article:

> *The threat didn't work. Following the testimony of Ruiz and others, the city settled with Fortunato for $205,000. The harassment not only continued for Ruiz; it became worse, according to court documents. She found a snake in her mailbox at home. Sexually explicit graffiti about her was scrawled on the department's gas pumps. Officers refused to provide her with backup. A rock of crack cocaine was planted in her patrol car. While working a security detail at a movie theater on Sheridan Street, she received an anonymous phone call. "He said he was going to kill me at the end of my shift," she remembers.*

In 2007, the Federal Bureau of Investigation busts four Hollywood cops who had dreams of being in the Mafia. FBI Special Agent Jack Garcia posed as a Mafia crime boss and soon had four Hollywood cops—the aforementioned Kevin Companion, Sgt. Jeff Courtney, Det. Thomas Simcox, and Officer Steven Harris—eating out of his hand. The officers helped move drugs and stolen goods, took bribes, and committed other crimes for the fake Mafia team. Companion took $42,000 in payoffs from Garcia and voiced his hopes that he could become a "made" mobster (an impossibility because he was half-Irish). All four officers were eventually convicted and sentenced to prison, but the investigation was scuttled early after Hollywood Police Chief James Scarberry learned about it and told several of his underlings, including Louis Granteed, the companion, friend and fellow sexual harasser who was then assistant chief of police.

"We were betrayed by the police chief," Garcia said after the Hollywood leak. "Could have gotten me and my guys killed. The chief claimed he didn't believe there was corruption in his department."

Thankfully the idiot Scarberry is gone, though, amazingly, Granteed remains in place as assistant police chief.

CHAPTER THIRTEEN
THE CODE OF SILENCE
(A CULTURE OF CORRUPTION)

"So, you think you want to come back here again?"
_____*Detective Sergeant Lyle Bien*_____

The main reason the HPD closed the Adam Walsh case and pinned his murder on the wrong guy was because they knew they could get away with it. Not only would no other department in the state of Florida do anything, but other departments such as the Broward County State Attorney's Office would even become their enablers by allowing them to be corrupt and backing them up. No one wanted to step on their toes, which included most of the media as well and that made the HPD feel invincible.

In solving this case, these clueless HPD detectives wanted to share their credit with no one, even though their homicide investigation skills were pretty much nonexistent. In the end, they would get credit for nothing except pinning a murder on the wrong person. Even if someone tried to point them in the right direction they would have none of it, as I know full well. This is why we have innocent people in our jails and prisons, even on death row. The Walsh family have been used and abused by the HPD. I'm sure if John realized the full extent of the cover-up, he would have blood shooting out of his eyes and a lawyer by his side.

On the 25th anniversary of Adam's death, the Adam Walsh Child Protection Safety Act was signed by President George W. Bush in a ceremony performed in the Rose Garden at the White House.

On July 27, 2006, Bill Bowen and I were featured on several of the news shows that were doing anniversary specials of Adam's kidnapping. At this time, WISN-12 News Milwaukee reporter Colleen Henry came to Hollywood. It would be the first time in twenty-five years that anyone had come with me to the mall so that I could show them what happened on July 27, 1981. When I appeared with Patrick Fraser on WSVN-7 News Miami, John Walsh saw the show and commented, "Even though it's a cold case, people are coming forward [referring to Bill and myself] saying they weren't taken seriously twenty-five, twenty-six years ago." John then asked Broward State Attorney Michael Satz to investigate the new Dahmer leads and was critical of the Hollywood police. There is nothing that I could find in the case files to show that Hollywood Police Chief James Scarberry did anything to investigate Adam's murder.

When John said, "The ball is in Michael Satz's corner," it didn't appear that Satz did much. John told reporters he couldn't believe that, after twenty-five years, he was still fighting for a competent investigation into Adam's killing. "That's a bitter pill for me to swallow. [As] someone who's a big supporter of law enforcement, that the law enforcement agency investigating my son's murder would. . . not interview people who thought they had important information about the case, it's really a tough thing." This statement is in complete contrast to his statement given after the closing of Adam's case (shown at the end of chapter six).

On November 2, 2007, Jim Scarberry resigned amid scandal. On November 3, 2007, Chadwick E. Wagner took over as police chief. When I heard there was a new chief, I was compelled to send him a letter congratulating him and requesting a meeting with regard to the Adam Walsh case. After not hearing from him, I left a couple of messages on his answering machine as well as with his secretary.

Days later, my phone rang. When I picked up, someone said, as if he were upset, "I hear you have been calling over here!" I asked what he meant and who he was. He said his name was Sergeant Bien from the HPD. He refused to give me a meeting, saying they were "too busy" and brushed me off.

In early 2007, my sister, Sondra Torres, called the Milwaukee Police Department. She told them my story and gave them my phone number. They assured her they would call me but never did. She also wrote to Florida state senator Bill Nelson. He responded by saying he would forward her information to the FBI. They never contacted her or me. I myself wrote a letter to the office of Florida Governor Charlie Crist. I then went to the Hollywood City Hall complaints department to file a complaint against the HPD.

At the complaints department, I talked to Cheryl LaHound. She sat down with me and listened to everything I had to say and insisted I come to the next board meeting. "The mayor will be there. You need to tell this to them," she insisted. She said the meeting would be within the next three days, and she would call me with the exact time. I left her with a portfolio full of information about the case.

I never did hear from her, so a week later I called back. When she answered the phone and I asked about the meeting, I was told, "Well, sir, if you have an issue with the Hollywood Police Department, you need to go to them to air out your problems." It was obvious someone had put Cheryl in check, so I went on and explained that my complaint was *against* the HPD. Not getting anywhere, I asked for my portfolio back. That was when she told me that I would have to go to the HPD to get it. "What? You gave it to them?" I asked.

This book was born out of that portfolio. The HPD now had some of the same information I have in this book. The sad part is that it didn't faze them one bit. They would still dismiss Dahmer as a suspect. What really bothered me was that the portfolio had some of my sarcastic remarks and scathing attacks against the HPD and how they have twisted and obfuscated facts in the case. I included a list of the lies and misstatements they'd been telling John Walsh and the media over the years. I even referred to them as Keystone Kops, the early 20th century slapstick silent-film comedies about a totally incompetent group of policemen.

Next, I went to the Broward County Medical Examiner's Office. I talked to Edwina Johnson, who was the chief investigator. She was involved in the Adam Walsh case from the beginning and listened to everything I had to say with great patience and interest. The meeting lasted well over an hour. Johnson knew a lot about the Adam Walsh case and all the players involved. The chief medical examiner, Dr. Joshua Perper was out of town, so Johnson assured me she would give him the information and he would call me.

Instead, Mrs. Johnson called back. She told me that Dr. Perper would do nothing without clearance from the HPD, and I would have to go to them first. It was also Mrs. Johnson who, soon after the ABC *Primetime* show aired in August 2007, returned Adam's remains to John Walsh at his request. She said it was one of the proudest moments in her life. In January 2008, at age fifty-six, Mrs. Johnson suddenly passed away.

Not wanting to give up, I called the Florida Department of Law Enforcement (FDLE) and talked to a very nice female detective. She listened to everything I had to say and set up an appointment the following Tuesday. One hour before the meeting when I was just getting ready to leave, the phone rang. It was the FDLE detective. She seemed very nervous.

"S-S-Sir, I—I need to cancel the appointment."

"Cancel or postpone?" I asked.

"Well, post-postpone."

"Postpone for when? Tomorrow? Next week?"

She replied, "I'm very busy, ah. . . ah. . . I'll call you back."

She never called back. But what made her so nervous? I think there had to be some communication with someone, and she was under orders to cancel my appointment.

A few minutes later, I received a call from, of all people, Sergeant Lyle Bien, who suddenly found time to give me an appointment. He said with a curt, angry, and sarcastic tone, "Okay, I'm going to give you that appointment now. Come in Tuesday, eight p.m."

This was the meeting that I had been fighting for since Adam's abduction. I would have to show up. I didn't want the HPD to say they tried to investigate the case but couldn't get cooperation from me.

At 8 p.m. on November 27, 2007, I was at the HPD. I met Chief Wagner. He shook my hand only after I put it out there and he had no choice. I could tell by the lack of direct eye contact that it wasn't a sincere handshake. I asked him to assure me that this would be an amicable meeting.

In a condescending tone, as if he were talking to a fifth-grader, he said, "These nice detectives are going to listen to everything you have to say and take notes."

Sometimes I think these cops don't realize how condescending they can be. The only amicable part of that meeting was when they offered me a Styrofoam cup of water, and even that offer was with a tone of condescension. I'm not totally stupid. I knew this wouldn't be an amicable meeting. I was even reluctant to drink the water they gave me, and I made sure I let some friends know the place and time of that meeting.

In their duplicity, during this one-and-a-half-hour meeting, Detective Lyle Bien and Detective Steven Sparkman acted more like Jeffrey Dahmer's lawyers than homicide detectives. Bien did most of the talking. I knew right away that Sparkman was there primarily as a witness. Since the meeting was not recorded, if this meeting ever became an issue, it would be the word of two upstanding Hollywood detectives against the word of a lowly citizen.

The meeting started with Bien using the "discredit the witness tactic." He admitted they'd made a lot of mistakes: "We all make mistakes. I'm sure you made mistakes, too."

Because of the smug look on his face, I knew right away where he was going with this. He had done a criminal background check on me and pulled up my records. Bien actually thought he could appeal to the side of me that got in trouble with the law many years ago, when I was in my early twenties, and I would understand or even have sympathy for their plight. I haven't always been a model citizen. Back on the streets of New York after my Southeast Asia tour as a security police officer in the K-9 core of the United States Air Force, I found it difficult to keep a job. I strayed to the wrong side of the law. However, taking money that didn't belong to me was a far cry from covering up a botched murder investigation. I was sentenced to five years plus another two years for escaping but turned myself in six months later. I served my time in Sing Sing and Elmira, where I had plenty of time to figure out the rights and wrongs of life. I don't care to elaborate further.

I find great irony in the fact that someone who strayed could apparently have more ethics and credibility than the people we pay to uphold our laws. I don't drink. I don't smoke. I minimize my swearing. I try to take care of my health. And most of all, I don't lie. I would also like to add, if I were an attention seeker, that would hardly give me reason to dedicate so much of my time and money to uncovering the truth.

At one point in the meeting, Mr. Bien asked me if I had gone into the mall to use the bathrooms. What an absurd question! Apparently, it was a made-up erroneous reference to gays hanging out there. I didn't even know where the bathrooms were, but I presume they were in the food court, as in most malls. And what if I did have need of the restroom? Where would this conversation have gone, and exactly what was he trying to imply? Even more important, what was the relevance? Apparently Bien didn't realize that, back in 1991, Jack Hoffman already tried the "making a witness not want to admit he was at the crime scene" routine. This is the kind of tactics the HPD resorted to. Remember, this meeting was just one year before they closed the case and pinned Adam's murder on a dead man.

As the meeting went on, I asked for a polygraph test … Mr. Bien told me, "A polygraph don't mean anything. It just means you saw what you think you saw."

Questions started spewing from me: "Does it mean, I just think I was at the mall that day? Does it mean, I just think I followed someone to the Sears toy department? Does it mean, I just think I went to the police in 1981?"

Sparkman jumped in, "Well, we have no proof of that."

I told them, "If you think I am making this up, then I've been making it up since 1981. Since then, I have told anyone who would lend an ear. In 1991, I gave Detective Jack Hoffman a list of phone numbers to call for verification, but he never called anyone. I could give you that list again, if you want it, sir."

Bein then asked me if my supervisor had advised me to go to the police back in 1981. I told Bien I was thirty-four back in 1981, and I was the supervisor. It was twenty-three-year-old Richard Herland who had advised me to go to the HPD. I then tried to impress Mr. Bien with my good memory. I told him that I remembered seeing him at a Gold's Gym in Oakwood Plaza, Hollywood, about eight years before.

Bien countered, as if this were more of a verbal sparring match than an interview, "So what? I remember you, too."

Because of this exchange and others like it, I've come to have what I would consider a healthy distrust of police, and I don't get along very well with them now. I really didn't want to be there with these cops, but this was something I had to do. I was doing this for Adam. I couldn't let the HPD get away with covering up this botched murder investigation, so I continued with the interview.

Just like a good defense lawyer not wanting to implicate his client, Bien would substitute Dahmer's name with "that person" or "this alleged person you say you followed." He would've made Dahmer's real lawyer, Gerald Boyle, proud!

He told me I was making it up about having an encounter and following someone to the Sears toy department because "if this person was at that point in the mall, you couldn't have been at that point you say you were at when you were following him. I know that mall as well as anyone." Then, with hindsight bias, he added, "Besides, a normal person doesn't follow someone around in a mall."

"Well," I retorted, "I'm not trying to be like anyone else. I did follow him, but only because in my heart of hearts, I knew someone might be in trouble. It's easy to criticize, especially with hindsight on your side, sir. If I could do this over, Adam would never have been abducted."

Bien kept throwing metaphorical crap against the wall, hoping I would be discouraged from pursuing it any further. The bottom line is that anyone who has seen that dead, dull look in Dahmer's eyes would never be so critical. His eyes had no life in them, as if he were extremely lonely. Even that isn't so accurate as it just can't be described. Bien is right: a normal person doesn't follow someone around in a mall.

Homicide detectives are supposed to work for the dead, yet these homicide detectives spent our interview acting like complicit purveyors of the odious offense of covering up an investigation while defending a dead psychopathic serial killer rather than seeking justice for Adam. Bien went out of his way not to mention Dahmer by name. It became obvious by Bien's selected wording, his tone, and his mannerisms that this interview was intended to get me to disappear and not implicate Jeffrey Dahmer. Bien even tried to convince me it wasn't Dahmer that abducted Adam.

When he asked me if I had seen the actual abduction of Adam, I told him no.

"Well, then, you can't say it was Dahmer." [This was the only time he actually mentioned Dahmer by name]. "It could have been anyone. Even if he was there, that doesn't mean he did it. You should just forget about it."

Acting like a big man in a small body, Bien continued to shout questions at me, and when I tried to answer, Bien would cut me off and shout, "You can't take it, can you?" and "How are you going to take it in court if you can't take it here?" What on earth was he talking about? Court? And who says I couldn't take it there? His strategy would get him nowhere. This little, dim-witted, wannabe ruffian thought I would be intimidated by his amateur thuggery. It was comical. All they succeeded in doing was to ratchet up my tenacity. Little did they know that everything they said would end up in this book, so everyone would be able to see what a great job these cops had done to reinforce the sullied reputation of a police department that has become fodder for media news articles about corruption.

I couldn't help but think how much Detective Bien reminded me of Rowan Atkinson's comedy character, Mr. Bean. There is no relation, in fact. Even the spelling is different—although I think Rowan Atkinson's Mr. Bean would've had a much better chance at solving this case than HPD's Bien.

Admittedly, I had my own sarcastic moments in that interview. When I was telling Bien about the only clerk in the Radio Shack being at the back of the store, Bien replied, "I don't believe you because I have been in many Radio Shacks, and I have never seen only one clerk; there are always at least two."

My response was, "You know what, you're right. I didn't think of that. It was around noon, and one of them could have been out to lunch." I knew my sarcasm wasn't helping, but in my defense, I was only feeding off his sarcasm. This meeting wasn't going anywhere anyway, and I resented Mr. Bien for calling me a liar. It might be that there are usually two store clerks on duty in Radio Shack. For all I know, one of them could've been in the stock room or actually had stepped out to lunch.

I guess it was time for them to change strategy. I was waiting for a watered-down version of the classic good cop/bad cop routine. Instead, they decided on the never-before-tried "threaten the witness with arrest" routine. At one point, Bien jumped up, flailing his arms about and shouting at me with as much gruffness as he could muster up from a five-foot seven-inch frame, "I could arrest you right now! How about that? You just admitted you were there! For all I know, *you* could have done it! You want me to arrest you?"

I remained seated as detective Bien backed up, folded his arms like the iron-pumping, bellicose little tough guy he thought he was, and said with a smart-aleck smirk, "So, you think you want to come back here again?" Feeling that I wasn't welcome, I answered, "Probably not without an attorney." He shouted at me again. "Oh, so now you need a lawyer?" Bien seemed to thrive on acting like the deceased Dahmer's unsolicited attorney.

At that point, the meeting was over and I was escorted out the front door. Obviously, the threat of arrest didn't work out so well for them. They were messing with the wrong witness. I was not and am not going to let them intimidate me. I wasn't there for anything I had done wrong. Actually, I would have loved for them to arrest me and make bigger fools of themselves than they already had. Adam deserved better than these cops investigating his murder. Obviously, it wasn't the Kiwanis Club gone awry that I was dealing with but very bad cops.

For example, I learned from listening to the CD audio section of the HPD case files that, not much more than a year before this meeting, during the summer of 2006, Bien and Sparkman went to Virginia and Long Island, New York, to stalk people with blue vans. This made no sense. I thought they had given up on the blue van a long time ago. In 2008, they switched back to the white Cadillac to please Joe Matthews and give closure to the Walshes. These sanctimonious cops walked around in their thick black shoes flashing their shiny badges with an air of arrogance, as though they thought they were better than everyone else. They weren't even at the crime scene, yet they seemed to act as if they knew more than the witnesses. Time and time again, these detectives would consider witnesses to be insincere, unreliable, confused, crazy, somewhat unstable, and, yes, even liars, along with whatever other defamatory terms they could conjure up. Why? We were just average people. What gave these detectives the right to look down their arrogant noses at us as we desperately tried to help them help the Walsh family?

The only thing I accomplished with my HPD rendezvous was to learn that none of these saviors of the downtrodden would breach the "Blue Code of Silence." Wagner, Bien, and Sparkman were all part of a cover-up that ran deep in this police department. As well, after this meeting it became more apparent than ever that none of these cops cared much about true justice for Adam and the Walsh family.

This only made me more tenacious than ever. In fact, I was so incensed I decided to pay for my own polygraph examination. I first went to a renowned polygraph service in Hollywood, Florida, but was told they did a lot of work with the HPD, and thus, it would be a conflict of interest. I couldn't even get a self-sponsored polygraph exam in the same town.

Eventually, I did find someone who was willing to do the polygraph examination, someone far from Hollywood and south of Miami who was honest and wouldn't kowtow to anyone. I include a partial excerpt of that test after this chapter. The polygraph examiner didn't have much good to say about the HPD investigation. Of course, I passed with flying colors—which is good, since I paid $650 for that test!

The FBI refused to get involved. I went to them so many times that they practically locked their doors when they saw me coming. When they did come out from behind their bulletproof windows and thick locked doors to talk to me, they told me it was a local case, even though Dahmer had crossed state lines—from Florida to Ohio to Wisconsin, and let's not forget to mention Germany. I was told, "The only way we could get involved is if we were invited in." I wanted to invite them in, but it was clear they weren't referring to me. It would have to be the HPD or the State Attorney's Office—the very same people that were covering it up.

My Personal Conclusion

If the HPD finds a dead person, they call the Medical Examiner's Office. The medical examiner collects the body and does an examination in order to make a determination of death. If the determination is homicide, the medical examiner relays those findings back to the HPD. There is discussion over the evidence. If the HPD arrests a suspect, it calls the Broward County Prosecutor's Office, so all three departments operate in full cooperation during the prosecution of the case. When one of these departments makes a mistake or goes rogue, none of the other departments is willing to step on their toes. They all work together. There is a symbiotic relationship between them. Whether you call it the "code of silence" or the "blue wall," it's the unwritten rule that all law enforcement departments stick together.

My letter to Chief Wagner. I suppose I could've done a better job writing that letter. Saying negative things about the HPD homicide detectives didn't exactly get me an open invitation by the chief.

November 20, 2007

To Chief Chadwick Wagner,

I would like to start by congratulating you on your new position. My name is Willis Morgan. I am writing you in hopes the Hollywood Police Department finally has someone that is willing to solve an old murder case. I was a witness to this crime. The problem is that the homicide detectives at the Hollywood Police Department are covering up facts and even lying to the media on national TV. The only reason I could think of as to why they would do this is they do not want to reopen the case and reveal how badly they mishandled this case from the beginning. They believed Ottis Toole when he said he did it, and they believed Jeffrey Dahmer when he said he didn't do it. They even managed to turn a blue van into a white Cadillac to suit Toole's vehicle. Then the biggest mistake of all, they dismissed witnesses and believed the statements of a serial killer. The reason I am writing to you direct is that some of the detectives are still with this department. I believe if they even see this letter it may never get to you. I have been trying to call you for an interview to no avail. It is my feeling none of the detectives in the homicide department wants me to get this interview.

Twenty-seven years ago, on July 27, 1981, I was in Radio Shack at the Hollywood Mall. Enclosed is my statement of the encounter I had that day. In 1991, when Jeffrey Dahmer's mug shot appeared in the Miami Herald, I had a name to put to that face. Indeed it was Jeffrey Dahmer that I encountered in Radio Shack. Also enclosed is a map of the path he took through the mall to the Sears toy department.

All the reasons Det. Jack Hoffman gave me back in 1992 to dismiss Dahmer as a suspect have since been proven to be false. Hoffman told me Dahmer couldn't have abducted Adam because "He was working ten hours a day, seven days a week, and never took any days off." The guy that hired JD has since been located by Art Harris, and he said that's not true. JD only worked part time as a busboy. He never worked weekends and was constantly being sent home for coming in disheveled.

I know for sure one day he wasn't working: Monday, July 27, 1981.

According to Jeffrey Dahmer's manager, he was paid on Fridays. It could be that he drank up his weekly pay over the weekends. By Monday, he would've been too disheveled to work and would've been sent home around 10 a.m., or just in time for a trip to the mall in the company's blue delivery van. As you may know, Adam was abducted at around 12:20-12:30 in the afternoon.

As you can see, I do not give up very easily when I'm sure about something. I have much more to say. This letter is a request for an appointment, not from anyone in your homicide department, but by you, directly.

Thanks in advance,
Willis Morgan

I can be reached by E-mail at [ll-*redacted*-ll@lll.com] or by phone at [ll-*redacted*-ll].

Copy of my polygraph exam.

SLATTERY ASSOCIATES, INC.
POLYGRAPH

FEDERAL & STATE
COURT QUALIFIED

Polygraph Report
Personal & Confidential

Person Requesting Examination:

Willis Russell Morgan

Date: December 07, 2007

Person Examined:
Morgan, Willis Russell.,W/M, 05/10/1947

Slattery Associates, Inc. File #07-2403(P)
Court/Case/File#

Issue at Examination:

This examination was scheduled to determine whether Willis Russell Morgan was exaggerating, or fabricating, details of an event that took place on July 27, 1981, which may be related to the kidnapping, and the eventual murder, of Adam Walsh a six-year-old youth. In preparation for this examination, Mr. Morgan supplied extensive documents related to his actions and observations on that day. Additionally, Mr. Morgan gives insight as to his motives, and rationale, for continuing to pursue a matter, which on its face would suggest that at least some public officials have tried to forget.

To summarize, Mr. Morgan said he does not claim to have seen Adam Walsh, or his kidnapping, on July 27, 1981, but clearly remembers an interaction with an individual, later identified as Jeffrey Dahmer, an infamous serial murderer, who lived and worked in the area, and at the time Adam Walsh went missing, was allegedly in the same department store from which Adam was taken. Mr. Morgan said it was only some time later that he realized the possible importance of his interaction with the individual, later identified as Dahmer, and so attempted to relay this information to law enforcement authorities. In his documents, Mr. Morgan clearly states that he tried on many occasions to give law enforcement and other public officials the information, which is in his possession, but instead was never taken seriously and generally has been rebuffed when attempting to give the information he possesses. For example, Mr. Morgan said he had long ago asked to undergo polygraph testing to verify the information he offered, but was refused the opportunity by law enforcement officials. Here today, Mr. Morgan said he feels so strongly about this matter that he has volunteered to self-sponsor and fund an examination and submit to polygraph testing to support the veracity of his statements and writings regarding the knowledge he claims to possess relevant to the disappearance of Adam Walsh.

8525 Northwest 53rd Terrace, Savanna Building, Suite 100, Miami, FL 33166
Phone: (305) 592-7917 · Fax: (305) 591-5963

Person Examined: Morgan, Willis Russell., W/M, 05/10/1947

Slattery Associates, Inc. File #07-2403(P)

Page 2

SLATTERY ASSOCIATES INC.

Date: December 07, 2007

Results/Conclusions:

Willis Russell Morgan was given a polygraph examination on this day, with four tests administered. After analysis of all the polygrams and all other relevant information, it is my opinion that there were no significant or consistent psycho-physiological reactions consistent with deception when Mr. Morgan answered the relevant questions found below. Accordingly, it is my professional opinion that **WILLIS RUSSELL MORGAN WAS TRUTHFUL** when he answered these questions.

Relevant Questions:

1. Have you made up any of the information in the folder you gave me? Answer – NO

2. July 27, 1981, was the person you seen walking into the toy Department of Sears, Dahmer?
   Answer – YES

3. Have you purposely falsified any information you've given me or the police regarding Dahmer?
   Answer – NO

Additional Information:

This examination was analyzed using a traditional review of the physiological data and by using a recent innovation in credibility assessment to objectively assess whether a client was truthful or deceptive during the examination. This "Objective Scoring System-Version 3" is based on empirical, peer-reviewed research with the relevant underlying statistical formulas, used for these analyses, having been reviewed by psychometricians at Queens University in Kingston, Ontario, Canada. Overall, the results of the examination found a probability of 0.049 (04.9%) that Mr. Morgan was deceptive, which translates into a 95.1% chance that he was truthful based on the recorded physiological data and questions asked.

Respectfully submitted,

John J. Palmatier

John J. Palmatier, Ph.D.
Polygraph Examiner

JJP
1 encl.

Letter from Florida State Senator Bill Nelson to my sister, Sondra.

United States Senate
WASHINGTON, DC 20510–0905

BILL NELSON
FLORIDA

March 16, 2007

Mrs. Sondra Morgan-Torres

Dear Mrs. Morgan-Torres:

Thank you for contacting my office regarding your brother's account of the Adam Walsh kidnapping and murder. I appreciate being made aware of your concerns. I have forwarded your correspondence to the Federal Bureau of Investigation for their review. They will contact you directly if they require any further information.

Again, thank you for contacting my office. I want you to know that as your United States Senator from Florida, I welcome the opportunity to serve you. If I can assist you with any other matter, please do not hesitate to let me know.

Sincerely,

Bill Nelson

BN/ctb

Enclosure

Letter from the Offices of the Governor.

**CHARLIE CRIST
GOVERNOR**

STATE OF FLORIDA

Office of the Governor

Citizen Services
THE CAPITOL
TALLAHASSEE, FL 32399-0001

www.flgov.com
850-488-4441
850-487-0801 fax

December 19, 2007

Mr. Willis Morgan
▇▇▇▇▇▇▇▇▇▇▇▇▇▇▇▇
▇▇▇▇▇▇▇▇▇▇▇▇▇▇▇▇

Dear Mr. Morgan:

Thank you for contacting Governor Charlie Crist. The Governor appreciates your concerns about the investigation of the murder of Adam Walsh and asked me to respond on his behalf.

Governor Crist thanks you for taking the time to share this information with him. Please understand, however, that the Governor's ability to intervene in this situation is limited. Governor Crist encourages you to continue expressing your concerns to the Hollywood Police Department. As you know, that department is handling the investigation of the Adam Walsh murder case.

Thank you again for writing. For information about the Governor's initiatives and to subscribe to the Governor's weekly "Notes from the Capitol" newsletter, please visit our Web site at www.flgov.com.

Sincerely,

Cole Hoopingarner
Office of Citizen Services

CH/cas

CHAPTER FOURTEEN
THE FLORIDA TURNPIKE
AND
THE WITNESSES

File photo left: courtesy of the Hollywood Historical Society

MILE MARKER 130

August 12, 1981, Vero Beach, FL: South Florida television newsmen interview an Indian River County sheriff's investigator at the scene where the severed head of six-year-old Adam Walsh was discovered by fishermen on August 10, 1981, in a canal next to the Florida Turnpike.

The Florida Turnpike

On Monday, August 10, 1981, the Walsh family heard the tragic news that a severed head had been found at 6:45 p.m. by two fishermen, Robert Hughes and Vernon Bailey. At first, the fishermen thought it was a doll's head floating in the water. They put their boat in the water and rowed over to it to discover it was human. They rowed back rather quickly to their truck and used the CB radio to call their office, which then called the Florida Highway Patrol. Homicide detective Donald Coleman of the Indian River Sheriff's Department conducted the initial investigation. The HPD responded to mile marker 130 with a photo of Adam, and a tentative identification was made. The head was then transported to the Indian River County Hospital.

John Monahan, a personal friend of the Walsh family, drove to the hospital to identify the severed head. A positive identification was made by Monahan that the severed head was that of Adam Walsh.

The head was then flown by helicopter to the Broward County Medical Examiner's Office. Dr. Wright conducted the postmortem exam of Adam Walsh's head. Adam's dentist, Dr. Marshall Berger, DDS, went to the medical examiner's office with Adam's dental charts. A positive identification was made through those dental records. The head was positively identified as Adam Walsh's.

Twenty-seven years later, after the HPD closed the case on Adam and I began searching the records, I located witnesses, Denis Bubb and Clifton Ramey, and a year later, Richard King and Tom Hayslip; all with information about the turnpike that would have proved useful in the case. Over the years, many of the detectives at the HPD made the claim that they had examined the full case files very thoroughly. Detective Smith made this claim after he took over in 1994 and both Matthews and Chief Wagner made the same claim when they closed the case on December 16, 2008. Yet none of these detectives ever called any of these witnesses. I had no problem finding their statements and I was able to locate all four witnesses even after so many years.

Witnesses Richard and Tom say they saw a blue van on Tuesday, August 4, 1981, and Denis and Clifton say they saw a blue van on Friday, August 7, 1981, between mile marker 130 and 131. The fact that the blue van was seen on two separate dates at this location might not be as relevant as the fact that the blue van was indeed at that location between the dates when Adam was abducted on July 27, 1981, and when Adam's severed head was found on August 10, 1981.

The week Dahmer disposed of Adam's head must have been a very traumatic one for him. He not only might have been sent home on Monday, August 3, but he might not have shown up for work on Tuesday, August 4, and possibly missed the entire week. No matter what the scenario was, it would have to include both August 4 and 7.

It was up to the HPD in 1981 not to ignore these witnesses and to take their statements seriously. Detective Ron Hickman did put out an updated BOLO (be on lookout) for the blue van. However, at this time, Detective Jack Hoffman had already deep-sixed the blue van, convinced that James Campbell was his suspect. At this late date, the best scenario must be partly conjecture, since after thirty years, memories fade and witnesses pass on. I put the pieces of the puzzle together, as the HPD detectives were unwilling or unable to do.

The Witnesses

On August 10, 1981, Denis Bubb heard about Adam's severed head being found off the Florida Turnpike near mile marker 130. Denis was a truck driver for the Publix supermarket chain and was driving his regular route north to the Yeehaw Junction (SR-60) exit at mile marker 149 with an empty double-tow (two-trailer truck). There, drivers would make the exchange for full double rigs that came from the Publix main warehouse in Lakeland, Florida, and then drive back to Publix's North Dade warehouse.

He recalled three days earlier, on August 7, around 12:30 a.m., he'd seen a suspicious blue van stopped on the swale area at that very same spot. The side door was open, and a white male was down by the canal with a flashlight. He saw the man take something round out of a bucket and throw it into the water.

On November 12, 2009, I met Denis at his home in Palm Bay, Florida, and asked him if anyone had ever contacted him or returned his call since he gave the HPD that phone tip. Denis said he received a return call within the hour but was told, "Yeah, yeah, we already know about the blue van. It has nothing to do with the Adam Walsh case."

I was the first to talk to Denis since then. Despite the HPD dismissing Denis's August 14 statement, I felt it had a lot of credibility as he was not the only one to spot a blue van at this location at the same time.

Homer "Clifton" Ramey, another driver for Publix, was also headed to Yeehaw Junction when he saw a "dark-colored van" stopped on the northbound side of the turnpike near mile marker 130. Denis had called Clifton on his CB radio and told him to check out the van that Denis had just passed and to check it out.

The only difference between Clifton's statement and Denis's is that Clifton saw the white male standing at the side door of the van and fumbling with a bucket in his hand. Clifton said he thought the man had an overheated radiator, except the hood wasn't up and the man was just standing there by the side door.

"I remember seeing him from the waist up, leaning into the van, as if he was fumbling with something. That's when I saw the bucket. He had the flashlight on it; it gave me some light." The van was also illuminated by the inside overhead light. Clifton also said the HPD returned his call within the hour. The detective thanked him for the tip and informed him that it was unrelated to the Adam Walsh case.

Actually, I had trouble locating "Clifford Ramey," as was written on the phone tip, until Denis told me his middle name is Clifton, not Clifford, and his first name is Homer. When I got home, I easily found Homer Clifton Ramey, now retired and living in Georgia.

I contacted Tom Hayslip in June 2010. Tom's recollection and meticulous note-keeping impressed me, as well as the effort he made to follow up with the HPD. It was Tom's suggestion that Dahmer could've been casing the spot out on August 4. An excellent suggestion, considering that Adam had been captive since July 27, 1981, and Dahmer had been in Lake Park, Florida, just seventy-two miles south of mile marker 130 on July 13, 1981.

It is very possible Dahmer could've been driving around with Adam's head in a bucket from August 4 until he disposed of it on August 7. Also this was just past midnight on Friday so this could have been Saturday morning on August 8. That would have placed the head in the water for only two days. Another possibility is that he could've gone back to his room at the Bimini Bay Motel and retrieved the head from his refrigerator. Of course, there is no evidence to support either of these assertions, but as suppositions go, they are logical.

Tom's statements to me (notes not included as per his request):

June 1, 2010

Willis,

At the end of my e-mail is the link to the overpass at mile marker 130 where I saw the blue van. It should be just north of Minute Maid Road overpass.

My notes, which I will send to you tomorrow, do not indicate the date I saw the van. However, the case notations you sent indicate I reported it as Tuesday, August 4, 1981, and I am confident that is correct. I am certain about the time of day and the location.

I will send you a PDF file of the original notes I made when I reported what I saw and a second set of notes I made in August of 2007, recalling the meeting with Jack Hoffman and the hypnotism session. Unfortunately, I failed to make any notes of that occasion when they occurred.

I must admit that I have mixed emotions about what you are doing. On the one hand, it is the right thing to do, as it may give many witnesses a sense of finality which we seek and correct a closed case. On the other hand, I worry that it might cause John Walsh to relive a nightmare he may have found peace with, if one can. I am sure you have considered this as well. I do know that one day the guilty party will stand before the Lord and be judged, as we all will. Likely, he already has.

I do admire your tenacity and can fully understand why you want to proceed; indeed I think I want you to. I would be interested in what you find, so you may send me any updates you want to send. Tomorrow, I will be sending the PDF from my work address, so please use my home e-mail address when you correspond.

Tom Hayslip

RIGHT: 1981 phone call by Tom Hayslip to the HPD

HPD-Adam Walsh case files: Roll 1, p. 3302

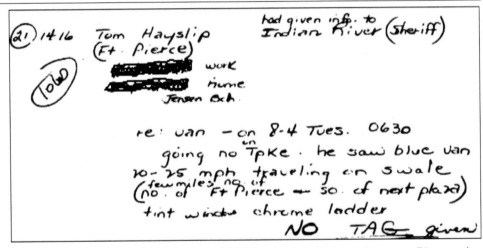

NOTE: None of the information Tom gave to Detective Hoffman made it into the case files, or it was removed in 1991 right after Bill Bowen, myself and others went to the HPD. This message, taken by operator number 1416, is one of the only mentions of Tom. Perhaps it was missed if Tom's records were expunged from the case files. I am not saying that happened; I am just saying it is possible.

Willis,

Attached to this e-mail are two sets of notes, one from 1981 and one from 2007.

1981 notes: After I read the article about finding Adam's head, I called the St. Lucie County Sheriff Lanie Norvell, who told me to call the Indian River County Sheriff's Department as the remains were found in that county. I drove the Florida Turnpike to confirm the location at which I spotted the van and record the mile marker, and then called the Indian River Sheriff's Office. They told me to call Hollywood detective Jack Hoffman, which I did. I gave him the description of the van and details of why I knew the time, etc. This would all have occurred between August 12 and August 14, 1981. No one ever called me, so about a year later, I again called my local sheriff and asked if he could get me an update, as it weighed on my mind that I should do more to be certain the information got into the case. He called me back and said he checked and was told that the van lead at the mall was not very reliable.

2007 notes: I did not record any notes at the time of the hypnotism, etc. However, seeing a similar van in Georgia in 2007 brought back the memory of Adam's death and caused me to return to my 1981 notes and record my recollection of those events. Expanding on the enclosed notes, my recollection these many years later is that I called Detective Hoffman and read him the 1981 notes I had made, and I believe he had me fax them to him, or I gave him a copy when he came to the hypnotism session, most likely around 4/26/1990 based on my margin notes that you can see on the 1981 notes attached. You may find all of this information should they send you more case records. If and when you do, let me know, and I will go into more detail about what all occurred. When you are researching this part, it may be useful to see if the name of a St. Lucie County detective Rick Browning appears, as my recollection is that he was involved in making the arrangements with Detective Hoffman. Also, I think the test was done in Ft. Pierce, or maybe Vero Beach.

I hope you find these notes useful in your pursuit; however, please do not share these notes with others without my written permission, as that will help me stay informed.

Tom

(NOTE: I could not find any of the notes Tom gave to Hoffman in the case files)

RIGHT: HPD- case files. Roll #1, p. 3111

This is a copy of another phone call received by the HPD. Richard King even said he could "describe the man" and was willing to undergo hypnosis. There was nothing in the case files to indicate that Richard was ever called back, and according to his wife Jeanne, the HPD never once in twenty-nine years returned his call. Richard worked for the Department of Transportation. Jeanne returned my call to tell me that Richard passed away in 2002. I only have Richard's phone call statement. Given the fact that he worked on the turnpike for the Florida Department of Transportation, Jeanne, said he would've been a great witness if he were still here. She told me, "He was very good with things like times and dates. . . If someone would have only listened to him, he would have made a great witness . . . Richard worked for the turnpike, and he would have known his mile markers."

DENIS BUBB
6890 CHARLESTON ST. HLWD 961-9291
DRIVER FOR PUBLIX
FRIDAY 8-7-81 AT 0030 HRS DENIS WAS DRIVING NORTH ON THE TURNPIKE. AT MILE MARKER #131, OBSERVED A LATE MODEL VAN PARKED ON THE ROADSIDE. SLIDING SIDE DOOR WAS OPEN AND A W/M WAS STANDING DOWN BY THE CANAL SHINNING A FLASHLIGHT INTO THE WATER. COULD NOT IDENTIFY VEHICLE OR W/M.

CLIFFORD RAMEY DRIVER FOR PUBLIX
20050 NW 15 AVE N MIAMI 653-3426
LATE MODEL APPROX 1978-79 VAN DARK COLORED, W/M WITH FLASHLIGHT STANDING BY OPENED SIDE DOOR.

ABOVE: HPD-Adam Walsh case files: Roll #1, page 3125

Why are these statements so important? Simple: now we have the blue van in *all three* locations:

- ✓ Where Jeffrey Dahmer worked.
- ✓ Where Adam Walsh was abducted.
- ✓ Where Adam's severed head was found.

WITNESS TIMELINE: MILE MARKER 130

August 4, 1981:

1: The blue van was first sighted near mile marker 130 at 6:30 a.m. driving very slowly at twenty to twenty-five miles an hour on the shoulder. Witness: *Thomas Hayslip*

2: The blue van was stopped on the shoulder at mile marker 130 around noon. A man stood at the back of the van. Witness: *Richard King*

August 7, 1981:

3: The blue van was stopped at 12:30 a.m. near mile marker 131. The side door was open, and a man was down by the canal with a flashlight and a white bucket. He took "something round" out of the bucket and threw it into the canal. Witness: *Denis Bubb*

4: The blue van was stopped at 12:35 a.m. near mile marker 131. The side door was open, and a man stood by the side door fumbling with a white bucket. Witness: *Clifton Ramey*

Perhaps in 1981, if the HPD had realized that what the blue van witnesses had seen at the location where Adam's severed head was found was relevant to Adam's abduction at the Hollywood Mall they may not have turned it into a white Cadillac when Ottis Toole confessed.

Also, for Toole's confession to be true, the head would've had to have been in the water since the day of Adam's abduction. In 1981, the original medical examiner, Dr. Ronald Wright gave a two-week window for how long Adam's head could've been in the water: from two days to two weeks. Now, it was ascertained to be only two or three days. On February 20, 2011, I called Dr. Wright and told him about the August 7, 1981, timeline. His response was that the date would be consistent with the evidence. For the severed head to have been in the water for only three days would have been within the lower end of the original estimate given by Dr. Wright.

Jack Hoffman even said, "Nobody believes that head was in the water for two weeks. I've handled lots of decomposed bodies. It's unbelievable what water, heat, and animals do to a body. . . The head also appeared to have been severed for a while, so the killer had likely kept the head for some time before putting it in the canal." It would seem that earlier on, Dahmer tried to keep the head of his victims for as long as possible because he didn't yet know how to save the skull.

NOTES ON THE INTERVIEW
WITH DET. DONALD COLEMAN
INDIAN RIVER CO. SHERIFF'S OFFICE

Det. Coleman advises that the remains were in such good condition that he immediately recognized them to be those of Adam Walsh. Det. Coleman states that the water at this location is very warm, there is little to no current, and the area is abundant in fish and wildlife. He recognized that the remains had no damage from fish, turtles, or alligators that he has seen in other remains found under similar circumstances. In his opinion, he believes the head had been in the water a day or two and certainly not more than a week.

ABOVE: Assessment of Lead Detective Donald Coleman cropped from the SAO case files (box 2, file 3, p. 250) at JusticeForAdam.com.

Art Harris talked to Carl Lord, one of the investigators for the Fort Pierce Medical Examiner's Office, where the severed head was first brought. He said evidence of sperm in a cavity of the head was found. It wasn't in the mouth, he said. It was found somewhere in the throat, according to *Jeffrey Dahmer's Dirty Secret,* p. 211. As previously established, we know Dahmer exhibited perversions of this nature. Although for every Mother Teresa, there's a Jeffrey Dahmer, the likelihood of two men not only willing to engage in this behavior but also living within driving distance of the Hollywood Mall when Adam was abducted is exceedingly small. According to Dahmer's defense lawyer, Gerald Boyle, "A criminal like [Dahmer] comes around every seventy-five years and, thankfully, isn't seen again for another seventy-five" (Elizabeth Gleick, "The Final Victim," *People*, December 12, 1994, vol. 42, no. 24).

In one of my conversations with Billy Joe Capshaw, it was suggested that Dahmer could've decapitated Adam before August 3, 1981, in the meter room. He then could've disposed of the body either in the dumpster or in the vicinity of mile marker 130 off the Florida Turnpike on August 4, 1981. He also could've kept the head as a trophy and even brought it back to his room at the Bimini Bay Motel and kept the head in the refrigerator, another Dahmer hallmark. Billy also came up with the suggestion that it could've been just before August 7 when Dahmer lost his motel room and needed to dispose of Adam's head. Dahmer did have the room at the time of Adam's abduction. In an interview with Detective Hoffman, Dahmer said he remembered hearing about Adam's kidnapping on TV while he was lying in bed in his room. That was one of the few statements Dahmer made that I believe.

That still leaves the body and, for that, I propose two possibilities. He could've put the body in some black garbage bags and disposed of them in the dumpster next to the meter room, or he could've put the garbage bags in the back of the van and disposed of the body in another location, maybe even along the turnpike, on August 4. He likely kept the head until 12:30 a.m. on August 7. Dahmer was known to have been not far from this area. Remember the Twin City Mall?

Jeffrey Dahmer could've been at the turnpike location for at least four hours on August 4, from 6:30 in the morning until at least noon, according to Tom's and Richard's notes. Could it be that Dahmer did get rid of Adam at this location? Yet, why was Dahmer standing at the back of the van on that afternoon? My guess was that he was retrieving body parts from the van for disposal. What actually happened, we'll never know.

When Denis and Clifton called the HPD on August 11, 1981, they were not sure of the detective's name they talked to when they were summarily dismissed. When Tom called the HPD on August 12, 1981, he was told by the Indian River County Sheriff's department to ask for Detective Jack Hoffman. Hoffman dismissed Tom then and didn't call him back until 1989, when Tom called St. Lucie County Detective Rick Browning, who might have been involved in making arrangements for Tom's polygraph examination given on July 19, 1989. Detective Hoffman showed up for the polygraph, but nothing much came of that meeting, even though the examiner said that, after going over the pre-test interview and review of the polygraph charts, it was his opinion that there were no deceptive responses when Hayslip was asked if he had seen a blue van and if he reported it to the police.

What we have here is a total lack of communication between detectives. The second lead detective, Ron Hickman, put out an updated BOLO on the blue van, dated August 14, 1981. Whatever went wrong, no one knows. When I called Ron Hickman at his Fort Lauderdale home in late June 2010, we talked about the Twin City Mall. Ron told me he remembered that incident but had nothing to do with it. "That was Hoffman that handled that," he said. I told him about the witnesses, and his response was, "I don't believe any of them."

I then moved on to the witnesses at the Hollywood Mall: Vernon Jones and his grandfather, who never made it inside the police station; Janice Santamassino, who almost ran into the back of the blue van and then locked eyes with Dahmer in the toy department; and Bill Bowen, who gave police the tag number and then followed up by calling the HPD to see if they wanted him to come in for an interview but was told to call back in two weeks. Hickman gave me the same response.

"I don't believe any of them, either; they are all lying." Then he added, "Our police department wasn't that bad."

I had to refrain from saying, "I beg your pardon, sir, but I think it was!" I explained to Detective Hickman that when Chief Wagner closed the case, he said detectives past and present believed it was Ottis Toole.

Hickman emphatically replied, **"They know I don't believe it was Ottis Toole!"**

I then asked him if he knew about the witnesses that saw a blue van at mile marker 130. They called the HPD two and three days before the updated BOLO on the 14th, and I asked if he would've dismissed them.

Hickman responded with an emphatic "Heck, no! That would have been important." He added, "This is the first I'm hearing about it." He told me he remembered that he had put out that updated BOLO, but no one told him about witnesses seeing a van at that site.

I explained who I was and about my involvement in the case. He then said he'd been on the case from the beginning, and he had never even heard of me. Then he remembered reading something about my lawsuit against the HPD and Joe Matthews in the paper and asked me, "Whatever happened to Matthews's report? I was flabbergasted when I read that the chief used that report and did not save a copy for the record."

I told him that Matthews said he "sent the only hard copy to Cuba and erased all his electronic copies."

"That's baloney! I don't believe that for one minute," Hickman said. At that point Hickman told me he had to go as it was time for church.

August 11, 1981

While Hollywood detectives raced up to mile marker 130 to investigate the severed head that had been found, Detective Connolly of the Plantation Police Department called the HPD to inform them of an attempted abduction of a three-year-old boy in their city (HPD case files, roll 1, p. 3136). Although this was on a Tuesday, the incident (case # 994-81-8) happened at 5:40 p.m. Dahmer usually got off work around 5:00 p.m., and this would've been more than enough time to get to Plantation and even drive around for a while.

The incident happened while three kids were playing in front of their house. One of the boys was approached by an unknown white male who tried to lure the child into a blue van. The child then ran into the house and told his mother, Deborah Pilkins, who called the Plantation Police. The suspect was described as a white male about six feet tall, thin build, with dirty blond long hair, wearing a blue long-sleeved shirt and blue jeans. (Most likely this was the same blue shirt Dahmer wore on July 13 in the Twin City Mall attempted abduction and on August 17 in the South Beach attempted abduction as well as when I had my second encounter with him.)

Due to the fact that the child, Paul Pilkins, was only three years old, police were unable to obtain any further information. When speaking with the other two kids, also three years old, police were again unable to get any more information except for the fact that the incident really took place.

Nothing in the Adam Walsh case files showed that Hollywood detectives ever called Deborah Pilkins. The full Plantation P.D. report can be read at JusticeForAdam.com.

All of this leaves me with the haunting thought: around 1991, did someone at the HPD spend more time looking through the files in order to see what to remove than actually trying to solve this case?

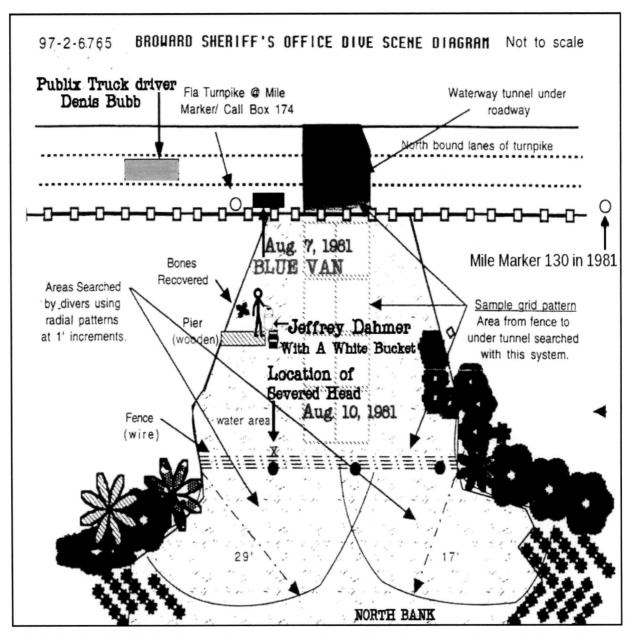

97-2-6765 BROWARD SHERIFF'S OFFICE DIVE SCENE DIAGRAM Not to scale

Publix Truck driver Denis Bubb Fla Turnpike @ Mile Marker/ Call Box 174

Waterway tunnel under roadway

North bound lanes of turnpike

Bones Recovered

Aug. 7, 1981 BLUE VAN

Mile Marker 130 in 1981

Areas Searched by divers using radial patterns at 1' increments.

Pier (wooden)

←**Jeffrey Dahmer With A White Bucket**

Sample grid pattern Area from fence to under tunnel searched with this system.

Location of Severed Head Aug. 10, 1981

Fence (wire)

water area

X

29'   17'

NORTH BANK

DIAGRAM ABOVE: The Florida Turnpike at mile marker 130 northbound diagram can be found in the SAO case files, Box 1, file 17

*The original SAO file diagram does not include the Jeffrey Dahmer sketch or the trucks.

*The bones that were recovered near the bridge turned out to be animal bones.

*The black circles along the fence are the fence posts.

In 1981, this location was mile marker 129.95 (rounded off to 130). Due to the extension of the turnpike to Homestead, Florida, all the mile markers have changed, and it's now mile marker 174.

CITY OF HOLLYWOOD, FLORIDA

INTER-OFFICE MEMORANDUM

TO: **ALL UNITS**   DATE: **August 14th, 1981**

SUBJECT: **Press release**

FROM: **DET. R. HICKMAN**   REFERENCE: **ADAM WALSH CASE**

Updated information received this date reference the vehicle suspected in the murder of ADAM WALSH is that the vehicle is a:

Late model Ford van, navy blue in color, with a black front bumper, chrome ladder mounted on the left rear, shiny flat-spoke mag wheels, tinted windows, with a rectangle window on the sliding door, passenger side, Florida tag, no spare wheel.

The suspect operating the vehicle is described as:

W/M, mid-twenties, 5'10" to 6', medium to heavy build, 180–200 lbs. Dark brown to black hair, medium to curly in style, mustache.

003926

PHOTO ABOVE: Florida Turnpike, mile marker 130, in 1981. Photo courtesy: HPD file photo

The footbridge was used to provide access to a water-measuring device that was monitored by the St. Johns Water Management District, which hasn't been used for quite some time. The area thirty years later has changed. In the photo below, the footbridge is dilapidated. The water level has dropped. The pond is overgrown with water hyacinth.

Photo below was taken from the road shoulder.
See the turnpike photo folder at JusticeForAdam.com for more photos.

Photo taken by me in 2011

PHOTO LEFT: In this photo, my Ford Aerostar is parked in the same location the blue van was parked when it was seen on August 7, 1981, by the two Publix truck drivers.

The footbridge is at the bottom right.

CHAPTER FIFTEEN
THE DAHMER WITNESSES

"Yes, I do have remorse, but I'm not even sure myself whether it is as profound as it should be. I've always wondered myself why I don't feel more remorse."

Jeffrey L. Dahmer

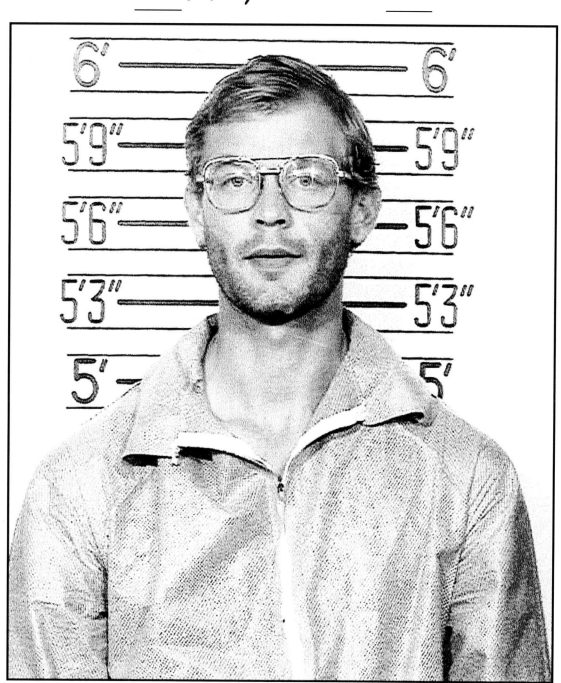

Booking photo of Dahmer with his glasses on is from the Milwaukee Police Department, July 24, 1991

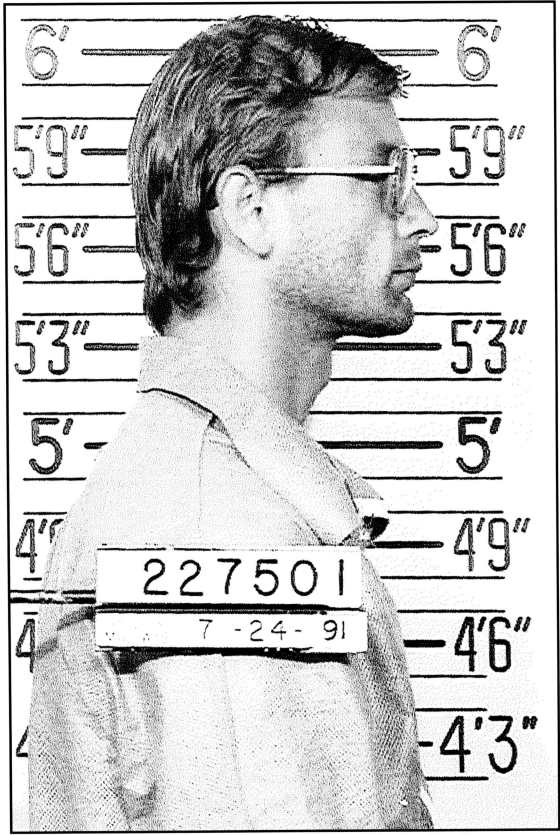

Profile with glasses: Jeffrey Dahmer dressed in his "suicide watch" outfit

NOTE: There are so many witnesses implicating Jeffrey Dahmer being in the toy department on the day of Adam's abduction that I won't mention all of them in this chapter, since some have already been previously mentioned and several more will be mentioned in the next chapter.

Witness Phillip Lohr

When the Adam Walsh Case was closed on December 16, 2008, I tried to get a copy of the two-CD-ROM set the HPD offered as their evidence in accusing Ottis Toole. They were only offering it to the media. When they asked me what media outlet I was from, I said, "I worked for the *Miami Herald*." I didn't lie; I had worked for the *Herald* for twenty-five years in the pressroom. Unfortunately, a *Miami Herald* reporter had already received a copy, and they were only giving out one per outlet.

Art Harris did manage to get a copy, though. He said he worked for the *Daily Business Review*, and there was no other reporter from that paper. After our meeting, Art and I went to Kinko's (since renamed FedEx Office), and I made a copy from his.

When I got home, I looked at the files for the very first time. I wanted to see where the investigators went wrong. While reading the case files, I was impressed at the comedy of the investigation. These detectives were running around nearly half the nation, interviewing all the wrong people for all the wrong reasons. Witnesses, right in their own back yard, had tried to tell them what happened, but they refused to listen.

I saw one of the letters I had sent to John Walsh care of *America's Most Wanted* in 1992 after the HPD dismissed Dahmer as a suspect. John Walsh had no idea the HPD was already in full cover-up mode at that time. HPD would never do much of anything with all the letters and tips *America's Most Wanted* would forward to them over the years.

What really caught my attention were the numerous witnesses from the Hollywood Mall and other locations. They were all there in the case files. I remembered that John Walsh had said on his show that no witnesses had ever come forward in his son's kidnapping. They were all there, and they were compelling. Individually, each account was a small window in time, but when I looked at them all together, I was able to put together a full timeline.

The real task would be to track down the witnesses and talk to them myself. I joined the free online ZabaSearch.com, Intelius.com, and PeopleFinders.com, but my best searches came from the free public county records. I started with the Broward County tax appraiser records.

I immediately found Phillip Lohr, a homeowner in Broward. I didn't have his phone number, so I went to his house. Phil wasn't home, but his wife, Mamie, was. At first, she was a bit leery. I showed up with a briefcase, and she couldn't imagine why I was there. As soon as I told her I was there about Phil's tip, she became very excited. She called Phil and asked him to come home right away. Mamie told me she couldn't understand why no one had ever called them before. She excitedly told me what she knew. In fact, she didn't stop talking until Phil showed up.

Phil told me the reason he didn't go to the police right away was because he'd convinced himself that there had to be other witnesses and because he hated thinking he was the one that could've stopped the kidnapping. Phil said, "I always felt guilty about making the wrong decision . . . I know absolutely it was Adam Walsh I saw . . . I am absolutely positive there was a blue van . . . I am equally positive Toole is the wrong man." When I showed Phil some photos and mug shots of Jeffrey Dahmer, he said, "I can definitely say, I cannot rule out Dahmer."

In Phil's statement, he had gotten some things wrong, as all the witnesses had, including me. Forget about the fact that Phil said the man he saw had a beard and glasses as he also said he was concentrating on the boy. By concentrating on the couple of things that are not consistent with what other witnesses said, the HPD easily found reasons to dismiss all the witnesses, which is exactly why they never got anywhere.

Phil was on his way to the Sears customer service desk. He was very angry because an unattended blue van was parked near the store entrance, up against the curb on the northbound traffic side, blocking all the traffic. Waiting to get around the van, he lost his parking space when another car pulled into it. He managed to get another space. When he went into Sears, he was even angrier, because he had to walk around this van that was the cause of the problem. As he walked into the west entrance near the toy department, he passed a small boy being carried by a dirty young man. The boy was shouting, "You're not my daddy! You're not my daddy!" The man replied, "I'm taking you to your daddy!"

Phil told me that, as he was watching this, he turned around and started walking backward, looking in disbelief. His boy was about the same age, and Phil was thinking that he would never carry his son like that. Phil said he wanted to intervene, but then he thought maybe the man was a stepfather or boyfriend.

He knew he had to remember this incident, but trying to remember both the man and the boy was too much, so he concentrated on the boy. "He had on a striped shirt, shorts. His face was covered with freckles, and his front teeth were missing. . . Also, I remember he had on a cap." Phil's description is exactly as Adam was described in the police incident report. Phil said the reason he decided to concentrate on the child was "just in case a child showed up missing." He then went to the service desk but quickly started having second thoughts. He ran back outside to have another look. When he got outside, the man, the boy, and the blue van were gone.

After hearing Phil's story, I called Art Harris. I told Art, "Guess where I'm at?" Then I told him he needed to get over here and listen to this story. Art arrived in about forty minutes. Phil repeated the same story nearly verbatim.

It should also be noted that since Phil saw Adam being carried out of the store, it's proof that security guard Kathryn (Shaffer) Barrack did not ask Adam to leave the store, as Joe Matthews would want you to believe. It's also clear that Adam was not wandering around outside in the parking lot by himself, as Ottis Toole said. When Phil went to Detective Smith, he was dismissed quickly and told what he saw had nothing to do with the Adam Walsh case. After Smith did his best to get Phil to disappear Phil went over his head to Sergeant Dunbar. Not getting any satisfaction from Dunbar, he went to the Broward County Prospector's Office. Investigator Phil Mundy was a Fort Lauderdale detective hired by the State Attorney's Office to look into the Adam Walsh case at a time when Jay Grelen sued to open the case files. Mundy first took Lohr's statement, then accused him of having an "attitude" and being "sarcastic."

I met Phil Lohr. I know Phil, and I have talked to him a number of times. Phil was a stand-up guy and a great witness who did his best to do his civic duty. This is what happens to a witness who is just adamant about what he saw! Either Investigator Mundy was in lockstep with the corrupt HPD, or he was in great dereliction of his fiduciary responsibility in getting justice for Adam Walsh. If I were a homicide detective, I would never simply dismiss Phil's statement.

One thing to notice when reading the printed transcripts of the taped statement is that Mundy had already dismissed Lohr before he even knew all the facts. For example, Mundy first heard about the blue van and the missing teeth of the abducted child in Lohr's statement. Yet he dismissed Lohr before the interview even started and only granted the interview at Lohr's insistence.

Phil Mundy's letter that was attached to the interview speaks for itself:

May 30, 1997

FROM: Phil Mundy

State Attorney's Office
Phone 305-831-6368
Pager 305-897-5288
Mobile 305-249-6619

To: Ralph J. Ray, Jr.

Attached for the file

Mr. LOHR had presented himself to Mark SMITH who, after hearing his story, tried to explain that the incident he was describing did not appear to have anything to do with the WALSH investigation. LOHR was not satisfied with that and complained about SMITH to Sgt. DUNBAR. Apparently LOHR was not satisfied with DUNBAR either, and found his way to our office.

I interviewed LOHR and came to same conclusion as Mark and tried to convey to Mr. LOHR that he should not feel guilty about not coming to the police fifteen years ago, because what he saw does not seem connected to WALSH. It seemed apparent from Mr. LOHR'S response, which bordered on sarcasm that the best solution was to simply take his statement.

In fact, LOHR cannot say it was Adam he saw, and his description of the man does not fit TOOLE. LOHR does not even know if he was at Sears on the same day as the WALSH abduction.

201 S.E. 6th Street, Fort Lauderdale, FL 33301

FULL STATEMENT: THIS IS GOING TO BE A WITNESS STATEMENT IN REGARD TO CASE NUMBER 96-02-262. THE FOLLOWING IS GOING TO BE THE STATEMENT OF MR. PHILLIP DAVID LOHR, L-O-H-R, WHITE MALE, DATE OF BIRTH JULY 7, 1955, AS GIVEN TO STATE ATTORNEY INVESTIGATOR PHILIP J. MUNDY. THE STATEMENT IS BEING TAKEN AT THE STATE ATTORNEY'S OFFICE, ROOM 630, ON TUESDAY, FEBRUARY 18, 1997, BEGINNING AT ABOUT 10:35 AM.

The following notations distinguish the two speakers:

PM: PHILIP MUNDY

PL: PHILLIP LOHR

****

PM: As an investigator with the State Attorney's Office, I have the authority to take your statement under oath. So I need you to raise your right hand. And do you solemnly swear or affirm to the statement you are about to give *to* be the truth, the whole truth, so help you God?

PL: I do.

PM: For the record, I need you to state your full name and date of birth.

PL: Phillip Lohr, 7/7/55.

PM: And your current home address, sir?

PL: (*IIII IIIIIIIIIIIIIIIII*) Street, Hollywood, Florida. [Redacted by me.]

PM: Mr. Lohr, as you are aware, our office is assisting in the investigation into the abduction and homicide of Adam Walsh. And just for the record, apparently you had some information that you felt you wanted to share with law enforcement, and that is what brings you here today in regard to that case, correct?

PL: That is correct.

PM: Would you tell me where you were and when you were there and, basically, what you saw in regard to the Adam Walsh abduction?

PL: Well, I could tell you what I saw, but you are the one saying . . .

PM: We are investigating the case.

PL: OK, when it was within a few days prior to helicopters in the general vicinity of the mall, I was walking into an entrance on the west side, into Sears, and I pretty much came face to face with a man who was carrying what I considered to be a large child. It didn't seem appropriate, for the size of the child, to be carrying him. As I walked by, I heard the child say, "You are not my daddy." This struck me as unusual, and I turned around and, in wondering what I should do, felt that perhaps I should at least try to get a description of the child. At first I tried to just take a look at everything, including the man. I finally just decided that, well, I will just go with the child that has a very round head, has noticeably predominant freckles on his face. I wouldn't consider him to be lightly freckled, yet he wasn't freckled all over his body or anything. He seems to have a very light pattern of freckles over his cheeks and going over his nose. At that time, I then decided that, well, they would have known if the child is missing, they will know the child, because he certainly didn't come there himself. So I made an attempt, as the man was still being blocked by other people coming in from going out, I made an attempt to get around by some lawn mowers to look at him from the side, and did the best I could to get a description of him. And at that point, I then went about my business, which was apparently to go over to the service counter area, and he was gone. I do recall, as far as relating the time, I do know that one of the reasons I didn't go out, or if it was Adam, was that it was daylight, and that was one of the reasons why I felt these things don't happen during these times.

PM: You don't have a recollection of the day of the week or [the] date and year that this incident occurred?

PL: No. Like I said, everything is based on the fact that I know it was just prior, within days, to the helicopters, and it was just within a day or two that I finally heard about the Adam Walsh abduction. When I caught the tail end of the newscast.

PM: The helicopter thing—did you see him the same day as you saw the man and the child?

PL: Absolutely not. No.

PM: When was the helicopters?

PL: This was afterwards.

PM: OK, I'm a little confused about that, then. You saw . . .

PL: Everything I am telling you transpired within the same week.

PM: OK, but that is what I am trying to get down. You saw the man and the child on one occasion?

PL: Correct.

PM: On one particular day?

PL: Correct.

PM: When did you see the helicopters?

PL: Within one or two days.

PM: That is what I am getting at. I was under the impression it might have been the same day.

PL: No, it wasn't the same day at all.

PM: It was a day or two later?

PL: Correct.

PM: The time of day you saw this gentleman and the child?

PL: I don't have a memory of looking at a watch or a clock. All I know is that I am still standing wondering what I should do, he has already gone out the door, and I know I said to myself, oh my gosh, here it is, broad daylight. What makes you think that something like this is happening? Like I said, the only reason, the only thing that unnerved me, was the child saying "You are not my daddy."

PM: Do you recall if it was morning or afternoon?

PL: Oh, this is going to be in the middle of the day. Towards afternoon. This is not morning.

PM: OK, it is not morning. Is it afternoon? After 12:00 p.m.? The best you can remember.

PL: It would only be my own impressions of the day, but I am going to have to go that it is from 12 noon to, say, 3:00 p.m. In other words, it is a bright day out. There is a brightness.

PM: The child you saw, let's take him, and then we will go on to the gentleman. Can you give me an approximation about how old you thought he was?

PL: I can only approximate that due to the size, and he is being carried. Like I said, he didn't seem to be the size that a father would just normally carry, as the means of traveling with your child. My son is six. I feel he is a bit too awkward for me to try and carry, so I am going to have to go that he is in the neighborhood of around six years, on height and weight.

PM: If you had to choose on this child's between being thin, medium and heavy, where would you put him?

PL: I would have to say medium. But once again, you have to just go with, the only way I could describe it as, he is too big for what you would think a dad would carry a son at.

PM: How about his hair color; do you remember that?

PL: It is brown, and I would like to lean towards the more chocolate or darker browns, but you can still tell it is brown.

PM: Forgetting about the freckles, if you can remember from his arms or the rest of his face and his neck, his complexion, how would you describe that? Was it . . .

PL: Forgetting the freckles?

PM: Yeah 'cause sometimes freckles influence people, and they want to say he was like tannish or dark complexion. What I am asking you, if you understand?

PL: I am trying to say that I'm no judge of skin colors or anything like that.

PM: You know pale, right. Pale would be light. Dark would be sort of a dark tan or Hispanic or even . . .

PL: No, he is not Latin.

PM: No, I understand that, I am just trying to make an association as to his complexion.

PL: Without the freckles. I don't have a word for you there. Like I said, I clued, I said it was the freckles. I can remember seeing them, and I said, gee, look at the freckles.

PM: You heard him say, "You are not my daddy," and you said the gentleman was carrying the child. Was the child, like, flailing away or fighting or . . .

PL: No. He was just simply making that statement, and he meant it. He did look kind of, oh, here we go for flustered, sweaty.

PM: The child?

PL: The child, yeah. He seems to be flushed, flustered, as if the impression struck me that perhaps the child had been crying, but that had been a few moments prior. There weren't tears or anything like that, it just struck me that you are not my daddy, and I am mad about the fact that now I am doing whatever I am doing. That is one of the impressions that I got from it. If that is what you mean by complexion, in other words a little flushed, flushed, he seemed to be a little flushed!

PM: Let me run down this gentleman that you saw, and could you give me an idea, and we are talking of course [about] a white male and a white child?

PL: Yes.

PM: The age of the gentleman, where would you put that?

PL: He seemed to be older than me at the time. Figure on roughly in the area of 25 years old, so I would have to put it about 30.

PM: How about height?

PL: I would say he is a little taller than me, but he does not exceed 6 feet. I am 5'7". Then again, I am wearing shoes, so maybe I am 5'8". Of course, he is wearing shoes, too.

PM: Again, if you had to pick between thin, medium, and muscular, where would you put this gentleman?

PL: I would have to put him at medium. It was nothing that told me he was muscular, nothing that suggested he was thin.

PM: Were you able to discern a hair color?

PL: Yes.

PM: Which was?

PL: Brown, with reddish tones.

PM: How about facial hair?

PL: Yes. He had longer sideburns, past his ears, and he also had the type of beard—how would you describe it? I don't know if a goatee is appropriate. I thought it may be a goatee on the chin, but this is a connected mustache to a short chin beard.

PM: Besides what we have talked about, was there anything about him physically that stood out?

PL: No. I would say he's got glasses. He does seem to have these little lines right at the corners of his eyes.

PM: You didn't notice if he was carrying anything besides the child?

PL: I did notice that he was not carrying anything.

PM: Did he speak to the child? Did you hear him speak to the child?

PL: I did hear him speak.

PM: Could you hear him?

PL: Well, I quickly did. I mean, he started to say something, but within the first two or three words I was already past him, and he is facing the other direction. His back is to me. He started to say something like, well, we or . . .

PM: You didn't see anyone that might have been with him?

PL: Oh, no, he was definitely alone with the child.

PM: And, alright now, because we are on tape and not drawing pictures, the entrance that you were going in where you encounter this individual and the child, which entrance is that?

PL: This is on the west side of the building. This is the lawn and garden entrance, which is just to the north of what would be considered the main entrance for that side. This takes you into where you are pretty much facing what used to be the service desk. There is also, like, a little area with plants, and then when you walk in, you see lawn mowers on the right and garden furniture on the left.

PM: After you passed the gentleman and he passed you, you didn't see where he went?

PL: He went out the door.

PM: I mean, after that, he is gone?

PL: No, because that is the reason why I know it is daylight, because, like I said, once he is gone, I still feel like maybe I should go outside and see if there is anything that is noticeable that would tell me that there is something wrong with the situation, and that is when I have a very distinct recollection of seeing the brightness of the day, and I say, oh, come on, here you are, and it is right here in broad daylight, there is probably nothing to worry about.

PM: Obviously there came a time when you learn of Adam Walsh being missing, and then of course when he was actually abducted. When you found out in the media, or however you found out, that the child was missing from the Sears, at what point in time did you associate what you saw with the possibility that it might have been connected to the Walsh abduction?

PL: You mean, I mean, immediately! I mean, they gave a description, and I believe they may have even shown that photograph, the baseball photograph.

PM: Just for the record, what we are referring to is a missing-person bulletin that was put out back in 1981, which contained a photograph of the Adam Walsh boy, both with a hat and without a hat. After you learned of the abduction of Adam, when Adam was missing, and you thought perhaps what you had seen had something to do with that? That was almost immediately that you saw . . .

PL: When I came in and caught the tail end of the newscast, and the picture was up, I felt that what I saw was possibly significant. That is what I mean as immediately. I started going, could that have been, you know, did what I see, could that have possibly been Adam?

PM: Did you go to the police with that information?

PL: No.

PM: Any reason why not?

PL: Well, I was forced to make a determination as to did I see something significant or was it not significant. And based upon that photo, I chose to presume that it wasn't going to be significant.

PM: I am a little confused. You found out about the Walsh abduction, and I thought you said that you thought this gentleman and child exiting the store, in your mind, could have had something to do with the Walsh abduction. Am I correct so far?

PL: Correct.

PM: But then you didn't go to the police, because you decided what you saw was not significant for the Walsh abduction.

PL: Well, see if I can put it in other words. I told you what I saw. And then within a week, I hear a child is missing. All of a sudden, gee, could that have possibly been the same child that I saw? I can't remember precisely what day it is because, as I told you in our interview previously to having the tape going here, that I was up there on many, many days. I do know that I was up there for at least three or maybe four days in a row. So I can't remember exactly what day it was. I look briefly at this photograph, and I don't see the freckles, which is one of the predominant things I took as one of the characteristic traits of him. And aside from that, I got a child who doesn't have all of his teeth in the front, and that is very, very common for children. Now, you add to that . . .

PM: Wait a minute, you lost me on the teeth part.

PL: Well, he was missing his, his teeth are arched. His teeth are just starting to grow in.

PM: The child you saw?

PL: The child I saw, yes.

PM: We didn't cover that before.

PL: Well, you didn't ask, and when . . .

PM: I know I didn't. If I don't ask, you should tell me.

PL: Yeah, like I said, I went with a very round head, gee, look at those freckles, his teeth was missing and they were kind of arched, just starting to grow in, and as I told you before, whether I implanted it or not, I believe that I chose his shorts as being khaki. And only because you could use the word "khaki" and everybody is going to go, yeah, that is what it was.

PM: So, taking all this . . .

PL: Listen, it boils down to, and I hate to bring it up, but it boils down to I was able to convince myself that it probably wasn't the same child, that the police probably have other witnesses, that I couldn't have been the only person that saw anything. Every reason in the book, just so that I don't have to say that I was the one that could have stopped the man. Now, you will have to understand that. OK, it is not something that I am happy to say on tape, alright, but even at the time, that same night that I saw, that came to my mind too. So it just basically boiled down to where the police don't need you, somebody else probably saw the same thing that you saw. Besides, what do I got to say? Just "you are not my daddy." And back then, I am presuming that maybe he kicked up a fuss previously, so, you know, you yourself said earlier that you had other people come forward, and you are very, very comfortable with what they had to say.

PM: It is a natural reaction.

PL: No, I mean, and over time, the fact that there was a van parked outside at the time . . .

PM: We haven't talked about this van yet. What does the van have to do with it?

PL: The van could have absolutely nothing to do with this, other than it being parked outside at the time. And since I never went outside to see where this man went with this child, all that I know, that that was one of the things that I remembered and recalled at the time of me catching the back end of the newscast. And ever since then whenever I am behind a van I start thinking.

PM: What can you tell me about the van you saw?

PL: It is one of those nicer vans with a picture window, and it has a teardrop little corner window, and that it is blue and that, I mean, like I said, it could be nothing, alright, but I have always considered that to have been sinister. And that maybe that guy just went right into that van.

PM: Where was the van parked in relation to the entrance you went into?

PL: Within 20 feet of the door. Right up against the curb.

PM: It was against the curb?

PL: Oh yes, that is the reason why I remembered it, because . . .

PM: Was somebody behind the wheel?

PL: Well, no. And the reason I remember it is because the van being parked there cost me my parking space I wanted to get. People were coming into my lane, stopping me from going forward, and there was a nice parking space right there, and this guy did a U-turn right into it. So then I had to swear at the van, drive around, and that is pretty much a precursor to me being in the frame of mind of wanting to start judging people when I finally did walk in the door, and saying, gee, look at this doting father carrying a child this size, and, you know, these are the little emotional things that make me remember this day. At any rate, to make a long story short with the van, every time we get behind a van, I eventually start to get bothered by should I have gone to the police, and every time that happens, I just put it out of my mind. I am tired of living that way. As I mentioned to you earlier, I do U-turns in the middle of the street because I quite frankly don't want to consider myself, you know, I don't want to go through another one. I don't want to actually end up being somebody that sees this thing twice.

PM: I can understand that. This will conclude the statement at approximately 11:00 a.m.

STATEMENT TERMINATED (SAO case files, box 8, file 23)

Witness Jennie Warren

After listening to Phil Lohr, I became energized and started wondering what other witnesses had to say. Back in 1981, Jennie Warren lived on Scott Street in Hollywood. She had moved only once since then and still lived only a few blocks from her old address. Again, I had an address but no phone number. Jennie is in her mid-eighties. I knew she would be apprehensive if I showed up without calling first, but I was compelled to do so anyway.

At 11 a.m., I knocked on Jennie's door. I heard a soft, quiet voice from behind the closed door say, "Yes?" I told her my name was Willis Morgan and I wanted to talk to her about something that happened in 1981. "You mean the Walsh case?" she responded. Now I knew I was at the right address, so I said "yes," and Jennie opened the door immediately.

I wasn't expecting what happened next. She started having an uncontrollable breakdown, crying really hard, her eyes welling with tears that ran down her cheeks. I didn't know what to say, so I just stood there, speechless. She cried and apologized, and then she cried again. Finally, she composed herself enough to say, "I'm sorry. I don't mean to bawl, but they just closed the case, and it wasn't him! It was the other guy!"

I didn't need to ask her who the other guy was. I knew who she was referring to. I showed Jennie my portfolio to put her at ease and assure her that I was there about the Adam Walsh case. She invited me in, and we sat down at the dining room table. I wanted to tell her about my involvement in the case, but I could see that she had a lot to say. She needed someone to talk to, so I let her do most of the talking.

Jennie Warren contacted police by phone in the early days after Adam's abduction, but didn't get any reply. Again, on October 30, 1995, Jennie called the HPD. Detective Mark Smith took the call. She told him she was calling about the Adam Walsh case and that she was in Sears with her three granddaughters the day Adam was kidnapped. Cheryl was fourteen, Ruthie eight, and Christina three—she was in a stroller pushed by Cheryl.

Smith had her come in for an interview, but it was not taped. In that interview, Smith had Jennie look at a photo array with six photos, Ottis Toole being number five. Jennie said she didn't recognize any of the photos to be the gentleman she saw at Sears. According to Jennie, Smith then pointed out the photo of Ottis Toole, and when she insisted it wasn't him, Smith tried to coax her, saying, "Are you sure? Because we have proof it was him."

She told him, "No, that's not him." Jennie said Smith did his best to get her to date and initial the back of the photo. She said she refused because "it wasn't him." Consequently, Smith dismissed her instead of dismissing Ottis Toole.

PHOTOS ABOVE: HPD and SAO file record: This is the photo array the Hollywood Police and the Broward County State Attorney's Office used to determine Adam's murderer. **NOTE:** Even after Jeffrey Dahmer was captured in 1991, his photo was never added to the lineup, most likely because witnesses like Jennie Warren would have picked him out.

It wasn't until nearly a year later, in 1996, after the media lawsuit prompted the release of the case files (and the SAO came to the aid of the HPD and tried to prevent the case files from being released), that she received a call from State Attorney Investigator Phil Mundy. After being interviewed by Mundy, she was dismissed again when she refused to implicate Ottis Toole. The taped interview took place on September 10, 1996, at her home in Hollywood.

Jennie said, without prompting, "I could have picked out the man, had the investigator placed his picture in the lineup with Mr. Toole. I wish my mind could take a picture, because it would be him, Dahmer."

According to Jennie, she entered Sears from the west entrance near the toy department. Ruthie wanted to go and look at some Barbie dolls, so they made a stop in the toy department. That was when she noticed a woman she would later come to know as Reve enter with Adam from the north entrance next to the service counter. Reve came directly to the toy department and dropped Adam off next to the video games. All the games had kids playing on them, so Adam just stood there, watching. Jennie said she left Ruthie there, as well. By coincidence, she left at the same time as Reve and in the same direction, until Reve turned to the right toward the lighting department and Jennie went to the service counter to pay her Sears bill.

Jennie took a number, but while waiting for her turn, she started thinking about the suspicious-looking gentleman in the toy department. He was just standing there watching the kids. She said, "He gave me an uneasy feeling. He seemed shy, and he had this look about him as if he was very sad or lonely." Jennie rushed back to the toy department to pick up the eight-year-old and then headed into the mall. "Even after I left Sears, I remember thinking how intent he seemed on being with the boys. He was standing right next to Adam, but Adam could care less. He just wanted to play the video games."

About thirty to forty minutes later, Jennie heard the first page on the Sears PA system for a missing child: "Adam Walsh, your mother is looking for you, please find the nearest sales associate . . ." She said, "I remember the announcement on the intercom because I stopped to give my granddaughters a lecture about safety and being alone."

I started going through my portfolio, showing her the information I had collected. When I came to a page with a front and side mug shot view of Dahmer, Jennie stopped me and said, "That's him! That's the man I saw. Only, he had his hair below his ears. I'm a beautician, and I notice all these things."

I asked Jennie if I could call Art Harris and explained, "He's a reporter, and he's writing a book about this case." With her permission, I called Art and asked him to come over. Because it was past lunchtime and I knew this was going to be a long day, I offered to buy Jennie lunch. We agreed on subs. I went to Publix supermarket right down the street, in the same mall Adam was abducted from. I get an uneasy feeling every time I even pass this mall, and the Publix was near the north entrance from where Dahmer had entered.

When I returned to Jennie's, Art was at her door. I could see that Jennie was starting to get a bit nervous. She called her grandson-in-law to come over. She told us, "Ben is on the way. He's a Hollywood police officer, you know."

As you can imagine, that gave me the willies, but as it turned out, Ben was a good cop. Jennie's full statement can be found in the SAO case files (box 1, statement 07.9). Sadly, Jennie passed away on September 16, 2012.

The Pottenburghs

1981

Initially, police collected the names of eight individuals who might have seen Adam at Sears. One was a ten-year-old boy named Timothy Pottenburgh, whose grandmother reported a suspicious incident.

Three days after Adam's abduction, Marilyn Pottenburgh called the HPD with a tip. Her call would be one of the few that were followed up. She said her ten-year-old son Timothy told her that he'd noticed something suspicious during their visit to the Sears store on the same afternoon that Adam Walsh disappeared.

Timothy's statement initiated the original BOLO for a blue Ford van with tinted windows, mag wheels, chrome ladder, and no spare tire on the rear. This BOLO would start the launch of the largest vehicle search in Florida state history. It was so extensive that even used-car lots and junkyards were checked for blue vans, and the VIN numbers were run for history checks. If you had a blue van and were seen making a U-turn, it was presumed you were trying to get away, so you would get pulled over and given extra scrutiny. If you had a blue van and sold it, you were trying to get rid of evidence, and that van was given extra scrutiny. Suddenly, practically every blue van in South Florida was suspect. Hundreds were checked and cleared. (Other statements contradicted the police BOLO and suggested the vehicle might have been a Dodge Ram cargo-delivery van, non-extended model).

Detectives immediately realized Timothy was describing the Twin City Mall suspect and his composite (shown earlier back on page 58 of Chapter Five) not only matched but was quite impressive for a ten-year-old. They asked his parents whether he had read about the story, and they assured detectives he had not. They also showed Timothy the Twin City Mall composites. Timothy said they looked exactly like the man he saw, only the hair was messier and curlier. (SAO case files, box 2, file 2, p. 26)

All the local news stations ran a re-enactment of an Adam look-alike being snatched and tossed into a blue van by a young, six-foot tall, white male perpetrator. Tips started to pour in. The offices of the HPD became disorganized in the deluge. This ragtag team of Hollywood detectives settled for writing tips on scrap paper, napkins, and even matchbook covers, with none of the calls from their cluttered desks being logged. Because of this chaos, nothing would develop from all the tips and thousands of man-hours of police work.

On August 14, 1981, Martin Segall hypnotized ten-year-old Timothy Pottenburgh. Timothy said a white man, about six feet tall, with dark brown hair and a mustache, was hanging around the toy department and reading a comic book. A short time later, a little boy—presumably Adam—was forced into a blue van.

Hollywood Police gave the following statement:

"The description provided by the second, adult witness [Eugene Menacho] strongly supported that of the ten-year-old boy [Timothy Pottenburgh]. He saw the same van near the same area of the Sears, and he also, under hypnosis, provided the same basic description of the vehicle," said Detective Jim Gibbons. "Now we have two people at the same time on the same day, and they're both saying the same thing. We feel very strongly this is our suspect."

With other witness statements that very strongly corroborate Pottenburgh and Monacho's statement, the case started off in the right direction. It was the lead detectives who derailed the investigation by injecting their own personal theories into the case and dismissing not only Pottenburgh and Monacho but also all other witnesses that didn't fit the detective's theories. This continued until the very day the HPD closed the case.

From the HPD case files:

Marilyn Pottenburgh, her ten-year-old son Timothy, and his grandmother, Carolyn Hudson, went to the Sears Mall to do some back-to-school shopping for Timothy on July 27, 1981. Marilyn stated, after shopping, they all went to the Sidewalk Café [food court] to eat. Marilyn also stated she didn't feel like walking all the way back to her vehicle, so Carolyn and Timothy walked back to retrieve the car from the Sears north entrance, then drove around to the east side and picked her up at the east-side, Sidewalk Café entrance. Timothy stated that, on the way back to the car, he and his grandmother stopped in the toy department of Sears, when he observed a white male in his twenties, 5'10" to 6' tall, loitering. Timothy also stated that the white male was holding a comic book in front of his face and was looking around the Atari games while in the toy department. After a short period of time, Timothy stated, he saw the man run out of the catalogue pick-up door [north exit]. *Then he ran to a navy blue van that was parked just northeast of the north door of Sears. Timothy and his grandmother then proceeded to walk to their vehicle, which was parked outside the north entrance. As they stepped off the sidewalk, the blue van almost hit them as it turned wildly around the northwest corner of Sears. Timothy then ran around to the west side of Sears to see why this man was in such a rush. It was at this time that the van stopped in front of the garden shop* (HPD case files, roll 1, p. 4851). [I surmise Dahmer might have exited from the west garden shop door instead of the north exit to avoid having to drag Adam out past the scrutiny of all the people at the service desk].

According to Marilyn Pottenburgh, she stayed in the mall to do some more shopping and was picked up at the east mall entrance, so she didn't witness the event in the parking lot. Carolyn Hudson, Timothy's grandmother, stated the only thing she witnessed was the blue van that almost ran her over as she was walking toward her vehicle with Timothy. Mrs. Hudson stated she didn't witness the other events on the west side of Sears her grandson Timothy reported. At a later date, on September 4, 1981, Carolyn Hudson was re-interviewed. This time, she wasn't positive of the time of day. She guessed it was around 1:15 p.m. that the incident occurred. Because of this, she would be dismissed.

Along with Hudson's dismissal went the blue van. Detective Hoffman suggested not letting the media know about the blue van being dismissed to keep the media busy and off their backs. Because of this, police departments throughout South Florida and the state continued searching for a blue van. Hoffman was also aware of this but thought it would be a good idea to keep everyone busy while he solved the case himself by going after the houseguest, James Campbell.

With the blue van dismissed, the investigators were left with nothing more than a bunch of dead-end leads. However, in 1983, Ottis Toole came along and saved the investigation. Finally, these detectives could climb out of their quagmire with a solid lead—and an easy confession.

Detectives would soon learn that Toole had a white Cadillac, and now things would start getting easy. They soon realized why they had been stumped for so long. They had wasted time and money running around looking for a mysterious blue van. All they had to do was turn that blue van into a white Cadillac to fit Toole's vehicle. This case was simpler than they could ever have imagined. Now all they needed was an Ottis Toole witness, and like a mushroom popping up after a Florida summer rainstorm, he would come, but not until 1996, long after Ottis Toole was dismissed as a suspect. In the next chapter, I'll show how this witness, William Mistler, would breathe life back into the Toole theory.

In 1981, during the early stages of the investigation into Adam's abduction, the original detectives didn't know about all the lost witnesses like me who were turned away from the front lobby of their own police department just days after Adam went missing. Nor did they know about the witnesses that didn't have their phone calls returned when they called the HPD with crucial tips, again, just days after Adam went missing.

In 2008, however, Detective Matthews did—or at least, he should have. Matthews himself said he was computer illiterate, so he took the paper copy of the case files and "put everything in chronological order. Then [he] read every page and every witness statement." Of the Pottenburgh statements, Matthews's assessment was, "I don't know what they saw, but it wasn't Adam." Matthews was so sure of his assessment that he wouldn't even bother to call the Pottenburghs for an interview. In fact, he felt so certain about his direction that he believed it wasn't necessary to call any of the key witnesses that were at the Hollywood Mall the day little Adam was abducted.

Witness Eugene Monacho

On Friday, August 14, 1981, Eugene Paul Monacho called the HPD to inform them that he had been on his way to Sears when he was almost involved in an accident with a blue van that was traveling at high speed. The van was driven by a man around twenty years old. Mr. Monacho informed Detective Hickman that the day was Monday, July 27, 1981, between 12:30 and 1 p.m.

RIGHT: Phone call to HPD from Eugene Monacho (correct spelling)

HPD case files, roll 1, p. 3134

According to the police files, Mr. and Mrs. Monacho were at the intersection of Hollywood Boulevard and Park Road, attempting to turn north onto Park Road. A speeding blue 1979 Ford van traveling westbound on Hollywood Boulevard almost struck Mr. Monacho's vehicle. According to Eugene, the driver was driving erratically, and his right hand was reaching behind the back of the driver's side seat. "His hand was going up and down. . . Something [was] behind the driver's seat. . . The driver appeared nervous, as if he didn't want to drive." Mr. Monacho attempted to get the tag number, but the vehicle was driving too fast and erratically. He was only able to get the last two digits, which he said were 6-4 or 4-6. Mrs. Francis Monacho was interviewed and said the time this took place was between 12:30 and 1 p.m.

I believe this was the van that Dahmer was driving. The timing is perfect, Eugene's description of the suspect matched the composite that Timothy Pottenburgh gave, and the suspect's arm movements suggest he could've been trying to keep Adam under control.

PHOTO RIGHT: Detective Sergeant Denis Nylon holds up composites from Eugene Monacho's description.
Photo by Maria Rosas, ©August 16, 1981.

When I saw these composites in 1981, I thought it was not the right suspect, but when I contacted Monacho at his Central Florida home, he told me he didn't get a good look at the driver because he was trying to avoid an accident and the driver was turned toward the back seat. Beyond that, Monacho was not much help.

Matthews had his own inexplicable lapses in judgment. When he accused the HPD of leaving a long trail of bungles, having turf wars, and general incompetence that would cause them to waste the first full month searching for a nonexistent blue van, he forgot to mention that he was part of that incredible incompetence. The big question is, did Matthews actually read these witness statements and then still discard them? Matthews said he called every living witness yet he never gave me and other witnesses from the Hollywood Mall a call as well he never mentions any of us in his book. None of these detectives was able to figure much of anything out, it seems. Their common sense lens was so far out of focus that they took tips from psychics while genuine witnesses were trying to call them with real tips, which they would ignore.

Even when it was clear the Twin City Mall composites matched the Hollywood Mall composites, the lack of communication between detectives at the HPD and their disorganization hampered the investigation. When the South Beach attempted abduction matched both the suspect and the blue van, they were about as lost as a stray puppy in New York City. When *four* witnesses saw a blue van at the location where Adam's severed head was found, these detectives gave preference to their own hypotheses, and even Joe Matthews's assumptions were flawed with confusion and illusion. He had no business accusing other detectives of a fault he shared with them.

In fact, Matthews would start his own book *Bringing Adam Home* off with a breaking news revelation on page twenty-six. Matthews said all the blue van leads were about as consequential to him as the sightings of the Loch Ness Monster. Matthews came to this conclusion without finding the need to call even one witness.

In 1981, Matthews, then a polygraph specialist and homicide investigator for the Miami Beach Police Department, was called in to consult on the case as early as four days after Adam vanished. Matthews claimed he was always clashing with the less-experienced lead investigator on the case, Detective Jack Hoffman. Matthews said he once asked the "less experienced" Hoffman what kind of organization he was running and explained that, in Miami Beach, he would've assigned a detective just to handle leads. Hoffman's response was, "When you go back to Miami Beach, you do it your way." Matthews tried over and over to interview Toole himself, but was always stymied by the HPD. Matthews was eventually taken off the case. In Matthews's opinion, HPD pulled him off when he "honed in on Ottis Toole."

This means Matthews was more of the problem than the solution. The other detectives had long since dismissed Ottis Toole as a viable suspect, nearly without exception. Matthews, the exception, continued to latch on to Toole. It's like the woman who was watching her son graduate from basic training. The woman standing next to her commented that one of the soldiers was out of step. The mother said, "That's my son; he's the only one in step." And like that mom, some people thought Detective Sergeant Joe Matthews was in step.

This was what Matthews had written about the blue van in his book: "The only solid lead that had come their way, the supposed sighting of Adam being dragged into a blue Ford van—had resulted in nothing but frustration for officers and area drivers alike. Police had checked a list of nearly seven thousand such vehicles sold in South Florida over the past three years, but nothing had come of it."

What was really interesting to read was John Walsh's take on the blue van. The HPD and Matthews did a really good job of getting John to believe "the blue van was a false lead, a bum steer, a dead end, an error" (*Tears of Rage*, pp. 94-95).

I decided to hear from Timothy himself. So I drove the five hours to Timothy's house in Central Florida. When I arrived, Timothy was sleeping. I explained to his wife, Michele, who I was and what I wanted to talk to Tim about. She woke him up immediately. One of the first things Tim told me was how badly they messed the case up. Tim said that he had been keeping up with the case. He even knew some of the other witnesses from news accounts. I showed him an 8-1/2" × 11" photo of Ottis Toole, and Tim scoffed at the notion that Ottis Toole could've been involved. He said, "Ever since they closed the case, I've been telling my grandmother they closed that case wrong."

When I showed Tim a photo of Jeffrey Dahmer in court, Tim said, "Yes, that was him, but he had a mustache." Next, I showed him the 1982 mug shot of Jeffrey Dahmer with the mustache. It was the mug shot that matched the Twin City Mall composite and the Hollywood Mall composite that Tim made when he was ten years old. He said, "It's been thirty years. I remember making that composite like it was yesterday, and that's him."

He also said that he was positive it was Adam Walsh that he saw. This was in complete contrast to what Detective Jack Hoffman said in 1981 and what Joe Matthews said in his book. I gave Tim a copy of *Bringing Adam Home* so that he could read it for himself. I just wanted Tim to know that Matthews, who calls himself a devout Catholic, was not to be trusted—not as a detective and not as a friend of John and Reve Walsh. With friends like Joe, John and Reve will never get true closure.

I have to wonder why Jack Hoffman never contacted Tim again when Dahmer surfaced in 1991, to ask him if he looked like the suspect. In 1994, when hotshot Detective Mark Smith took over the case, he never bothered to call Tim either and in 2008, when Matthews put together his Matthews Report, he never gave Tim or anyone else a call.

After talking to many witnesses, I've become adept at judging people, and I can say unequivocally that Timothy Pottenburgh is an upstanding witness. Tim generally avoided talking about the case because it had affected him so much and because it bothered him that the police tried to make it seem as if the witnesses didn't know what they were talking about.

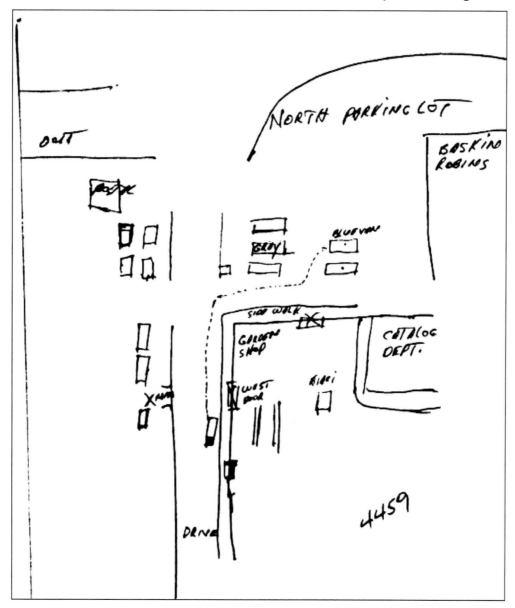

ABOVE: This is the drawing of the north parking lot from Timothy's statement (HPD case files, p. 4856), showing where the van was parked in the north parking lot and the west parking lot where it stopped next to the garden shop. This also matches where Phillip Lohr, Bill Bowen, and Janice Santamassino said the van stopped. It also matches where I said Dahmer had to have parked his vehicle, near the north entrance door where he entered the mall. This depiction isn't to scale in any way and is only meant as a general description. I also include my own diagram with the path Dahmer took through the mall and Sears.

PHOTO ABOVE: This is the main south entrance of the Hollywood Mall.

PHOTO BELOW: HOLLYWOOD MALL—Aerial view courtesy of Hollywood Historical Society.

HOLLYWOOD
POLICE DEPARTMENT

File Photo: The Hollywood Historical Society

HOLLYWOOD MALL DIAGRAM

This diagram isn't to scale and is only from my memory.

*The CVS Pharmacy next to Publix was not there in 1981.

1: Location where I parked.

2: I entered the mall from the east food court entrance.

3: I went to Waldenbooks for about 20 minutes.

4: After Waldenbooks, I went to Radio Shack.

5: This is where Jeffrey Dahmer parked the blue van.

6: The north entrance to the mall.

7: This is the southeast interior entrance into Sears.

8: The toy department.

NOTE: Numbers 4, 7, and 8 show Dahmer's path from Radio Shack to the toy department.

9: The catalog desk and service area.

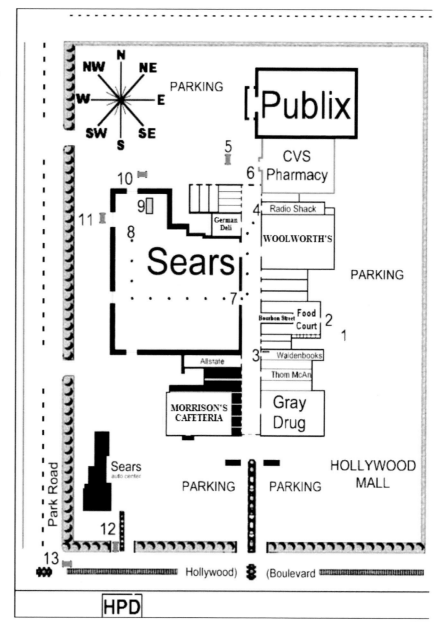

10: The north entrance into Sears.

11: The west garden center entrance to Sears. This is the location where Dahmer stopped the van, ran back into the toy department, grabbed Adam, and left.

12: The SW exit from the mall parking lot. This is a right turn only.

13: The intersection where Dahmer almost had an accident with Eugene Monacho.

PHOTO ABOVE: The Sears toy department. Adam was abducted from the west side Sears exit door seen at the top right.

PHOTO RIGHT: The garden center from the outside. Dahmer parked the blue van by this curb facing south and blocking northbound traffic. He then went into the toy department to abduct Adam.

SAO file photos.

PHOTO LEFT: This is the north parking lot, looking west toward Sears (now Target). Jeffrey Dahmer was parked in the first row of vehicles to the right. My photo from 2007.

PHOTO ABOVE: North entrance to Sears (SAO file photo). The location where the brown AMC Gremlin is parked is also the area where Reve Walsh parked her 1979 gray Checker and where the Pottenburghs parked. It was at the curb where Timothy and his grandmother were almost run over by Jeffrey Dahmer.

Witness Vernon Jones

PHOTO RIGHT: Vernon Jones, photo taken by me in 2008

I first located Vernon Jones's father, and he gave me Vernon's phone number. I called Vernon and made arrangements to meet at my place. I then called Art Harris and gave him Vernon's phone number. Art called Vernon and rearranged for us all to meet at his place. When I finally met Vernon, I would learn just how much the Adam Walsh kidnapping had affected his life.

Art showed Vernon photos of Jeffrey Dahmer. When Vernon looked at a double front and side-view mug shot of Dahmer, his eyes welled up. All these years, he'd never realized that this could've been the guy.

Vernon was nine years old in 1981. He was visiting his seventy-eight-year-old grandfather, Otis Williams, who lived in Hallandale, Florida, not far from the Hollywood Mall. His grandfather was in the landscaping business. He was always in need of tools and liked to go to the Sears tool department. On July 27, 1981, Otis took him to Sears. Video games were brand new in 1981, thus making Sears a very popular place among young people in the neighborhood. The tool department was next to the toy department. Nine-year-old Vernon was more interested in playing the video games, so Otis let him stay and play some games while Otis went tool shopping.

Vernon was playing an Intellivision baseball game with Adam. Adam was to his right, and to his left was a white man who kept hissing at him. He said, "He was trying to get my attention and saying something like, 'Psst! Hey, hey,' and motioning to me to come." Vernon remembers looking at him and thinking to himself, *You talking to me? Man, I'm not going with you.*

Just then, Vernon heard a crack. When he turned back to the game, Adam had hit a grand slam home run and won the game. Vernon said he was upset about losing to a much younger kid but blamed it on the man distracting him. Adam was sporting a wide grin for beating the bigger kid. Vernon put the controls down and went around to the other side of the aisle to play Donkey Kong, leaving Adam to himself. While playing Donkey Kong a bit later, Vernon saw the man take Adam by the hand as he walked past him. At nine years old, he didn't give it much thought. Right after that, his grandfather came for him, and they left.

Vernon said he couldn't remember if it was that evening or the next evening that his grandmother called him into the living room. The news was on, and they were doing a segment about a small boy abducted from the Sears toy department.

His grandmother said, "Vernon, you were in the mall this day. Did you see this boy?"

Vernon remembered seeing the boy on the news and shouting to his grandfather, "Grandpa, Grandpa! That's the boy I was playing with!" When his grandpa asked if he was sure, he replied, "Yes, sir."

On the way to work the next morning, Vernon's grandpa, Otis Williams, took him to the Hollywood Police Station. Vernon would never forget what happened next. Otis was holding his hand and walking to the entrance. There was a large, heavyset cop hanging out near the entrance to the station.

Otis, being a fast walker, accidentally brushed up against the officer and immediately apologized, saying, "I'm sorry, sir." Vernon said he never knew the officer's name but remembered his gun belt and his huge belly. "I'm here about the kidnapping at the mall," Otis tried to explain.

The officer then spat a huge wad of tobacco at his grandfather's feet. Vernon described how he remembers it splattering all over his grandfather's shoe. "Listen, boy, I don't have time for this," said the officer.

Vernon told me he couldn't understand why the officer was calling his grandfather "boy" when he was so much younger. It was his first experience with racism. Otis grabbed his grandson's hand and left.

That was how the HPD lost another good witness. In 1994, HPD would hear from Vernon again. He wrote a heartfelt letter to John and Reve Walsh, care of *America's Most Wanted*. He apologized and explained that he was too young to understand what happened that day when that man walked out with Adam.

The Walshes forwarded the letter to the HPD, who never even bothered to call Vernon. It would be years later (at a time when the HPD and the SAO were in full cover up mode) before investigator Phil Mundy would do an interview. After that interview, Mundy wrote: "Interview revealed JONES has no knowledge of crime . . . Mr. Jones was also shown the photographic line-up which includes the photo of Ottis Toole, and he was unable to identify him. This would indicate that Mr. Jones was in the store after the kidnapping." Really? That's the explanation then?

In Vernon's interview with Phil Mundy, Vernon gets some descriptions wrong, such as the man's age, but the interview conducted by Phil Mundy was on September 24, 1996, fifteen years after the event. Vernon was only nine years old in 1981. Had they interviewed him then, he might have had a much better recollection.

The important thing was that he was indeed there with Adam, especially in light of the context of what other witnesses say. Again, no one witness will get every aspect of the case correct. Vernon got the man's age wrong, and no one knew for certain what color shirt the suspect was wearing. There were so many different guesses.

After the Adam Walsh kidnapping, Vernon's parents enrolled him in karate school to better protect himself. He now has a black belt and his own school of self-defense. He speaks at child safety and youth crime-watch seminars and conventions all over the U.S. He always talks about what happened to Adam. "It could have been me," Vernon said. He believes he might even have been a target before Adam. "At least one hundred to two hundred chiefs of police around the country have heard my story, but Hollywood never called me. What does that tell you?"

The full statement of Vernon Jones's interview by Mundy can be read on the HPD CD (file 2) and also in the SAO case files ("Statement of Vernon Jones," box 1, file 8.10) at JusticeForAdam.com. On the following pages are some records from the HPD case files:

Philip Mundy's two-page investigative report # 10:

Investigative Assignment #96-02-0262   September 27, 1996

INVESTIGATIVE REPORT #10

TO: RALPH J. RAY, JR.
          Chief Assistant State Attorney

FROM: PHILIP J. MUNDY
          Investigator

SUBJ: Statement of Vernon Jones

RE: Homicide Investigation of Adam Walsh

ENCL: Transcript of Statement of Vernon Jones

****

Mr. Vernon JONES' sworn statement was taken on September 24, 1996 in which he describes being in the Sears department store in Hollywood on the day of Adam Walsh's kidnapping/murder.

Upon reviewing the facts set forth by Mr. Jones, who was age nine at the time of the incident, it does not appear that Mr. Jones was present at the same time Adam Walsh was in the store. Mr. Jones relates that he was playing at the video games and there was only one other child in the area at the time who later left the store with an adult male. Mr. Jones does not identify this child as Adam Walsh. In addition, Mr. Jones cannot recall the time of day he was there but seems to remember that after leaving the store with his grandfather they went to have something to eat. This would indicate that Mr. Jones was in the store after the kidnapping.

Investigative Assignment #96-02-262   Page -2-
Investigative Report #10

Further, Mrs. Kathryn Shaffer BARRACK has related going to the video game area where she found a total of four children, two white and two black males. All of these children, one of whom she has identified as Walsh, were ejected from the premises by Mrs. Barrack.

Mrs. HAGAN has indicated in her statement that there were between three and five children at the video games as she passed thru and she has identified one of the children as Adam Walsh. In addition she identified Ottis TOOLE as standing there talking to Adam Walsh at the time. Mr. Jones only makes mention of a man who was standing off to the side who later left with the other child.

Mr. Jones was also shown the photographic line-up which includes the photo of Ottis TOOLE and he did not identify anyone.

INV. PHILIP J. MUNDY

cc: Det. Mark Smith, Hollywood P.D. with enclosure

Vernon's heartfelt letter to Reve and John Walsh:

May 16, 1994

John or Reve Walsh
America's Most Wanted
P.O. Box Crime T.V.
Washington, D.C.   20016-9126

Dear Mr. or Mrs. Walsh,

I truly do not know were to begin in this letter, so I will formally introduce myself. My name is Vernon M. Jones Jr., born in Hollywood, Florida on May 3, 1972. During my summer months as a child, I would spend time with my grandfather mowing lawns on Bal Harbor and enriching my intellect through the generosity of a kind philanthropists whom we worked for. As a reward for my hard work, my grandfather would constantly take me to the Sears store in Hollywood Mall, to play video games, visit my father and family who worked there and eat at Morrison's Cafeteria.

•As you may suspect by now, I was playing Atari and Intellivision with your son Adam, on that eventful day in July. The reason why I am informing you of this is to give you my sincere apologies for my being too young and naive to realize that I possibly could have made a difference in the outcome of your families life. Being a young black male in America made it so that when I approached people in the Mall about the stranger that approached myself and Adam that day, I was constantly shunned and not taken seriously about my concerns. As you know, the tragic event led to an American outrage and awakening concerning their children. My own parent's preceded to further my enthusiasm for the martial arts, by enrolling me in a formal class thereafter.

Recently when speaking at the 7th Annual National Youth Crime Prevention Conference, held here in Miami, I addressed the crowd concerning the incident's of our past. I shared with over 1500 strangers, that the child in which many of them read of years ago, could have been myself, or in the least bit been tragically accompanied by me. And in doing so, I realized that I truly owed Adam and your family for all of the positive things that you have done for our nation. By the code of honor that I have been raised to believe in, I would like to offer myself as a small substitute for your son, Adam. I know this may be baffling to you, but to me it means more than you can imagine.

I can only hope my plea for a bit of your valuable time and understanding is heard. I understand that this letter may be read by many individuals before it reaches your own personal hands. Therefore, I do ask of the first individual who reads this, to respect my privacy and sincerity, and see to it that the Walsh family receives this letter as soon as possible.

Enclosed is a rough draft copy of the speech that I used at the National Conference and a brief biography used in a recent program. I do not wish to cause any ill feelings or gain any sort media attention. I personally have what the Japanese call a spiritual bushi"warrior" that will not allow me to rest, until I have communicated with you. Thank you for your time and again my sincere regards.

Sincerely,

Vernon M. Jones Jr.
Field Coordinator

Enclosure

9200 South Dadeland Blvd., Suite 320 • Miami, Florida 33156 • Telephone: (305) 670-2409 • Fax: 670-3805

Black Lotus Academy of the Martial Arts:

Taishi Vernon M. Jones Jr.

Considered an excellent example of a new generation of martial artists, Taishi Jones, is a dynamic speaker and instructor with nearly a decade of teaching experience. As an internationally renowned youth crime prevention consultant, he has addressed thousands of Law Enforcement Personnel, students and policy makers. Recently acquired through the Office of the Governor of Florida, he is the Field Coordinator for Youth Crime Watch of America. Utilizing his prowess in Ju-Jitsu, Shotokan, Tae Kwon Do and Aikijitsu, he has promoted the martial arts in every possible fashion: ranging from open tournaments, W.U.K.O. events, self-defense seminars and conferences, this 22 year-old entrepreneur is truly versatile.

Black Lotus Academy of the Martial Arts
16155 S.W. 117 Avenue #15
Phone 305-378-0077

Memo by Vernon Jones:

Playing home video games in the Hollywood Mall on that eventful day with young Adam Walsh prior to his abduction, brought about the realization that "It could have been me", at an early age in life. Instances such as this are constant reminders of the growing epidemic of crime in our schools and communities. The Youth Crime Watch or Varsity Patrol programs empower students, such as myself, with the techniques and components needed to take control of our own school environment. Advisors such as the dearly departed Assistant Principal, Dr. Vic Nardelli, and Officer Bill Flannagan, are the "sparkplugs" that can motivate students into taking charge, with the support from the administration. But it is we, the students who must lead, nurture, and own the program. For without us, the students, the Youth Crime Watch program will not flourish; but without this spectacular program, every students chance of even existing is dramatically reduced. We are informed that every student has earned the right to a safe learning environment and Youth Crime Watch has therefore earned our sincere gratitude for making it all possible.

Dedicated to the Memory of

Dr. Vic Nardelli and Officer Bill Flannagan

By:

Vernon M. Jones Jr.

Witness Janice Santamassino

Janice Santamassino was another easily found witness. She was a property owner in Broward County. I noticed another name on the warranty deed to her house that I recognized: Ed Weinert. I met Ed over thirty-four years ago. When I first started at the *Miami Herald* as a trainee, he was a journeyman pressman but left soon after I started. Again, I had an address but no phone number, so I went to Janice's home and knocked on her door. A house sitter answered and told me Janice was out of town for two weeks. When I went home, I passed the phone number on to Art Harris.

When I contacted Janice by phone after several weeks, she told me Art Harris had already talked to her, but she was more than willing to tell me her story, as well. She invited me over. When I told Janice I worked at the *Miami Herald*, she confirmed that Ed also worked there, although Ed was not so quick to remember me.

On Monday morning, July 27, 1981, Janice went to Kinney Shoes to buy a pair of sandals for her four-year-old daughter, Lori. She parked on the west side of the mall and had to go through Sears to get to the mall. She was upset because there was an "old beat-up blue van" parked illegally outside the west entrance of Sears, blocking traffic. Since she didn't expect a vehicle to be parked there, she had to jam on her brakes in order not to hit it. She mentally noted the tag number of the van and was planning on reporting it to mall security to have it towed. But once she entered Sears, the idea left her.

She entered the toy department and saw two video games on the right-hand side. Her daughter Lori wanted to play. A young boy wearing an oversized hat, shorts, and a striped shirt was already playing and even took time to explain to Lori how to play. Janice would later realize that the boy was Adam. "We were there for a good ten minutes or so. . . I began to wonder why a small boy was unattended, all by himself." Janice wanted to leave, but Lori wanted to play with Adam for five more minutes. Janice, being on vacation, firmly told her no, reminding Lori that they had planned to spend the rest of the day at their pool. Janice led Lori by the hand away from the games. Going through the toy department and heading into the mall, she passed the next toy aisle and noticed a man in the aisle. His head was down, and he seemed to be looking at or reading the label of a handheld toy. As she passed him, he looked up at her, and they locked eyes.

"I was thinking how out of place he looked. He was scary looking." She grabbed her daughter's hand and briskly walked away. "It was spooky. He just gave me a bad, uncomfortable feeling." And he didn't look as though he belonged in a toy department, all by himself, shopping for toys. Janice described him as being about six feet tall, with sandy brown messy hair and no glasses. "He was a disheveled wreck." Janice didn't find the shoes she wanted at Kinney Shoes, so she went back to Sears and bought a pair of sandals at the Sears shoe department. To this day, Janice has kept that shoe box with the price of $4.99 on it.

She heard the announcement for a missing boy. On the way out of Sears, she saw a woman by the service counter, and there was a man standing beside her. The woman looked distraught and was leaning on the counter, crying. The boy at the video games was gone, and so was the creepy guy in the toy aisle. Janice left Sears and went home, thinking the child would show up. On the way out, she noticed that the blue van was gone as well. Later that evening on the news, she heard about the kidnapping and remembered the man she'd gotten two good looks at: "One from the side and one straight on when we locked eyes." Janice realized she'd seen Adam. She called the police that evening and then again the next day. She mentioned the van and said she recalled only a portion of the tag number that she had memorized earlier. Janice told the unknown HPD detective that she was willing to be hypnotized to try to remember the rest of the tag number. The detective took her name and phone number, made statement notes, and told her they would get back to her. No one ever called. Not in 1981, not in 1991, not in 1996, and not even in 2008, when they closed the case. Nowhere in the case files will you find a statement given by Janice Santamassino. The Hollywood police have steadfastly refused to interview her.

On September 21, 1996, *America's Most Wanted* aired what it believed to be its final show. For the first time since the show went on the air on February 7, 1988, John Walsh profiled the tragic murder of his six-year-old son, Adam. The reason Adam was not profiled earlier was because the HPD had asked John to keep quiet so it wouldn't interfere with their investigation, even though many suspects in other cases had been captured because those cases were profiled. The entire one-hour show was about the Adam Walsh case. It was narrated by John Turchin from WSVN-TV, the Fox affiliate station in Miami. Unfortunately, the show was based on information and facts gathered by Detective Joe Matthews, portraying Ottis Toole as the perpetrator of Adam's abduction, using the white Cadillac. The show ended with Turchin asking viewers to call the show's hotline, 1-800-CRIME-TV, if they had any tips. John Walsh said he was proud of the way the program on Adam had turned out and said, "How could anyone who had seen it doubt what had really happened?" John was oblivious to the fact that Joe Matthews's reasoning was off-kilter.

Even though the show was slanted, Janice was not swayed by the white Cadillac and called to tell *America's Most Wanted* about the dark van inappropriately parked near the west entrance to Sears. She also told them about the "weird, out-of-place" looking man in the toy department and mentioned that she had called the HPD in 1981. *America's Most Wanted* forwarded her information to where else, the HPD. To this day, they have never called her. Art Harris's call was the first time anyone had ever called her, and of course my call was the second.

When I showed her some of the same photos of Dahmer that Art had already showed her, she told me for sure it was him. "The profile photo looks exactly as what I saw when he was looking down at the toy he was holding only his hair was a little bit messier." To this day, Janice Santamassino has not been interviewed by authorities, and now, they will never get that chance. Sadly, on August 25, 2013, Janice passed away peacefully at her Hollywood, Florida, home.

PHOTO RIGHT: Janice Santamassino. Photo courtesy of Ed Weinert

FUGITIVE _Adam Walsh_ DATE _9/21/96_

OPERATOR _Meredith_ TIME _10:58_

☐ AMW
☐ FJ
☐ Other

When and where did you see him? _Hollywood, FLA_

Why do you believe it's him? Caller saw (Because she parked By Toy Entrance _next to van_)
A DK Color Van was parked there (Maybe Blue)
W/ curtains in windows
(Old - Beat up Van)

What was he doing? It was → 11:00am – (Morning Hours)
around

Where is he now? Caller reported this information to Hollywood Police that night Adam disappeared.

What else can you tell us about the fugitive? Caller had seen Adam playing near the arcade. When she walked in, and 10 to 15 mins later, she heard on the loudspeaker he was missing

May we give your name and telephone number to law enforcement agents? ☐ YES
They may wish to call you back for more information. ☐ NO

Name _Janice Santamissino_ Please characterize the caller _____

Location _____ _(w)_

Phone ████ ████ ████

Witness Bill Bowen

PHOTO RIGHT: Bill Bowen standing in the spot where Jeffrey Dahmer "found" a dead man. Photo taken by me in 2007

I didn't have to look up Bill Bowen. I had known Bill for a number of years, ever since Art Harris gave me his phone number in 2004. I realized witnesses were not supposed to talk to each other because they could cross-contaminate their statements, but at this point, I didn't think it mattered any longer. I'd also met Bill several times on different TV shows about the Adam Walsh case.

On July 27, 1981, Bill was going to the Sears service desk. Before he even made it into the store, he witnessed a white male, approximately twenty years of age, struggling while lifting a young boy up by one arm. The man violently "slung him into a blue van, like a sack of potatoes." The boy resisted the man as best he could.

Bill said he didn't get a good look at the child because the man was between him and the child. According to Bill, the boy was screaming, "No, I'm not going! No, I don't want to go!" And the man screamed, "Yes, you are!" Then the man threw the boy into the van. Before Bill realized what was happening, the man jumped into the driver's seat and sped away. At first, Bill thought he could've been an older brother.

However, this guy was so violent that Bill decided to run over and get the tag number. Unfortunately, the van screeched off so fast that Bill was able to get only a partial tag. In fact, Bill still remembers the smell of burning rubber. After so many years, Bill is no longer so positive about the tag number. Back in 1981, though, he did remember the tag number when he gave it to the police.

Bill went into Sears to change his billing address and left. The next day, Bill heard about the kidnapping. The same day, someone broke into his apartment so he called the police to file a report. When they came to his apartment, Bill also told them about the kidnapping at the mall. That was when he gave them the tag number.

Over the next several days, Bill kept calling the HPD to see if they wanted him to come in for an interview. He kept getting an answering machine and leaving messages. Finally, after about the fifth or sixth time, he got a live person. Bill told them he was calling about the kidnapping at the mall. He wanted to know if they needed him to come in for an interview. He was told by the person on the phone to call back in two weeks because, "The person you need to speak with is on vacation." Bill explained that he was moving to Birmingham, Alabama and told them, "That's why I went to Sears to change my billing address." The person on the phone said that the best they could do was to take his name, address, and phone number, and someone would get back to him. Bill moved to Birmingham. He never did get that call.

Ten years later, on Sunday, July 28, 1991, Bill was reading the *Birmingham News*. In the paper appeared an article about a man that was arrested in Milwaukee for committing some crimes that most people couldn't even begin to comprehend. There also appeared a profile photograph of Jeffrey Dahmer and his denial of any killings outside of Wisconsin and Ohio.

When Bill saw this photograph, he got a flashback of the incident that he'd witnessed at the Sears in the Hollywood Mall back on Monday, July 27, 1981. Bill said, "It hit me like a baseball bat! That was the man in the Sears parking lot with the blue van." After getting answering machines and the run around in 1981, Bill drove 780 miles back to Hollywood, Florida at his own expense, with the *Birmingham News* in hand to report this to the HPD. He was referred to Detective Hoffman. One of the first questions Hoffman asked him was, "Why are you coming in now? Why didn't you come in 1981?" Bill explained to Hoffman all the phone calls he'd made and that he had left his forwarding address. He also explained about the tag number he gave to a uniformed police officer.

After that interview with Detective Jack Hoffman, the HPD would never again interview Bill or even give him a call. If the police had returned Bill's calls back in 1981, Bill could've given them more information about the blue van, the tag number, and the suspect.

Incidents like this led John Walsh's lawyer to say that HPD investigators were "the biggest bunch of bungling idiots since the Keystone Kops. We may never know for sure the full extent of their incredible incompetence, but we can conclude that it was really bad."

Bill had to insist on being interviewed so that he could give a witness statement. Hoffman finally relented otherwise Bill's name might have never made it into the case files. And only after Bill insisted did Detective Hoffman go grudgingly across the street to the mall so that Bill could show him what happened. But according to Bill, Hoffman didn't seem to be interested in anything he had to say. "He really didn't care," Bill said. When they were done, Hoffman told him, "Thanks for helping, but we have our man." Jack Hoffman never did explain what man he was talking about and he had already dismissed Ottis Toole.

Although the HPD reported to the press that they were "baffled by the lack of leads," if they had followed up on Bill and the other witness leads, they could've captured Jeffrey Dahmer. All those murders in Milwaukee would've never happened. Bottom line: Jeffrey Dahmer should have been arrested, tried, convicted, and sent to Florida's death row.

Bill's interview with Detective Hoffman can be viewed in the SAO case files (box 3, file 1, p. 188).

NOTE: My interview is right after Bill's, starting on p. 204.

Security Guard Kathryn Jean Shaffer-Barrack

In 1981, Kathryn Shaffer was a Sears security guard. She was seventeen years old and Adam's kidnapping would be blamed on her youth and inexperience. She was accused of kicking Adam, along with several other kids, out of the Sears store and into the parking lot, unattended.

PHOTO RIGHT: In the center of this photo is the Sears north entrance. The service desk is just to the right of the north door. File photo HPD

According to the HPD case files, Kathryn Shaffer started at her shift at noon. Kathryn described how, on July 27, 1981, at about 12:30 to 12:45 p.m., she was called to the toy department regarding a disturbance at the Atari video games. Arriving at the location, she encountered two black children and two white children. She asked the children if their parents were in the store. When they replied in the negative, she told the children they would have to leave the store. She watched as the two black children walked out the exit at the south end of the store, and she then watched as the other two white children exited the store via the north doors. Mrs. Shaffer explained that, at the time of the occurrence, she was shown photographs but did not identify Adam Walsh as one of the children she ejected from the store.

Kathryn would turn out to be one of the more difficult witnesses for me to find. Since 1981, she had moved from South Florida to Lakeland, in Central Florida, and on to the Carolinas. Finally, I got some tips that she had moved to Tennessee. The tips seemed to be consistent, so I started concentrating on the best tips from Tennessee. I not only managed to find her, but I got her phone number, as well. Though it was one of the more difficult searches, it would be mostly for nothing. When I called, her husband Todd Barrack answered but didn't have much to say. He was angry that I'd found them. Todd told me he was sick and tired of *America's Most Wanted* and people in the media tracking him down and couldn't believe I was able to find them. I won't say the address or even the town they live in, as I want to respect their privacy.

However, I thought I was doing this for Kathryn. I wanted to let her know that she'd had nothing to do with Adam's kidnapping. Phillip Lohr saw Adam being carried out the west exit. According to Vernon Jones, he didn't see any of the boys, black or white, fighting while Adam was there, but he did see Adam leaving toward the west exit with that same person that was hissing at Vernon. Also, Bill Bowen saw Adam being dragged by one arm to the blue van by the west exit. Timothy Pottenburgh and Janice Santamassino also verified the blue van parked at the west exit. Mia Cockerham (next chapter) saw Jeffrey Dahmer take Adam by the hand and leave.

Todd was quite blunt with me and said, "The case is closed; it's already been solved. . . Leave us alone." He then asked me what news outlet I was from. When I told him I was a witness, he seemed to be incensed that I would even be interested. Maybe after Matthews contacted Kathryn on behalf of *America's Most Wanted* for his interview, he left her so distraught that she became unwilling to talk. Back in 1981, John Walsh was so convinced that security officer Kathryn Shaffer kicked Adam out into the parking lot unattended that he filed a lawsuit against Sears for negligence. The suit was later dropped for personal reasons. If the HPD had given John the correct information from Shaffer's original statement, when she said the boys went out the north and south exits, not the west exit, maybe the Walshes wouldn't have filed that misguided lawsuit in the first place.

Unfortunately, the HPD as well as Joe Matthews used Shaffer as their convenient scapegoat, and to this day, Joe Matthews has the Walsh family convinced that Shaffer put Adam out of the Sears and into the parking lot (*Bringing Adam Home*, p. 239). Even if Shaffer, over the years, convinced herself that she might have put Adam out, Matthews should have known better. The Hollywood Police say Adam was abducted from the west exit. Even Ottis Toole seemed to know Adam was abducted from the west exit. Shaffer never sent any of the kids out the west exit. The problem was, Matthews didn't even believe there was a blue van and refused to contact any of the witnesses that said there was one. Thus, none of the abovementioned witnesses (except for Kathryn Shaffer, although he used her as his own personal scapegoat) are in Matthews's book, which was based on his own report, the Matthews Report.

If Joe Matthews believes I am slandering him, then he knows what to do. I would love to get him in front of a civil jury. A civil jury wouldn't have to worry about being held hostage to what is politically expedient, as judges sometimes can be. All anyone needed to do was to listen, and this case could've been solved a long time ago—and correctly, I might add.

WITNESS TIMELINE

These times stated by Hollywood Sears employees and witnesses below may not be exact and are only copied from their statements in the case files except for Vernon Jones, Janice Santamassino and Mia Cockerham because the HPD refused to interview them. But we can put together a pretty good timeline from all these witnesses relevant to Adam's abduction.

Reve Walsh: When asked if she could be mistaken about arriving at Sears around 12:30 p.m., rather than an earlier time of 11:30 a.m., she said "anything's possible." Reve said she may have been inaccurate in her estimates because she wasn't wearing her watch that day.

Joanne Braun worked at the catalog and service desk. She stated that she recalled a gray Checker vehicle parked near the north entrance door between 11:30 a.m. and noon. She also recalled seeing Reve Walsh walk past the catalog department holding a little boy by his hand HPD case file (roll 1, p. 73 and p. 4868).

Willis Morgan: I'm positive it was Jeffrey Dahmer I encountered in Radio Shack at the estimated time of 11:30 a.m. to 11:40 a.m. I then saw Dahmer walk into the Sears toy department at around 11:40 a.m. to 11:50 a.m.

Jennie Warren saw Reve enter Sears with Adam and drop him off at the toy department.

Angel Gans relieved Betty Gutberlet in the lamp department at 12:00 noon. She said that at approximately 12:05 p.m., Mrs. Walsh inquired about a lamp that was on sale. Gans checked the storeroom but didn't have the lamp in stock. Mrs. Walsh then left the lamp department at 12:20 p.m. to 12:25 p.m. (HPD case files, roll 1, p. 4865).

Mary Hagan went to Sears around 12:00 p.m. She saw Dahmer talking to Adam. You will read her statement in the next chapter.

Janice Santamassino saw Jeffrey Dahmer and Adam in the toy department.

Timothy Pottenburgh saw Dahmer standing in the toy department.

Vernon Jones played a video game with Adam.

Timothy Pottenburgh saw Dahmer in the north parking lot retrieving the blue van and driving to the garden side west entrance.

Mia Cockerham saw Dahmer take Adam by the hand and walk him away from the video game. You will read her statement in the next chapter.

Vernon Jones saw Adam pass with Jeffrey Dahmer going toward the west exit.

Phillip Lohr saw Dahmer carrying Adam out of the store.

Bill Bowen saw Adam being tossed into the blue van.

Jenny Rayner worked the switchboard and handled the store intercom system. She stated that, at approximately 12:20 p.m. to 12:25 p.m., she received a telephone call from a woman who identified herself as Reve Walsh. Mrs. Walsh stated, "I was supposed to meet my son Adam in the toy department; he's not here. Can you page him?" Rayner paged Adam but got no response. She paged him again at 12:40 p.m. with no results. Rayner stated that Mrs. Walsh called her back and asked her to page Adam again. At 1 p.m. Rayner paged Adam again. Martha Crube relieved Rayner at 1:15 p.m. and continued to page Adam until 3:30 p.m. with no results (roll 1, p. 4866).

Eugene Monacho almost had an accident with Jeffrey Dahmer between 12:30 p.m. and 1 p.m.

Andrew and John Sotillo, cousins, went to the mall at 12:15 p.m. to have lunch at the Sidewalk Café in the food court. The Sotillo boys had to be at David Park for a tennis match at 1 p.m. They walked to the park by going through the Sears store. Andrew and John stated that while they were walking past the Atari video games, they stopped to play. While playing the video game, they witnessed an incident involving two black youths. The time was 12:45 p.m. They recalled the time because they had to be at David Park in fifteen minutes. Eventually, the Sotillo cousins moved back to Venezuela. Sears sent four of their attorneys to Caracas to interview them.

Security guard Kathryn Shaffer: Although Joe Matthews used Kathy as one of his key witnesses in order to close the Adam Walsh case, I list her here because nothing Joe said in his book added up. She asked the boys to leave the toy department after Adam had already been abducted.

Kathryn stated that she recalled an incident between 12:30 p.m. and 12:45 p.m. at the Atari video game located near the toy section. She witnessed a fight between two white boys and two black boys. "One black child slapped the ten-year-old white child." Shaffer said one of the black youths became verbally abusive toward her, and she instructed all four kids to leave the store.

Shaffer said she sent the two black kids out the south door exit near the men's department and the two white kids out the north exit by the catalog department. Shaffer also stated, after seeing a photograph of Adam, that she was sure the younger white male juvenile was not Adam (HPD case file, roll 1, p. 70 and pp. 4866-67, September 2, 1981).

The following is an excerpt from a 1996 interview with Investigator Phil Mundy.

STATEMENT: Kathryn Barrack, September 15, 1996

KB: I was called to the toy department for a disturbance with the children who were fighting over the electronic games there. That [was] not an uncommon thing. Upon arrival, there were four little boys—two white boys, two black boys—fighting over the game.

PM: Pushing, shoving kind of thing?

KB: No, you know, they wouldn't take turns, obviously. At the time, the black boys were the ones playing the game and continued telling the little white boys that, they were going, "OK, just a minute, just a minute," saying they were going to surrender the game but would not.

PM: And what did you do to resolve that?

KB: I asked the children playing the game, the two little black boys, if their parents were in the store. They both answered me with a no answer, and I pointed to doors out the opposite end of the store and told them, "You two, out those two doors."

PM: Did the boys leave out those two doors?

KB: Yes.

PM: Did you see what the other two boys did?

KB: I then asked them, "Are your parents in the store?" Assuming they were together, and the older of the two told me no. So I said, "You two, out those two doors," and pointed at different doors.

PM: And what did they do?

KB: They left out those doors.

NOTE: The opposite two doors would be the *north* and *south* doors, **not** the *west* garden center exit where Adam was abducted from.

James Martin was thirteen years old when he went to visit his mother, who worked in the Waldenbooks store in the mall. From there, he went to Cozzoli's in the food court to have a slice of pizza and a Coke for lunch. Then he walked down to Woolworth's to look at some model cars. From there, he went to Sears. At approximately 12:45 p.m. or 12:50 p.m., he went into the toy department to play the Atari video games. James stated that he witnessed two black males who tried to take the controls from an eight-year-old white boy. At that time, he states, a female security guard walked up to the two black kids and talked to them, at which time they left (HPD case file, roll 1, p. 70 and p. 4867).

This would mean Dahmer could've hung around for about fifteen minutes or so in the toy department before retrieving the blue van and abducting Adam. I believe Adam was dropped off in the toy department around 11:40 a.m. to 11:50 a.m. Between 12:18 p.m. and 12:20 p.m., Adam was abducted. That means Adam was in the toy department for about twenty-eight to forty minutes.

When security guard Kathryn Shaffer observed the incident in the toy department at 12:45 p.m., Adam had already been missing for around twenty-five minutes. Dahmer was already in his van with Adam, and the evidence I found implied that he was most likely on his way back to the meter room. According to the record in Detective Mark Smith's third supplemental report, some people attempted to place blame on Shaffer and she became hesitant to discuss the matter. In Smith's report, he said Shaffer now admitted that she could've put Adam out the west-side garden center exit. Either Smith had all his information wrong, or someone managed to get Shaffer to change her original statement. Shaffer's full statement can be found in the SAO case files ("Statement of Kathy Shaffer," box 1, file 12).

PHOTO ABOVE: Sears: Southwest view. Photo from SAO file. This is the parking lot road Dahmer took to Hollywood Boulevard.

North Parking Lot

SEARS FILE DIAGRAM: The numbers are added by me. (Diagram from SAO file)

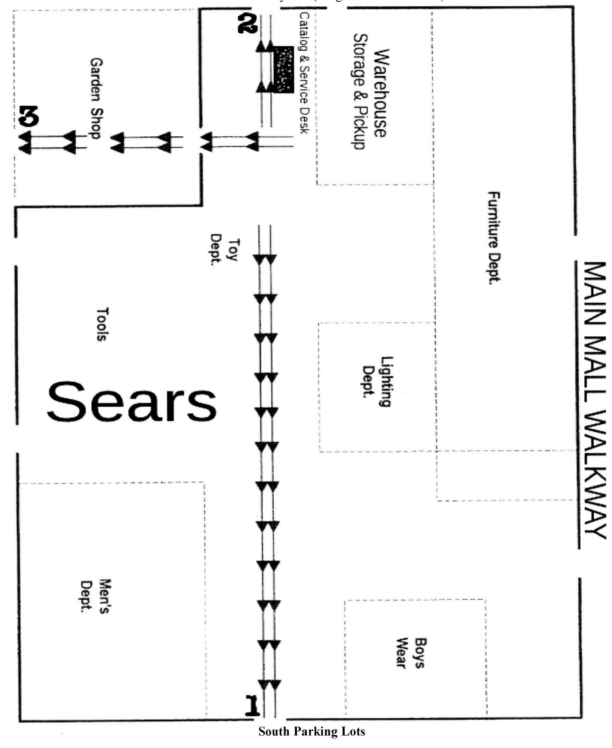

South Parking Lots

1: The two black children walked out the exit at the south end of the store.
2: The two white children exited the store via the north doors.
3: Adam Walsh was abducted from the west garden center exit.

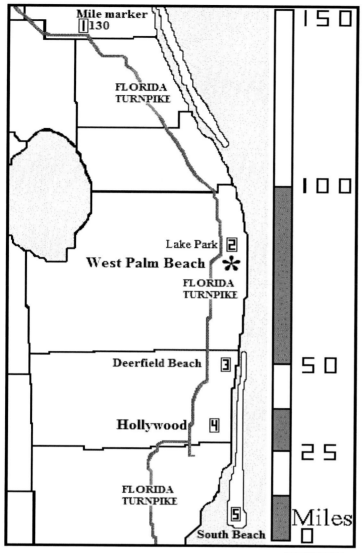

Southeast Florida Map

1: Florida Turnpike, mile marker 130—This is the location where Adam's severed head was found and witnesses spotted a blue van on August 4 and 7, 1981.

2: Twin City Mall—This is the location of an attempted abduction on July 13, 1981. Ten-year-old Terry Keaton managed to get away. Witnesses gave a composite that matched the Hollywood Mall composite.

3: Deerfield Beach—Witness called police when she saw the Twin City Mall composite on TV. She witnessed an attempted abduction of a female child of approximately five years old, possibly on the same day as the Twin City Mall attempted abduction.

4: Hollywood Mall—Location of Adam Walsh abduction on July 27, 1981.

5: South Beach—Attempted abduction of a ten-year-old boy on August 17, 1981.

Area Map

This map shows the proximity of the Hollywood Mall to the location where Jeffrey Dahmer lived and worked. My Hallandale house was about halfway to the mall from

Sunshine Subs.

1: Sunshine Subs
2: Bimini Bay Motel
3: Mr. Pizza
4: My house
5: Hollywood Police Station
6: Hollywood Mall
7: Kmart

CHAPTER SIXTEEN
THE TOOLE WITNESSES

PHOTO LEFT: Ottis Toole, 1983. File photo from the Broward County State Attorney's Office

"No, I didn't kill Adam Walsh."
_____*Ottis E. Toole*_____

Now that you have met the Jeffrey Dahmer witnesses, I'd like you to meet the Ottis Toole witnesses. After Jeffrey Dahmer was arrested in 1991, witnesses came forward implicating him in Adam's abduction. When Detective Mark Smith took over the Adam Walsh case in 1994, the Hollywood police could no longer maintain they had no witnesses implicating Dahmer. Smith now dished out the HPD's new spin, saying "We have Dahmer witnesses, but we have even more Ottis Toole witnesses." The following are the Toole witnesses from the HPD's own case files. Either the HPD lied, or they are fudging their numbers by counting all the Duval County Jail inmates incarcerated with Toole. These inmates said Toole did it because he told them so. The common rumor around the jail that Toole killed Adam is not evidence. The evidence that he had nothing to do with Adam's murder is in the HPD's own case files.

Ronald Collins said that, while he and Toole were cellmates, Toole spoke of killings in which he was involved, but none involved children.

Bobby Lee Jones first met Toole around March 1981, when they worked together for a short time for Southeast Color Coat Roofing Company. He said that, on one occasion, Toole blurted out that he'd killed two children, and he dismembered one with a large knife after beating the child. Jones gave little regard to Toole's statements. Jones would meet Toole again in 1983 at the Duval County Jail.

Lee Hodges was seventeen years old and doing time for auto theft in 1983. His cellmates were Bobby Lee Jones and Ottis Toole. He recalled Toole discussing murders in which he was involved, but none concerned Adam Walsh.

James Collins was another coworker at Southeast Color Coat Roofing Company, as well as a cellmate. He remembered Toole being inquisitive about the repercussions a child murderer might face from his fellow inmates. However, Collins's interview only lasted eleven minutes because he became hostile.

James Poole reported Toole as having said he was in the child repossession business. This statement seemed to be isolated, as detectives didn't acquire a similar statement from anyone else.

Boyd Earl Gilbert was a cellmate of Toole's at the Butler Transient Unit. Boyd said Toole claimed to have earned a living committing arson for people who wanted to collect insurance money. He also said Toole told him he visited South Florida several times and killed a policeman's son there.

James Dover worked at a gas station in Hollywood. He said he saw Toole in his gas station about one to two years before Adam's abduction.

James Redwine, a Jacksonville man, contends Toole wasn't anywhere near Broward County on the day Adam disappeared. According to Redwine, Toole spent July 27, 1981, at the rooming house where Toole lived. "He was up here that day," Redwine said in an interview. "Ain't no way he could have drove there or back. . . That's the truth. I ain't got a reason to lie." Yet the Hollywood police dismissed Redwine because he could not prove Toole was there.

Paul Ruiz, Travis County Texas district attorney investigator, said he had a taped confession from Henry Lee Lucas, who stated that Ottis Toole told him he'd killed Adam Walsh. On October 19, 1983, Ruiz also interviewed Ottis Toole about a case in Austin. In that interview, Ruiz asked Toole to think about kids. Toole stated, "I don't think I could kill a kid, you know, little kids like seven, eight, nine, ten years old. I may, and could, have killed fourteen-, fifteen-, sixteen-year-olds." When Ruiz asked Toole if he'd told someone about killing a kid and cutting off his head somewhere in Florida, he laughed and said, "I wouldn't do that, not to a little kid."

The following is an example of how Ottis Toole responded during that first interview with Ruiz on October 19, 1983, 9:41 a.m. EDT.

Ruiz brings up killing of kids.

Toole: I don't think I could kill no kid. [NOTE: Toole defines "kids" as under 10 years old.]

Ruiz: Did you tell someone you kidnapped a kid and cut off his head?

Toole: I kidnapped a kid and cut off his head?

Ruiz: Did you?

Toole: I wouldn't do that [laughter] . . . I wouldn't do that . . . not to a little kid. I wouldn't kill a little kid.

On October 20, 1983, Ruiz interviewed Toole again. This time Toole said he did kill Adam but couldn't remember what he did with the body, because "all the body parts seemed to be all jumbled up." The interviews can be found on the HPD CD-2 at JusticeForAdam.com.

Erica Toole was only six years old when Adam was murdered. Years later, when Erica was twenty, she was interviewed by Detective Smith. She told Smith that she always knew her Uncle Ottis had murdered Adam. Erica also said the entire family believed Ottis Toole to be responsible for the death of Adam Walsh. Then she added that neither she nor her family had anything to base that on other than what they had heard, read, or been told.

Sarah Christine Paterson called *America's Most Wanted* months after Ottis Toole died of liver failure on September 15, 1996. She talked to Joe Matthews, who also forwarded her name and phone number to the Broward County State Attorney's Office. Two months later, in a November 6, 1996, telephone interview with Philip Mundy, Sarah claimed her uncle, Ottis Toole, gave her a deathbed confession admitting to killing Adam Walsh but refused to tell her where Adam's body was. That happened in December 1995, nearly eleven months earlier, when she visited Uncle Ottis. Sarah told Mundy that she couldn't say for sure if he did it or not, because she wasn't there.

She also referred to Joe Matthews as a jerk and told Mundy that if he ever heard from Mr. Walsh or that other one, Matthews, to tell him that he's a jerk.

"You mean Matthews?" Mundy asked.

"Yeah, Matthews. He's a jerk," she replied.

Sarah's statement is at JusticeForAdam.com in the SAO case files ("Sarah Paterson Statement," box 1, file 19.17).

Phil Mundy also disputes Toole's deathbed confession. "I don't think Toole, in my estimation, made what I would call a dying declaration. If John Walsh wants to believe he made a deathbed declaration, fine. And I can't blame the guy for wanting to think that."

Toole's death took the Hollywood police by surprise, and they lost their opportunity to do a deathbed interview. When John Walsh heard about Ottis Toole's passing, he was incensed that the HPD hadn't notified him. He had wanted them to get a deathbed confession.

Barry Gemelli worked in the infirmary where Toole passed away. Of course, once someone passes on, anyone can claim they said anything. In Joe Matthews's book, he said that Barry Gemelli had told him that he overheard Ottis Toole confess to Adam's murder. Not true!

Hollywood detectives conducted an inquiry following Toole's death. They went up to the Lake Butler Prison Hospital where Toole died and interviewed all the people providing health care for him. Not one person stated that Toole made any such confession.
SAO case files: Box 2, 01. / NEWS ARTICLES Walsh Adam, p. 140

The following was what Barry Gemelli had to say in an interview with Phil Mundy on September 23, 1997. He made this statement just two years before Barry himself passed away on July 23, 1999.

"I saw this show where John Walsh had made the comment on the program that, when Ottis Toole died, you know, he died carrying all this information with him. Nobody knows anything. He never opened up and he didn't state anything, and I kind of sat here kind of, like, in awe, like that's not the case" (SAO case files: Box 8, "Statement of Barry Gemelli," file 36, p. 2).

Lead Detective Jack Hoffman said, with regard to Toole's deathbed confession: "No reason why the person would have withheld that information from the police." Hoffman also accused Walsh of making up the deathbed confession in an attempt to cope with the murder, saying Walsh was "just trying to get this off of his conscience." Then he reiterated, "I stand on my professional career that Ottis Toole didn't do it."

Gerard John Schaefer, The man behind Ottis Toole's confessions was a Martin County ex-deputy sheriff known as "the killer cop." He acted as Toole's jailhouse lawyer and actually admitted that he wrote letters posing as Toole and demanding $50,000 from John Walsh for Adam's remains "so you can get them buried all decent and Christian." Toole was illiterate and, thus, unable to write those letters himself. Schaefer claimed Toole told him everything, and he believes Toole. Detective Matthews wrote, "Although Schaefer wrote those letters, let there be no doubt Toole was responsible for Adam's murder" (*Bringing Adam Home*).

PHOTO RIGHT: Ex-deputy sheriff Gerard John Schaefer mug shot from Broward County file

In a bid to get one of those field trips to Hollywood, Schaefer told investigators that he represented Ottis Toole in all further matters and that he would have to be present at all interviews conducted with Toole in the future. Should Toole be taken out on location, Schaefer indicated to the investigators that he must accompany Toole and law enforcement agencies. That never happened.

If you recall, FBI Agent Bill Hagerty, along with Hollywood Lead Detective Jack Hoffman, interviewed Ottis Toole on October 7, 1991 (referenced in this book on pages 75-76). The following statement was what the Broward County State Attorney's Office had to say about that interview in their *Adam Walsh Investigative Report*.

October 7, 1991
    Toole is interviewed at Florida State Prison (FSP) by Detective Hoffman and FBI Agent William Hagerty and he denies killing Adam and claims he never left Jacksonville in July, 1981.

    Toole tells them he has been befriended by Gerald Shaffer who is writing a book with Sandra London. Toole tells Shaffer he did not kill Adam but Shaffer urges him to say he did for the sake of the book.

LEFT: Cropped from the SAO case files (box 2, file 3)

Schaefer was convicted in 1973 of two mutilation murders but is believed to be responsible for at least thirty more killings. A sadistic sex beast by nature, Schaefer would lure young women off the roads with the help of his badge to rape, torture, mutilate, and murder them. He enjoyed tying his victims to trees and leaving them there while he went to work as a police officer. Teeth, jewelry, and clothing from several missing girls and young women were found in a trunk in his mother's attic, and he once gave his wife a suede purse that belonged to one of his victims. After he was convicted for the first-degree murder of two teenage girls, Schaefer's wife divorced him and became engaged to his defense attorney, although Schaefer retained the attorney to continue handling his appeals.

Schaefer's downfall came when he received an emergency call on his radio just as he was tying two young hitchhikers to a tree in the woods. When he returned, he found that the girls had escaped. Schaefer telephoned his boss, telling Sheriff Richard Crowder, "I've done something foolish. You're going to be mad at me." Schaefer explained to his sergeant that he just wanted to teach the two young girls a lesson about the dangers of hitchhiking. Crowder ordered him back to the station and went looking for the girls, finding them both still in handcuffs as they emerged from the forest. Returning to headquarters, Crowder fired Schaefer on the spot and arrested him, charging him with imprisonment and two counts of aggravated assault.

When a reporter asked the sergeant how Schaefer had made officer of the month, the sergeant said they were a small police department, so they rotated the award. Schaefer also considered himself a bit of a novelist. In prison, he published a collection of lurid tales of sex and gore that he marketed as a mail-order book called *Killer Fiction*. Oddly enough, Sondra London, an old high school girlfriend who helped Gerard with his writings, subsequently became engaged to Danny Rolling, another sadistic killer who was executed in 2006 by lethal injection on Florida's infamous death row. He had killed and grotesquely mutilated five students in Gainesville, then deliberately posed them to shock whoever discovered them.

On December 3, 1995, Schaefer was found dead in his cell at the Florida State Prison in Starke. He had been stabbed numerous times around one eye and slashed across his throat. His sister, Sarah Schaefer, claimed that her brother was murdered because of information he'd obtained on the murder of Adam Walsh. Gerard Schaefer had told police that Toole had made a full confession to him and that he used a bayonet to kill Adam Walsh. Authorities, though, believe Gerard's death was linked to money he collected for his activities as a jailhouse lawyer.

On the following pages are:

1: The letter Gerard Schaefer penned for Ottis Toole to John Walsh

- The only time Toole had anything to do with this letter was when he signed it. John Walsh, as well as Assistant State Attorney Kelly Hancock, said they could get a conviction based on this letter alone. Evidence that Schaefer penned this letter for Toole was something easily overlooked. The small "**x**" to the left is Ottis Toole's signature.

  If Toole had actually penned this letter himself, why would he have had to put an "**x**" in the location where he was to sign his name? Detective Matthews also placed this letter in the gut photo section of his book as some of his apparent proof implicating Toole, although Matthews cut the letter off short just above the small "**x**" where Ottis Toole signed his name.

- More letters from Gerard Schaefer can be read in the SAO case files (box 2, file 4) at JusticeForAdam.com.

2: The RETYPED 1988 letter from Detective Hoffman to Chief Richard Witt, with reference to Gerard Schaefer's complicity in Ottis Toole's confessions.

October 4, 1988

Dear Walsh,

My name is Ottis Toole. I'm the person who snatched, raped & murdered and cut up the little prick teaser, Adam Walsh, and dumped his smelly ass into the canal. You know the story but you don't know where his bones are- I do.

Now you are a rich fucker, money you made from the dead body of that little kid. Oh, he was a sweet little piece of ass! I want to make a deal with you. Here's my deal. You pay me money and I'll tell where the bones are so you can get them buried all decent and Christian.

I know you'll find a way to make sure I get the lectric chair but at least I'll have money to spend before I burn. If you want the bones of your little cockteaser you send a private lawyer with money for me. No cops. No State attorneys. No FDLE. Just a private lawyer with a written contract. I get $5,000. as "good faith" money. Then when I show you some bones I get $45,000. You get a lawyer to make up a paper like that.

If you send the police after me before we make a deal then you don't get no bones and what's left of Adam's hot pussy can rot. I remember how the little bitch was crying for his mommy when I was ramming out his asshole. I love to fuck a boy, and then I love to kill them. Now you want his bones or not? Tell the cops and you don't get shit.

Sincerely,

Ottis E. Toole

OTTis E. TOOLE, 090812
P.O. BOX 747
STARKE, Fla- 32091

001600

CITY OF HOLLYWOOD, FLORIDA

INTER-OFFICE MEMORANDUM

TO: Chief Richard Witt
Deputy Chief R. S. Davis
Major B. W. Davis

DATE: October 24, 1988   FILE:

SUBJECT:

FROM: Det. J. Hoffman
Homicide Unit

REFERENCES:

This detective received a telephone call on 10/24/88 from Sgt. Richard Scheff of the Broward County Sheriff's Department.

The nature of this call pertained to the recent trip to Raiford Prison by Sgt. Scheff and Sgt. Fantagrassi.

During the week of 10/17/88. Sgt. Scheff and Sgt. Fantagrassi went to Raiford Prison to conduct an interview with prisoner, Gerard J. Schaffer. Mr. Schaffer recently wrote letters to various police departments, including the Broward Scheriff's Department. In these letters, Schaffer states that he is a cellmate of Ottis Toole and also does legal appeals for fellow inmates.

Mr. Schaffer tells how Ottis Toole has spoken to him frequently about the Adam Walsh murder. Mr. Schaffer believes that Toole is telling him the truth. Toole also gave Schaffer a handwritten confession to the Walsh murder.

According to Sgt. Scheff, after interviewing Schaffer, it is his opinion that Schaffer is strictly interested in this matter because he thinks he would be entitled to the reward money offered by the Walsh family. Schaffer believes the reward money is in excess of $100.000.00.

Gerald Schaffer informed Sgt. Scheff that he represents Ottis Toole in all further matters. Schaffer stated he must be present at all interviews conducted with Ottis Toole in the future. Should Ottis Toole be taken out on location, Mr. Schaffer indicates that he must accompany Toole and the law enforcement agency.

Gerald Schaffer informed Sgt. Scheff that Ottis Toole told him that he used a bayonet to commit the Walsh murder. This bayonet was taken from Ottis Toole's sister's residence in Jacksonville.

Sgt. Scheff and Sgt. Fantagrassi proceeded to locate Toole's sister. Upon doing this, Toole's sister was interviewed by these detectives. Toole's sister informed Sgt. Scheff that she had obtained the bayonet in question in 1979. This bayonet has been hanging on her mantel since the year she obtained it. According to her, if Ottis would have taken this bayonet she would have been fully aware of it. She assured the detectives that the bayonet has never left her residence.

Ottis Toole's sister agreed to cooperate by furnishing the bayonet to the Sheriff's Department to be forwarded to the crime lab.

It is the opinion of Sgt. Scheff and Sgt. Fantagrassi that Gerard J. Schaffer is interested in this matter strictly for his own personal benefits. There is no evidence at this time to link Ottis Toole to the Walsh murder.

JH/ab

005189

Mary H. wanted to remain anonymous, so her last name was redacted from the file records except for the H. Only after the release of the second CD-ROM was her full name revealed, possibly by mistake or because she had passed away at eighty-five years of age in 2006. Mary Corbett Hagan said she had gone to Sears around noon for the lamp sale. Everything in her statement was accurate except for one thing: she saw Dahmer not Toole. The HPD assumed it to be Toole. Now, no one will be able to talk with her. The following are excerpts from the HPD case files. Mary's interview was conducted by State Attorney Investigator Philip Mundy on September 5, 1996.

MH: The man had on jeans, and maybe they were kind of faded out a little. I don't know. Just, he wasn't very well kept. He didn't look like he should have been talking to this child. He was kind of humped over, and he is not trying for anybody else to hear . . . It was disgusting because if that was one of my grandchildren or anyone, I wouldn't want him talking to someone who looked like that. . . He was so unkempt, he looked like a bum. . . He didn't look like somebody that took baths. . . Everything about him looked like, well, like somebody that sleeps out or something. . . He didn't look good; that's all I can say . . . He was very tan. . . When he looked at me, he kept this stupid grin on his face, but in his eyes he had a dull, blank look.

PM: Where did you go after that?

MH: I went to the lamps to look at the lamps. . . When I left the lamps, I went through the same part, and there wasn't any of the children there, and when I looked—I was going to look again at that character—and so saw he was gone, and so was the children, all of them.

PM: When was the first time you found that there was something wrong?

MH: I heard in the evening on TV. I heard they were searching for Adam Walsh . . . The mother was searching for him, and everybody was searching for him . . . I didn't think much of it . . . I thought he was just lost . . . Then I didn't pay attention anymore; then a neighbor told me they found the head, and I really became upset. . . I told Frank [Mary's husband] when he came home from Europe, and he said, "Well, we will go up and talk to the police."

PM: How come you didn't go to the police sooner?

MH: I didn't want to go by myself, so I waited for my husband to come home . . . We went to the station, but there were a lot of people, and somehow I started trying to tell the police. He made a few notes, but he didn't ask me anything.

PM: This was right at the police station?

MH: Yes, at the police station . . . There was one sitting at a desk when we went in.

PM: On the first floor?

MH: Yes.

PM: Was he in uniform?

MH: Yes, but I don't think he ever took down my name . . . He didn't listen to me . . . He made me feel like he thought I wanted attention, like I was making up a story . . . That's the way I felt, so I didn't tell him so much.

PM: What happened after that?

MH: Nobody ever got in touch with me.

PM: Nobody from the Hollywood Police Department?

MH: No, nobody.

When I read Mary's statement, I knew that must have been the same cop I'd talked to. Officer Presley had taken condescension to a whole new level when I tried to tell him what happened. It was as if he didn't believe anything I said. He wanted, even demanded, proof that I was there. He asked for a receipt as proof. I didn't have one, but only because I didn't buy anything. Like Mary, I also had the feeling that he thought I had come in just for attention.

Mary's description of the suspect is exactly the same as mine, and I didn't conform my statement to match hers in any way. My statement and description have always been consistent. The date of my taped statement is October 25, 1991. Mary's statement was taken in 1996 and can be located in the HPD case files (roll 1, p. 2705). Also, Mary's full statement can be located in the SAO case files: box 1, file 05.7, STATEMENT OF MARY CORBETT HAGAN.

Mary's timeframe was right. Everything about her statement was sincere and accurate. Even Phil Mundy had this to say when he found out that the HPD thought Mary H. might be nothing more than a liar and a fraud: "If Mary H. is a fraud or a liar, it would be one of the major disappointments of my career." The HPD should know people who are quick to accuse others of lying are normally inveterate liars themselves.

So, that leaves the question, how did Mary pick Toole's photo out of a six-photo lineup as being the man she saw in the Sears? The answer is very simple: she didn't. She did pick out Toole but only because she was influenced by what she saw on the news and TV. At that time, Ottis Toole was getting a lot of publicity and a lot of smokes for saying he did it. The HPD detectives were saying he did it. The media was saying he did it. So how could they all be wrong? Knowing these investigators, I'm sure there might've been a little prompting on their part as well. One thing you can bet on: Dahmer's photo wasn't in that line-up. It didn't need to be, since Dahmer said he didn't do it.

Mary wrote a letter to John Walsh. Thinking the HPD knew what they were doing, that letter was forwarded by *America's Most Wanted* to the HPD. Detective Mark Smith called her but dismissed her without giving her a taped interview. At this time, Smith might have been trying to steer the investigation away from Jeffrey Dahmer.

SAO investigator Phil Mundy has maintained that he knew right away when he interviewed Mary H. that she was a legitimate witness. What convinced him the most was the minute she described Adam's flip-flops. Then, when she described the grin the disheveled man had, Mundy knew she was describing Toole. Since he had met Toole, Mundy felt he knew Toole's mannerisms. Mundy maintained if Toole were still alive, the case could've been brought to a successful prosecution.

However, the original lead detective Jack Hoffman said, although he was no longer in charge of the case when Mary came forward, she couldn't have seen Toole, because she said she saw him inside Sears. Toole has always maintained he never entered Sears but snatched Adam from the parking lot. That was the one thing consistent in Ottis Toole's statements.

Mary came forward the second time after Hoffman had been removed from the case, though he had been in charge when other witnesses tried to come forward but were summarily dismissed because their statements did not conform to what Toole and Dahmer were saying. Years later, Joe Matthews would latch onto Mary as a key Ottis Toole witness that helped close the case. From everything that I know and have read, such as other witness timelines and statements about this case, I would submit, it was most likely Jeffrey Dahmer Mary had seen. Ottis Toole himself has said he abducted Adam from the parking lot and never been inside the toy department. Also, Toole had long since been eliminated as a suspect.

The full interview can be found in the SAO case files ("Statement of Mary Corbett Hagan," box 1, file 5, p. 7).

Larry Leon Waldo actually exonerates Ottis Toole. Although I've listed him as an Ottis Toole witness because Matthews used Waldo as another one of his pivotal witnesses, Larry, an acquaintance of Ottis, claims that he celebrated his birthday with Toole on July 27, 1981.

Detective Robert Dunbar and Detective Francis Hogan of the HPD interviewed Larry on November 2, 1983, at his Hollywood, Florida, apartment where he'd since moved. Records show that Larry did have an arrest record for D.U.I. and no driver's license on June 10, 1982. That arrest record also shows his address as 141 W. 10th Street, Jacksonville. This would be eight blocks from Betty Goodyear's boarding house, where Ottis was living at the time, and Betty Goodyear stated that she did know Larry Waldo.

These two detectives concluded in their report that they believed Larry was mistaken and might have been with Toole in 1982 as opposed to 1981, because they believed Larry was a troubled individual burdened with both psychiatric and alcohol problems. In their opinion, "This would bring into question Waldo's ability to recount past details with any accuracy." So they must have figured the date could be corrected for him.

It's true: Larry did have problems, but it was those problems, as well as his social standing, that put him in the company of someone like Ottis Toole. To say Larry was mistaken about the date of July 27, 1981, might have been a mistake on the part of the detectives.

Larry would remember that date because July 27, 1955 was his birth date. Larry Waldo died on May 2, 1990. His interview can be found in the SAO case files ("Larry Leon Waldo," box 7, file 1, July 6, 1998).

Arlene and Heidi Mayer called the HPD to say they had an encounter with Ottis Toole at a Kmart located at 651 South State Road Seven, just under two and a half miles southwest of the Hollywood Mall, three days before Adam Walsh was kidnapped

After the now-defunct *Hollywood Sun Tattler* newspaper ran an article on the Adam Walsh case in its Saturday, October 22, 1983 edition with a photo of Ottis Toole saying he confessed, Arlene Mayer called the HPD to say she thought she and her daughter, Heidi Mayer, had a run-in with Toole. At first, the HPD believed them because they both managed to separately pick out the photo they saw in the newspaper of Toole from a six-photo lineup, at which time they were requested to sign and date the back of the photo as confirmation.

On July 24, 1981, Arlene was shopping with her twelve-year-old daughter in Kmart, around 6 p.m. to 7 p.m., when a man kept staring at Heidi and following them around the store. He then asked Heidi if she wanted to ride in his shopping cart. In 1983, when Ottis Toole confessed to Adam's abduction, his photo made its way to the front pages of the local newspapers. When Arlene and Heidi saw the photo, they thought it could've been the person they'd encountered at the Kmart, and they called the HPD to tell them they now realized that man to be Ottis Toole.

However, Ottis Toole was on a bus between Newport News, Virginia, and Jacksonville, Florida, at that time. The not-so-bright HPD would eventually dismiss the Mayers, even though they shouldn't have. In 1991, when Jeffrey Dahmer made the papers, the Hollywood investigators wouldn't have enough sense to connect the dots to him or deliberately might not have wanted to. It could've been Dahmer that the Mayers encountered that day. The HPD should have gone back to the Mayers and shown them Dahmer's composites, photos, and mug shots, even if only to exclude him. Only they never did, no doubt as a result of Dahmer having already been rejected as a suspect. At a time when Ottis Toole was trying his best to take credit for Adam's abduction, never once in any of his confessions did he mention the Kmart incident. Nor did the detectives ever question him about it.

One of the reasons Hoffman and Hickman eliminated the Mayers as witnesses and didn't mention the Kmart incident to Toole was that they knew that encounter had nothing to do with Ottis Toole. The record showed that, on July 25, Toole arrived in Jacksonville, and it had been clearly established that the Kmart incident happened on Friday, July 24, 1981. Even the incorrigible Matthews admitted, in his own book on page 115, "This makes the failure to corroborate Toole's encounter with Heidi Mayer all the more confounding." Yet it wouldn't stop Matthews from rebuking Hoffman and Hickman's conclusions and coming up with his own.

Matthews concluded that the Mayers didn't know what the heck they were talking about and must have been confused. Matthews said so himself, in his book, and even took it upon himself to change the date of the Kmart incident from July 24 to July 25 in order to fit his own personal timeline. That still doesn't work, as Toole didn't arrive in Jacksonville until the afternoon of July 25, and he couldn't have made it to Hollywood so quickly, unless his hotrod Cadillac had wings.

In his book, Matthews made strong accusations against Detective Hoffman, who I presume wouldn't defend himself because of his own incredible incompetence. Matthews said of Hoffman, "Ego was involved and tunnel vision . . . And the tunnel vision is that you come up with your own hypothesis as to what took place, and you work that case to validate your own hypothesis." This brazenly bold statement was made without shame, considering the fact that Joe Matthews's methods of deduction were to simply ignore all the facts.

On August 10, 2010, I contacted Heidi Mayer by e-mail:

August 10, 2010

Dear Heidi Mayer,

My name is Willis Morgan. I am independently investigating a cold case that was given to the media by the Hollywood Police Department. Your mother called the Hollywood Police about an incident that occurred at the Kmart located on State Road 7 on July 24, 1981. I would like to talk to you and your mom about that incident and show you some composites. There has been new evidence uncovered, and I think you and your mom could be of some help in this case.

Please give me a call at **1-III-III-IIII**.

I am trying to put closure to a 29-year-old cold case, and I believe the incident you and your mom reported may be related to this case.

I appreciate your help,

Willis Morgan

Email: **IIIIIIIIIIIIIIII@.IIIII**.com

On August 10, 2010, Heidi responded:

Mr. Morgan,

First I would like to know who you are and who you work for before I go any further with this conversation. No offense but for the last 30 years I have dealt with this matter and I was under the impression that the case was closed and I would not have any more contact about it anymore.

Sincerely,

Heidi Mayer

I wrote her back with the following:

August 11, 2010

Heidi,

I worked 25 years for the *Miami Herald*. I am retired now but I am also one of the witnesses in the Adam Walsh abduction. I believe I may know the person you had that incident in Kmart with on Friday July 24, 1981. It could not have been Ottis Toole because the records show he was in Newport News Virginia on Friday, July 24, 1981, and arrived in Jacksonville Fl. only on Saturday, July 25, 1981.

Please look at the included composite and let me know if you think this could be the person you encountered that day in Kmart.

There are other witnesses that encountered this person in the same area at about the same time you had your encounter. When I hear from you, I will send you more information.

I appreciate your help,

Willis Morgan

Phone: ▌▌▌-▌▌▌-▌▌▌▌

Email: ▌▌▌▌▌▌▌▌▌▌▌▌▌@▌▌▌▌.com

On August 11, 2010, Heidi replied:

Everything that I have known that I can remember was Otis O'Toole [sic]. I have been through this enough with this in my life and I would appreciate it if you will just understand I don't want to discuss this anymore. I have finally put this in the past and moved on with my life.

Heidi Mayer

On August 12, 2010, I went to Arlene Mayer's home in Hollywood, Florida. I talked to her husband Wayne, and he told me that Arlene had passed away on June 25, 2006. Before I could even explain to Wayne about the case, his first response was, "They sure messed that case up!"

I then explained the case to him and showed him the composites from the Twin City Mall and the Hollywood Mall. Wayne looked at them and said they looked exactly like the person that his wife described, though of course, that wasn't evidence. He did confirm that the encounter at Kmart was on Friday, July 24, 1981. Wayne emphasized it was on Friday, and not any other day, because Friday was the day of the week he always dropped his wife and daughter off at the Kmart. Wayne said that he would drop off his wife and daughter, and then pick them back up two hours later. He didn't see the incident.

In one of Arlene's interviews, she did say it could've been on a Saturday. However, with Arlene passed away and Heidi not wanting to talk (after the HPD and Joe Matthews ran her through the wringer for so many years), there was no way to know for sure if they actually saw Jeffrey Dahmer. We do know for certain that they didn't see Ottis Toole, and Jeffrey Dahmer's weekends started around 5 p.m. on Friday. Dahmer was known to be on the prowl from Palm Beach to South Beach, and it appears that sometimes Dahmer would take the bus and sometimes the blue van. But really, after more than three decades, all this leads us into is suppositions, something I blame the HPD for.

William Mistler would rekindle the Toole theory. In another tip generated from the *Sun Tattler*, on July 7, 1991, at a point when Ottis Toole was eliminated as a suspect, William Mistler called the HPD. Mistler had read an article by Major J.B. Smith of the HPD. The article said the HPD did the most thorough investigation before eliminating Ottis Toole as a suspect in the Adam Walsh abduction and homicide.

In Mistler's first statement, dated July 29, 1991, he said he was at the Hollywood Mall the day Adam was kidnapped. The reason he gave for not coming forward sooner was because he read about a blue van being the suspect vehicle, so he thought what he had seen had nothing to do with the Adam Walsh abduction. Mistler went to Sears around 10 a.m. to 11 a.m. to buy some camping equipment. He and his family were going on a camping trip that evening.

Hotshot cold-case detective Mark Smith commented, "This statement is significant because, if accurate, it represents the only known eyewitness account of the abduction."

Mistler said that, while he was in the parking lot, he noticed a "grandfather-like figure, between fifty and sixty years old," get out of a white Cadillac and walk up to a boy that seemed to be about seven to ten years old. Mistler stated, "Ottis Toole never touched Adam. He never got within two feet of Adam. Toole just kneeled down and talked to him . . . When he got up, Adam followed Toole to the car and got in the passenger side." Mistler wasn't able to describe Adam's clothing. All he remembers was Adam's "white shoes." Yet Mistler said, "If I'm wrong, I'll stand on my head and spit out quarters."

Later on in the afternoon, around 3 p.m., Mistler went back to Sears with his family to pick up some more supplies. When he entered the store, he noticed a woman that looked really distraught, and there was a man with her. He heard an announcement paging Adam. His nine-year-old son Jason remarked, "Hey, that's John Walsh, Adam's dad." Mistler lived only a few blocks from the Walshes, and their kids played at the same park. According to the son, John used to bring Adam to the park a lot. Mistler then paid for the items he'd bought and left on his camping trip. It would take ten years before Mistler called the HPD to tell them his story. "I'm the guy who saw Ottis Toole take Adam Walsh from the curb outside the Sears store that day and put him inside a car."

When the HPD asked him to take a polygraph, he agreed without hesitation. While no record of that initial July 30, 1991 exam itself remains in the case file, the examiner, Detective Philip Diecidue, said the results were inconclusive. The HPD then tried to place him under hypnosis, but on August 2, 1991, a doctor from the psychological service unit said he was unfit to be hypnotized. They then drove Mistler back to Sears to jog his memory as to Adam's clothing, but Mistler couldn't remember anything. Both the State Attorney's Office and the HPD dismissed Mistler as a viable witness because his story kept changing.

In 2011, years after William Mistler had been dismissed as a credible witness, Joe Matthews would latch onto him like a parasite that latches onto a host and exploits it for valuable resources, spending over eight pages of his book breathing life back into Mistler as a star witness (starting on page 172 of his book). Matthews states that Mistler was at Sears twice that day, once at 3 p.m. and also more than two hours earlier. Matthews must have known that Mistler was at Sears for the first time between 10 a.m. and 11 a.m., before Adam was abducted. That was between four and five hours earlier, way more than *two*. Matthews was just trying to make his early timeline fit close to Adam's abduction time, like trying to fit square pegs into round holes. Adam was abducted between 12:15 p.m. and 12:20 p.m. in the afternoon.

Mistler was able to pick out Ottis Toole in a photo lineup, but only because he'd been watching TV and reading articles from news media sources, and that was good enough for the HPD. However, after a review of Mistler's statements, on February 23, 1996, he was again asked to take a polygraph exam, to which he agreed. In one investigative case summary report located in the SAO case files (box 8, file 5, p. 21) and dated February 26, 1996, the following pertinent questions were proposed to Mistler during the course of that exam given by polygraphist/investigator Terrill "Terry" L. Gardner.

* Did you lie when you said that you personally observed Ottis Toole in a dark-over-white Cadillac in July of 1981? **No**.

* Did you lie when you said that you personally observed Ottis Toole put a young boy in a dark-over-white Cadillac in July of 1981? **No**.

The following is the opinion of polygraphist/investigator Terrill "Terry" L. Gardner of the exam.

In the examiner's opinion, the subject's response on his polygraph indicated consistent reaction to the aforementioned questions.

It is further the opinion of this examiner that the subject was not being truthful when he stated that he personally observed Ottis Toole with Adam Walsh and a dark-over-white Cadillac in July of 1981.

In another interview and polygraph exam given by Terry Gardner dated March 19, 1997, William Mistler insisted he was being truthful in 1991 when he first came forward:

William Mistler: Yeah, Jack Hoffman tried to sell me a bag of s--t, they were lying to me. They f--kin' knew I was telling the truth. I want to make that clear.

This can be found on the HPD CD-2 file titled "DOC001y__6 MISTLER" at JusticeForAdam.com.

This statement was cropped from a letter dated June 28, 1996, by Philip Mundy to the State Attorney's Office: "It was also brought to light during this interview that Mr. Mistler has never made a formal identification of Adam Walsh. In fact, further questioning on this subject brought out that Mr. Mistler cannot say that it was indeed Adam Walsh that he saw on July 27, 1981, outside the Sears store."

Joe Matthews and the HPD used this confused, marijuana-smoking (a daily habit by his own admission), potty-mouthed key witness to close Adam's case. Remember, Mistler first came forward when serial killer Jeffrey Dahmer made national headlines. Witnesses, including myself, went back to the HPD to let them know that it was Jeffrey Dahmer that was at the Hollywood Mall at the time Adam was abducted. Could it be that someone was trying to steer the investigation away from Jeffrey Dahmer at a time when witnesses were coming forward?

Notice how they brought Mistler to the Hollywood Mall all on their own, in order to jog his memory—not once, but several times. Yet they wouldn't extend that courtesy to me when I implicated Jeffrey Dahmer. Detective Hoffman only grudgingly went to the mall for Bill Bowen after Bill insisted he go. If Bill or I were to have implicated Ottis Toole instead of Dahmer, I could only imagine all the attention the HPD detectives would've doted upon us.

I went to William Mistler's house and knocked on his door. When I explained to William why I was there, he did not want to talk to me. He told me, "That case has been solved and closed, and I've got nothing to say to you." I wasn't so quick to give up. I knew this would be the one and only chance I'd have to talk to him. I tried to show him some information I had in my portfolio that I always carry around with me, but he was not interested. He simply repeated, "I've got nothing to say to you." Then he closed the door, leaving me standing there … and so I left. I never did get any quarters.

Information on Mistler can be found in the SAO case files ("Interviews of the Mistler Family," box 1, file 1, p. 2 and "NEWS ARTICLES Adam Walsh," box 2, file 1, p. 65).

Joel Cockerham: According to Joe Matthews, Joel called the *America's Most Wanted* hotline after they ran the September 21, 1996 special program depicting Ottis Toole as the culprit in Adam Walsh's abduction. Joel explained that until he saw the show, he hadn't realized it, but now he thought he could've been the boy that was kicked out of the store with Adam.

Matthews claimed that he talked to Joel at some length. In Matthews's book, it appears he latched onto Joel's statement as proof that Adam was "kicked" out of Sears. In fact, Matthews thought this was the fuel that would reignite the investigation. According to Matthews, eight-year-old Joel was playing Asteroids with Adam when the trouble started with the kids who wanted to take the controllers away.

PHOTO RIGHT: Joel Cockerham.

According to *Bringing Adam Home* (p. 219), when *America's Most Wanted* aired that segment, Joel's sister, Mia, who was nine in 1981 (actually, the book got it wrong; Joel was nine and she was ten), and was with Joel in the toy department, clapped her hand to her mouth. "That's him," she told Joel. "He had more hair then, but that's him."

When I contacted Mia on September 18, 2014, and showed her composites and mug shots of Jeffrey Dahmer, she said, "I'm absolutely positive that was the person." It was the 1982 mug shot that did it for her. Mia said she was the little blonde girl in the toy department when she met Dahmer. In his book, Matthews leaves readers to assume he talked to Mia Cockerham (now Taylor). She says that never happened. She told me she had never told *America's Most Wanted* or Matthews that she saw Ottis Toole. In fact, Mia has never talked to anyone. "Matthews made that up, or he may have twisted something around that Joel said to make it sound like it was Toole. What I have consistently said was that Toole was way too old, and the person I saw had a lot more hair." Mia also said Joel never played Asteroids. "He wouldn't even have known how to play the game. He only watched others play."

Mia's Story

In 1981, Mia's family lived out in the east Everglades. They had no electricity (and thus no television), no telephone, and no communication with the outside world. In fact, her family didn't even know Adam had been abducted until weeks later, when they purchased a newspaper and read about it. Every now and then, her father would bring the family to the city so he could go to the Gulfstream Park racetrack in Hallandale and the Hollywood dog track. During one of those trips, on July 26 and July 27, 1981, he dropped the family off at the Hollywood Mall when it opened in the morning. Several hours later, he returned to pick them up. On Sunday, July 26, Mia was in the mall with Joel, her mother Peggy, and her two older brothers. While their mother shopped just yards away, Mia and Joel walked over to the toy department. That was when Mia saw a strange man. As Joel and Mia were in the toy department, the security guard came over to get the older kids to hush up. Mia and Joel then went to find their mom. "As we were walking toward the mall/Sears exit, a man stepped in front of us, inappropriately close, with this toy in his hand, and asked Joel if he knew how to play a ball-in-the-hole game." It was a silly question, Mia said. "I had a weird feeling about this guy. He was really creepy looking." She smelled stale beer on his breath. When Dahmer tried to talk to Joel, she said, "There's Mom. Let's go … Thankfully, our mother was close by, and we ran to her."

It was at that time the female security guard showed up a second time and told everyone to be quiet again, and the man headed out the west exit. It was also at that time her two older brothers joined their mom as well. On the way out of the west exit, she saw a blue van parked at the curb. She also saw the same dirty man standing next to it. Mia said if it hadn't been for her mother and the security guard showing up, her brother would have been abducted. "He was definitely targeting my brother." On Monday, July 27, 1981, Mia went to the mall again with her mother and Joel. This time, her older brothers were not with them.

Mia: "The next day, Monday, July 27, 1981, we were again at the mall and saw the same man, wearing the same dirty clothes as the day before, talking to a child, who I believe was Adam Walsh, as we were leaving the mall. My brother Joel asked my mother if he could stay with his friend whom he spoke to earlier—the child who we saw and believe to be Adam—however, she said, 'No, his dad is here now.'

"He was really close to the kid [Adam], leaning over and talking to him. He leaned down, took his hand by his fingertips, as he was talking to him." The little boy looked confused, and she didn't hear him say anything as he was led away to the left toward the west exit.

PHOTO RIGHT: Mia Taylor. Photos of Mia and Joel are courtesy of Mia Taylor.

Mia's statement was in complete contrast to what Matthews claimed in his book *Bringing Adam Home*. Whoever talked to Joel at *America's Most Wanted*, or Matthews himself, may have taken what Joel said out of context. Ever since that day, Joel has been haunted by Adam's abduction. Ten years after the incident, Joel had a psychological breakdown. He was put on medication and was in and out of hospitals right up until the day he sadly took his own life on October 4, 2006, at the age of thirty-four.

Mia Taylor: "After it was announced in 2008 that Ottis Toole was found to be the suspect, now, as then, when I saw the photograph of Ottis Toole, I did not recognize him as the person I saw that day. The disheveled person I saw was younger and had more hair."

Authorities have never contacted Mia, neither the HPD nor Joe Matthews. That again says a lot about the credibility of the HPD as well as the credibility of the Matthews Report that was used to close Adam's case.

CHAPTER SEVENTEEN
THE EVER-ELUSIVE
MATTHEWS' REPORT

PHOTO LEFT: Joe Matthews (promoting his book). Photo of Matthews taken March 16, 2012

Joe Matthews's conclusion that Ottis Toole murdered Adam helped police and prosecutors to close their investigation. The now-retired Matthews first met John Walsh when the HPD hired his company, the Southern Institute of Polygraph, to polygraph John Walsh and James Campbell in 1981. At that time, he was also a homicide detective for the Miami Beach Police Department. The Walsh family said he worked the case until its December 16, 2008, closing.

The Hollywood police closed the Walsh case on the basis of the four-hundred-page report Matthews compiled. Once the case was closed, Matthews gave a copy of his manuscript to a coauthor to have it formatted into a book. His manuscript was his own interpretation of police documents. These are the same police documents that can be downloaded for free at JusticeForAdam.com. Now everyone can come to his or her own conclusions.

Matthews befriended John Walsh and was hired onto John's show *America's Most Wanted* for twelve years as an on-screen senior criminal investigator. In 2006, at the Atlantic Hotel in Fort Lauderdale, John arranged to meet with Matthews, who had previously investigated Adam's murder. Reve wanted Matthews to reinvestigate the case and have it closed in a conclusive way. She told John, "I don't care if you go to work just to pay the bill of this private investigator."

Whether Egotistical or Eager to Placate the Walshes …

Matthews had a chance to set the record straight. Instead, for egotistical reasons or in his eagerness to placate the Walshes, he authored his own narrative of events and took it upon himself to become the chief propagandist for the Ottis Toole theory as he contrived evidence and twisted facts in what may have been a diabolically clever scheme he hatched up that would please the Walshes. Then he used useful idiots at the HPD to get the case closed. Reve herself said she didn't want to go to her grave not knowing, yet Matthews seems to be okay with her not knowing the truth. He also perpetrated a hoax, most likely in order to make himself into a superhero and make some money in the process.

Although the Walshes believed it was Ottis Toole, it was undoubtedly Matthews who helped solidify that belief. Joe Matthews made up his misguided fictional report and presented it to the new, inexperienced, as well as incompetent chief as the truth at a time when this police department was the perfect soil for Matthews to grow his Ottis Toole theories. When Wagner actually accepted and agreed with his report (especially since it didn't point to Jeffrey Dahmer), Detective Sergeant Joe Matthews's ego had to have been lifted to the heights of delusional euphoria and then he thrived in the limelight when news publications like *USA Today* called Adam's closing "redemptive for the Walshes." And as for John Walsh, he had one of these quintessential bumbling, stumbling, lying detectives right in his midst all along.

Common Sense Was No Friend Of Matthews

According to one *Sun-Sentinel* article dated March 4, 2011, by Chauncey Mabe, Matthews thought his manuscript was too technical for the general audience. Joe Matthews commented about his eponymous Matthews Report: "As worldly as I thought I was as a homicide investigator, I was very naive when it came to publishing my manuscript. I expected to make it required reading for criminal justice programs." Whatever Matthews does, he shouldn't congratulate himself too much. He's not all that good.

Matthews claimed he used "good, old-fashioned police work" to solve the case. He also said, "I'm probably one of the very few people who ever read all ten thousand pages and put it in some sort of order, and I started from the very beginning."

Well, Mr. Matthews, I also read the entire case file, and I came to an entirely different conclusion. Matthews was either incredibly stupid or a fraud. The Matthews Report that he made up is based on not much more than rumors, innuendos and deception on Matthews's part. Also, if he'd really read the entire case file, Matthews would know that the page count (excluding the photo box) was just over seven thousand pages—there was no need for him to inflate his ego. The HPD first came up with the inflated page count of ten thousand back in 1995, likely in order to convince the court they needed more time to investigate the case. As well, it could've been close to ten thousand pages before 1991, when Jeffrey Dahmer was captured and some evidence vanished. This leaves me with the haunting thought that someone at the HPD may have removed roughly three thousand pages from the case file.

Matthews considers himself a seasoned cold-case homicide detective, but the very basic tenet of investigating a cold case homicide is to use due diligence and call all the witnesses. Matthews said he'd painstakingly reviewed every scrap of information in the files, but he never gave me, and others like me, a call. Instead, Matthews just called the ones he cherry-picked to satisfy his own theatrical conclusion that pushed for Toole's post-mortem condemnation as Adam's killer.

The coauthor of *Bringing Adam Home*, mystery writer Les Standiford, wrote, "In doing what hundreds of cops before him—including the FBI and the Florida Department of Law Enforcement—could not, marks him as a very remarkable and honorable individual indeed. I would call him a hero. For parents who have lost a child in whatever manner, I do not think there is ever such a thing as closure. But the Walsh's [sic] certainly feel great gratitude for what Joe Matthews did, and as John Walsh has said, 'At least now the not-knowing is over, and a different phase of life can begin.' "

Clearly, without question, Joe is a remarkable hero, but only in his own story. What Standiford doesn't seem to understand is that the FBI never tried to solve the Adam Walsh case. Since they were not asked to assist by the HPD, there was no evidence showing that Adam was brought to another state, and there was no ransom note, the FBI refused to get involved. That case belonged to the HPD to solve and only the HPD.

When asked about me, Bill Bowen, and other witnesses implicating Jeffrey Dahmer, Matthews said, in support of his book, *Bringing Adam Home*, "People are entitled to their opinions. But the information I provided that officially closed the Adam Walsh murder investigation was not based on my opinions or what the lead investigator documented as facts in his reports. I conducted an independent investigation and was able to prove beyond any reasonable doubt—based on direct and circumstantial evidence which cannot be disputed—that Ottis Toole abducted and murdered Adam. Only because of those facts was the case officially closed."

Whether exploitative or stuck on stupid, Matthews, a braggart and a buffoon, produced his self-serving opportunistic Matthews Report resurrecting Ottis Toole as the murderer of Adam Walsh. Smitten with his smoking gun, Shroud of Turin discovery, Matthews presented this report to the HPD on April 30, 2008. That agency reviewed the report as a part of its official investigation of the murder and accepted Matthews's conclusion that Ottis Toole murdered Adam Walsh. That police department then provided the report to the Broward County State Attorney's Office for its review, and that agency also reviewed (and agreed with) the report as a part of its official investigation.

"It's going to be tough," Chief Wagner told John Walsh, "but I've got broad shoulders, and I'm going to do it on national television."

On December 16, 2008, the HPD announced—with John, Reve, and Adam's siblings present—that their investigations of the murder would be closed, based in part on the Matthews Report. In actuality, the case was closed based fully on Matthews's self-serving report. At that press conference announcing the closure of the case, the HPD explained that they had closed their investigation because Matthews had provided conclusive evidence that Toole was the murderer and no further investigation was needed. The State Attorney's Office agreed. (Morton's letter to Wagner was Exhibit A in my lawsuit).

In a letter to the *Miami Herald* in March 2009, Chief Assistant State Attorney Charles Morton Jr. wrote, "The material and reports in the Hollywood Police Department's investigation of Toole contains substantial and documented investigative information that tracks Toole's whereabouts and his opportunity to have committed the crime. This was neatly and skillfully pointed out in an investigative file created by retired detective Joe Matthews and presented for my review."

Stupidity Would Make Matthews Famous

Using John Walsh's name, Matthews had such influence over the incorrigible chief as well as the ineffective Mr. Morton that he could've convinced them to indict a ham sandwich. Later—and I should add, only after I filed a lawsuit—Morton would start backpedaling and say that he only meant that he agreed with Chief Wagner's right to use exceptional clearance to close the case, and not with the Matthews Report. A copy of this response to the *Miami Herald* was attached as Exhibit B in my lawsuit.

The *Miami Herald* reported on March 28, 2010, "The decision to close the Adam Walsh murder case was based in part on an 'independent investigation' and a report by a retired cop and Walsh family confidant. But authorities retain no copy of the report, so its conclusions cannot be reviewed."

They quoted Barbara Petersen, president of the First Amendment Foundation. She said Matthews's files are "clearly a public record . . . That's stunning that they would make the decision to close a case based on documents they now claim are not public record . . . If they were allowed to view the records, they then become public records subject to disclosure and retention under public records laws."

Hollywood spokeswoman Raclin Storey also stated, "Matthews let the HPD review his findings, but he did not provide us with a copy of his work," and Janice Williams, records custodian for the State Attorney's Office, states that Matthews's files were returned to his attorney, Kelly Hancock, who said he returned the files to Matthews. John Walsh also held up a copy of the Matthews Report on the CBS *Early Show*, the very day after it was announced that the case had been closed.

Once I filed the lawsuit, everyone, except John Walsh himself, would begin to put distance between themselves and the bottom-dwelling Matthews. It is my understanding that Matthews claims that he investigated the Adam Walsh case without being paid, simply because he thought it had to be done. Even if Matthews worked pro bono to come up with his fake investigation that took him two years and nine months to complete, he has a lot of explaining to do.

My Demand for Production of the Matthews Report

On April 12, 2010, I retained the law firm of Hunton & Williams LLP to assist in obtaining access to the records that Matthews had provided to the HPD and the Broward County State Attorney's Office. I wanted to be afforded the same opportunity as the HPD and the State Attorney's Office to review the Matthews Report and come up with my own conclusions.

Keep in mind that my primary goal for this lawsuit was never profit or personal gain of any kind. My primary goal was simply justice for Adam Walsh. Eventually, I want the HPD to reopen the Adam Walsh case and then close it correctly.

In May 2010, my attorney, Thomas Julin, was on a conference call with the HPD's lawyer, Joel Canter, and Assistant State Attorney Charles Morton, who in concert called Joe Matthews, creator of the ever-elusive report. Matthews then came up with the fabricated story that he didn't have a copy of the report because he gave the sole copy of it to his book publisher. He went on to say that his publisher was in Cuba and that he didn't know when his publisher would be returning. He added that he would make an attempt to find out.

The reason he gave for giving the only copy to his publisher was that he was afraid I would steal it. He accused me of stalking him. I twice went to his place of business in Davie, Florida, for the purpose of talking with him. I wanted to give him the opportunity to let me see his report before I took legal action. I also brought with me my own documents and wanted to go over them with him. I never imagined Matthews, who made up a report going against a mountain of evidence as to who abducted Adam, was going to give up his report. However, I felt it was necessary to give him that chance.

The first time I went to Joe Matthews's place of business, his secretary, Mary Alvarez, unlocked the door and invited me in. She'd assumed I was there to inquire about his latest business venture, LifePrint DNA kits. She told me to come back at 2 p.m. "That's when Mr. Matthews should be back." I noticed she had a paperback version of John Walsh's book *Tears of Rage* on her desk. I couldn't help myself and asked her some questions about the book and then told her that was what I was there about.

I went to lunch down the street at Home Town Buffet and returned at 2 p.m. When I approached the apparently always-locked, semi-transparent glass door, I could see only the back of Mary as she scurried off to a back room. It was my impression that she had called Matthews while I was at lunch, and he might have told her not to let me in. An easy conclusion to come to when I add to the fact that Joe never showed up at 2 p.m. I left and decided to come back one more time just in case I was wrong about my conclusion.

The second time, I parked away from the glass door and walked from the side to the door so that I wouldn't be seen in advance. When I put my face right up against the glass door, I could see in. This time, I made eye contact with Mary, and she still got up and went to the back room. A few seconds later, Joe's son, Greg Matthews, came to the door and let me in. He was actually quite courteous. Greg explained that he didn't get involved in his father's business. He also assured me that his father didn't want to talk to anyone about that case. At that point, I decided to let my attorney handle it. Rather than show his report to anyone, Matthews hired an attorney. This looked like the biggest red flag of all to the fact that Joe Matthews knew his report was bogus.

On April 16, 2010, Joel D. Cantor, counsel for the HPD, responded in writing to my attorney's request for the Matthews Report: "My client [the HPD] does not have a copy of the requested report. Based on your request, it is our intention to officially demand that this report be made available for your client's inspection. Although I intend to author this official demand later today, I cannot accurately predict how quickly Mr. Matthews will respond with a copy of the report. Please be assured that once we are advised that the report is available for inspection, I will contact you immediately."

My attorney responded, letting Cantor know that willing and knowing violation of the public records law was a crime, and that if the department were serious about obtaining the report from Matthews, it could use its law enforcement authority to do so.

My attorney asked Mr. Cantor to also produce Mark Smith's personal memorandum evaluating the report. It was attached to the Matthews Report when it was sent to Chuck Morton for his review. Cantor said he'd searched and been unable to locate a copy. *Miami Herald* reporter David Smiley had previously asked for the report and also had been told the same thing. Chuck Morton then had a different story regarding the Smith memo. Morton suggested to my attorney that he might have lost it in connection with a trip to Orlando for surgery. He admitted that he saw it and read it. Failure to maintain a copy of that report was a further violation of the public records law. I'm willing to bet someone has a copy but doesn't want it to be seen, because of its glowing review of the Matthews Report.

Joel Cantor then called my attorney to say that Chief Wagner was very upset that Matthews had placed him in that position. Cantor said that the chief wanted the report made available and that he was doing nothing to "harbor" or "assist" Matthews. Once the HPD and SAO realized

Matthews wasn't giving up his report, they decided that the Matthews Report was worthless to their investigation.

Janice Williams, public records custodian for the defendant state attorney, responded on April 21, 2010, with this letter to my attorney:

"[O]ur office does not have a copy of the 'report' you have requested. However, based upon your request, we contacted Mr. Kelly Hancock, Counsel for Mr. Matthews on Thursday April 15, and again on April 20. We have made a demand that a copy of Mr. Matthews's 'report' be made available to you for inspection. We were advised that Mr. Hancock communicated our demand to Mr. Matthews." A copy of this response was attached as Exhibit C in my lawsuit.

Kelly Hancock responded by saying, "Please be advised that I do not and have never represented Joseph Matthews."

On April 26, 2010, the defendant state attorney's office wrote to the defendant Matthews: "We request that pursuant to Chapter 119, Florida Statutes, you make the subject manuscript or report available for inspection by Mr. Julin . . ."

Even by May 13, 2010, Matthews hadn't made his report available for inspection. On this date, my attorney placed a second conference call with Joel Cantor and Charles Morton, and jointly called Matthews again to ask that he make the report available. During this telephone call, Matthews acknowledged that he'd received the multiple requests for access to the report, but asserted that he'd destroyed all electronic copies of the report due to his fear that the plaintiff (me) would break into his office and steal the report.

He asserted that only one written copy of the report remained and claimed that he'd given that copy of the report to his coauthor (who apparently needed it to write Joe's book) and that the coauthor had taken it to Cuba, where it remained. Matthews asserted that he was reluctant to show the report to the plaintiff (me) due to concerns that the plaintiff would make the report available to the *Miami Herald* or other media. I took this to be a hidden message suggesting that he had it but just didn't want anyone to see it.

Morton said that others would be entitled to request access, too, but for now, Mr. Morgan was the only one who had made a request, and his obligation was to show it only to Mr. Morgan. Both Cantor and Morton explained to Matthews that the manuscript had to be returned and made available because it was a public record. Matthews then agreed that he would produce the manuscript. He said his coauthor would be in Cuba for only a short time longer and that he would call his wife to find out exactly when he would return. Matthews would then contact Morton to arrange the production of the manuscript for inspection at a mutually agreeable time and place.

In a call days later, Matthews's attorney ultimately agreed that he would arrange for the production of the report to the plaintiff alone, at a mutually agreeable time and place, for a maximum time of one hour, with the stipulation that the plaintiff didn't bring a pad or pen and didn't take notes. Plus, the plaintiff would have to drop the lawsuit. He also said Matthews would contact his coauthor to find out when he would be returning to the United States with the report, and then he would contact Morton to let him know when the report would be produced.

Matthews was counting on me not being able to absorb the four-hundred-page report in one hour, and of course he was right. Obviously, I turned this offer down, and Matthews never did make the report available for inspection. Further efforts by my attorney to obtain a copy of the report from any of the [soon to be] defendants have been futile. At this time, it would appear that the defendants are acting in concert with each other to conceal public records in order to avoid public criticism of their erroneous conclusion that Ottis Toole murdered Adam Walsh.

My message here to Joe Matthews is that honesty would have been a much better decision on his part, because once he started down that path of lies, it led to more lies to cover up the lies he had already told. Although he is not exactly Legion of Valor material, Matthews needs to understand that lying is not free. There are consequences.

Matthews took advantage of the HPD's blunders. It was one inept detective taking advantage of an even more inept police department. Joe Matthews is far from the hotshot, intrepid sleuth that he portrays himself to be.

Ironically, Les Standiford, Joe Matthews's coauthor on *Bringing Adam Home*, said, "At first, Matthews approached a textbook publisher to use his manuscript as an instructional book for law enforcement in order to prevent the mistakes made by police in the case from happening again." Really? Since I started asking to see his report, he has refused to produce it for me, the HPD, other law enforcement agencies, or for anyone else to view.

I don't know exactly what transpired at the Miami Beach Police Department, but they might have had good reason to demote Matthews from detective sergeant to a regular uniformed police officer after twenty-nine years of service and not long before his regular retirement.

When Matthews confronted Patricia Schneider, the major in charge of the detective bureau, and demanded to know why he was being demoted, since he was getting along fine with those above him, the major said she'd heard he couldn't get along very well with Dick Witt over at Hollywood P.D. He could choose between demotion or retirement. Joe Matthews chose early retirement, thus bringing to an end his illustrious career as a Miami Beach homicide investigator. He said so himself in his book *Bringing Adam Home* (pp. 202-206).

I'm also mindful that the State Attorney's Office conducted the biggest, most incompetent and fake investigation into Adam's murder that any prosecutor's office could possibly conduct. In particular, I am talking about Chuck Morton. The SAO was very good at dragging its feet until things quieted down.

In the past years, the SAO has been asked for documents in writing by Art Harris. Mr. Morton sent Art letters of denial in 2006 and 2007 stating that the case was still being investigated. Only then would his office call one of the real witnesses, Bill Bowen, most likely in order to make his investigation seem genuine. Morton left a message on Bill's answering machine asking Bill to call him back at the phone number Morton left, because he wanted to interview Bill and would even pay for his trip to South Florida. When Bill returned the call, no one answered, and no one ever called him back even though Bill left his cell phone number.

Mr. Morton did interview me once, with his investigator, Terry Gardner present. It happened after the twenty-fifth anniversary media blitz started by Colleen Henry's story as well as Patrick

Fraser's story of Adam's abduction aired. The meeting took place at the 17th District Court building, room 665, in downtown Fort Lauderdale. After that interview, during a short conversation with Gardner, I received nothing more than monosyllabic answers and a cold stare, as if he loathed me. And it was only after John Walsh told reporters he couldn't believe that, after twenty-five years, he was still fighting for a competent investigation into Adam's killing did that interview take place. John said, "The ball is in Michael Satz's corner," imploring Sat's office to interview people who thought they had important information about the case.

The Evidence

On the following pages are the evidence reports from the Florida Department of Law Enforcement (FDLE) showing the many tests they did proving that Adam Walsh was never in Ottis Toole's 1971 white Cadillac Sedan DeVille.

The roll of undeveloped film Matthews received from the FDLE is referenced on the last page. There were no big secrets; those photos just didn't mean anything to anyone except Detective Sergeant Joe Matthews.

The FDLE reports can be read in the Broward County State Attorney's case files (box 7-HU-06-98, volume IV, file 18). The evidence that Matthews had for his "Shroud of Turin" idea is located right after the FDLE report.

FLORIDA DEPARTMENT OF LAW ENFORCEMENT

ROBERT R. DEMPSEY
COMMISSIONER

JACKSONVILLE REGIONAL CRIME LABORATORY
120 PLATEN ROAD
P.O. BOX 4999
JACKSONVILLE, FLORIDA 32201
9 November 1983

TELEPHONE
904/359-6390
(SC) 694-6390

TO: Honorable Sam Martin
        Chief of Police
        Hollywood Police Department
        3250 Hollywood Blvd.
        Hollywood, Florida 33021

FDLE Lab No. 83 10 43357
(Sub 03 and 04)
Agency No.   81-56073

Robert R Dempsey

Robert R. Dempsey
Commissioner

ATTN: Detective Jack Hoffman

RE: TOOLE, OTTIS
        Death Investigation
        WALSH, ADAM
        BROWARD COUNTY
        07-27-81

James M. Pollock Jr.

James M. Pollock, Jr.
Crime Laboratory Analyst,
Serology

"SUBPOENAS PERTAINING TO THIS CASE SHOULD
REFER TO FDLE LAB NO. 83 10 43357."

REFERENCE:

This report has reference to the following exhibits which were delivered to
the Laboratory on 3 November 1983 by Glenn Abate (Submission 03) and by
Detective J.W. Terry (Submission 04).

EXHIBITS:

Submission 03

        One sealed brown paper bag containing exhibits #7 thru #14 from
        carpets and padding in 1971 White Cadillac Sedan de Ville,
        VIN 6834910134601

#7   One sealed manila envelope containing "carpet sample #1 from driver's
        side"

#8   One sealed manila envelope containing "carpet sample #2 from driver's
        side"

#9   One sealed manila envelope containing "carpet sample #3 from driver's
        side"

#10   One sealed manila envelope containing "carpet sample #4 from driver's
        side"

005823

Honorable Sam Martin
Page Two
FDLE Lab No. 83 10 43357

EXHIBITS (cont.):

#11   One sealed manila envelope containing "carpet sample #1 from rear
       floorboard

#12   One sealed manila envelope containing "carpet sample #2 from rear
       floorboard

#13   One sealed manila envelope containing "carpet sample #3 from rear
       floorboard

#14   One sealed manila envelope containing "carpet sample #4 from rear
       floorboard

Submission 04

#15   One sealed brown paper bag containing "machette with canvas sheath"

RESULTS:

Exhibits #7 thru #14

The "carpets and padding from the front and rear floorboards of the 1971
White Cadillac Sedan de Ville" were treated with luminol, a presumptive
chemical test for bloodstaining. Areas of strongly persistent luminescence
were noted on the portion of "carpet from driver's side", on the portion of
"carpet from left rear floorboard", and on the "padding underneath the
carpet from left rear floorboard". These results as well as separate
chemical tests demonstrated the presence of a trace of bloodstaining on
these carpets and padding. There was an insufficient amount of blood for
further tests.

Exhibit #15

Chemical tests on the blade edge of the "machette" demonstrated the presence
of a trace of bloodstaining in a quantity that was insufficient for further
testing.

Chemical tests for bloodstaining on the "canvas sheath" were inconclusive.

REMARKS:

Debris from the "machette blade" and from the "canvas sheath" will be
forwarded to the Microanalysis section of the Tallahassee Regional Crime
Laboratory. Results of their analysis and the disposition of the evidence
will be the subject of a separate report.

JMP/ch

cc: Detective J.W. Terry, Jacksonville Sheriff's Office

FLORIDA DEPARTMENT OF LAW ENFORCEMENT

ROBERT R. DEMPSEY
COMMISSIONER

P.O. BOX 1489
TALLAHASSEE 32302
TALLAHASSEE REGIONAL CRIME LABORATORY

TELEPHONE
488-7880

22 December 1983

TO: Honorable Sam Martin
Chief of Police
Hollywood Police Dept.
3250 Hollywood Blvd.
Hollywood, Florida 33021

ATTN: J. Hoffman

RE: TOOLE, Otis
Death Investigation
WALSH, Adam
BROWARD COUNTY

FDLE LAB NO. 83 10 43357
AGENCY NO. 81-56073

Robert R Dempsey

Robert R. Dempsey
Commissioner

Reginald R Hurchins

Reginald R. Hurchins
Crime Laboratory Analyst, Microanalysis

"SUBPOENAS PERTAINING TO THIS CASE SHOULD REFER TO FDLE
LAB NO. 83 10 43357."

REFERENCE:

This report has reference to the following exhibits which were delivered
to the laboratory on November 8, 1983 via Certified Mail #P276000227
(Submission #01 and Submission #03).

EXHIBITS:

#1   Hair collected from headrest area of front passenger seat

#2   Vacuum sweepings from front seat area

#3   Vacuum sweepings from rear seat area

#4   Carpet standard

#5   Hairs from carpet under front seat

#6   Vacuum sweeping of carpet under front seat

#15a   Debris removed from blade of 'machette'

#15b   Tape lift of debris from blade of 'machette'

#15c   Sample of canvas sheath

FLORIDA DEPARTMENT OF LAW ENFORCEMENT

P.O. BOX 1489
TALLAHASSEE 32302

ROBERT R. DEMPSEY
COMMISSIONER

TALLAHASSEE REGIONAL CRIME LABORATORY

TELEPHONE
488-7880

25 January 1984

TO: Honorable Sam Martin
Chief of Police
Hollywood Police Dept.
3250 Hollywood Blvd.
Hollywood, Florida 33021

FDLE LAB NO. 83 10 43357
AGENCY NO. 81-56073

Robert R Dempsey

Robert R. Dempsey
Commissioner

ATTN: J. Hoffman

RE: TOOLE, Otis
Death Investigation
WALSH, Adam
BROWARD COUNTY

Linda A. Hensley

Linda A. Hensley
Crime Laboratory Analyst Microanalysis

"SUBPOENAS PERTAINING TO THIS CASE SHOULD REFER TO FDLE
LAB NO. 83 10 43357."

REFERENCE:

This report has reference to the following exhibits which were transferred
to the Tallahassee Laboratory on 08 November 1983 via Certified Mail No.
P276 000 227 (Submissions #01 and #03); Submission #04 on 23 November 1983
via Certified Mail No. P276 000 241 and Submission #06 on 21 November 1983
via Certified Mail No. P446 862 136.

EXHIBITS:

#1   Hairs from "backrest area of front passenger seat"

#2   Vacuum sweepings from "front seat area"

#3   Vacuum sweepings from "rear seat area"

#5   Hairs from "carpet under front seat"

#6   Vacuum sweepings of "carpet under front seat"

#15A   Debris from "machete and canvan sheath

#15B   Debris from "blade of machete"

A   Head hair standard from Walsh

005813

Honorable Sam Martin
Page Two
FDLE LAB NO. 83 10 43357

RESULTS:

The hairs recovered from Exhibits #1, #2, #3, #5, #6, #15A and #15B were
compared to the hairs in the head hair standard from Walsh (Exhibit A) and
were found to be different from the hairs in the standard.

REMARKS:

The above exhibits will be returned to the submitting authority at the
first opportunity.

LAH:rjb

FLORIDA DEPARTMENT OF LAW ENFORCEMENT

ROBERT R. DEMPSEY
COMMISSIONER

JACKSONVILLE REGIONAL CRIME LABORATORY
120 PLATEN ROAD
P.O. BOX 4999
JACKSONVILLE, FLORIDA 32201
14 November 1983

TELEPHONE
904/359-6390
(SC) 694-6390

TO: Honorable Sam Martin
       Chief of Police
       Hollywood Police Department
       3250 Hollywood Blvd.
       Hollywood, Florida 33021

ATTN: Detective Jack Hoffman

RE: TOOLE, OTTIS
       Death Investigation
       WALSH, ADAM
       BROWARD COUNTY
       07-27-81

FDLE Lab No. 83 10 43357
(Sub 01, 03, 05)
Agency No.   81-56073

Robert R Dempsey

Robert R. Dempsey
Commissioner

Glenn W. Abate

Glenn W. Abate
Crime Laboratory Analyst,
Crime Scene Section

"SUBPOENAS PERTAINING TO THIS CASE SHOULD
REFER TO FDLE LAB NO. 83 10 43357."

REFERENCE:

This report is in reference to a vehicle processing done by the Jacksonville
Crime Scene Unit as requested by Detective Jack Hoffman of the Hollywood
Police Department.

SCENE:

On October 20, 1983, the Crime Scene Unit went to the Wells Brothers Used
Car Lot located at 4334 Brentwood Avenue, Jacksonville, Florida. Parked on
the lot was a white 1971 Cadillac Sedan de Ville, VIN 683491Q134601 and
bearing no license tag.

On October 31, 1983, the vehicle was delivered to the Jacksonville Regional
Crime Laboratory at 120 Platen Road, Jacksonville, Florida for further
processing.

ASSISTANCE RENDERED:

On October 20, 1983 the interior of the vehicle was processed for serological and microanalytical evidence. The seats, carpets, and trunk were
sprayed with luminol, a chemical presumptive test for trace amounts of
blood.

005815

Honorable Sam Martin
Page Two
FDLE Lab No. 83 10 43357

ASSISTANCE RENDERED (cont.):

On November 2, 1983, the interior and exterior of the vehicle was photographed. The interior carpets were removed for further luminol spraying and
collection of serological and microanalytical evidence. The vehicle was
then given to the Latent Print Section for processing.

ITEMS COLLECTED:

The following items were collected on October 20, 1983:

1- Hairs collected from backrest area of front passenger seat

2- Vacuum sweepings from front seat and floor area

3- Vacuum sweepings from rear seat and floor area

4- Carpet standard

The following items were collected on November 2, 1983:

5- Hairs from carpet under front seat

6- Vacuum sweepings of carpet under front seat

7- #1 cutting from driver's carpet

8- #2 cutting from driver's carpet

9- #3 cutting from driver's carpet

10- #4 cutting from driver's carpet

11- #1 cutting from left rear floorboard carpet

12- #2 cutting from left rear floorboard carpet

13- #3 cutting from left rear floorboard carpet

14- #4 cutting from left rear floorboard carpet

DISPOSITION OF ITEMS:

All items were turned over to the Evidence Intake Section for distribution.

Items 1 through 6 were assigned to the Microanalysis Section of the Tallahassee Regional Crime Laboratory.

Items 7 through 14 were assigned to the Serology Section of the Jacksonville
Regional Crime Laboratory.

005816

Honorable Sam Martin
Page Three
FDLE Lab No. 83 10 43357

DISPOSITION OF ITEMS (cont.):

Results of the examinations will be the subject of a separate report by the
appropriate section.

REMARKS:

On October 20, 1983 the spraying of luminol gave positive indications on the
left front and left rear interior floorboard carpets. These non-descript
areas were photographed and sketched.

On November 2, 1983 the carpets were re-examined with the application of
luminol. The areas of luminescence were photographed and samples were
taken. A report on the results of the luminol sprayings will be issued from
the Serology Section of this laboratory.

Four (4) rolls of 120mm and one (1) roll of 35mm color negative film were
used to photograph the scene.

The film will be developed by laboratory personnel and the negatives
retained in the files of this department.

GWA/ch

cc: Detective J.S. Terry, Jacksonville Sheriff's Office

Junk Evidence: Joe Matthews and his "Smoking Gun"

On the rear floorboard of the car—where Toole admitted to tossing Adam's severed head—pictures show the bloody outline of a face. Matthews said, "I have a blood transfer from Adam's face onto the carpet—you can actually see his image. It's as clear as the Shroud of Turin, Veronica's veil. It's clear" (*Bringing Adam Home*).

The November 2, 1983, luminol negative photo on this page is the photo from the FDLE. Matthews also received these photos and the image on the following page is the same as this one, but after Joe Matthews, flipped, inverted and zoomed in on a fraction of the image. Only then, with an apparent total absence of reasoning, does Matthews have his Eureka moment and make the claim this is Adam Walsh in his book *Bringing Adam Home*.

This photo can also be seen on the Florida Department of Law Enforcement DVD. It's the second photo on the DVD. All the photos on the DVD are exactly the same photos that Joe Matthews received from the FDLE. The FDLE DVD can be viewed at JusticeForAdam.com

BEFORE

PHOTO ABOVE: DVD file photo from the Florida Department of Law Enforcement. Color photos at JusticeForAdam.com (Somewhere in the photo above is the photo on the right)

AFTER

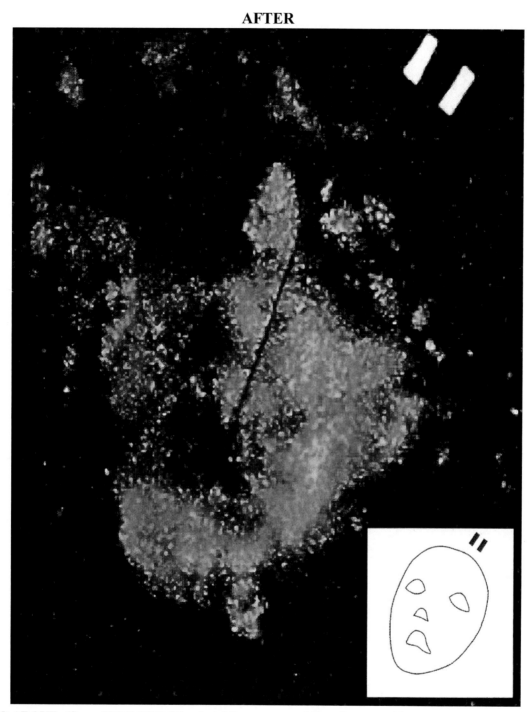

PHOTO ABOVE: (Same FDLE-DVD File photo) Image scanned from *Bringing Adam Home.*

The line that runs through the original FDLE image can be used as a reference and is the location Joe focused on before he flipped and rotated it to become his own image. HarperCollins Publishers added the sketch outline insert in order to help readers find Adam's face.

NOTE: The same double marker appears in both photos indicating how the photograph has been rotated and inverted; at the bottom left of the FDLE photo and the top right of Mr. Matthews's photo.

CHAPTER EIGHTEEN
THE SECOND LAWSUIT
2010—2011

<u>Headline:</u> Thursday, June 3, 2010 | *DAVID SMILEY* | *Miami Herald*

Adam Walsh witness sues for investigation report

A witness in the 1981 abduction and murder of 6-year-old Adam Walsh wants to see a missing investigation report that was key in the controversial 2008 decision to declare the case solved.

CLERK OF THE COURTS
BROWARD COUNTY 17TH JUDICIAL CIRCUIT OF FLORIDA

Case Summary

Broward County Case Number: **CACE10023089**	State Reporting Number: **062010CA023089AXXXCE**
Court Type: **Civil Division - Circuit Court**	Case Type: **Declaratory Judgment**
Incident Date: **N/A**	Filing Date: **06/01/2010**
Court Location: **Central Courthouse**	Case Status: **Disposition Entered**
Magistrate ID / Name: **N/A**	Judge ID / Name: **03 Rodriguez-Powell, Mily**

*Style: **Willis Morgan Plaintiff vs. Chadwick E Wagner, et al Defendant***

Party Detail

Party Type /	Party Name	Attorneys / BarID ★Denotes Lead Attorney
Plaintiff	Morgan, Willis	★Julin, Thomas Richard Retained BarID: 325376
Defendant	Matthews, Joseph	★Panza, Thomas Francis Retained BarID: 138551
Defendant	Satz, Michael J	★Silvershein, Joel Michael Retained BarID: 608092
Defendant	Wagner, Chadwick E	★Cantor, Joel David Retained BarID: 362093

Unlike Jay Grelen in 1995, when he sued the HPD for case records, I had no newspapers backing me up with a team of lawyers. My attorney, Thomas Julin, was the same attorney that represented Grelen and the *Mobile Press Register* in 1995, only this time, he was on his own. We had a thirty-minute hearing set before Judge Mily Rodriguez-Powell on Friday, July 16, 2010, at 10:30 a.m. in the Broward County 17th District Courthouse, room 998, 201 S.E. 6th Street,   Fort Lauderdale, FL.

This was akin to walking into the lion's den for my attorney. He was going up against three top lawyers for the top law enforcement agencies in Broward County. When they spoke, the judge would take copious notes. Yet, when my attorney spoke, she seemed to be in a bored daze, as though she didn't want to be there with this case on her docket.

My argument was the Matthews Report was a public record because police and prosecutors alike had received and reviewed it before closing the case. Wagner and Broward State Attorney Michael J. Satz countered that the public had no right to see the report because it was "worthless" to their investigation, and it hadn't been worth keeping a copy. Matthews's lawyer, Fort Lauderdale's Tom Panza, said his client refused to produce a copy.

Introduction to Defendant Matthews's Attorney

Tom Panza is a well-known South Florida attorney and lobbyist who has enriched his pockets defending police scandals and corrupt top cops who are quick to spend our tax dollars getting themselves out of trouble. As a lobbyist, Panza has been known to donate large sums of money to politicians, police, and judges alike.

In Florida, laws limit individual contributions to $500. According to the *New Times Broward—Palm Beach*, to get around campaign finance laws, Panza did what's known as bundling. He contributed the maximum amount of money, many times over, using names such as his six-year-old daughter and even younger son, as well as his wife. Her catering firm Dottie's Delight would also donate, and so on.

Tom Panza has no problem subverting campaign laws for the sweet payoff of favoritism in court, as well as to get cases defending some of Florida's largest ever scandals. One of Panza's big clients was the Broward County Sheriff's Office, which was accused of falsely clearing cases to make it look like they were doing a great job, similar to what the HPD did in the Adam Walsh case.

A Defense Beyond the Pale

Sure enough, prominent lobbyist Tom Panza argued that the Matthews Report wasn't used by the police and the state attorney in connection with their official investigations. Panza also claimed that Matthews wasn't the custodian of the record.

In what appeared to be a coordinated effort between the HPD and the SAO, Joel Silvershein, attorney for defendant Satz at the State Attorney's Office, argued that Matthews was the custodian of the report, but denied knowledge of whether it was a public record. The state attorney admitted that Chuck Morton viewed the report but denied that he used it as a part of his official investigation. HPD attorney Joel Cantor argued that defendant Wagner asserted that he'd decided to "exceptionally clear" the case before he received Matthews's "personal memoirs."

Wagner admitted that he had met with Matthews. Matthews gave him a copy of his memoirs and asked him to read it. Wagner passed on the copy to Mark Smith who advised that "the memoirs were really nothing more than a 'regurgitation' of the facts and investigative findings by members of the Hollywood Police Department involved in the Adam Walsh investigation over the previous twenty-seven years."

Smith claimed, "The memoirs served no genuine purpose and had no value to the Hollywood Police Department and so were not retained." Smith also stated that Wagner observed Matthews in possession of the memoirs several weeks later during a meeting with representatives of the State Attorney's Office.

Notice how Matthews's Report suddenly became his "personal memoirs." The reference was new and had only been used since I had demanded them. The argument was quite extraordinary, considering their response when my attorney first requested the Matthews Report, ordering Matthews to produce the document. Remember, they were all getting paid with our tax dollars to uphold our laws.

The First Amendment dictates that, "Congress shall make no law . . . abridging the freedom of press," thereby entitling us to public records, bills, and documents. Florida's open government and public records laws lead the nation in providing public access to government meetings and records. Government must be accountable to the people. The Florida Constitution, which sets forth our rights as citizens of this state, provides that the public has the right to know how government officials spend taxpayer dollars and make the decisions affecting our lives. The principle of open government is one that must guide everything done in government for its public.

Florida statutes expansively define "public record" to include "*all documents, papers, letters, maps, books, tapes, photographs, films, sound recordings, data processing software, or other material, regardless of physical form, characteristics or means of transmission, made or received pursuant to law or ordinance or in connection with the transaction of official business by any agency*" (Fla. Stat. sec. 119.011(1), 1995).

These laws serve no purpose when we have a police department that thinks it is above the law and judges that don't uphold the law. Clearly, Chief Wagner received the Matthews Report. The police chief's letter to Chief Assistant State Attorney Charles "Chuck" Morton, asking him to read over Matthews's report, was included as an exhibit in my lawsuit. The reply letter from Morton back to Chief Wagner, stating that he had received and reviewed the Matthews Report, was also included as Exhibit A in my lawsuit. Janice Williams, Public Records Custodian for Michael Satz at the State Attorney's Offices even sent Matthews a letter demanding Matthews to make his report available for inspection by Willis Morgan. That letter was Exhibit C in my lawsuit. These letters can be read on the following pages.

CITY of HOLLYWOOD, FLORIDA

POLICE DEPARTMENT · 3250 HOLLYWOOD BOULEVARD · ZIP 33021-6967

"A Leading Force in Professional Law Enforcement"

Accredited by The Commission for Florida Law Enforcement Accreditation

Chadwick E. Wagner
Chief of Police

December 2, 2008

Charles Morton, Esq.
Chief Assistant State Attorney
201 S.E. 6th Street
Sixth Floor
Fort Lauderdale, Florida 33301

Re: Criminal investigation exceptional clearance of the abduction
      and homicide of Adam Walsh

Dear Mr. Morton:

For several months, we have painstakingly reviewed the details of the Adam Walsh abduction and homicide investigation in consult with homicide investigators, past and present. As a result of our recent meeting, Assistant Police Chief Mark Smith was tasked to review the independent investigation submitted by retired Miami Beach Homicide Detective Joe Matthews regarding the abduction and homicide of Adam Walsh and he has shared his thoughts in the form of a memorandum directed to my attention which I have attached for your review. As a result of this exhaustive review, which included the investigative process over the past twelve (12) years since the Adam Walsh files were disclosed for inspection, it is my intention to exceptionally clear this investigation with the conclusion that there is adequate probable cause to arrest Ottis Toole for the abduction and homicide of Adam Walsh if he were alive today. I believe your office supports this position and I am appreciative of your recent assistance and guidance.

The professional relationship between your office and our Agency cannot be underestimated and I wish to thank you in advance for the support and assistance your office has provided during the term of this investigation.

Respectfully,

CHADWICK E. WAGNER
Chief of Police

CEW:lw

Hollywood
All-America City

Our Mission: We are dedicated to providing municipal services for our diverse community in an atmosphere of cooperation, courtesy and respect. We do this by ensuring all who live, work and play in the City of Hollywood enjoy a high quality of life.

MICHAEL J. SATZ
STATE ATTORNEY
SEVENTEENTH JUDICIAL CIRCUIT OF FLORIDA
BROWARD COUNTY COURTHOUSE
201 S.E. SIXTH STREET
FORT LAUDERDALE, FL 33301-3360   PHONE (954) 831-6955

December 9, 2008

Chief Chadwick E. Wagner
Hollywood Police Department
3250 Hollywood Boulevard
Hollywood, Florida 33021-6967

Dear Chief Wagner:

We have received your letter and your Assistant Police Chief's, Mark Smith, memorandum both dated December 2, 2008 in which you are advising us of your intent to exceptionally clear the investigation involving the death of Adam Walsh. As I understand it, it is your intention at this time to close what has been an extensive and continued investigation by your agency in following numerous leads, both past and current. You have concluded that based on the totality of the evidence you have gathered today, there is "probable cause" to arrest Ottis Toole, if he were still alive, for the July 27, 1981 kidnapping and murder of Adam Walsh.

As you know, over the years our office has also conducted its own investigation and assisted you as well in investigating this heinous and atrocious crime. Based on the totality of the evidence we have gathered and reviewed, we agree with your conclusion that there is "probable cause" to arrest Ottis Toole for Adam Walsh's death. We have not found there to be legally sufficient evidence to arrest any other persons whose names have been mentioned as possible suspects.

We have reviewed the additional evidence and materials presented by retired Detective Sgt. Joe Matthews and have considered your critical comments concerning some of the conclusions Mr. Matthews has reached. We are also mindful of the fact that due to some past investigative errors, a successful prosecution may be difficult to achieve if Ottis Toole were alive today. Nevertheless, this does not take away from the fact that there is legally sufficient evidence today to establish "probable cause" to arrest Ottis Toole. Because Ottis Toole is deceased, we understand your decision to exceptionally clear the case. However, keep in mind that should there be any other credible and convincing evidence presented in the future that is sufficient to arrest any other suspects, we will not hesitate to prosecute, despite the position we are taking today.

Sincerely,

CHARLES B. MORTON, JR.
Chief Assistant State Attorney

CBM, jr/kf

EXHIBIT "A"

March 25, 2009

To: Mr. David Smiley, The Miami Herald

In response to the areas you proposed to cover when you requested an interview, please accept my following comments; you may include any of my comments in your article if you choose to do so:

The delayed Dahmer identifications certainly add intrigue and mystery to Adam Walsh's tragic death. They may form the basis for the writing of a book or a murder mystery novel, but they do not come close to supporting the filing of criminal charges.

When prosecuting an individual for a crime, especially one as serious as the Adam Walsh murder, the law requires that the evidence and circumstances lead to a reasonable and moral certainty that the accused, and no one else, committed the crime.

Recent studies in the science of eyewitness identification lend support to the argument that eyewitness identification evidence is among the least reliable forms of evidence in criminal prosecutions. The delayed Dahmer identifications would raise serious legal and moral questions in a potential prosecution of Dahmer for Adam Walsh's horrific death. The moment in which an eyewitness views and identifies a criminal suspect is a significant juncture in the possible criminal prosecution of that person. The length of time between the crime and the identification is one of the critical legal factors in determining the admissibility and accuracy of identification evidence. This factor has been embedded in our nation's criminal justice case law for well over a half a century. Identifications made years after the crime is committed are "extremely unreliable" and can be effectively destroyed in court under thorough cross-examination. Such identifications would have to be corroborated by overwhelmingly credible evidence in order to have "probable cause" to prosecute the suspect for that crime – e.g., credible admissions by the suspect or credible and indisputable physical evidence that directly links the suspect to the criminal act. When questioned, Dahmer, who had nothing to lose by admitting his guilt, did not admit to killing Adam Walsh and there is no credible and indisputable physical evidence directly linking Dahmer to Adam Walsh's death.

It is evident to me over the course of the investigation that the witnesses who have identified Dahmer are confident in the accuracy of their identifications. However, the science of eyewitness identification studies show that "confidence" alone is a rather poor predictor of accuracy of identification.

The material and reports in Hollywood Police Department's investigation of Toole contains substantial and documented investigative information that tracks Toole's whereabouts and his opportunity to have committed the crime. This was neatly and skillfully pointed out in an investigative file created by retired Detective Joe Mathews and presented for my review. Mathews' investigative file was also presented to the Hollywood Police Department and reviewed by Assistant Police Chief Mark Smith, who worked tirelessly on the Adam Walsh case. The facts surrounding Adam Walsh's

EXHIBIT "B"

March 25, 2009

disappearance corroborated with objectively documented circumstances of Toole's whereabouts and conduct immediately before and after the crime gives rise to a "reasonable ground of suspicion to warrant a cautious person in the belief that Toole committed the crime" - the legal definition of "probable cause."

Keep in mind that having legally sufficient "probable cause" to believe that someone has committed a crime does not mean that an arrest should or must be made. As I pointed out in my December 09, 2008 letter to the Hollywood Police Department that, due to a concatenation of circumstances, it would be difficult to achieve a successful prosecution against Toole if he was alive today.

On the other hand, even if one believes Dahmer killed Adam Walsh, it would be impossible to achieve a successful prosecution against him if he was alive today given the legally insufficient evidence to even file charges.

You should also keep in mind that exceptionally clearing a case is a police decision not a state attorney decision. My letter simply advised the Hollywood Police Department that our office understands the reasons for their decision to exceptionally clear the case; nevertheless, I pointed out at the end of my letter that "should there be any other credible and convincing evidence presented in the future that is sufficient to arrest any other suspects, we will not hesitate to prosecute".

I hope this information helps you to give a complete and objective perspective to your article.

Chuck Morton

EXHIBIT "B"

MICHAEL J. SATZ
STATE ATTORNEY
SEVENTEENTH JUDICIAL CIRCUIT OF FLORIDA
BROWARD COUNTY COURTHOUSE
201 S.E. SIXTH STREET
FORT LAUDERDALE, FLORIDA 33301-3360   PHONE (954) 831-6955

May 5, 2010

Mr. Joseph Matthews

Re: Public Records Request for Joe Matthews' Adam Walsh Report

Dear Mr. Matthews:

This correspondence is in reference to a request by Mr. Thomas Julin, Esq. on behalf of Mr. Willis Morgan for "inspection and copying of the manuscript or report..." prepared by you regarding your work on the Adam Walsh homicide. The request by Mr. Julin, made pursuant to Chapter 119, Florida Statutes is entitled "Public Records Request for Joe Matthews' Adam Walsh Report," and is attached hereto for your review.

Our office is not in possession of the manuscript or report. We therefore demand that pursuant to Chapter 119, Florida Statutes, you make the subject manuscript or report available for inspection by Mr. Julin, at a time and place coordinated by you or your legal representative and Mr. Julin.

It is our understanding that Mr. Kelly Hancock, Esq., no longer represents you in this matter. Therefore, if you have retained other counsel, please advise them of your receipt of this letter. Should you or your legal representative wish to contact our office, please call 954-831-7913 so that we may discuss this matter if necessary.

Sincerely,

Janice Williams

Janice N. Williams
Public Records Custodian

CC: Kelly Hancock, Esq.
        Krupnick Campbell et al
        12 SE 7th Street Suite 801
        Fort Lauderdale, FL 33301

        Joel Cantor, Esq., Police Legal Advisor
        City of Hollywood Police Department
        3250 Hollywood Boulevard
        Hollywood, FL 33021

        Hunton & Williams LLP
        Thomas R. Julin, Esq.
        1111 Brickell Avenue, Suite 2500
        Miami, FL 33131

Exhibit "C"

These moronic cops were actually so stupid they put these incriminating letters in the Adam Walsh case files so anyone could read them. They never realized at the time that these letters would come back to implicate them in an incriminating manner now that they were being sued.

Broward circuit judge Mily Rodriguez-Powell dismissed my suit in August. It should've been irrelevant whether the chief used the Matthews Report or made up his mind before his department accepted and read the report. It should've also been irrelevant that the report was nothing more than a regurgitation of what they already knew. The fact that they accepted and read it alone makes the report a public record. Their assessment that the Matthews Report was "worthless" in itself should be meaningless. Deciding something to be worthless does *not* exclude it from being eligible for the public record.

At the end of that hearing, while everyone was gathering their papers, including the judge, I sat there watching the lawyer representing the State Attorney's Office, Joel Silvershein. He was the only one not gathering his things. He was just sitting there staring straight ahead at the judge. Then I realized why. When the judge looked up, she locked eyes with Silvershein and nodded in acknowledgment. As subtle as it might have been, to me, it was about as subtle as a flying brick! Silvershein then gave the judge a half wink in open court and said, "I'll see you in court later." Only after the judge nodded back with a cute little look of affirmation did Silvershein gather his belongings. This implied to me that they saw each other on a regular basis. For all I know, Silvershein and the judge might even share the same water cooler from time to time. And here I am, trying to sue the State Attorney's Office all by myself!

On August 4, 2010, Judge Rodriguez-Powell ruled, "There is simply no evidence that the document was used in transaction of, or the course of, government business." In my eyes, I would view it as her being incapable of understanding—or, more likely, unwilling to understand—our sunshine laws. People only hide something when they have something to hide. She sided with the defendants and ordered my case dismissed with prejudice. She completely discarded Florida records law in order to favor the State Attorney's Office, whose offices are in the same building. And if she favors the state attorney, she would have to favor the HPD and Matthews. This is why they say you can't fight City Hall!

Judge Rodriguez-Powell could've been influenced to rule against me by the facts that the top law enforcement agencies were arguing against the release of the Matthews Report, and that no media outlets were asking for its release as in the 1995 lawsuit. My only recourse would be to file for an appeal, and this time, I would try to obtain some support from others. Otherwise, the 4th District Court of Appeal in West Palm Beach might be inclined simply to overlook Adam's case and let the ruling stand.

This case should've been impossible to lose, yet I lost. Judge Mily Rodriguez-Powell might have been too weak to make the right call. She might have let cronyism and politics get in the way of making the correct ruling. I don't know, but I can't help but think the judge put her own career ahead of Adam's justice. In the end, I'm sure Judge Rodriguez-Powell will come to realize that on July 16, 2010, when she turned her courtroom into a kangaroo court, she wasn't on Adam's side.

The State Attorney's Office

With Dan Christensen's approval, I'm including the following article that ran in the free online news site *Broward Bulldog*, to explain the type of state attorney's office that Michael Satz had been running.

January 14, 2010, at 11:23 PM

Finkelstein says Satz favors bigshots, police over "everyday citizens"

By Dan Christensen, browardbulldg.org

Howard Finkelstein

Photo courtesy of: Howard Finkelstein

Office of the State Attorney,
17th Judicial Circuit,
Broward County, Florida

Michael Satz

In what's shaping up as an extraordinary clash of legal titans, Broward Public Defender Howard Finkelstein has accused Broward State Attorney Michael Satz of routinely violating defendants' rights and applying a double standard of justice in the county.

For years, the state attorney has given favorable treatment to police officers and "influential or wealthy" citizens facing prosecution, Finkelstein alleged in a six-page letter sent to Satz on Tuesday. The letter asks Satz to provide better training for prosecutors and to establish new office procedures.

"It is imperative that the Broward State Attorney's Office treat all persons it considers for criminal prosecution equally. The two systems of justice in Broward County must end," said Finkelstein, an assistant public defender in Broward since the 1980's.

The Broward County Association of Criminal Defense Lawyers sent its own letter to Satz on Thursday saying it "strongly" backed Finkelstein, who is best known throughout South Florida as Channel 7's "Help Me Howard."

Satz, who like Finkelstein, is an elected constitutional officer, counterattacked on Wednesday.

In a written reply, the prosecutor instructed the public defender that he'd misinterpreted the law. Satz said Finkelstein's accusation that Broward prosecutors give special treatment to a favored few was "both false and irresponsible."

"The members of the State Attorney's Office work hard to represent all citizens of Broward County who are victims of crime, regardless of their station in life," wrote Satz, Broward State Attorney since 1976.

Underlying the Finkelstein-Satz dispute is a tussle over evidence—who gets to see it and who decides who gets to see it.

According to Finkelstein's letter, Broward prosecutors "either through neglect or by design" have until recently failed to disclose favorable evidence to criminal defendants as required by law, particularly evidence of police misconduct.

Such evidence, known as *Brady* material, can sometimes be used by the defense to exonerate or to impeach the testimony of a police officer on the witness stand.

The term comes from a 1963 Supreme Court decision in *Brady v. Maryland*. The court held that prosecutors who suppress evidence favorable to a defendant who asks for it violate due process of law.

Local questions about the state's obligation under *Brady* arose Sept. 6 when Assistant State Attorney Sheila Alu e-mailed a *Brady* disclosure regarding one case to a counterpart at the Public Defender's Office, Finkelstein said. The information was a list of police officers under investigation by Satz's office.

Finkelstein's office hadn't seen the list before, even though those officers were listed as witnesses in other open cases.

Public defenders reviewed hundreds of closed cases in which those officers were listed as defendants, but no *Brady* disclosures by the state were found, Finkelstein wrote.

The Public Defender's Office filed public records requests seeking the names of all police officers investigated since 2006 and again found no disclosures.

Finkelstein cited a number of examples of investigations of police officers that were not disclosed but should have been. In some cases, Finkelstein also questioned why those officers were not prosecuted—and wrote that it appeared as if the decision not to prosecute was used as an excuse not to disclose the existence of such cases as *Brady* material.

"Fort Lauderdale Police Officer Daniel Zavadil and Lauderhill Police Officer John Lafontant both admitted to forging names and falsifying police reports, yet they were not prosecuted and no *Brady* notices were filed," he wrote.
"Margate Police Officer Joseph Devito was determined to have filed a false police report after hitting a pole with his assigned police car. Four BSO deputies and the Margate Chief of Police were involved in the investigation, yet no *Brady* notice was filed."

"It appears that the Broward State Attorney's Office gives great deference to law enforcement; it would clearly have filed charges if the same allegations were made against a civilian," Finkelstein wrote.

Satz's office recently changed the way it handles *Brady* requests, and since then hundreds of disclosures have been made, Finkelstein said. In all, more than 300 officers have been identified by the state in either *Brady* notices or investigation close-out memos sent to the Public Defender's Office.

"We have received more *Brady* notices in 12 weeks than we have in the past 30 years," Finkelstein wrote.

Prior "systemic nondisclosure" is "of particular concern" when it comes to closed cases, Finkelstein told Satz. The reason: people convicted of crimes who did not have access to favorable information that's only now been disclosed have either limited or "in most instances, no remedies available."

Satz did not provide a detailed rebuttal regarding the *Brady* issues but told Finkelstein he intends to send him a further response "based on specific facts."

Satz's office has long said it will not file criminal charges in a case unless there is a reasonable likelihood of conviction.

But according to Finkelstein, police officers and others get special treatment from Satz in that regard.

"Although the office espouses a filing standard of 'likelihood of conviction,' that standard has two distinct meanings. For everyday citizens, the 'likelihood of conviction' filing standard means nothing more than probable cause. For police officers or other influential or wealthy citizens, 'likelihood of conviction' means that the State Attorney's Office cannot possibly lose the case."

Satz denied that accusation, saying the same standard applies "to all persons accused of crimes, whether they are rich or poor, a police officer or a civilian."

Satz said that in 2009 his office reviewed more than 25,000 felony cases and tens of thousands of misdemeanor and juvenile cases for the filing of criminal charges.

"In each and every one of those cases our policy was—and is—to do the right thing for the right reason. This has always been our policy. Your allegations are misguided and an insult to every assistant state attorney in this office," Satz said.

CHAPTER NINETEEN
THE APPEAL
AND
JUSTICE FOR ADAM

PHOTO LEFT: Joe Matthews, the star in his story, posing for my sister Jorain. Photo taken March 16, 2012

From November 14 to 21, 2010, the Miami International Book Fair made prerelease copies of *Bringing Adam Home* available to the public. I managed to get a copy, and of course, I made it available to my attorney, Tom Julin, who told me he was "mesmerized" by its contents.

I stopped into Barnes & Noble. I asked the girl behind the counter if she'd heard of *Bringing Adam Home.* She told me, "Oh yes, it was so good! I can't believe that detective solved that case all by himself." I then asked her where she had gotten her copy. She said the publisher sent it to the store, and the store let employees have the prerelease copies of books to read.

I asked her if she had a computer with access to the Internet. We then moved to another computer, and she did a Google search with the key words *Willis Morgan, Joe Matthews,* and *lawsuit.* An article came up, and she started reading. "What is going on?" she asked. By the end of our exchange, she told me I could have her copy and she would bring it in the next day.

Matthews's Obsession with "Closure"

In the prerelease copy of the book, Matthews claims to have unearthed startling new evidence about the 1981 murder of Adam Walsh. I included portions of this book in my public records appeal to my lawsuit that challenged the sworn testimony by Chief Chad Wagner.

Matthews, with coauthor Florida International University creative writing director Les Standiford, made the claim that Matthews found ghastly evidence amid ninety-eight old 35 mm photo negatives dredged from the files of the Florida Department of Law Enforcement (FDLE).

The photos supposedly were taken by state agents shortly after Toole's initial confession as they searched his 1971 Cadillac using luminol, a spray-on chemical that detects traces of iron in the blood. The book said the agents never ordered prints from the negatives, and the evidence was apparently never viewed by Hollywood detectives.

Also, the book said several old photographs contain overlooked evidence traced in a blue (luminol) glow. Yet one chilling picture stood out: a "glowing blue image pressed into the carpet—was the outline of a familiar young boy's face, a negative pressed into floorboard carpeting, eye sockets blackened blank cavities, mouth twisted in an oval of pain. It was Adam's face, etched in his own blood, as stark as any fragment of bone; and the cry that issued from his battered lips was as damning an indictment as anyone might ever hear . . . Poor Adam—the truth singing to the world at last" (*Bringing Adam Home*).

And that is why Les Standiford was the creative writing director at Florida International University! I won't even try to match writing prose with Les. I only want the true story told.

Matthews said when he first looked at that photo he glanced away, not sure whether to trust his eyes, but he double-checked to be certain because what he was looking at chilled him—it was Adam. I think Matthews wanted to see Adam, so he saw Adam. It's like looking at ink spots in a psychiatrist's office in which anyone can see anything (the Rorschach test). Maybe that was why Chief Wagner never mentioned the photo when he closed the case.

John Walsh said of the photos: "I'm not going to look at them . . . I don't think any parent wants to do this. They're good evidence that Toole was the killer, and Joe has every right to write the book. He helped close that case."

When a luminol solution is sprayed on surfaces, it reacts with metal ions, such as iron, which is stored and transported by hemoglobin (red blood cells). Very small iron concentrations on a surface, as little as one part per million, are enough to catalyze luminol chemiluminescence, causing a glow. However, luminol sensitivity only indicates the presence of a catalyst. A glow does not mean there's blood present. The luminol compound also reacts with other substances, such as saliva, rust, potassium permanganate, animal proteins, vegetable enzymes, and other organic fluids and tissues. Matthews also needs to explain how a non-flat object such as a severed head can leave a facial image on a hard, flat surface. Luminol is only an investigative tool. It cannot be admitted for evidence in court. The Florida crime lab went over that car with a fine-toothed comb and found only drops of blood in amounts too insignificant to be tested.

I don't want to accuse the Walshes' knight in shining armor of being deliberately deceptive, but that is my conclusion. The outline Matthews saw could've been something as simple as metal parts placed on the floorboard or even the car's metal floorboard under the carpet. Matthews was a seasoned detective, and even rudimentary crime scene investigation (CSI) should've told him this. He also needs to explain how the photo he compares to the Shroud of Turin changed from the original photo he received from the FDLE to the one he inverted, flipped, and cropped before publishing it in his book.

The image of Adam's face that Matthews compares to the Shroud of Turin wasn't in the prerelease promotional copy of *Bringing Adam Home* that he refers to as the "uncorrected proof," after I filed a lawsuit. However, an eight-page photo insert is included in the 304-page hardcover edition that went on sale on March 1, 2011, by HarperCollins Catalogs.

According to Matthews, on a bright spring afternoon late in April 2008, he arrived at the office of Hollywood Police Chief Chad Wagner with a thickly bound sheaf tucked under his arm. Excited at his accomplishment, Matthews then presented his findings to the new police chief.

Wagner was curious as to why such evidence hadn't been examined before. Matthews told him he couldn't explain that. Wagner then assured Matthews, "I'll read every page" (*Bringing Adam Home* pp. 261–262). Matthews felt that he'd done everything he could under the circumstances. It wasn't his call now. He would wait and see if Wagner wanted to proceed on the basis of what he'd presented in his report.

The book said that, on November 14, 2008, one month before the closing of the case, Wagner called a meeting at the Broward County State Attorney's Office to go over the report and the FDLE crime scene photos. Nine people were present: Chief Wagner, Assistant Chief Louis Granteed, Captain Mark Smith, Hollywood Police legal advisor Joel Cantor, Detective Sergeant Joe Matthews, Broward Chief Assistant State Attorney Chuck Morton, John and Reve Walsh, and their attorney, former Broward prosecutor Kelly Hancock.

According to *Bringing Adam Home*, Wagner called the meeting to discuss the report compiled by Sergeant Matthews. "Would anyone in the room," Wagner asked, "object to the conclusions in the report that Matthews had placed before them?" The meeting led to unanimous agreement that the investigation would be "exceptionally cleared."

However, Joel Cantor said in an interview on Monday, January 3, 2011, with reporter Dan Christensen, that he attended no such meeting and had seen no crime scene photos with Adam's image. "I've never heard that, but wow, if that's part of Joe's story, so be it." That leaves me to wonder what John and Reve Walsh themselves think of Cantor's denial. Someone wasn't telling the truth.

Coauthor Les Standiford said the ongoing litigation prohibited him from discussing details about the book, including the photo with Adam's image. "I certainly think it is dramatic," he said. "But you don't make a decision based on one photograph; you look at the tapestry. People are going to have to read the book for themselves and decide for themselves." What Les needs to understand is that Matthews's entire book is a woven tapestry of either deception or confusion, with the presumptive goal of making Matthews into a hero.

Yet when a reporter from the *Miami New Times* asked Les a question about an investigation by the *Miami Herald* in March 2010, Les would reveal in his answer what limited understanding he had of the Adam Walsh case.

The Miami New Times: After police closed their investigation, the *Miami Herald* published a story implicating Jeffrey Dahmer in the abduction. What is your take on that investigation? Any major holes you see?

Les Standiford: The Adam Walsh case was so momentous to the country at large and went unsolved for so long that it is no surprise that people began to develop what might be termed extra-logical theories to "solve" the case, much as we see in alternative versions of the Kennedy assassination and "truther" accounts of 9/11. It is a diverting coincidence that Jeffrey Dahmer did reside in Sunny Isles, Florida, at the same time that Adam Walsh went missing, and authorities from Florida did question him following his arrest on other charges back in the early '90s. But Dahmer denied any involvement in the crime, and police never found any evidence to the contrary.

It's no wonder Standiford calls *Bringing Adam Home* "a story that had to be told." Adding, "The Walsh's [sic] put their trust in the police for a long time. That's the saddest thing of all." This is true, but equally sad is the trust the Walshes put in Joe Matthews.

HarperCollins suggested changing some names to protect against litigation, but both Standiford and Matthews wanted no part of that. Standiford said, "We were not making things up. This was all out of the record. It is what it is, and it can all be backed up. . . If I wrote this as fiction, no one would believe me."

What bothered me more than anything was what Matthews said on pages 282-3, where he claimed he made a comparison of the mug shots of "harmless . . . preppy-looking" Dahmer with Toole's photo. He said he thinks the two "new" witnesses (referring to Bill Bowen and myself) actually saw Ottis Toole, not Dahmer. Remember, it wasn't just Bill and I that saw Dahmer that day. Compared to Toole, a Yankee Stadium full of credible witnesses had implicated Jeffrey Dahmer.

Whenever people tell me about some famous person they met, I tell them, that's nothing, I met Jeffrey Dahmer. Then I get to watch the look on their face. I also met Cassius Clay (before he changed his name) in Times Square, New York. He even talked to me. He asked if I knew where Joe Frazier was. A few years later, he found Joe in Madison Square Garden. I was once stuck in an elevator with Kurt Russell at the old *Miami Herald* building in downtown Miami during the filming of the 1985 movie *The Mean Season*. Kurt and I had to pull the elevator doors open to get out. If I had to describe what Clay or Russell were wearing, I wouldn't be able to, but I know it was them the same way I know it was Jeffrey Dahmer I encountered in Radio Shack.

Matthews should stay on his side of the fence with his two cents. I am confident about who I encountered. Matthews thought we only realized it was Jeffrey Dahmer a decade later, in 1991, after we learned of Dahmer's activities in Milwaukee. I always knew it was "that guy" from "that day" in 1981. I just didn't know his name until 1991. Again, I'm forced to add that I was not a "new" witness. I went to the police just two days after the abduction, and Bill called the police no less than five times after giving them the tag number! Bill also went back to the police in 1991. If Matthews had read the case files as he said he did, he should've known that. At the very least, he could've called us. I really don't need this gladiator of logic telling me who it was I encountered on that day in 1981.

My attorney, Thomas Julin, asked the 4th District Court of Appeals in West Palm Beach to reverse Judge Mily Rodriguez-Powell's order. Tom argued in a December 20 court filing that the book in which Matthews claims credit for finding the "evidence that finally and conclusively" identified Toole as Adam's killer and "persuaded" Wagner to close the case undercuts both Wagner's statements and the judge's ruling. "It begs the question of who is telling the truth," my attorney said. He also asked the appeal court judges to review portions of *Bringing Adam Home* that he filed for me, under seal, in order to give all the defendants a chance to respond. The following is a summary of the pages relevant to my lawsuit from the book *Bringing Adam Home: The Abduction that Changed America.*

The book reports that the HPD asked Miami Beach Police Department Detective Sergeant Joe Matthews, an expert regarding polygraphing, to work on the Adam Walsh investigation as early as July 31, 1981 (p. 6). Matthews did further work on the investigation for the HPD in September 1981 (pp. 63-67).

In August 1991, Matthews met with HPD Captain Gil Frazier and criticized the investigative work previously done by the HPD on the Adam Walsh investigation. Matthews obtained Frazier's agreement to allow him to conduct a formal investigative interview of suspect Ottis Toole (p. 182).

That interview took place three years later, on August 15, 1994. HPD Detective Mark Smith recommended that the HPD conduct an interview of Toole with Matthews present (pp. 189-190). After receiving that recommendation, Chief Richard Witt went to the Miami Beach Police Department and negotiated an interagency agreement that would allow Matthews to work with the HPD on the Adam Walsh investigation (pp. 199-201). Matthews then began working alongside Mark Smith for the next year (pp. 198-199, 201).

Matthews prepared to conduct the investigation of Ottis Toole, but on the morning the interview was to take place, Witt told Matthews that an HPD detective, not Matthews, would conduct the Toole interview (pp. 199-201).

Matthews retired from the Miami Beach Police Department and then worked in collaboration with John Walsh to conduct an investigation of the Adam Walsh murder (pp. 216-220, 230-234). Matthews went to the office of HPD chief James Scarberry on February 21, 2006 (p. 234) and informed the chief that he'd been asked by John Walsh to reopen the case and to conduct a complete, independent investigation to prove conclusively who had kidnapped and murdered Adam (p. 236). When Matthews asked Scarberry for his help, Scarberry "gave his okay," agreeing that Matthews "would have access to everything in the department's files." Scarberry assured Matthews that Mark Smith, the detective in charge of the Adam Walsh investigation, "would provide whatever help he needed" (pp. 236-237). The HPD then transferred all case file documentation to Matthews (p. 237). Matthews reviewed the documentation, interviewed numerous witnesses, and examined physical evidence (pp. 237-251).

On May 25, 2006, Matthews asked the HPD to turn over to him photos taken by the FDLE of the search and analysis of suspect Ottis Toole's Cadillac (p. 252). The car itself had been lost. When the HPD reported that it didn't have the photographs, Matthews discovered that the FDLE had the undeveloped film, instead (p. 253). On June 27, 2006, the FDLE provided Matthews with ninety-eight never-before-seen photographs of the Cadillac (p. 253). Matthews had "hit pay dirt" (p. 254). The photographs showed Ottis Toole's bloody footprints, his machete soaked in blood, and an outline of Adam Walsh's face etched in his own blood in the carpet of the Cadillac's floorboards (pp. 253-258, 273-274).

Wagner replaced Scarberry as police chief in November 2007 (p. 260). In late January 2008, Matthews "told Chief Wagner that he was well along on a cold case investigation of the murder of Adam Walsh that had been authorized by Chief Scarberry" and that he "looked forward to presenting his report to Chief Wagner" (p. 261).

Late in April 2008, Matthews appeared in Chief Wagner's office "with a thick, bound sheaf tucked under his arm" (p. 263). When he handed over the report to Wagner, he stressed the importance of the FDLE crime scene photos he'd had developed for the first time (p. 264). Wagner told Matthews he would find out why the HPD hadn't previously obtained the photos (p. 264).

On November 14, 2008, Chief Wagner called a meeting at the Broward County State Attorney's Office, attended by Assistant State Attorney Chuck Morton, Assistant Chief of the HPD Louis Granteed, HPD Captain Mark Smith, HPD legal adviser Joel Cantor, former Broward prosecutor Kelly Hancock, and Detective Joe Matthews (pp. 271-272).

The book asserted that the Matthews Report describes extensive evidence overlooked by the HPD over the years, but the outline of Adam's face found in the photographs of Toole's Cadillac "was an emotional haymaker" (p. 274). "After everyone in the room had delivered their estimations of all that Matthews had presented, Wagner had his mandate, and it was unanimous" (p. 274). "All agreed that the investigation of the homicide of Adam Walsh would— pending the approval of Broward County State Attorney Michael Satz—be exceptionally cleared" (p. 274).

On December 10, 2008, Chief Wagner called Matthews to report that Satz "had reviewed Matthews's report and had made his call in response" (p. 275). Wagner asked Matthews if he would like to inform John and Reve Walsh and invite them to a press conference on December 16, 2008, at which Wagner would announce the decision to clear the case (p. 275).

The book concludes with an allusion to Assistant State Attorney Chuck Morton's letter to the *Miami Herald* in 2010: "Joe Matthews had finally pieced together such a web of corroborating evidence against Ottis Toole, one that had been validated by Assistant Police Chief Mark Smith and others at HPD, Morton pointed out to reporters" (p. 283).

My attorney received an order from the 4th District Court of Appeal over the weekend of January 15, 2011, in which it not only denied the motions to strike our reply brief that Joe Matthews and Chad Wagner filed, but also denied our request to take judicial notice of Joe Matthews's book. Tom said he wasn't too surprised by either order. It likely meant that the court would rule fairly quickly on the basis of the primary argument that we made in the briefs—that Matthews's report was a public record because Wagner received it and asked Mark Smith to review it as a part of the police department investigation. "I still think this is a strong argument," Tom told me.

I am sure the HPD regrets the day they ever brought Matthews into their investigation. They were doing just fine botching case #81-56073 up all by themselves. Bringing the abysmally clueless Matthews into the fold was kind of like entrusting the safety of chickens to a predator that eats chickens. Matthews used the chief to get the case closed, and then turned around and wrote in his book that the chief could never have closed the case by himself. I would bet this made Chief Wagner feel pretty darned stupid. If he'd known the things that were going to be said about him and his department, maybe he would've done a whole lot less to get the case solved, rather like his predecessors.

On March 1, 2011, *Bringing Adam Home* went on sale. Joe Matthews continued with his insidious agenda, making his rounds on the talk shows with Reve and John Walsh. Reve commented on Joe's Shroud of Turin, evidence: "To me, it was the one thing that a mother knows, is that this is their child, that this picture is their child. . . This is the piece of evidence that ties everything together for me, and I can go to my grave knowing that not only that I did everything I could but that I found my answers in that photo."

Bringing Adam Home: An Amazon.com Review

"Standiford dutifully tells the story of what happened that day and in the almost thirty years since. Aided by the police detective who finally pieced the puzzle together, the author meticulously details what happened to Adam and all of the players involved, including scores of incompetent cops interested more in their egos than solving the murder of an innocent child. There are times that I was so angered by the tales of these egomaniacal officers, I had to put the book away to calm down."

The above book review is one of many reviews posted on Amazon.com. This review is right on target, except for one thing: Detective Sergeant Joe Matthews was part of the unforgivable bungling and conspiracy to cover up the real facts of the case. Matthews did lambaste the lead detective, Hoffman, and claims to have "bumped heads" with him over the years. He also said the case started off wrong from the very beginning because they had the wrong detective on the case (this was a reference to Hoffman). Kind of reminds me of that old proverb about the pot calling the kettle black!

When Joe Matthews requested photos from the Hollywood Historical Society to use in his book, he clearly signed a form stating that the photos he received may not be altered, cropped, or obfuscated (without further permission).[2] The women at the Society told me Matthews never did give them a copy of his book. I felt bad enough that I gave them one of my copies of his book. When they looked at it, they were pretty angry. Matthews had cropped the photo of Detective Ron Hickman without permission. Matthews had to crop Hickman's photo because Hickman was holding up a composite of a suspect that looked more like Jeffrey Dahmer than Ottis Toole (see page sixty-four for the uncropped version of the photo, as required by the Hollywood Historical Society).

I wondered if they would take legal action, but was told that the Historical Society was too small an organization. Instead, all the ladies wanted Matthews's phone number so they could chastise him. I only mention this as a testament to Matthews's character. If Matthews could do this to these very helpful ladies at a nonprofit organization, then he was also capable of taking advantage of others, such as the Walsh family, for his own personal gain.

On July 25, 2011, I received notice from my attorney that the 4th District Court of Appeals finally had gotten around to scheduling the oral argument on the appeal from the circuit court order dismissing the complaint. It was set for 9 a.m. Monday, September 19, 2011, in West Palm Beach, Florida.

July 27, 2011, was the thirtieth anniversary of Adam's abduction. Les Standiford and Joe Matthews took full advantage of the day and gave an 8 p.m. book signing speech at a church in Cooper City, Florida. On the same day, my friend Maria Beltran called me to say she had purchased two tickets for us to see the ABBA concert at the Hard Rock in Hollywood. The time

---

[2] The photo of Adam holding the baseball bat in my book was approved with type on the actual photo by the Hollywood Historical Society only because I received written permission from the original photographer, Michael Hopkins, at Gerlinde Photography, Hollywood, Florida. Also below the user's signature, the form states: "The user named above will provide a copy of any printed document using our photo(s) to the Hollywood Historical Society for our archives."

was 8 p.m., the same day and time as Matthews's speech. I needed a photo of Matthews for my book so I had to talk Maria out of the ABBA concert and go with me to get a photo of Matthews. Maria agreed and gave the tickets to a friend.

Maria wasn't able to get Matthews's photo, as Les and Joe were very adamant about no one taking photos. In fact, when they said that, another woman with a camera just got up and walked out. It wasn't much of a speech. Les read several pages from the book and then turned to Matthews and said, "Okay, it's your turn." Matthews said a few things about the case and then took a few questions.

Maria said they seemed nervous and gave very short answers. I think they knew about that September court date and wondered if it had messed up their tempo. No media showed up, and only about thirty people came to whom they sold twenty or so books, four of them to Maria. Matthews would need to sell a lot more books than that to pay for his legal fees. The taxpayers had footed the bill for the HPD and the SAO, but Matthews was on his own. The HPD and the SAO should have sued Matthews for their legal fees, although it would be a tough lawsuit, since they should have kept a copy of Matthews's report for the record in the first place. Besides, I don't think the HPD or the SAO really cared about using up taxpayers' dollars.

I'm not one to give up so easily. Matthews made himself a big part of the Adam Walsh case. A book about this case without his photo would not be complete. Matthews, ever the entrepreneur, came out with the paperback version of his book and went on a promotional book signing tour again. On March 9, 2012, he was at Books & Books in Coral Gables, Florida. Maria and I went with my friend Geno Mondesir. Since they might remember Maria, the plan was for Geno to go in, listen, and get some photos. Maria and I would wait in the car.

After a few minutes, I couldn't help myself. Since I could see that Joe and Les were isolated in a separate back room like two happy rats in a cheese factory, Maria and I went in. We stayed out of sight near the entrance to that room just to hear for myself what they were saying. Nearly the entire speech was Joe Matthews bombastically mocking my lawsuit, my attorney, and the *Miami Herald*. Over a chorus of whispered oohs and aahs from a spellbound audience, Matthews claimed that the suit was "ridiculous on its face and was not only dismissed, but with prejudice." He went on to explain that meant the judge found the complaint to be "unfounded and baseless." Matthews said, "This attorney wanted twenty-seven years of my work to do with whatever he wanted." In his newfound supreme confidence, Joe held up his manuscript for everyone to see that it was still in his possession, not in Cuba. Unfortunately, the cell phone photos Geno took were not of great quality.

On March 16, 2012, I got another chance to get a good photo. This time I double-teamed Matthews and sent my friend Dolores Abad and my sister Jorain Patronie to a bookstore named Murder on the Beach, Delray Beach, Florida. They went in separately, several minutes apart, both armed with cameras ready for action. With some innate ability at deception, Matthews changed his story from his previous book signing. He made the astonishing claim that it was the *Miami Herald* that filed the lawsuit, and that my attorney worked for the *Herald*. He said he could prove it because the same attorney had sued once before on the side of the *Herald*. He also claimed I was an agent for the *Herald* on assignment staking out his business. His proof was the three-way 6 p.m. private conversation he had with my attorney and the State Attorney's

Office that made it onto the front page of the *Miami Herald* the very next morning. The article claimed that his report was "hidden in Cuba." Yeah, the story was given to the *Herald*. However, that didn't make me an agent and my attorney worked only for me.

"Oh my!" one woman exclaimed.

At this event Matthews said he never told the *Herald*'s attorney that he'd sent his report to Cuba, but rather that his coauthor was in Cuba. It was the attorney that twisted everything around when he "reported back to the *Herald*." Everyone laughed along with Matthews, except Dolores and my sister. Matthews became so scared, he said, that he changed the locks and installed a high-tech security alarm system at his business office. He also threw his computer into a canal because he was afraid "the *Herald*'s agent" would break into his business and steal all his work.

Applause! Applause!

Matthews even mocked the HPD. For a good laugh, he referred to Police Chief Richard Witt as "Dick" and then explained, "That's his name." In fact, he mocked the good chief so much that one woman in the audience even referred to the chief as Chief Twit when she asked a question, which of course got lots of applause. Matthews then excoriated the old lead detective, adding that if he'd had the information he had now back then, the original lead detective, Jack Hoffman, would've been arrested for misconduct.

According to Matthews, Toole was arrested on an unrelated homicide. Since police already had Toole on a few cases, he decided to just tell them about the rest. Had proper procedure been followed, this case should've been wrapped up several months after Toole first confessed.

Matthews claimed that Jack Hoffman was upset because Toole knew too much about Adam's abduction. Instead of saying maybe he committed the homicide, Jack accused Jacksonville Detective Buddy Terry of giving Toole information, costing Terry his job.

Matthews admitted that he'd contacted Detective Lyle Bien and asked Bien to call the FDLE to ask for the photos that Matthews had discovered. "But when I called Bien back two weeks later and asked him if he had called for the photos, Bien asked, 'What photos?'" He then called Chief Witt and was told they couldn't be found. This went on for some time. "Finally, I decided to call for myself," he said, explaining he got the photos on his own. "Had Bien called and gotten the photos like I had asked him to, he would have looked at them out of curiosity, and he would have seen Adam's face first. He could've gotten all the credit for solving the case, and he would have been the hero. But he didn't do it; he refused to do anything," Matthews claimed. "What else could I do? I didn't want the credit, but someone had to do it." Matthews then sheepishly accepted the resounding applause from the audience and a standing ovation.

Okay, I was eavesdropping. I won't say how, but the trip was worth it. Nothing thrills me more than to hear one bad cop bashing another bad cop like Mr. Bien.

Matthews bragged about his book. "Les wrote it exactly the way I feel," Matthews said and then added that it was the only book he reads. Ha-ha! The audience laughed along with this already charisma-challenged detective as he injected insipid humor into his performance. Matthews might not admit it, but I'm pretty sure he'll end up reading my book.

In the end, this book signing was nothing more than a one-hour psycho-babbling amateur comedy show and a clear presentation of Matthews's willingness to fabricate everything. If Joe Matthews was as pious as he portrays himself to be, with an honest report and book, he wouldn't need to change his narrative to a fictionalized version of events. End of story.

PHOTO LEFT: At a bookstore named Murder on the Beach, Delray Beach, Florida on March 16, 2012

Photo taken with my camera by someone in the audience named Dolores

My sister had to contain herself as she talked Joe and Les into posing for this gotcha photo.

PHOTO RIGHT: Joe Matthews autographing his story

PHOTO LEFT: Les, happily endorsing Matthews's story

FOURTH DISTRICT

July Term 2011

WILLIS MORGAN,

Appellant,

v.

CHADWICK E. WAGNER, Chief of Police of the City of Hollywood, Florida,

MICHAEL J. SATZ, State Attorney for the Seventeenth Judicial Circuit in and for Broward County, Florida, and **JOSEPH MATTHEWS,**

Appellees.

No. 4D10-3433

[October 12, 2011]

More than a year after Judge Mily Rodriguez-Powell derailed justice for Adam, on October 12, 2011, the 4th District Court of Appeals would follow suit by affirming that judgment. The three-judge panel consisted of Dorian K. Damoorgian, Jonathan D. Gerber, and Krista Marx. They rendered a decision after hearing an oral argument given by my attorney, Thomas Julin. In the approach they took, they didn't even bother to acknowledge the admissions of either the police chief or the state attorney in their pleas that they received.

They examined the Matthews Report to determine whether it contained evidence relevant to the investigation. In closing the case, Chief Wagner even said he agreed with the findings in the Matthews Report. The admission of the chief that he asked Detective Smith to review the report should be regarded as more than sufficient to establish that the record should be disclosed. The finding that the record wasn't of use to the investigation is irrelevant to the ultimate legal issue of whether the public has a right to view the record for itself.

During the oral argument by my attorney, Judge Marx reiterated Chief Wagner's claim: "But the chief said he didn't use it." That shouldn't even be an issue legally. Either she was that inept or she was just another one of the enablers that allowed the police department to lie and cover up facts in this case.

Even though the 4th District's decision contains many errors, the way the court wrote the opinion makes it very difficult to obtain further review. It seemed to me that the court simply wanted the Adam Walsh investigation to be over and no longer subject to public scrutiny. In order to achieve that result, they folded like a cheap card table and neither squarely addressed the primary arguments my attorney made nor critically evaluated the arguments of the state attorney, Chief Wagner, and Matthews.

My attorney argued that the evidence that the Matthews Report was used to close the Adam Walsh case was in Joe Matthews's own book. Tom Panza argued that the book was the prerelease uncorrected version and corrections needed to be made before publication. Apparently, the court agreed with that argument. When the book went on sale, I bought a copy and checked for corrections. Not one change had been made. At the end of the hearing, I asked to speak to the court, and I was told with particular disdain to, "Shut up and sit down!"

This is the court system we have. Howard Finkelstein was right. It is nearly impossible for an average citizen to get justice, not only from the State Attorney's Office but also from the courts. Adam will never get justice if left to the whim of our courts. The 17th District Court and the 4th Court of Appeal ran roughshod over Florida public record laws with deliberate disregard for my right as a private citizen to view records that clearly are a public record.

In doing so, they've applied a double standard of justice. Patrick Fraser, WSVN-TV MIAMI, once told me that the court just didn't want to hear the case because of intellectual laziness, but as I see it, our legal system ignored the letter of the law in favor of the individual discretionary interpretation of its application. This has led to uneven administration of the law based on everything from age to social status to race.

The final *en banc* rehearing from the 4th District's full twelve-judge panel would be denied. That denial was succinct and brutal, as the 4th Court of Appeal simply preferred to rubber-stamp the decision of the 17th Court. The decision can be read in full in the lawsuit section of my "Extra Files & Photos" file titled "Oct. 12, 2011, 4th COURT OF APPEAL—DECISION" at JusticeForAdam.com.

I came to the realization that our courts in South Florida were all a part of the culture of corruption, and they never had any intention of ruling in favor of a common citizen. Both the 17th District Court and the 4th District Court of Appeal ignored the essential facts presented in evidence and made their decision based on what was safest for their own careers. In doing so, they did their best to avoid the merit of the case and sided with the half-truths and ludicrous folly presented by the defense. This isn't a justice system; it's just a system.

Exculpation but Not Exoneration

The case is over. I was unable to get justice for little Adam in our courts. They say an appeal is when you ask one court to show its contempt for another court, but the 4th District Court of Appeal wasn't about to do that for Adam, me, or any other ordinary citizen. The trial wasn't a total waste of time, though. What I did succeed in doing was to reveal to everyone why Adam will never get justice from the HPD, The State Attorney's Office and not even our court system.

Unlike Judge Moe's decision in 1996, it is erroneous conclusions like this that enable and embolden state departments to be brazenly corrupt. The greatest threat to the rule of law comes from within our legal system itself. And Adam's case was a great example of the appalling failure of our justice system. So now I will appeal to an even higher court: the court of public opinion.

The moral of this story: Never take on a government office or department without some "big guns" backing you up, even if it's a case that should be impossible to lose! Not that I didn't try. No one was interested in justice for Adam. It was an old case, I was told over and over again. Originally, I even wanted this case to be a class action, but I was unable to get any witnesses to join. I was given reasons like: "I live in Hollywood, and I don't want any problems with the police in case I ever need them"; "I'm too old"; "I'm too busy"; or "My family doesn't want me to get involved."

Over-Hyping Horror

Free from his legal morass, Joe Matthews carried on with his contrived hypothesis. Nothing is more obscene than Matthews's own imagination and suspicions. On one radio talk show with Joseph Cooper, WLRN-FM 91.3 Miami, Matthews even made the claim that Ottis Toole ate part of Adam. On Tuesday, December 20, 2011, Matthews got to be the leading star that he has always wanted to be, on the *Investigation Discovery* (ID) TV channel.

Cold Case

The ID show was about the Adam Walsh abduction and how Detective Joe Matthews put all the pieces of the puzzle together that got the case closed. Matthews was beaming with the pride of thinking he had the puzzle all figured out. In reality, he was so far out in left field with his cockamamie Ottis Toole theories that he wasn't even in the ballpark.

In one depiction, the show had the Sears security guard putting Adam out of the store! Matthews should have known it never happened that way. His version of events was totally made up and obfuscated. At the end of the show, he said, "If Ottis Toole was alive today he would be arrested, tried, and most likely convicted." I presume if Toole were alive today, Joe Matthews would do his best to see Ottis Toole put back on death row, even for something he didn't do.

Florida has a long history of falsely accusing and wrongly convicting suspects in our criminal justice system, putting innocent men in prison and even on death row. In December 2000, after spending fourteen years on Florida's death row, Frank Lee Smith was finally cleared of the 1985 rape and murder of eight-year-old Shandra Whitehead, exonerated by DNA. Appallingly, the police and prosecutors did their best to get a witness to say it was Frank Smith, even after she said she wasn't sure, very much as Detective Smith tried to do with Jennie Warren in the Adam Walsh case, when the HPD tried to pin Adam's murder on Toole.

The police will tell a witness that they are sure a suspect committed the crime, because they have "proof." Not wanting a murderer to be set free, some witnesses will feel it's their civic duty to make that identification, although not Jennie Warren. As in Ottis Toole's case, people with intellectual disabilities or below-average intellectual function are particularly vulnerable to being wrongfully convicted. With their desire to please authority figures, they are very susceptible to being influenced during interrogation, and sometimes they confess to crimes they didn't commit. Most law enforcement officials receive training in how to properly question these suspects, but in Ottis Toole's case, the police and prosecutors didn't seem to concern themselves with this formality. They just wanted a conviction.

Frank Townsend was another great example of the kind of case where police take advantage of low IQ. His mental capacity was equivalent to that of an eight-year-old and they cajoled him into confessing. The Broward Sheriff's Office even took Townsend to some of the murder scenes so that Townsend could show them what happened. After Assistant State Attorney Kelly Hancock prosecuted Townsend, it would take twenty-two years of Townsend's life before he would be exonerated with DNA and another suspect was captured (October 30, 1988|BY JONATHON KING). Keep in mind, Kelly Hancock was the same attorney that gave John and Reve Walsh advice and the same attorney that sat next to Joe Matthews at the December, 2008 conviction of Ottis Toole. I only mention these cases to show that Adam's case isn't an aberration—rather more of a common occurrence in Florida. There are other cases like these where cops and prosecutors go after the downtrodden to make themselves look good, and not just in Florida. The Adam Walsh case was just one of them. Only, no one went to prison in the Adam Walsh case. Ottis Toole had already died in prison before ex-cop Joe Matthews and the HPD pinned Adam's murder on him.

I might not have been able to get a copy of the Matthews Report, but I was able to get a copy of the Broward County state attorney's files for the Adam Walsh case.

When I first contacted the State Attorney's Office to request the Adam Walsh case files, I was told that they would first have to hire an attorney to have the files redacted and I would have to pay for that. I told them that was okay, just send me the bill. The next time I called, they told me the attorney would need a secretary and I would have to pay for that as well. Okay, send me the bill, I told them again. Of course this was all illegal. Had they actually sent me a bill, I would have taken legal action. I started going in person to the records department. I wanted them to know I was not going to give up. The case had been closed, and I could not be denied access.

On January 4, 2012, I received a call from Susan Seltzer, public records custodian for the State Attorney's Office. She told me that all eight boxes (7,812 pages) of the records had been sent to CopyScan to be put onto a CD-ROM. I did pay for the services of CopyScan and on January 17, 2012, I finally received these records, after eight months of hounding them with phone calls, e-mails, and going down in person to the records department, without assistance from my attorney. That itself was an achievement! Those files can now be viewed for free at JusticeForAdam.com.

"Hollywood Police Frame Girl After They Rear-End Her Vehicle"

In July 2009, Chief Wagner gave a media conference about the HPD's latest scandal. Wagner asked for the public's patience and said he was conducting an internal investigation. "I realize and understand those that feel a sense of betrayal over this incident," Wagner said. "And I ask each and every one of you to allow this investigative process to run its course and to have confidence that this matter will be investigated accurately and professionally."

Wagner's intent, in my opinion, was to rely on the media's short attention span and simply let things die down. He only said something after the video made national news when public defender Howard Finkelstein released the clip to a legal affairs blog, setting off a YouTube sensation. An article by Sofia Santana, *South Florida Sun-Sentinel* (7:13 p.m. EDT, July 31, 2009), said Finkelstein leaked the video because he felt the public, defense attorneys in particular, should know about the incident.

"I really do believe their intent was to keep it quiet," Finkelstein said of the HPD.

Here's what happened: A police officer rear-ended a car, which was stopped at a stoplight. The veteran officer didn't want to mess up his career, so he and three others decided to mess up the life of twenty-three-year-old Alexandra Torrensvilas. Alexandra admitted having a couple of beers, so the officers conspired to make it seem as though Alexandra was at fault. The officers claimed she swerved in front of the officer that hit her. She was arrested for DUI and cited for an improper lane change. The charges against her were dropped because the officer that hit her was the same officer that gave her the breathalyzer test.

He and three other officers then tried to fake the reports to make it look as though the car that was rear-ended was at fault. Their dashboard camera would give them away. Throughout the tape, the cops acknowledged that what they were doing was illegal, but one cop observed that, when you are the law, nothing is wrong with bending the truth. Now Alexandra has filed a civil suit against the Hollywood Police.

At the end of that meeting, when Wagner started taking questions, the media let him have it! "How do you expect us to believe anything you say? This department has no credibility!" one reporter shouted.

The Chief tried to project a professional persona while repeating textbook lines that a chief is supposed to say after an incident like this, but he fell far short of a sterling moment as he awkwardly fumbled his way through that question. Then it was my turn. I raised my hand . . . but quickly realized I just had to shout my question louder than everyone else, so I did: "Sir . . . Sir! How do you think this scandal will affect the credibility in your closing of the Adam Walsh case?"

At that point the chief recognized me and said, "This case has nothing to do with that case." He then turned to his minions lined up behind him and said, "Let's get out of here."

The chief and all his henchmen went for the exit door at the same time and collided with one another trying to get the door open. They truly looked like a modern-day version of the Keystone Kops. And these perpetually incompetent modern-day cops, who seemed to have an attraction to unashamed humiliation, scandals and an FBI sting operation on their department, would've given those guys at Keystone Film Company a real run for their money.

Court order denying my appeal:

IN THE DISTRICT COURT OF APPEAL OF THE STATE OF FLORIDA
FOURTH DISTRICT, 1525 PALM BEACH LAKES BLVD., WEST PALM BEACH, FL 33401

December 1, 2011

CASE NO.: 4D10-3433
L.T. No. : 10-23089 03

WILLIS MORGAN   v.   CHADWICK E. WAGNER, ETC., ET AL.

Appellant / Petitioner(s),   Appellee / Respondent(s).

BY ORDER OF THE COURT:

ORDERED that appellant's motion filed October 27, 2011, for rehearing, clarification, certification and rehearing en banc is hereby denied.

I HEREBY CERTIFY that the foregoing is a true copy of the original court order.

Served:

Patricia Acosta	Thomas R. Julin	Richard A. Beauchamp
Thomas F. Panza	Joel D. Cantor	Joel Silvershein
Jonathan D. Kaney, I I I		

kb

Marilyn Beuttenmuller
MARILYN BEUTTENMULLER, Clerk
Fourth District Court of Appeal

CHAPTER TWENTY
FINAL SUMMATION

"We really don't think we have a good solid witness that saw what happened to Adam."
_____*Captain Mark Smith*_____
Quote from A&E TV show on Nov 8, 2013

The Audacity of Lies

Captain Mark Smith: "But those witnesses, whom police interviewed in 1992 after Dahmer was arrested in other murders, didn't provide any new leads . . . Dahmer repeatedly denied having a role in Adam's death. The official line is he didn't kill Adam."

Smith also said, "If we found no more on Jeffrey Dahmer, and I don't believe we will find any more than this circumstantial evidence we have now, we would never get to a conviction. I don't believe we'd ever get to an indictment" (WISN-12 Milwaukee, February 5, 2007).

Captain Tony Rode, Hollywood Police spokesman, told the Miami *Daily Business Review* that Arthur Jay Harris's theory that Jeffrey Dahmer killed Adam Walsh "is not new at all." Rode said, "Police interviewed the two witnesses who claimed they saw Dahmer in 1991, and again a few years ago when Harris came to the police with his theory." This isn't true.

Captain Mark Smith, on August 15, 1994, composed a memo that said, "Due to the amount of time since the incident, it would be virtually impossible to set out and try to establish new suspects or motives." A year later, in 1995, when a lawsuit was filed against the HPD, he suddenly found "new suspects." Later on, in another statement, he would say, "The best thing about cold cases is that the older they get, it actually works in our favor. We do get some tips but none that have panned out. To this day, we're still actively pursuing tips." (HPD case files)

Captain Mark Smith: "There are people who say they saw Jeffery Dahmer . . . I'm convinced he didn't do it . . . There's more people that say they saw Ottis Toole, who I'm not totally convinced is involved in this case. So we have a group of people saying the same thing on two different people" (WSVN-7 Miami, Thursday, February 1, 2007).

The Miami Herald: "Fort Lauderdale Detective Philip J. Mundy, who interviewed Toole, doesn't think he is lying . . . 'Under proper questioning, I don't think this man will admit to a homicide he didn't participate in. If he did commit one, I'm inclined to believe he would be truthful.'" (October 30, 1983)

It's really hard to wrap your mind around Mundy's statement. Ottis Toole was America's most notorious lying serial confessor! Yet one of John Walsh's attorneys, Kelly Hancock, thought Mundy was doing a great job in the investigation of Adam's case and even extolled the virtues of Mundy in a letter he sent to John Walsh. On the following page is that must-read letter.
(SAO case files, box 3, file 02, p. 4)

KRUPNICK CAMPBELL MALONE
ROSELLI BUSER SLAMA & HANCOCK
A PROFESSIONAL ASSOCIATION

JON E. KRUPNICK*
WALTER G. CAMPBELL, JR.*
KEVIN A. MALONE*
RICHARD J. ROSELLI*
THOMAS E. BUSER*
JOSEPH J. SLAMA*
KELLY D. HANCOCK
LISA A. McNELIS

LOUIS R. BATTISTA
IVAN F. CABRERA
ROBERT D. ERBEN
KELLEY B. GELB
CAROL J. HEALY
SCOTT S. LIBERMAN
ROBERT J. McKEE

* BOARD CERTIFIED
  CIVIL TRIAL LAWYER

SUITE 100
700 SOUTHEAST THIRD AVENUE
FORT LAUDERDALE, FLORIDA 33316
TELEPHONE (954) 763-8181
MIAMI (305) 944-4472
FAX (954) 763-8292

50 SOUTHEAST FOURTH AVENUE
DELRAY BEACH, FLORIDA 33483
TELEPHONE (407) 395-3253

R. SUSAN MADERA
ADMINISTRATOR

MICKIE DONNELLY
CLAIMS ADMINISTRATOR

ELAINE P. KRUPNICK
OF COUNSEL

REPLY TO: FORT LAUDERDALE

April 3, 1996

Mr. John Walsh
STF Productions
5151 Wisconsin Avenue NW
Washington, DC 20016

Dear John:

I have spoken with Ralph on a couple of occasions. As you know, they sent photographs to you to see if you and Reve can identify anyone. Ralph requested that you contact the Hollywood detective and advise him about the photographs.

Ralph told me that he has Phil Mundy working on the case with him. I feel we are very fortunate to have Phil. He was a homicide investigator for years with the Fort Lauderdale Police Department and has been with the State Attorney's Office for quite a few years. I worked with Detective Mundy on numerous first degree murder cases and he was always extremely competent and very dedicated in pursuing his case. Hopefully, with his assistance and Ralph Ray supervising the investigation, they will be able to focus in the right direction.

If you have any questions, please do not hesitate to contact me.

Very truly yours,

Kelly D. Hancock

KDH/jb

002003

Chief Wagner Steps Down

Hollywood Police Chief Chadwick Wagner retired at the early age of fifty-two at the end of January 2013, after five years as chief. According to BrowardBulldog.org, the online newspaper, Wagner left amid reports of significant friction with his new bosses at City Hall—City Manager Cathy Swanson-Rivenbark and her top assistant, Frank Fernandez, the new director of public safety.

"They are making his life miserable every day," said Jeff Marano, senior vice president with the Broward County Police Benevolent Association. "He's not getting along with them, and they have asked him to leave a little earlier than he'd planned," said the head of another police department who spoke on condition of anonymity.

Just a week later, Wagner was hired as a captain with the Broward Sheriff's Office.

Changing of the Guard

Now, with this police chief gone, I would make one more attempt to get the justice Adam deserved. I called the city manager's office and asked to speak with the city manager or assistant manager. After I explained who I was, I was put on hold for several minutes, and then I was told Frank Fernandez would get back to me. In February 2013, I sent the city manager's office the certified return receipt letter posted on the following page.

In mid-January 2013, a new interim police chief, Major Vincent R. Affanato, took over. He was selected from the rank and file of the HPD by Frank Fernandez. I tried to get an appointment with the new chief and even sent him a similar letter, without response. On March 26, 2013, Fernandez's office did call me and set an appointment for April 4, 2013. I was told Chief Affanato would be there, but he never showed up.

My one-hour-plus, 9 a.m. meeting was with Fernandez alone. However, I finally had a meeting. Fernandez was hired as the assistant city manager and public safety director for the city of Hollywood, effective August 13, 2012. Previously, he had worked as a police practices expert consultant for the United States Department of Justice as well as with the Miami Police Department.

During the meeting, Mr. Fernandez seemed to be obsessed with wanting to know if I had an attorney. Because of his insistence on wanting to know, I had a feeling he was just on a fishing expedition for information and wouldn't follow up on anything. My instincts were backed up by the fact that Fernandez kept propping up his selection of the new interim police chief. He told me the new chief was an upstanding and honest cop that wasn't involved in the case during its inception. The new chief would help Fernandez told me.

I had to remind Fernandez that Wagner was not part of the initial investigation, either. I advised Fernandez, when he did get a permanent chief, to get someone with thick skin and a good track record from out of state. I explained what happened to Chief Witt when he tried to clean up the corruption at the HPD. Of course, at the time, I had no way of knowing Fernandez himself was to be the new chief of police at the HPD.

Meeting request with the City of Hollywood Management Office:

Appointment Request Letter

February 8, 2013

Office of the City Manager
2600 Hollywood Boulevard
Room 419
Hollywood, Florida 33022

Cathy Swanson-Rivenbark
City Manager

Frank Fernandez
Assistant City Manager—Public Safety

Dear Cathy Swanson-Rivenbark:

My name is Willis Morgan. I am one of the witnesses in the Adam Walsh abduction case.

I would like to request an opportunity to meet briefly with you at your office to discuss the incorrect closing of the Adam Walsh case.

On December 16, 2008, the Hollywood Police closed the case based on a report that ex-Miami Beach detective Joe Matthews put together. This report has not been made available, but a book titled *BRINGING ADAM HOME*, based on that report, was published in 2010.

According to the many witnesses, including myself, the person named Ottis Toole, whom Detective Joe Matthews and the Hollywood Police said murdered Adam Walsh, did not commit this crime. I, as well as many others, saw another serial killer at the Hollywood Mall on July 27, 1981. His name is Jeffrey Dahmer. I had a face-to-face encounter with him and watched as he walked into the Sears toy department around 12:00 noon.

Thank you in advance for your consideration of this request.

Should you or your staff have any questions in the meantime,
I can be reached by phone at [|||-*REDACTED*-|||] or by e-mail at [|||-*REDACTED*-||@|||.*com*].

Thank you.
Sincerely,
Willis Morgan

Fernandez seemed to be more interested in what my motives were than the facts in the case. My motives aren't even relevant. The facts in the case are what are important. When he wanted to know if I was a book writer, I let him know that I was writing a book and he was going to be in it. I wanted this office to understand that anything I said about them was based solely on what they did. I was hoping the city manager's office might want to put distance between themselves and the HPD. At the end of that meeting, Fernandez told me he was going to start by requesting the closing report from the HPD.

I wished him luck and told him that, if he got it, I would give him $100. I had gone to the HPD records section, filled out the records request form for the closing report, and found that a closing report simply doesn't exist. I was told by records department supervisor Lieutenant Millares that what was on the CD that I already had was all there was. In fact when I mentioned Adam by name, another detective standing nearby said, "Adam Walsh?" When I turned to him and asked if he knew about this case, he said, "Oh yeah, but you're not getting me involved in that case I wouldn't touch it with a ten foot pole." It was as if he knew this closing was a scandalous debacle.

As for Fernandez, either he is too busy trying to clean up the ongoing scandals at the HPD or he doesn't think much of my resolve to disseminate the truth. I sent him a follow-up letter thanking him for the meeting and for his offer to help in getting the case reviewed and closed correctly, but I've yet to hear from him again.

While the city manager's office wanted to get rid of Chief Wagner, justice for Adam wasn't high on any list. In mid-August 2013, Fernandez took over as the new Hollywood chief of police. Fernandez referred to himself as "a cop's cop," but I bet, even with his newfound position, he won't do anything to correct the wrongdoing his predecessor did in closing the Adam Walsh case because his police department never did put Adam high on any priority list.

And, Finally . . .

John Walsh has been a real-life superhero and crusader for justice. Many bad guys have been taken off the streets, and many lives have been saved due to his efforts. Let it never be forgotten that John didn't do it alone; Adam, too, must get much of the credit.

When John said it was the "not knowing" that was the hardest, he might not have realized it was the not knowing that was the problem. When you don't know, *you imagine* . . . and when you're surrounded by detectives and prosecutors feeding you misinformation and outright blatant lies, your imagination can run awry.

> John Walsh: "It never seemed to occur to the cops that the most maddening part about Toole's confessions—his inconsistencies and fuzzy recall—might actually have a reasonable explanation. Any normal person would certainly remember having committed a homicide. Factor in his heavy drinking and drugging, and it makes sense that he might not be able to remember exactly what he had done with the body of one victim out of the hundred or so killings that he had been a party to." (*Tears of Rage*).

I can only hope John and the Walsh family read this book. Perhaps it will have a profound effect on them. Maybe John will realize that when he suggested to Detective Jack Hoffman that Jeffrey Dahmer could be responsible, he was right! Even Jeffrey Dahmer's own father would later write in his book, *A Father's Story*, that when Dahmer was convicted of child molestation, it occurred to him that his son would "never be more than a liar, an alcoholic, a thief, an exhibitionist, a molester of children."

Mistakes, Incompetence, and a Cover-Up

I have always been willing to accept the challenge of getting justice for little Adam. With a sense of purpose, I have climbed all the obstacles and jumped the hurdles the Hollywood police and others have put in front of me, and I haven't given up yet! In closing, I would like to say one last word to the court of public opinion: Don't be fooled by Joe Matthews or the HPD. Like Jeffrey Dahmer, they are master manipulators. They have fooled a lot of people for a lot of years. Please, don't let yourself be one of them.

If Adam never gets his justice from these agents of mass incompetence or our court system in Florida, maybe, just maybe, this book will give Adam a small semblance of justice, because the truth has a way of standing on its own. And if the truth sweeps the nation like a Florida hurricane, maybe then the HPD and Joe Matthews will feel contrite enough to give a genuine apology for what they have done to the Walsh family.

I might now be an old retired guy with a tenacity problem, but even after this book is published I will continue to be the voice of clarity as an advocate for Adam. It's my fervent wish that this book finally puts to rest any doubt that it was indeed Jeffrey Dahmer who abducted and murdered little Adam Walsh. The real question for the HPD to answer is why their police department lost its capacity for honesty and integrity while becoming the best friend, defender, and ally of one of America's most notorious serial killers. They don't owe me an explanation. They owe it to Adam's parents and siblings.

I'm not necessarily any cleverer than anyone else. I just had the distinct advantage of being there. I witnessed that guy walk into the toy department. I only wanted to corroborate what I have been telling everyone all along. I wanted to eliminate any doubt as best I could so that everyone would believe me. I've been through a lot of aggravation, sweat, and tears putting this book together, and the evidence I present forms a compelling wall of guilt pointing only to Jeffrey Dahmer.

It has always tugged at my heartstrings when I hear witnesses say they didn't intervene because they thought Adam's abductor was an older brother, stepfather, or even his dad. Because of the encounter I had with Dahmer, had I gone a little further into the toy department, I would've known better. I could've done something.

At least now the frustration of never being heard has been lifted. In my parting words to the HPD detectives and Joe Matthews, I will say what they have done by wrongly closing Adam Walsh's case without interviewing any of the witnesses was truly pathetic.

I have lived with the pain and guilt for well over three decades, thinking I should've been the one that prevented Adam's abduction. I feel I let Adam down, even though I never met him. Then I remind myself that if it hadn't been Adam, it would've been someone else. Someone was going to have a very bad day that day.

Until Adam gets his justice, I will always be a *Frustrated Witness!* Thanks for listening to me.

WORDS OF ENCOURAGEMENT

Congratulations, Willis, on pushing this rock farther up the hill.

You need no affirmation from me, but I'll offer it. What a concise, literate and compelling narrative with which you have, to my layman eyes at least, blocked all routes of escape.

Jay Grelen (*Arkansas Democrat Gazette*)

Willis—I hope you will continue with your quest to expose the true facts regarding the murder of Adam Walsh. Detective Matthews and the Hollywood Police Department did a grave disservice to justice, which can be undone only by citizens like yourself who are devoted to the cause. Please feel free to call on me for help again as you continue.

Tom Julin (The Hunton & Williams LLP Law Firm)

Willis, the truth always takes longer to prevail, but it always does. Lies, on the other hand, always spread fast and rule likewise, but in the end, corruption is discovered and dismantled in its full ugliness for good. I am glad that people like you exist to bring some light into such a sad case. I think what you do is very honorable and your persistence will prevail.

With kind regards, Sondra Schalk (German-English Translator and Contract Court Interpreter)

Willis,

You did more work in putting this together than some of the investigators did in trying to find Adam's killer.

Take care, Patrick

Patrick Fraser (WSVN-TV MIAMI)

Willis,

I, like you, believe it was JD and nobody can change my mind. I still believe they will find additional evidence one day. My whole objective of this is to try and convince people that it "was" JD. I'm as sure as you are.

Thanks, Denise (Witness Denise Smith)

Recommended Books

The books I recommend are first-person accounts, written by people directly involved with Adam Walsh, Jeffrey Dahmer, or the HPD. The exception is *Stalking Ottis Toole.*

1: THE PRIME TARGET—Sopa Princewill 2008

This is Sopa's story. It's a first-person narrative of his time as manager at the Oxford Apartments, with a fascinating and gruesome insight into the everyday life of resident Jeffrey Dahmer.

2: SERIAL KILLER'S SOUL—Herman Lee Martin 2010

Herman served time in the cell next to Jeffrey Dahmer. Once you get past Herman's deep religious convictions, this book is an interesting account of Jeffrey Dahmer's time at Columbia Correctional Institution.

3: ACROSS THE HALL —Vernell Bass 2011

Bass gives a first-hand account of what it was like to live across the hall from one of the world's most evil serial killers.

4: A FATHER'S STORY—Lionel Dahmer 1994 by Baramin Group, Inc.

Lionel tells his poignant story of life with his son, Jeff Dahmer.

5: TEARS OF RAGE—John Walsh and Susan Schindehatte 1997

John tells his heartwarming story of Adam from a father's perspective.

6: STALKING OTTIS TOOLE—Dr. Tim Gilmore 2013

Dr. Gilmore does a great job finding the real Ottis Toole, not the police puppet. Ottis Toole was a dimwitted arsonist who never meant to kill anyone yet was a master farceur as a serial confessor. It's hard to know which Ottis was Ottis until you read this incredible book.

7: BRINGING ADAM HOME—Les Standiford with Joe Matthews 2011

This book is written with inventive imagination and filled with fictitious prose that trumped cold, hard facts. Based on a very true story, it is told by an unchecked ego. I recommend it with mixed feelings. On the one hand, I hate to see Joe make money on his novel; on the other hand, it is relevant to the erroneous closing of the Adam Walsh case.

TOOLE'S KNOWN TIMELINE RELEVANT TO ADAM WALSH

June 15, 1981: Ottis Toole and Henry Lee Lucus give blood in Houston Texas.

June 19, 1981: Lucas steals a pickup truck in Jacksonville.

July 22, 1981: Lucas is arrested by Maryland Police for the stolen pickup truck.

July 22, 1981: Toole is a patient in Riverside Hospital in Newport News, Virginia.

July 24, 1981: Toole is discharged from Riverside Hospital.

July 24, 1981: Toole gets bus fare to Jacksonville from The Salvation Army.

July 24, 1981: Toole makes a phone call from Newport News at 3:20 p.m.

July 24, 1981: Incident happens in Kmart in Hollywood, Florida, around 7:00 p.m.

July 25, 1981: Toole arrives in Jacksonville sometime on Friday.

July 27, 1981: Adam Walsh is abducted.

July 31, 1981: Toole pays his rent.

August 1, 1981: Toole reports an assault to Jacksonville Police, case # 388323.

October 21, 1983: Police announce that a convicted murderer, Ottis Elwood Toole, has confessed to killing Adam. Toole said he used a bayonet to cut off the boy's head. Toole said he and his homosexual lover, Henry Lee Lucas, had traveled the country, killing nearly two hundred people. Lucas was in a Texas prison for murder convictions when Adam was abducted, and skeptics say Toole confessed to killing Adam because he wanted to outdo his lover.

October 26, 1983: Despite two days of searching, Adam's body isn't found where Toole says he buried it. Hollywood Police Chief Sam Martin says investigators will have a difficult task making a case if the boy's remains are not found.

October 27, 1983: Toole's state-appointed lawyer stops all further interviews with Toole.

August 5, 1984: Toole is sentenced to death for an arson murder in Jacksonville, which is later reduced to life in prison.

August, 1994: Hollywood detective sergeant Mark Smith takes over the Walsh investigation and finds that crucial Toole evidence has been lost.

September 15, 1996: Ottis Toole dies at Raiford Prison from cirrhosis of the liver and AIDS. He has been ailing for many years.

December 16, 2008: Chief Wagner closes the Adam Walsh case, pinning the murder on Ottis Toole.

March 01, 2011: Detective Sergeant Joe Matthews's "nonfiction" book goes on sale, effectively portraying himself as a real-life hero in the case.

GERMANY TIMELINE

Plus notations in Dahmer's military file that reflect counseling

May 21, 1960: Jeffrey Dahmer is born.

September 16, 1962: Billy Joe Capshaw is born.

June 18, 1978: First known murder by Dahmer occurs.

October 13, 1978: David Rodriguez arrives in Baumholder.

December 29, 1978: Dahmer enlists in the U.S. Army.

January 12, 1979: Dahmer reports for duty in the U.S. Army. He starts his training at Fort McClellan in Anniston, Alabama, to become a military policeman.

May 11, 1979: Dahmer is sent to army medical school at Fort Sam Houston, Texas.

July 13, 1979: Dahmer is sent to Baumholder, West Germany, to serve as a combat medic.

October 29, 1979: Billy Joe Capshaw joins the U.S. Army.

November 2, 1979: Unidentified woman's charred and mutilated body is found near Bosenbach.

November 22, 1979: Dahmer has his first Thanksgiving in Baumholder.

February 4, 1980: Preston Davis leaves Germany.

February 24, 1980: Billy is assigned a room with Dahmer.

May 30, 1980: Dahmer is cited for Article 15: failure to obey a verbal lawful order as well as drunk and disorderly. The punishment imposed is a forfeiture of pay of $100 per month for a two-month period.

July 31, 1980: Christine Ebelshäuser is murdered in Pirmasens.

August 2, 1980: Dahmer is picked up by military police for intoxication and receives a written reprimand.

August 8, 1980: Dahmer is caught going through the Bachelor Enlisted Quarters (BEQ) refrigerator stealing food.

August 8, 1980: Dahmer receives disciplinary action for alcohol abuse.

August 11, 1980: Dahmer receives disciplinary action for alcohol abuse.

August 30, 1980: Dahmer is counseled for loud music in the barracks.

September 2, 1980: Dahmer receives disciplinary action for alcohol abuse.

October 1980: Dahmer goes to Oktoberfest.

November 27, 1980: Dahmer has his second Thanksgiving in Baumholder.

November 27, 1980: Erika Handschuh is murdered.

November 30, 1980: Erika Handschuh is found frozen in the snow near Bad Kreuznach.

December 8, 1980: Dahmer is so intoxicated prior to starting duty that he can't even stand up.

December 20, 1980: Dahmer receives disciplinary action for alcohol in the barracks.

December 22, 1980: Dahmer is cited for Article 15: drunk and disorderly. He arrives for duty heavily intoxicated.

December 23, 1980: Dahmer receives disciplinary action for alcohol abuse. He fails to perform his assignment.

February 2, 1981: Billy goes to the hospital for a broken foot.

February 5, 1981: Dahmer is ordered into an alcoholic rehabilitation program, but he refuses treatment.

February 23, 1981: A double murder occurs fifty-five miles east of Baumholder.

March 7, 1981: Dahmer receives disciplinary action for alcohol abuse. He is reported for formation in improper uniform. He is sent back to the barracks. It is noted that he is in a shambles and doesn't report back for duty.

March 9, 1981: Dahmer receives disciplinary action for alcohol abuse and refusal to obey a direct order.

March 24, 1981: Dahmer is hastily removed from his room and sent to Fort Jackson, South Carolina, for debriefing.

March 26, 1981: Dahmer is discharged from the U.S. Army. The same day, he arrives in Miami.

April 16, 1981: David Rodriguez leaves Baumholder.

July 26, 1981: Billy gets a phone call from Dahmer at 9 p.m. Baumholder time (3 p.m. Miami time).

October 29, 1981: Billy is honorably discharged from the U.S. Army.

FLORIDA TIMELINE

1981:

MARCH

- March 26: Jeffrey Dahmer is discharged from the Army.
- Same day: Dahmer moves to Miami Beach.
- Same week: Dahmer takes a room in Miami Beach for a short time.

APRIL

- Dahmer moves out of his apartment after he runs out of money.

MAY

- Dahmer sleeps on the beach and begins dumpster diving for food.

JUNE

- Late June: Dahmer is found eating out of the dumpster behind Sunshine Subs shop by the store manager. He is given something to eat.
- Days later: Dahmer is found eating out of the dumpster again and is given a job by the manager as a part-time busboy.

JULY

- Early July: Dahmer gets a room at the Bimini Bay Motel.
- July 7: Dahmer finds a dead man out by the dumpster.
- July 13: Dahmer makes an attempted abduction at the Twin City Mall.
- July 20: Monday, one week before Adam's abduction, Dahmer is seen in the Hollywood Mall Sears by Denise Smith.
- July 24: Dahmer might have attempted an abduction of a twelve-year-old girl in the State Road 7 Kmart in Hollywood, Florida.
- July 26: Sunday, one day before Adam's abduction, Dahmer is seen in the Hollywood Mall Sears toy department by Mia and Joel Cockerham.
- July 27: Dahmer calls Billy Joe Capshaw (8:00 a.m. EDT) in his Germany barracks. He tells Billy that he is in Florida.
- July 27, Monday morning: Dahmer is seen in the Hollywood Mall by Vernon Galbraith.
- July 27, around noon: I encounter Dahmer in the Radio Shack.
- July 27, around noon: Numerous witnesses see Dahmer in the Sears toy department.
- July 27, 12:15-12:30: Adam Walsh is abducted from the same mall.

AUGUST

- August 4: The blue van is seen by two separate witnesses off the Florida Turnpike near mile marker 130, just north of the Minute Maid Road overpass.

- Early August: Dahmer might have lost the room at the Bimini Bay Motel.
- August 7: about 12:30 and 12:34: Two separate Publix truck drivers witness a "white male with a blue van" at Florida Turnpike mile marker 130.
- August 7: About 12:30 and 12:34, two separate Publix truck drivers witness a "white male with a blue van" at Turnpike mile marker 130.
- August 10: Adam's severed head is found by two fishermen.
- August 11: Denis Bubb and Clifton Ramey call the Hollywood Police Department and tell them about the blue van observed at mile marker 130 on August 7.
- August 11: Chief John Atwater calls the HPD to tell them of the Twin City Mall incident.
- August 11: Detective Connolly of the Plantation Police Department calls the Hollywood Police Department to inform them of an attempted abduction of a three-year-old boy in their city.
- August 12: Jane Houvouras calls the HPD to inform them of the incident in the Twin City Mall.
- August 12: Ginger Keaton calls the HPD to inform them of the incident in the Twin City Mall.
- August 14: Detectives Hoffman and Nylon of the HPD go to the Twin City Mall to investigate the attempted abduction on July 13, 1981.
- August 17: Dahmer attempts to abduct an eleven-year-old boy in South Beach.
- August 19: I have my second encounter with Dahmer.
- August 27: Hollywood Police say they are "stumped" and scale back investigation to two detectives saying, "It can't go on forever."

SEPTEMBER
- Late September: Dahmer is fired from the Sunshine Subs shop.
- Late September: Dahmer returns to Ohio.

OHIO

OCTOBER
- October 7: Dahmer is arrested by the Bath, Ohio, Police Department.

NOVEMBER
- Dahmer drives from Bath, Ohio, to Hot Springs, Arkansas, to visit Billy Joe Capshaw.

1982:

AUGUST
- August 8: Dahmer is arrested by the Milwaukee Sheriff's Department for disorderly conduct.

ADAM WALSH CASE CHRONOLOGY

December 26, 1945: John Edward Walsh is born in Auburn, New York.

1970: John Walsh moves to Hollywood, Florida.

July 10, 1971: John Walsh and Reve Drew are married.

November 14, 1974: Adam John Walsh is born in Miami Shores, Florida.

July 27, 1981: Adam Walsh is abducted from the Sears toy department at the Hollywood Mall.

July 29, 1981: John and Reve seek the help of psychic Micki Dahne.

August 10, 1981: Adam's severed head is found in a canal 120 miles north of Hollywood.

August 12, 1981: A $100,000 reward is posted for information leading to the arrest of a suspect.

August 15, 1981: A funeral is held for Adam with an empty small white casket, because his severed head is kept as evidence.

August 27, 1981: Hollywood Police scale back their investigation to two detectives.

July 1982: Reve gives birth to her daughter, Meghan Jane.

October 12, 1982: Congress passes the Missing Children Act, which establishes a toll-free missing children's hotline. President Reagan signs it. The law mandates the creation of a national clearing house of computerized information to aid parents of missing children.

July 22, 1983: John and Reve Walsh sue Sears, Roebuck & Co. over Adam's abduction.

October 10, 1983: The television movie *Adam* premieres on NBC.

October 11, 1983: Brevard County detective Steven R. Kindrick telephones the HPD and says an inmate in the Duval County Jail wants to talk.

October 21, 1983: Police announce they have a suspect after Ottis Elwood Toole confesses to killing Adam and becomes a national sensation.

October 26, 1983: Police give up searching for Adam's remains at the location Ottis Toole pointed out for them.

November 21, 1983: John and Reve Walsh drop their lawsuit against Sears for personal reasons.

February 11, 1984: Carpet samples from Ottis Toole's car are returned to the Hollywood Police.

May 1984: John Walsh hosts the PBS documentary *A Parent's Greatest Fear*.

May 1984: Ottis Toole is sentenced to death for an arson murder in Jacksonville.

June 13, 1984: The National Center for Missing and Exploited Children (NCMEC) is opened by President Ronald Reagan in a Rose Garden ceremony. The national twenty-four-hour toll-free hotline 1-800-THE-LOST is also started.

December 1985: Reve has another son, Callahan Drew.

February 7, 1988: *America's Most Wanted* debuts on the Fox network.

August 13, 1992: Hollywood detective Hoffman questions Jeffrey Dahmer, but Dahmer denies any involvement in Adam's abduction.

August, 1994: Hollywood detective sergeant Mark Smith takes over the Adam Walsh investigation and discovers that crucial Ottis Toole evidence has been disposed of from the evidence room.

September 1994: Reve gives birth to son Hayden.

January 1995: *Mobile Press Register* reporter Jay Grelen requests access to the dormant Adam Walsh case files.

May 18, 1995: Thomas Julin files a lawsuit against the HPD on behalf of the Mobile Press Register Inc. and reporter Jay Grelen.

October 18, 1995: Judge Moe says Hollywood Police have until February 16 to produce a viable suspect in the case, or they must make their case files public.

February 16, 1996: Judge Moe orders the HPD to open the Adam Walsh case files.

September 15, 1996: Ottis Toole dies in prison from AIDS-related cirrhosis of the liver.

September 21, 1996: *America's Most Wanted*, recently canceled by Fox, airs its 427th show, profiling Adam's case. Two months later, the show is reinstated.

October 1997: John Walsh publishes his book, *Tears of Rage*.

December 16, 2008: The HPD officially closes the Adam Walsh case pinning Adam's abduction and murder on Ottis Toole.

June 1, 2010: A lawsuit is filed by me in the 17th District Court in Fort Lauderdale against the HPD. The State Attorney's Office and Detective Joe Matthews are also named as defendants.

August 4, 2010: My lawsuit is dismissed with prejudice by the 17th Court in Fort Lauderdale, Florida.

March 1, 2011: Joe Matthews's book *Bringing Adam Home* goes on sale.

May 16, 2011: *America's Most Wanted* is canceled after twenty-three years. The final episode is aired on June 18, 2011.

October 12, 2011: The 4th Court of Appeals rubber-stamps the decision of the 17th Court.

July 27, 2015: My book *Frustrated Witness!* goes on sale.

—END—